GERMANY
2000 YEARS

GERMANY
2000 YEARS

KURT F. REINHARDT

Professor of Germanic Languages
Stanford University

REVISED EDITION

VOLUME II

The Second Empire and the Weimar Republic

F R E D E R I C K   U N G A R   P U B L I S H I N G   C O.
New York

THIRD PRINTING, 1962
REVISED EDITION

CONTENTS

VOLUME II

The Second Empire and the Weimar Republic

CONTENTS

LIST OF MAPS AND ILLUSTRATIONS

PART V. THE RISE OF THE SECOND EMPIRE

1750–1822	Prince Hardenberg, Prussian chancellor (1810–1822)
1755–1813	Gerhard Scharnhorst, Prussian chief of staff
1757–1831	Baron vom Stein, Prussian cabinet minister (1807–1808); dismissed at the request of Napoleon
1773–1859	Prince Metternich, Austrian chancellor and minister of foreign affairs (1809–1848)
1810	Foundation of the University of Berlin
1812	War between France and Russia; defeat of Napoleon's "Grand Army"
1813–1815	The War of Liberation
1813	War of the "Great Coalition" (Prussia, Austria, Russia, England) against Napoleon — Napoleon's defeat in the "Battle of the Nations" (*Völkerschlacht*) at Leipzig — Denmark and the states of the "Confederation of the Rhine" join the coalition
1814	The campaign in France and the first Peace of Paris — Abdication of Napoleon
1814–1815	Congress of Vienna — Reorganization of Europe — The "Holy Alliance"
1815	Napoleon's return from Elba, the "Rule of 100 Days," and the Second Peace of Paris — Napoleon's deportation to St. Helena — Foundation of the German *Burschenschaft*
1817	The Wartburg Festival of the *Burschenschaft*
1818–1819	Enactment of constitutions in Weimar, Bavaria, Baden, and Wurtemberg
1819	Assassination of Kotzebue by Karl Sand — The "Carlsbad Decrees"
1820	The "Final Act" (*Schlussakte*) of Vienna
1823	Convocation of the Provincial Estates of Prussia
(1825–1855)	Nicholas I, tsar "of all the Russias"
1830	"July-Revolution" in France and German revolutionary movements — Enactment of constitutions in the electorate of Hesse and the kingdom of Saxony
1833	Enactment of constitutions in Brunswick, Hanover, and Oldenburg
1834	Foundation of the German *Zollverein* (Customs Union)
1835	The first German railroad, from Nuremberg to Fürth
1835–1848	Ferdinand I, emperor of Austria, son of Francis I
1840–1861	Frederick William IV, king of Prussia, son of Frederick William III
(1846–1878)	Pope Pius IX
1847	Convocation of the United Diet (*Vereinigter Landtag*) of Prussia in Berlin — Foundation of the Hamburg-America Line
1848	Publication of the "Communistic Manifesto" by Karl Marx (1818–1883) and Friedrich Engels (1820–1895); "February-Revolution" in Paris and "March-Revolution" in Germany: revolt in Vienna and flight of Metternich; street fighting in Berlin; convocation of

a Prussian National Assembly; the Frankfurt Preliminary Parliament votes for the convocation of a German National Assembly; revolt in Baden; opening of the German National Assembly in St. Paul's Church in Frankfurt (May); renewed street fighting in Berlin; election of Archduke John of Austria as imperial administrator (*Reichsverweser*, 1848–1849); uprising in Frankfurt; Vienna surrenders to imperial troops; abdication of Emperor Ferdinand I

1848–1916   Francis Joseph I, emperor of Austria, nephew of Ferdinand I

1848–1850   The duchies of Schleswig-Holstein rise against Denmark

1848–1849   Promulgation of constitutions for Prussia and Austria

1849   The Frankfurt National Assembly offers the hereditary imperial crown to King Frederick William IV, who refuses to accept — Revolutionary uprisings in Dresden, the province of Baden, and the Palatinate

1850   Publication of the revised Prussian constitution — Treaty of Olmütz between Austria and Prussia, in which Prussia relinquishes her plans for a union of German states under Prussian leadership

1851   Restoration of the German Confederation (*Deutscher Bund*)

(1852–1870)   Napoleon III, emperor of the French, nephew of Napoleon I

1852   Treaty of London, determining the order of dynastic succession in Denmark and the duchies of Schleswig-Holstein

(1853–1856)   The Crimean War

1854   Establishment of the House of Lords (*Herrenhaus*) with "Three-Class-Suffrage" (*Dreiklassenwahlrecht*) in Prussia

(1855–1881)   Tsar Alexander II of Russia

1855   Prince William of Prussia, brother of Frederick William IV, becomes regent of Prussia

1857   Foundation of the North German Lloyd

(1859)   War between Austria and Sardinia

1861   Promulgation of a new constitution for Austria — Foundation of the Prussian *Fortschrittspartei* (Progressive Party) under the leadership of Virchow

1861–1888   William I, brother of Frederick William IV, king of Prussia and (1871–1888) German emperor

1862   Otto von Bismarck-Schönhausen becomes prime minister (*Ministerpräsident*) of Prussia

1862–1866   Constitutional quarrels in the lower house of the Prussian Parliament

(1863)   The Polish revolt

1863   Diet of the German princes in Frankfurt, Emperor Francis Joseph I of Austria presiding — Foundation of the General Association of German Workers (*Allgemeiner Deutscher Arbeiterverein*) by Ferdinand Lassalle (1825–1864)

1864   War between Prussia-Austria and Denmark and Peace of Vienna — Foundation of the "First (communist) International" in London by Karl Marx (dissolved in 1876) — (The "Second International," founded in 1889, disintegrated during World War I [1914–1918]. The "Third International," on a strictly communistic basis, was created in 1919 with its center in Moscow) — Pope Pius IX publishes the *Syllabus of Modern Errors* to refute the principles of Liberalism and Socialism

1865   Convention of Gastein between Austria and Prussia concerning Schleswig-Holstein

1866   The "Seven Weeks' War" or "German War" between Prussia and Austria: battle of Königgrätz; truce of Nikolsburg; treaty of Prague — Secret defensive treaties of the southern German states with Prussia

1867   Foundation of the North German Confederation

1869   Foundation of the Social-Democratic Party under the leadership of Wilhelm Liebknecht (1826–1900) — (Opening of the "Vatican Council" in Rome; declaration of papal infallibility in *ex cathedra* promulgations on matters of faith and morals; indefinite prorogation of the Council in 1870)

1870–1871   The "Franco-Prussian" or "Franco-German" War — Capitulation of Sedan and capture of Napoleon III; overthrow of the French monarchy; siege and capitulation of Paris (Sept., 1870, to Jan., 1871)

(1870)   Italian troops capture Rome and deprive the papacy of its temporal possessions (Sept.) — Rome becomes the capital of a united Italy — The pope refers to himself as the "prisoner in the Vatican"

1871   Proclamation of the German empire in the Hall of Mirrors in Versailles (Jan. 18) — Peace of Frankfurt — The first German *Reichstag* (Imperial Diet) — Promulgation of the *Reichsverfassung* (Imperial Constitution) and the *Reichs-Strafgesetzbuch* (Imperial Penal Code) — Foundation of the German Center Party under the leadership of Ludwig Windthorst (1812–1891)

Chapter 13

NATIONAL LIBERATION AND
POLITICAL RESTORATION

Reforms in Prussia. While Austria had come out of the first phase of the Napoleonic Wars weakened but not broken, Prussia had lost more than half her territory, having been reduced to but four provinces: Brandenburg, Pomerania, Prussia, and Silesia. Her economic life was completely paralyzed by the immense war indemnities and by Napoleon's "Continental Blockade" of England (decree of 1806), which made it impossible for Prussia to continue the lucrative export of agricultural products to the British Isles. The catastrophe of Jena and Auerstedt (cf. p. 325 sq.) made the political leaders of Prussia realize the mistakes and omissions of the past decades and made room at last for those unselfish and patriotic men who had long voiced their prophetic warnings in vain.

a) Reform of the State: Stein and Hardenberg. Baron Karl vom Stein was the descendant of an old Westphalian family of Imperial Knights, who had preserved the medieval tradition of knightly independence as well as the idea of a unified and centralized German realm under imperial leadership. "I have but one fatherland," he said, "which is called Germany. . . . With my whole heart I am devoted to it, and not to any of its parts." Opposition to the ambitions of the territorial princes, who in the past had given so many proofs of their national unreliability, was therefore part of his social heritage. He was deeply convinced of the necessity and social significance of a moral regeneration of the German nobility, which he considered as an essential factor in any attempt to rescue Prussia and Germany from their deepest humiliation.

In his autobiography Karl vom Stein appears as a man of action whose political realism was inspired by the religious conviction that the State was a moral organism and that everyone of its members was called by Providence to fulfill a definite social function in the service of the commonweal. The salvation of Germany, he believed, could never be brought about as long as Austria and Prussia, the great historical powers, could not be reinstated in their prerogatives of undisputed leadership. He therefore looked upon the several secondary German states which owed their existence to Napoleon with apprehension and disgust, considering them the greatest obstacles to a German rebirth.

In 1804 Stein received an appointment as Prussian Minister of State in the General Directory and was given charge of the departments of finance and economics. He immediately seized the opportunity to carry out some of the much-needed reforms. An edict of 1805 decreed the suspension of the inland duties in Prussia which had proven one of the major stumbling blocks to the development of a unified national economy. The substitution of private ownership of industrial enterprises for State ownership served to break down the economic system of the mercantile State (cf. p. 328 sq.), and the elimination of the corporate restrictions of the guilds was to prepare the way for the introduction of the principle of freedom of trade.

Stein's *Memoir* of 1806, in which he demanded the reorganization of the Prussian cabinet and the whole governmental system for the sake of greater efficiency and responsible leadership, went unheeded until the collapse of Prussia had verified his prophecy that "the Prussian State will either be dissolved or lose its independence, and . . . the love and respect of the subjects will entirely disappear." Stein, who had been dismissed by a royal cabinet order in January, 1807, as "an obstinate, defiant, stubborn, and disobedient state official," was called back in July of the same year, the day after the conclusion of the Peace of Tilsit (cf. p. 326). In October he published his first great Reform Edict, having as its main objectives the abolition of serfdom, the free exchange and disposal of landed property, and the free choice of occupation. Up to this time, two thirds of the population of Prussia had been bound to the soil, unable to leave their homes of their own free will and obliged to render personal service to the manorial lord. In the rural districts the medieval feudal system had survived essentially untouched. It was still illegal for a member of the nobility to engage in trade or to hold citizen or peasant lands. And it was likewise impossible for a peasant or burgher to acquire mortgages on the estates of the nobility. It was therefore a revolutionary innovation when the Edict of 1807 declared that "every inhabitant of our states is competent . . . to possess . . . landed estates of every kind" and "every noble is henceforth permitted . . . to exercise the occupations of a burgher; and every burgher or peasant is allowed to pass from the burgher into the peasant class or from the peasant into the burgher class."

Stein recognized in the sudden and unparalleled breakdown of Prussia the result of a political and social system of bureaucratic and feudalistic tutelage. A partly paternalistic, partly absolutistic form of administration had gradually loosened the mutual bonds of loyalty and unselfish devotion between the people and their government and had bred an attitude of irresponsibility and indifference among all classes of the population. Stein's program of national regeneration received its directives from his clear-sighted diagnosis of the national disease. It became the supreme goal of his short-lived political career to forge out of a reborn Prussia a powerful instrument for the future unification of a greater Germany that was to include Austria.

Although the ethical convictions of the political philosophy of nineteenth-century liberalism (cf. p. 523 sqq.) were embodied in Stein's edict, it would be a mistake to assume that he identified himself with the doctrines of Adam Smith (cf. p. 514 sq.) or the French Physiocrats (cf. p. 329). When we read that "it is just as much in harmony with the indispensable demands of justice as with the principles of a well-ordered national economy" to eliminate everything that hitherto has prevented the individual to attain to that amount of prosperity that he is able to reach in accordance with his capacities, we must not forget that in Stein's opinion only a nation that consisted of free personalities was capable of enlisting the co-operation of all classes and groups. Liberalism for him, then, was a means to an end, not an end in itself. This explains why, for instance, he refused to make the peasants the absolute masters of the soil, but embodied in his reform program certain restraining clauses which were intended to prevent the reduction of peasant holdings to mere merchandise, and to safeguard the continued existence of a healthy landowning peasantry. Thus the purchase and sale of peasant holdings was made dependent on the consent of the government. As far as the entailed estates of the nobility and the law of primogeniture (right of the eldest son to inherit real estate) were concerned, their integrity was to be preserved because Stein believed that an independent, landowning nobility was likewise essential for a healthy State organism. Economic liberalism, on the other hand, as well as the theories of the French Revolution aimed at the confiscation, dissolution, or partition of all entailed estates. It was precisely because of Stein's attempt to steer a sane middle course between conservatism and liberalism that he antagonized both the conservatives and the liberals. As the progressive features of his reform program became more conspicuous, the nobility indignantly began to look upon him as a traitor to his own caste and an avowed "Jacobin" (revolutionary radical, so named after the "Jacobin Club" of the French Revolution, whose meetings were held on the premises of the "Jacobin" [Dominican] monastery).

In the year that followed the publication of the Reform Edict, Stein bestowed on a large number of cities the *"Magna Charta"* of self-government (1808), thereby restoring to them the autonomy that they had possessed in medieval times. In his constitutional reform of city administration the Prussian minister followed the model of the French Revolution, eliminating the merchant and craft guilds and substituting, for the privileges of birth, capital and private property as the principle of social organization. Jews and members of the armed forces were excluded from citizenship, the former for racial, the latter for professional reasons. Members of both categories were considered as "denizens" (*Schutzverwandte*). They were forbidden to own real estate, were excluded from trade and industry, and had no share in city administration.

Late in 1808 Stein was dismissed a second time, upon the interception of a compromising letter that he had addressed to Count Wittgenstein at the court of the elector of Hesse, and in which the Prussian prime minister openly tried to enlist support in Hesse and Westphalia for the incipient revolt against Napoleon. Stein's property was confiscated by the French emperor and a price was set on his head, but before fleeing to Austria he had drawn up his "political testament," a circular letter in which he set forth the ideas that had inspired his reforms. Some of the demands contained in this political document were not realized until 1848, when the March Revolution (cf. p. 527 sqq.) forced, among other things, the establishment of a Prussian parliament, the suspension of the manorial police, and the abolition of patrimonial jurisdiction. The political result of Stein's dismissal was a closer co-operation of Prussia and Russia and the temporary aloofness of Prussia in the struggle for liberation, which for the time being had to be carried on almost exclusively by Austria.

Stein was succeeded in office by Altenstein (1808–1810), whose feeble and inefficient administration was in turn superseded by the appointment of Karl von Hardenberg as State chancellor of Prussia. Despite the divergency of their political philosophies, Hardenberg's name remains closely associated with Stein's reform program which he continued and in some respects completed. A native of Hanover, he considered, like Stein, Prussia as his adopted country and devoted his great political and diplomatic talents to the cause of its liberation, consolidation, and aggrandizement.

Hardenberg was a docile pupil of the enlightened *"Philosophes"* (cf. p. 368 sq.), a statesman endowed with irresistible personal charm, combining a profound knowledge of human nature with an unshakable belief in the sovereign and autocratic rights of the great political leader. Living in forced retirement after the Peace of Tilsit, he composed his famous *Memoir* of 1807, a counterpart of Stein's document of the preceding year. Its quintessence was the demand for social and economic reorganization, in accordance with the principles of an enlightened individualism and, at the same time, the call for a strongly centralized State bureaucracy, with special provisions for some form of "national representation."

Shortly after having taken over the office of State chancellor he issued a number of financial laws, designed to bring about a "revolution from above." A special edict decreed the secularization of all Church property, both Catholic and Protestant, extending the more limited secularizations of 1803 (cf. p. 325). The amount realized by the sale of ecclesiastical estates was applied to the reduction of the national debt. The new tax bills of 1811 introduced a general ground tax, extended the excise (consumers') tax and the duty on luxury articles over the entire country, and proclaimed complete freedom of trade, subject only to the payment of a license tax. Hardenberg agreed with Adam Smith that unlimited competition was "the best incentive and regulative principle of industry." The bases of the new legislation were equality before the law, freedom of ownership, and freedom of contract. Opposition to the new legislation was vociferous, especially among the nobility and the big landowners. They regarded Hardenberg and his associates as "aliens," who were trying to transform the "honest State of Prussia into a new-fangled Jew-State."

In accordance with the changing agricultural theories and methods Hardenberg worked out a series of new agrarian laws. Albrecht Thaer, who had made a name for himself by the publication of his book on *The Principles of a Rational Agriculture* (1809–1812), in which he applied the economic theories of Adam Smith to a scientifically improved cultivation of the soil, was asked to carry out the new agrarian laws. By making the profit motive the basic principle of agriculture the new system dealt the deathblow to the patriarchal economic ethics of the past. According to Thaer "the most perfect agriculture is the one which draws the greatest profits from its activities." Here, too, the representatives of the landed nobility protested against a new system of rationalization, defending the spirit of patriarchal order and sentimental attachment to the soil. With Adam Müller (1779–1829, cf. p. 498 sq.), their spokesman, they tried to preserve or revive a romantic-feudalistic ideal of agrarian organization and management. For them agricultural activity was a moral "office," performed in the service of State and community, and they thought that there was an essential difference between factory and farm, between trade and agriculture. They therefore objected to Thaer's cool impersonalism which cut the ties that were binding the landowner to the soil. With Martin Luther and a majority of medieval economists they saw in the patriarchal system of agriculture a divinely established order, the basis of family and State alike, an order that was arbitrarily threatened and disturbed by the innovators who replaced personal service and obligations by the servile devotion to the impersonal power of money. They were quite generally opposed to the modern preponderance of trade and manufacture over agriculture and pleaded for the restoration of the corporative system of medieval economy. "Knighthood and peasantry are about to perish, and in the end there will be nothing left but merchants, tradesmen, and Jews" (Adam Müller).

It was due to Hardenberg's personal energy, and the great political power that he wielded as chancellor of the State, that he won his victory over the forces of conservation. In his edict of 1812 he went so far as to open the way for the Jews to acquire citizenship and to enter the academic and civil services.

b) Reform of the Army: Gerhard Scharnhorst. The crushing defeat of the Prussian armies at Jena and Auerstedt (1806) had shown the weakness and inadequacy of the military system that had been created by the kings of Prussia in the period of State absolutism and enlightened despotism. In the year (1807) in which Stein headed the Prussian cabinet and worked out the principles of his social and political reform program, he also laid out the general ground plan for a thoroughgoing military reform. He was fortunate enough to find a congenial collaborator in Gerhard Scharnhorst, who, combining sound theory with practical experience, became the creator of the modern armies, recruited from the people and consolidated by patriotic devotion to a common cause. The victories of the colonial armies of North America over the English mercenaries had conclusively proven the superiority of armed forces that were inspired by popular sentiment and loyalty to a common fatherland. But Scharnhorst was convinced that, if the traditional soldierly training and discipline of the Prussian military machine could be preserved and harmonized with the new patriotism, the military might of the new Prussia would become impregnable.

A native of the state of Hanover, Scharnhorst entered the Prussian military service in 1801 and became director of the military academy in 1804. In his writings he elaborated the new military science whose principles provided the bases of military training and strategy down to Moltke (cf. p. 534) and von Schlieffen (cf. p. 635). In his *Memoir* of 1806 he emphasized the significance of moral incentives for successful warfare, designating personal courage and individual responsibility as absolute requisites of soldierly conduct. Taking the revolutionary armies of France as a model, he demanded the creation of a national army in which every citizen was called to military service. This new citizen army was to be founded on the soldierly virtues of courage, gallantry, and honor and was to provide equal opportunities for all. Dishonorable forms of punishment were to be abolished and rewards for bravery in the ranks were to be encouraged. "Sacrifice and fortitude are the pillars of national independence," he wrote. "If our hearts no longer beat for these, then we are lost, even while we still ride on the waves of great victories." These words were written before the defeat of the Prussian armies, and Scharnhorst, like Stein, had to hear himself denounced as a "Jacobin" radical. But even if Scharnhorst's capacities had been duly appreciated, if his counsel had been heeded and he had been given the supreme command, it would probably have been too late to turn the tide.

Scharnhorst's time came when the Peace of Tilsit had been concluded and Prussia had ceased to be a great power. The king, convinced at last of the need of military reform, made Scharnhorst the head of the military commission, and his ideas bore fruit not only in the ensuing War of Liberation (1813) but in the wars of 1866 (cf. p. 539 sq.) and 1870–1871 (cf. p. 542 sqq.) as well.

The military reform was carried out in several stages, each step forward calculated to make the most constructive use of those accomplishments and institutions of the past that were worth conserving. The idea of universal military service had come into being as a measure of national self-defense in the days of the French Revolution, and its acceptance in Prussia was born of the same motive. The principle of conscription itself was nothing new in Prussia, although hitherto it had been beset with too many discriminations as to classes and persons, exempting large groups of the population and working great hardships on the peasants who provided by far the largest contingents of the conscript armies.

Side by side with conscription the system of recruiting and voluntary enlistment was still in existence and imposed a heavy burden on the state treasury. Military discipline was enforced by a brutal penal code that provided severe punishments, including whipping and running the gauntlet, for minor offenses. The humanitarianism of the enlightened age had stopped short of the military barracks, for the simple reason that the political power of the "enlightened despots" rested on a rigidly disciplined army.

The French Revolution had for the first time made legal equality the basis of conscription, while Napoleon reintroduced the system of limited selective service by legalizing exemptions and service by proxy.

The military reforms of Stein and Scharnhorst attributed primary importance to the necessity of limiting membership in the future armies of Prussia to Prussian citizens. The reform plan of 1807 called for a standing army and a national militia, side by side. When Napoleon prohibited the formation of a militia, the reformers realized that their only alternative was the transformation of the standing army into a citizen soldiery (*Volksheer*), in which all citizens, irrespective of class and position, were obliged to serve. At the same time it was absolutely essential for the new army to combine the traditional spirit of order and discipline with the modern ideals of citizenship, human dignity, legal equality, personal freedom, and voluntary service. The new patriotism was to be wedded to the old Prussian military virtues. The military reform therefore included a complete program of education.

The outgrowth of these considerations was the creation of an army of the line and, side by side with it, the so-called *Landwehr* (militia) and *Landsturm* (general levy of the people). The army of the line was based on the principle of universal military service without exemptions. The *Landwehr,* consisting of some 150,000 men between the ages of twenty and thirty-five, was an army of reservists, and the *Landsturm* signalized the general mobilization of the male population in their entirety for the service of their country. The idea of a "total war" of the people was developed in Ernst Moritz Arndt's (cf. p. 480) stirring pamphlet, *What is the Meaning of Landsturm and Landwehr?* (1813.) The "*Landsturm*" accordingly was to include all men over thirty-five. Their services were to be employed only within the confines of the national boundaries, they were to wear no uniforms and were to use any suitable weapon. The real meaning of the creation of the *Landsturm* was then the virtual obliteration of the distinctions between soldiers and civilians, a "*levée en masse*" in which no one was willing to give or could hope to receive any quarter.

Stein and Scharnhorst knew perfectly well that the military reform could only succeed if the traditional exclusive hold of the members of the nobility on the commanding positions in the army could be broken, if class distinctions were eliminated, and if nobility and citizenry could be welded together. They were absolutely firm in their conviction that the only alternative was a radical reform or none at all. Scharnhorst therefore ruthlessly purged the officers' corps of all those commanders who owed their positions to social prestige rather than personal qualification. Only two of the 143 generals who belonged to the Prussian army in 1806 were allowed to continue in service in the War of Liberation of 1813. One of the first resolutions of the newly appointed military commission reads as follows: "In time of peace only technical knowledge and training, and in time of war only the highest type of bravery, activity, and circumspection can establish a claim to a commanding position. It is therefore necessary that all individuals in the entire nation who possess such qualifications be entitled to aspire to the highest posts of honor in the army."

It was this attempt to break down the privileges of the nobility that met with the strongest opposition of the military clique, whose members were anxious to perpetuate their families in the military leadership of the nation and who suspected Stein and Scharnhorst of "Jacobin" tendencies. The reformers, on the other hand, believed in the principle of competition and considered it the duty of the State to enlist the services of all citizens in accordance with their capacities. It was this part of the military reform program that was only partially and temporarily realized; after the War of Liberation the nobility regained their dominant position in the army.

c) *Educational Reform: Wilhelm von Humboldt.* Shortly before Stein, giving way to Napoleon's pressure, had to resign his post in the Prussian cabinet, he persuaded the king to appoint Wilhelm von Humboldt (1767–1835), Prussia's ambassador to the Vatican (1802–1808), as head of the Ministry of Education (*Kultus und Unterricht*). In his youth Humboldt had associated with the humanistic circles of Weimar and had acquired fame as the author of treatises on aesthetic subjects and as a translator of Greek tragedies. He was a man of sensitive character, highly cultured, many sided in his interests, and cosmopolitan minded. Owing his own education to private tutors, he had never attended a school and was therefore not specially prepared for his new position. Up to the time of his appointment as minister of education (1809) he had been out of touch with the program of the reformers and had to offer no definite program of his own. It needed a good deal of moral persuasion to make him accept the proffered cabinet post, but he soon grew into his task and became the creator of the modern system of "humanistic" education in Germany.

To fall in line with the social and political reforms the new educational program had to combine the ideas of the German Enlightenment and Classical Idealism of the eighteenth century with the new nationalist and liberal ideologies. The term "national education" (*Nationalerziehung*) had been coined by the philosopher Johann Gottlieb Fichte (1762–1814, cf. p. 500 sq.) who, in the winter of 1807–1808, had delivered his impassioned *Addresses to the German Nation* in Berlin, under the very eyes of the French army of occupation. In these discourses Fichte blamed the unconcern and selfishness of the individual citizens for the downfall of Prussia, and called for the reconstruction of the fatherland by means of sacrifice and devotion and by the steeling of the national will. He referred to Pestalozzi's (cf. p. 377) educational endeavors, to bridge the gap between an educated intelligentsia and the common people, and recommended a unified school system (*Einheitsschule*) as the most solid foundation of a uniform national education.

Pestalozzi had specified the cultivation of a healthy family life as the indispensable basis of a social and national commonwealth and had described the school as the family's natural complement, whereas Fichte assigned to the school an independent and all-inclusive function that necessitated the radical severance of the ties between home and school. This made the education of the child the exclusive prerogative and responsibility of the State. As Scharnhorst had made the State the master of the bodies of the nation's youth, through universal military service, so Fichte's universal and unified school system was designed to make the State the master of their minds and consciences. Both men were convinced that the moral incentives that the State had to offer would result in a spirit of voluntary submission to the State as a supreme moral absolute. The immediate practical outgrowth of these ideas was the creation of a tripartite system of education, consisting of elementary schools (*Volksschulen*), "humanistic" secondary schools (*Gymnasien*), and universities (for graduate and postgraduate study). The exclusive academies for young noblemen (*Ritterakademien*) and the military schools for the children of soldiers (*Garnisonschulen*) disappeared.

Wilhelm von Humboldt's personal accomplishment within the larger framework of the educational reform was the combination of the educational ideals of the New Humanism (cf. p. 403 sq.) with the doctrines of Pestalozzi. He emphasized the creative aspects in the process of learning and the elements of personal spontaneity that constitute true knowledge and wisdom. Both Pestalozzi and the New Humanists were advocates of "formal discipline," insisting on the basic significance of a harmonious exercise and development of mental faculties and rejecting the idea of specialization, professionalism, and utilitarianism in education. They argued that a well-balanced and liberally educated mind was the most suitable and useful instrument in mastering any scientific, practical, and professional problem and situation. For Humboldt, language in particular was a means for the creative development of intellectual forces and faculties, a material symbolization of spiritual realities. In his philosophical speculations on the nature of speech he made the attempt to demonstrate that the languages of different peoples were the truest manifestations of their national individuality (cf. Herder, p. 396 sq.). It was for this reason that he made the study of languages, ancient and modern, the basis of secondary education. That he attributed major importance to the study of the languages of antiquity was due to his conviction that in the thought and speech of the Greeks and Romans the ideal of *Humanität* was most completely and most impressively conveyed to the student.

Humboldt's ideas on higher education received their official sanction in the "statutes for classical education" (*Gymnasialverfassung*) of 1812. The curriculum of the *Gymnasium* was to consist of a ten years' course, and the compulsory major subjects of instruction were to be Latin, Greek, German, and Mathematics. The minor subjects that were to round out the course of liberal and general education were likewise compulsory. At the end of the ten years' course the student was to undergo a comprehensive oral and written examination, the successful passing of which was to be made a prerequisite for his entering a university. Thus secondary education and university education were strictly and organically correlated, and all professional and vocational training was excluded from the *Gymnasium* and relegated to the universities and polytechnical institutes of university rank. For the time being, this standardized type of classical or humanistic education seemed to carry the day, while the more scientifically and technically oriented "Realschulen" (cf. p. 361), stemming from eighteenth-century Enlightenment, were temporarily pushed into the background.

The rehabilitation of the academic standing of the German universities after a long period of decline took its start from the foundation of the Universities of Halle (1694) and Göttingen (1734). The latter institution in particular was destined to become the cradle of modern scholarship and modern science. The Göttingen faculty were instrumental in building up one of the finest libraries in the world, and in 1751 they founded the "Scientific Society" (*Sozietät der Wissenschaften*), which was closely affiliated with the university.

The ideal contents of the new humanistic scholarship were supplemented by the addition of the new idealistic philosophies (cf. p. 499 sqq.) which had their central meeting ground in Jena, where Fichte (cf. p. 500 sq.), Schelling (cf. p. 501 sq.), Hegel (cf. p. 502 sqq.), and Friedrich Schlegel (cf. p. 475) proclaimed their gospel of the unity of all the sciences and the universal mission of higher education. According to Schelling, it is the function of a university to provide authoritative guidance in the search for truth and to pursue knowledge, not for any practical or utilitarian reasons, but strictly as an end in itself.

The attempted university reform in Prussia was abruptly brought to a halt by the collapse of the State, entailing the loss of some of the most prominent institutions and the suspension of others. However, King Frederick William III expressed the feelings of the intellectual elite of his people when he said: "The State must replace its material losses by spiritual gains." Shortly after Prussia's defeat a royal edict was published that commanded the establishment of a general institute of higher learning, in affiliation with the Academy of Sciences in Berlin. Wilhelm von Humboldt, too, felt that such a leading institution in the capital of Prussia could achieve a great deal in restoring the moral prestige of the State: "The foundation of a great and well-organized university which, if it succeeds, must draw students from all parts of Germany, will be one of the most efficient means to win for Prussia the attention and respect of Germany." Thus the creation of the University of Berlin (autumn, 1810) was chiefly the fruit of Humboldt's ideas and endeavors. When the new university opened its portals, Humboldt was no longer in office. The appointment of Hardenberg as State chancellor in June, 1810, had killed his hopes for a truly independent ministry of education. Further co-operation between the two men proved impossible, and Humboldt returned to the diplomatic service, accepting the appointment as Prussian ambassador in Vienna.

In his educational ideals Humboldt anticipated the pet theory of educational liberalism, the concept of an education without ulterior purpose (*"zweckfreie Bildung"*), of a "knowledge without presuppositions" (*voraussetzungslose Wissenschaft*). But although these and similar slogans proclaimed the absolute objectivity of knowledge and science, the intellectual battles that were fought between the "liberal" representatives of multiple schools of thought were as fierce as ever.

For Humboldt, as for the other leading thinkers of the early nineteenth century, the ideal university was to fulfill the dual function of teaching and research. The high standard of the German universities in the nineteenth century was due to the fact that they were able to realize this ideal demand. These institutions succeeded not only in rearing successive generations of great scholars but also in preparing their students for the complex tasks of national and community life. The pre-eminent teacher was regarded as a kind of apostle, whose teachings became living realities in his disciples. The average professor, on the other hand, developed more and more the characteristics of the specialist and scholarly expert. With the growing specialization of the sciences and professions in the later nineteenth century, and with the ultimate failure of the educational reformers to achieve a new synthesis of science, philosophy, and religion, the idea of scholarship frequently degenerated into an unhealthy preponderance of theory over life, resulting eventually in an abstract and sterile intellectualism. Such a development was bound to bring down upon the German universities sooner or later the Nemesis of thwarted emotions and instincts, the revolt of the telluric forces of "blood and soil." The educational program of the national-socialist revolution reflected this violent reaction against the divorce of scholarship and life, but, because of a similar one-sidedness, it utterly failed to offer the much-needed corrective.

d) *Physical Education: Ludwig Jahn* (*1778–1852*). The educational reform required the mobilization of both the moral and physical strength of the people. The idea of a self-responsible, self-active, and harmonious personality could only be realized if the training of mind and body received an equal share of attention. Ludwig Jahn (the *"Turnvater"**) made it the major concern of his life to restore the German *Volksgeist* on the basis of the strictest physical and moral discipline. After years of restless wander-

* Father of gymnastics.

ing Jahn had accepted a teaching position in one of the Berlin secondary schools and in 1811 he started the gymnastic training (*Turnen*) of several hundred students on the *"Hasenheide"* in the outskirts of Berlin. This group of young people formed the nucleus of a nationwide organization of young athletes, united by a common national ideology and strengthened in their spirit of solidarity by their association and intercourse on frequent journeys across the country, in game and play, in athletic drill and gymnastic festivals. The members of the *Turnerschaft,* recruited from every class and calling, uniformly regimented in dress and equipment, and adopting identical slogans, developed into a homogeneous social force and potential fighting unit for "folk and fatherland." Jahn's idea of a self-sufficient national democracy was pugnaciously intolerant and made him hurl abuse and invective against Frenchmen, courtiers, and Jews alike. But in his blunt and rude sincerity he contributed to the growing assimilation of classes and social groups and aided in the educational reform by injecting moral motives into the lives and thoughts of students in secondary schools and universities.

Military Reforms in Austria and the War of 1809. The "Three-Emperors' Battle" at Austerlitz of the year 1805 (cf. p. 325) had sealed the downfall of Austria but had also cleared the way for the forces of reform and regeneration. Count Philip Stadion (1763–1824), a native of Mainz and like Stein the descendant of an old family of Imperial Knights, took the lead in the Austrian reform movement. He was a statesman who loathed the leaders of the French Revolution as much as he hated Napoleon, their heir and self-appointed executor.

At the time of Austria's decisive defeat the Austrian lands were in a more literal sense than any other European territories exclusive possessions of their native dynasty, the Hapsburgs. Nobles and great magnates were more numerous and more influential there than anywhere else. It was therefore for the time being very difficult, if not impossible, to break down the privileges of birth, to free the peasantry, and to carry out those social and political reforms that marked the rebirth of Prussia. It was for these reasons that the reforms in Austria had to confine themselves chiefly to the reorganization of the army. Thus Austria, with her territories free from enemy occupation, could prepare herself more directly and more thoroughly for the future War of Liberation.

The man who was Stadion's chief collaborator and who at the age of twenty-five had been hailed as the "liberator of Germany" was Archduke Charles, the brother of Emperor Francis (cf. p. 324 sq.). After the Peace of Pressburg (cf. p. 325) Charles assumed the supreme command of the Austrian armies and took over the Ministry of War. He had distinguished himself in the campaigns that preceded the defeat and his genial personality endeared him to civilians and soldiers alike.

Anticipating Scharnhorst's reforms, Archduke Charles firmly established the principle of universal military service, reformed the military penal system, and restored military discipline and morale on the basis of individual responsibility. Like Scharnhorst he recognized the significance of a strong army of trained reserves, supplementary to the army of the line. Thus the "Patent" of 1808 decreed the organization of a *Landwehr,* and both Stadion and Archduke Charles prepared their people for an immediate uprising against Napoleon.

In the same year, 1808, there occurred the heroic and memorable rebellion in Spain, where Napoleon had forced the abdication of King Charles VI and placed his own brother Joseph on the Spanish throne. The Spanish uprising was Napoleon's first serious setback. It was aided by an English expeditionary army under the Duke of Wellington (1769–1852), and it could have led to Napoleon's overthrow if Prussia's irresolute king had followed the example of Spain and Austria and had lent his ear to the advice of Baron vom Stein. Instead, Frederick William III, turning to a policy of appeasement, deserted the cause of national liberation and left Austria, Germany, and Europe at the mercy of the superior might of the French emperor. The shame of the Austrian defeat and the Treaty of Schönbrunn (cf. p. 326) is mitigated by the bravery with which this first phase of the War of Liberation was fought by the Austrian people, and more especially by the glorious uprising of the Tyrolese peasants and shepherds who under the leadership of Andreas Hofer offered all Europe an example of inspired patriotism. Andreas Hofer, the heroic innkeeper of the Passei Valley, was eventually captured, court-martialed, and shot (1810), the Tyrolese rebellion was quelled, and the Austrian war lost; but the cause of freedom had won the crown of martyrdom and the sacrifices were not in vain.

Napoleon and England. In the meantime, however, Napoleon's conquest of Europe had proceeded apace in breath-taking strides. When he was named First Consul of the French Republic in 1799, France had already obtained control of Belgium, Holland, Switzerland, and the left bank of the Rhine. Northern and southern Italy had been reduced to the status of French protectorates within the new system of political alliances. After the plebiscite of 1804 had bestowed upon Napoleon the imperial title, he began to carry out his revolutionary designs for a "new order" in Europe. In 1805 he went to Milan and, like Charlemagne, usurped the "iron crown" of the ancient Lombard kings, investing his stepson, Eugène Beauharnais, with the dignity of a viceroy. In 1806 he created the kingdom of Naples and Sicily and enthroned his brother Joseph as its ruler. The remaining Italian territories, including the Illyrian provinces, Rome, and the Papal States, were annexed by France during the following three years.

In Germany as in Italy Napoleon's policy was dictated by the principle *"divide et impera"* (divide and rule). By sowing the seeds of discord between North and South and by making capital of the venality of some of the German princes he won the material and moral support of a number of South German principalities and gained a strangle hold on the German lands in their entirety. In the Treaty of Pressburg Napoleon's German allies received territorial awards and Bavaria and Wurtemberg were given the status of kingdoms. The emperor of the French proclaimed himself the protector of the newly created puppet states which were united in the Confederation of the Rhine (*Rheinbund*).

And yet, despite this almost unprecedented accumulation of power in his hands, Napoleon realized that his triumph remained incomplete and insecure unless he succeeded in breaking the British domination of the sea lanes and in making England acquiesce in the "new order" of Europe. In order to strike against this last and most formidable opponent Napoleon assembled a fleet of transport ships in the French channel ports and prepared for an invasion of the British Isles. He was convinced that once he dominated the English Channel the road to world domination was clear and unobstructed. But quite unexpectedly he abandoned his invasion plans and in a surprise move marched his armies to the interior of Germany, defeating an Austrian army at Ulm (Wurtemberg). One day after this battle the English under Admiral Nelson achieved a major triumph in the destruction of the French and Spanish naval forces at Trafalgar (1805), thereby ending once and for all Napoleon's hopes of gaining a victory over England by means of military conquest. The only avenue that remained open for the French emperor was the prospect of defeating England by cutting off her trade. But in order to carry such an economic war to the finish, Napoleon's domination of the European continent had to be complete. Thus the defeat and partial occupation of Prussia was followed by the creation of the "Grand Duchy of Warsaw" out of the territories of Prussian Poland, and the establishment of a new "kingdom of Westphalia" that included the Prussian lands west of the Elbe and some of the smaller states of northwestern Germany, and that was to be ruled by Napoleon's brother Jerome. With his influence and control extending to the coasts of the North Sea and the Baltic, and having broken up and defeated the Third Coalition (cf. p. 325), the emperor was at the height of his power and seemed to have become truly invincible.

But while the subjected peoples of Europe were smarting under the yoke of the conqueror they were eagerly waiting for the first opportune moment to throw off their chains and regain their independence. The major flaw in Napoleon's calculations was his underestimation of the strength of some of his opponents, especially of the tough fiber and cool determination of the freedom-loving British nation, which set all its inherited tenacity against the Corsican emperor's gigantic onslaught.

Napoleon's Decrees of Berlin (1806) and Milan (1807), promulgating the so-called "Continental System" and forbidding all British imports to European countries, were intended as a knockout blow against British trade. England was to be brought to her knees by social and commercial disintegration and by political revolution.

However, the "Continental System" turned out to be a boomerang: England's answer was the "Orders in Council" by whose directives ways and means were found to utilize the leaks in the "Continental System" to force English wares upon the European markets while at the same time cutting off the export trade of France and her protectorates. Lacking sufficient naval strength, Napoleon was neither able to enforce his paper blockade against the British Isles nor to cope with the tremendous productive capacity of industrial England which with its power-driven machinery was just beginning to reap the fruits of the "industrial revolution" (cf. p. 548 sq.). Thus the economic war against Great Britain yielded no decisive results for either side and showed all the appearances of a stalemate.

The Break With Russia and the War of 1812. In 1810, after having divorced Josephine, his first wife, who had failed to bear him the much-desired heir to the imperial throne, Napoleon married Marie Louise, the daughter of the Austrian emperor, Francis I. In 1812, he forced Austria into a military alliance with France.

By that time the Franco-Russian alliance, dating back to the Peace of Tilsit (1807) had become a meaningless scrap of paper. Napoleon's own cynical disregard for international treaties and loyalties encouraged a like opportunism on the part of his nominal allies. The young Russian Tsar, Alexander I, resented Napoleon's annexation of the North German coastal regions, extending from the Dutch border to the Baltic, as well as the restoration of a Polish puppet state, bordering on the formerly Polish territories now owned by Russia. Alexander threw down the gauntlet to the master of continental Europe by promising the Poles national independence under Russian protection and by declaring Russia's exemption from the system of the continental blockade against England.

Napoleon realized that Alexander's acts jeopardized the success of his whole political scheme and endangered his hegemony over Europe. Russia's attitude was tantamount to a declaration of war, and in the summer of 1812 Napoleon's "Grand Army," consisting of more than 600,000 men and including large contingents of Bavarian, Swabian, Saxon, Prussian, and Austrian troops, marched through northern Germany and Poland against Russia. Pressing on to Moscow, they found the city deserted and huge conflagrations of mysterious origin. This combined with the shortage of food supplies and equipment caused such consternation and confusion in the ranks that Napoleon was forced to give the order to retreat. The homeward march through the frozen Russian steppes became a ghastly epic of horror and privation, with less than one fifth of the "Grand Army" escaping the icy grip of winter and the harassing attacks of the Russian Cossacks. Napoleon had staked his all on one card and had lost.

The War of Liberation. Europe had watched the progress of the Russian campaign with bated breath, but when the news of the colossal disaster found its way into the various capitals, the first incredulous amazement soon gave way to a feeling of relief and renewed hope. The Napoleonic myth crumbled almost overnight. When the emperor arrived in Warsaw, he was fully aware of the gigantic proportions of the catastrophe, but the force of his will was unshaken and he showed genuine greatness in defeat.

a) *Prussia and Russia.* The destruction of the "Grand Army" was a world-historic event that immediately set in motion the political leaders of the subjugated peoples of Europe. At the outbreak of the Franco-Russian War Karl vom Stein had accepted an invitation of Tsar Alexander and had traveled from his exile in Austria to the general headquarters of the Russian army in Wilna. He acted as the tsar's chief councilor and submitted to him a detailed plan for the organization of a grand uprising in the rear of the Napoleonic armies. This plan provided for the landing of English and Swedish troops in northern Germany, to aid the German peoples in their struggle for liberation. Count August von Gneisenau (1760–1831), quartermaster general and the leader of the Prussian war party, was sent on a diplomatic mission to Sweden and England, while Ernst Moritz Arndt's (1769–1860) literary talents were enlisted for propagandistic purposes.

Stein was convinced that the liberation and eventual unification of Germany could only be achieved if the uprising of the masses was directed by a central national committee that disregarded the wishes and selfish ambitions of the German princes who, as members of the Confederation of the Rhine, had in his opinion usurped a sovereignty to which they were not entitled. They were to be reduced to the status of members of the Reich and subjects of the emperor: "Whenever the princes therefore do or command anything that is contrary to the interests of the fatherland . . . their subjects are absolved from their oath of allegiance" (Stein). Against much opposition Stein succeeded in making Alexander amenable to his ideas. In the *Petersburg Memorial* of 1812 he outlined his military and political strategy and demanded specifically the destruction of the Confederation of the Rhine and the creation of a unified and independent Germany. He repeatedly called attention to the corrupting influence of the petty princely courts, accusing the princes of having undermined the people's sense of justice and dignity and of having made themselves and their subjects the laughingstock of Europe. "In this moment of great decisions," he wrote, "I am absolutely disinterested in the fate of the dynasties; they are merely instruments; it is my wish that Germany become great and strong in order to regain her national independence."

In December, 1812, General Yorck von Wartenburg (1759–1830), the leader of a Prussian auxiliary corps, signed on his own responsibility the Convention of Tauroggen which in effect amounted to the conclusion of a nonaggression pact with Russia and presented the Prussian king with a *fait accompli.* Although Yorck was subsequently dismissed and the Convention of Tauroggen repudiated by Frederick William III, a revolutionary step had been taken that carried with it its own irrepressible momentum. Meanwhile Stein had arrived in East Prussia and, as the emissary of the tsar, had taken over the provisional administration of this province and proclaimed the formation of *Landwehr* and *Landsturm*. This was another revolutionary act and, like Yorck's nonaggression treaty with Russia, designed to force the Prussian king into a war for Prussia's freedom.

Early in 1813 the assembled deputies of the provincial estates of Prussia listened to the declarations that Stein made as the representative of the tsar. Yorck was present and called for a crusade against the French. From then on events moved fast: on Hardenberg's advice, Frederick William, in an attempt to escape the surveillance of the French army of occupation and also to be nearer to Alexander's headquarters, exchanged Berlin for Breslau, the capital of Silesia. Scharnhorst was put in charge of the rearmament program. To speed up the negotiations that were carried on between Prussia and Russia, the tsar gave Stein orders to proceed to Breslau and, though he was given a cool reception by Hardenberg and the king, the result of his visit was an alliance between Prussia and Russia (Treaty of Kalisch). On March 10, the birthday of the late Queen Louise, Frederick William proclaimed the creation of the decoration of the "Iron Cross." On March 15 Alexander I arrived in Breslau and on the following day war was declared against France. The Prussian king issued the stirring proclamation *"To My People,"* reminding his subjects of the sufferings of the past and naming the precious objectives of the great struggle: freedom of conscience, honor, independence; freedom of commercial enterprise; and a rebirth of the arts and sciences.

The armed citizenry was represented in the contingents of the *Landwehr,* while the academic youth in large numbers enlisted voluntarily in the "Free Corps," especially in those districts that were most familiar with the hardships of foreign occupation and the yoke of the conqueror. Theodor Körner (1791–1813) left his native Saxony, whose king had decided to throw his country's lot in with Napoleon, to join the "Free Corps" of Major von Lützow and to serve the cause of freedom with "lyre and sword." As a poet and human character he symbolized the fervent idealism of German youth, and as a soldier he realized the crowning ambition of his life by dying a hero's death on the battlefield. When in his verse he glorified the War of Liberation as "a crusade, a holy war,"* he merely gave poetic expression to a universal conviction. But Körner belonged to that relatively small group of patriots who with the purity of their enthusiasm fanned the spark in the hearts of their fellow countrymen, so that it grew into a devouring flame.

The joint forces of the Prussians and Russians were commanded by the Russian Marshal Kutusoff, while the Russian General Wittgenstein and the Prussian General Blücher were in charge of the divisional command. Yorck was exonerated and entered Berlin at the head of his corps, jubilantly greeted by an aroused populace. Napoleon, on the other hand, could still count on the support of the Confederation of the Rhine and, with the aid

---

* "Dies ist kein Krieg, von dem die Kronen wissen,
  Es ist ein Kreuzzug, 's ist ein heiliger Krieg."

of their contingents and a newly recruited army of the line, marched quickly through Germany and met and defeated the allied armies at Lützen and Bautzen, on Saxon soil. The Russo-Prussian forces retreated from Saxony and were in grave danger of being outflanked, when Napoleon committed what he himself later characterized as the greatest stupidity of his life: he entered into an armistice of two months' duration, declaring himself willing to renounce his claims to Poland and to relax the continental blockade.

b) *Austria's Policy and War Aims.* These two precious months permitted Prussia to complete her armaments, while at the same time Austria under the leadership of Count Stadion and Prince Metternich withdrew from her alliance with France and made preparations to enter the war on the side of the allies.

An offer of Metternich to mediate was coupled with definite demands for territorial adjustments and restitutions and amounted practically to an ultimatum. In a personal interview with the Austrian chancellor in Dresden, Napoleon admitted that it was impossible for him to give up any of his conquests, because he could not afford to face the French people with a confession of even partial failure. When nevertheless he finally accepted the Austrian offer of mediation, he did so in order to gain time for more extensive preparations.

In the meantime, England's promise of aid and Sweden's entry into the coalition fundamentally changed the character of the war and turned the odds against Napoleon.

If the war had begun as a struggle for national liberation and self-determination, this original aim was partially changed by Austria's entering the ranks of the allies. What Metternich wanted was not a reorganization of Europe in accordance with national aspirations, but a restoration of the European balance of power, on the basis of historical and "legitimate" dynastic and social claims and relationships. The Austrian empire was a conglomerate of diverse nationalities which had been brought together and held united by a century-old dynastic policy and by the prestige of the Hapsburg crown. Metternich realized that the victory of the principle of national self-determination would of necessity lead to the dissolution of the foundations of the Austrian monarchy. But in formulating Austria's war aims the Austrian chancellor looked beyond the boundaries of his own country: he foresaw that the peace and order of Europe would be jeopardized by the countless new complications and antagonisms that would arise out of the triumph of nationalism. As a member of a cosmopolitan-minded European aristocracy Metternich clung to the heritage of the cultural and political traditions of a European commonwealth of nations and considered Napoleon's claims to hegemony as "outside the pale of nature and civilization."

Prussia and Austria were united in their opposition to the creation of a universal super-State that threatened by its uniform structure to suppress all individualism and political independence on the European continent. As against the universalism of the Napoleonic monarchy Prussia and Austria defended the ideal of European solidarity. But while Baron vom Stein wanted to build the new Europe on the principle of the new nationalism, Metternich still hoped for the conservation of the historico-political structure of the pre-Napoleonic epoch. This contradiction in the ultimate war aims of the two German nations remained invisible as long as Prussia and Austria fought side by side against the common enemy, but they became strikingly evident as soon as the victory was won.

c) *Napoleon and the New Military Strategy.* In the age of Absolutism and Enlightened Depotism the armies had been the exclusive creation and property of the rulers. Their moves were scientifically calculated, their services methodically and rationally employed. In their build-up and strategy the "cabinet wars" of the absolutistic princes were artistically conceived chess games that aimed less at the destruction than at the paralyzation of the enemy. Frederick the Great was the first military leader who occasionally broke with the traditional rules of warfare and developed a new offensive strategy. But the new methods were perfected by the generals of the French Revolution and especially by the greatest of them, Napoleon Bonaparte. Under their leadership the masses of the citizen armies acquired a new significance in defense and attack, until Napoleon's military genius learned how to combine to the best advantage the methodical warfare of the absolute monarchs with the psychological assets of the new citizen morale in the army. He knew that the masses could be most effectively used if they were inspired by the ideals of personal devotion to a common cause.

The result was a new military strategy that aimed at the annihilation of the enemy, achieved by the force of superior numbers and by a relentless offensive initiative that dictated the law of action to the opposing armies. Napoleon's forced marches, his surprise movements, and his flexible maneuvering were aided and quickened by a well-trained army of polytechnicians, pioneers, and engineers.

The Prussian generals of the War of Liberation were Napoleon's most docile disciples, and Clausewitz (1780–1831) in particular systematically developed the principles of the new strategy in both theory and practice.

d) *The Liberation.* When the end of the brief armistice came the allies were agreed upon a definite strategic plan. The main army, under the command of the Austrian Marshals Schwarzenberg and Radetzky, was stationed in Bohemia and consisted of Austrian, Russian, and Prussian troops. In their camp were the three allied monarchs, the tsar, the emperor of Austria, and the king of Prussia. A second army under Marshal Blücher stood in Silesia, and a third, under the unreliable Bernadotte (1764–1844),*

---

* Jean Baptiste Bernadotte, a native of France, began his career as one of the generals of the French Revolution, served under Napoleon in Italy and Germany but later on deserted the cause of the French emperor. In 1810 the Swedish estates elected him as crown prince of Sweden and in the same year King Charles XIII adopted him as his successor. He ruled Sweden as Charles XIV (1818–1844).

covered the city and district of Berlin. The three combined armies surrounded Napoleon in a semicircle which, according to the plan, was to close in on the French emperor from three sides. For the first time in his military career Napoleon found himself deprived of the initiative. The clever maneuvering on the part of the allies was designed to avoid a decisive battle until the strength of their opponent would be sufficiently sapped and worn down.

After ten days of skirmishing the French Marshal Macdonald walked into a trap. After crossing the river Katzbach he was attacked by Blücher and his army annihilated. In several minor encounters Silesia was cleared of French troops and an enemy attack on Berlin repulsed.

The main army, in the meantime, was approaching Dresden, the capital of Saxony. Napoleon hurried north in forced marches and attempted an encircling movement. After two days of undecisive fighting the allies carried out a voluntary tactical retreat. But Napoleon failed to follow up this strategic advantage and instead resumed his former advance on Berlin.

The war at this juncture had only lasted two weeks and already the victory of the allies was practically assured. Napoleon had lost more than one third of his army and the morale of the French troops was badly shaken. The allies were gradually gaining superiority in numbers and materiel. Napoleon knew that his only salvation lay in attack and a battle in the field, but none of the allied generals would do him the favor of exposing their armies to such an onslaught. To effect the eventual unification of their forces in a concerted and crushing offensive, they had first to decide on the most favorable terrain to deliver the final blow. In the meantime, the striking power of Napoleon's armies was further weakened by the desertion of Bavaria, which went over to the allies.

Following Blücher's advice the allied armies now began to converge on Leipzig. As they approached from north and south, Napoleon in a desperate move turned northward to attack the united forces of Blücher and Bernadotte. But Blücher's and Gneisenau's strategy not only frustrated Napoleon's counteroffensive but cut off his retreat, so that at last the emperor decided to march upon Leipzig and to accept the battle at the place where it was forced upon him.

The first day of the battle of Leipzig was undecisive. But on the following day the allied ranks were strengthened by reinforcements and the French were driven back into the suburbs of the city. Napoleon, realizing his desperate position, attempted to negotiate an armistice, but his delegates were not even received by the allied commanders. On the third day, Bernadotte's army advanced and closed the gap between the Silesian and Bohemian contingents. While the battle was raging the Saxon and Swabian troops went over to the allies and thus contributed their share to Napoleon's defeat.

On the following morning the concerted attack of the three allied armies on the retreating troops of the enemy was completely successful and the three monarchs and their generals met on the market square of Leipzig. Napoleon withdrew in the direction of the Main river and gained his last victory on German soil when he brushed aside a Bavarian army that had tried to cut off his retreat.

The larger part of Germany was freed from the enemy, and the allied headquarters were moved to Frankfurt. The Confederation of the Rhine was dissolved, and much against the wishes of Baron vom Stein the disloyal German princes were allowed to retain their thrones. Those who had been deposed by Napoleon were reinstated in their domains. The three Hanseatic cities, Hamburg, Bremen, and Lübeck, as well as the old imperial city of Frankfurt, were given back their autonomy and their senatorial administration.

If the allies had followed up their victory, they could have crushed Napoleon so completely that an extension of the war into the following year would have been unnecessary. But hardly had the battle of Leipzig been won when the old discords and rivalries among the allies came to the fore again and gave the enemy the needed time for partial recovery. Metternich considered the annihilation of Napoleon as undesirable from the point of view of the European balance of power. He still hoped for a peace that would break the hegemony of France without denying to her the satisfaction of certain legitimate historical aspirations. Blücher and Gneisenau, on the other hand, maintained that Napoleon's "crimes" called for the overthrow of his regime and the destruction of his military power. Blücher's goal, therefore, was the capture of Paris, followed by the dictation of merciless peace terms. Metternich sensed in these proposals a revolutionary radicalism that seemed to endanger the very principle of monarchical rule, and in the environment of the Austrian chancellor Blücher's headquarters were disdainfully referred to as a "nest of Jacobins."

After much futile bickering and more or less academic disputes the campaign of 1814 finally got under way, Blücher advancing along the shores of the river Marne and the main army following the course of the river Seine. At the same time negotiations with Napoleon's plenipotentiaries were begun at Châtillon. But even now, when final victory was within certain grasp, Blücher's army, owing to the lack of unity among the allies, suffered several severe setbacks that filled Napoleon with new hope. He made one last attempt to intercept the supply lines of the allies and, that failing, withdrew in the direction of Paris, this time followed by the reunited allied armies. On March 31, 1814, Paris surrendered, the allies entered the city, and the war was ended. Napoleon, who had taken up quarters in near-by Fontainebleau, agreed to abdicate to make way for the restoration of the Bourbon dynasty. Talleyrand, the former Gallican*

---

* The term *Gallicanism* refers to certain nationalistic and monarchical tendencies in the Catholic Church of France (Gaul) which received their clearest formulation in the Declaration of the French Clergy of 1682, drawn up by Bossuet. Its four articles demand that the authority of the pope be restricted to ecclesiastical affairs and assert the superiority of a general Church council to the pope (Conciliar Theory).

bishop, who had left the Church and deserted the Monarchy to serve first the Revolution and then Napoleon, returned now as the Bourbon King Louis XVIII's confidant and minister of foreign affairs, and concluded the peace treaty of Paris between France and the allied powers. The new king of France was the brother of the unfortunate Louis XVI who had been executed in 1793.

The terms of the Peace of Paris were very lenient: no war indemnity was imposed and France was allowed to retain all the territories that she had possessed in 1792, including Alsace, and she even received some territories that had not belonged to her former monarchs, such as Avignon, the duchy of Savoy, and the county of Zweibrücken. This leniency on the part of the allies was due to the fact that the restoration of the Bourbons was supposed to ensure peace and stability in Europe and that therefore everything must be done to make the new rulers appear true to their assumed role as saviors of the honor and the territorial integrity of the French nation. The deposed emperor was granted a pension and sovereign rights over the small island of Elba in the Mediterranean, not far from his native Corsica.

e) Alsace and the Rhine. Metternich's call for the restoration of historically "legitimate" political structures in Europe found an echo even among those romantic writers whose ardent nationalism was in other respects diametrically opposed to the cosmopolitan ideals of the representatives of the old European aristocracies. Arndt and Görres (cf. p. 480) no less than Baron vom Stein and other leading German patriots were fighting for the establishment of a national democracy within the borders of the old German empire. Motivated by the dual impulse of the reawakened historical sense and a vigorous national consciousness, they were the first among their countrymen to advance a program of *Machtpolitik* for the realization of legitimate national aspirations. And yet, when these national leaders directed their appeal to the ancient frontier district of Alsace, it was most surprising and disappointing to them to find that the population failed to respond. The same people who in the eighteenth century had still loyally adhered to their German political and cultural heritage had been almost completely won over by the political and social reforms of the Napoleonic era. The peasants enjoyed the newly gained freedom of person and ownership and the middle classes cherished the freedom of trade and commerce that was guaranteed by the unified and modern legislation of the centralized administration under the French regime. This lukewarm attitude of the Alsatians was one of the reasons that prevented the return of Alsace to Germany under the terms of the Peace of Paris.

But with Alsace lost, the German patriots were all the more solidly united in their historic claims for the possession of the Rhine as "Germany's river, not Germany's boundary" (Arndt). The Rhine became a symbol of German nationalism in the era of Liberation and Romanticism (cf. p. 468 sqq.). Even in ancient Roman times both banks of the river had been settled by German tribes, and all the past greatness and glory of the Empire was mirrored in its placid and majestic waters, in the ancient cities that lined its shores, the magnificent cathedrals that towered above the plains, the rugged castles whose ruins recalled a proud and virile past. Here it was that the patriotic German felt it his sacred duty to keep eternal watch against the encroachments of the "hereditary enemy," the French. For Arndt, the Rhenish districts and the Rhenish people represented the heart and the soul of Germany. The river was the artery from which the whole organism received its lifeblood. It was in the recently liberated city of Coblenz, the city of his birth, that Joseph von Görres (1776–1848) edited the *Rhenish Mercury,* a political review that established the fame of its author and editor as the first and foremost of great German publicists, and to which Napoleon referred as "the fifth of the Great Powers of Europe." In the pages of Görres' *Mercury* the contemporaries could read about the historic and cultural significance of the left bank of the Rhine and they could derive new hope and confidence from the prophecies of Napoleon's downfall and the coming liberation and unification of Germany.

f) The Congress of Vienna (1814–1815). The victory of the allies over Napoleon brought to a temporary halt the revolutionary era that had begun with the French Revolution of 1789. The first phase of the struggle between the European monarchies and the principle of the sovereignty of the people ended with a triumph of the defenders of autocratic and authoritarian government. The German people at large had never submitted to any great extent to the intellectual trends of the period of Enlightenment (cf. p. 368 sqq.), and most of the leaders of the movement of Classical Idealism (cf. Chap. 12) had stressed the values of historical continuity and inherited traditions. Thus the forces of the European counterrevolution, when they assigned to the Congress of Vienna the task of the reorganization of Europe, met with sympathetic response on the part of Germany.

The new order of Europe was to be based on the principles of permanency and stability, and Prince Metternich was the statesman whose political ideas dominated that illustrious assembly of great and small powers. The "dancing" Congress of Vienna, unequaled in modern times in its splendor and extravagance, was a social rendezvous of European aristocracy, convoked to celebrate the resurrection of the *ancien régime.* The gay and frivolous elegance of the ancient imperial metropolis on the Danube provided a most suitable background.

The feeling of social equality that had characterized the period of the national uprisings against Napoleon was forgotten as soon as the victory was won, and the traditionalist sentiment of the people accepted the return of social distinctions and privileges as something necessary and unavoidable. The aristocracy, on the other hand, had "learned nothing and forgotten nothing." They were convinced that their rule would be safe and secure if they only succeeded in preserving the people's trust in a divinely instituted system of authoritarian governance. According to Talleyrand, only he who had experienced the period before 1789 was able to appreciate fully "the sweetness of human existence." Among the advocates of the restoration movement the French philosopher Joseph de Maistre (1754–1821) was the only one whose conservatism was enlightened by a statesmanlike vision that was able to look beyond class distinctions and social prejudice. He recognized the constructive values of a temperate nationalism and traditionalism, whose forces must be implanted in the larger organism of human society. For him the notion of a united "mankind" was no empty abstraction: he visualized it as a "society of nations," devoted to the moral advancement of each of its members and to the perfection of their collective association.

The Congress of Vienna had hardly begun its deliberations when the separate interests of the four great European powers — Russia, Prussia, Austria, and England — again asserted themselves openly. France, defeated and internally weakened, was temporarily eliminated from the game of European power politics. As far as England and Austria were concerned, their interests seemed to run parallel. The first Peace of Paris had given England all she needed and wanted: the continental blockade had failed; and the acquisition of Egypt, Malta, Heligoland, the Cape of Good Hope, and other colonial territories made Great Britain the unassailable mistress of the Seven Seas. To compensate Holland for the loss of Capetown and Ceylon, Belgium was arbitrarily united with Holland, to form the kingdom of the Netherlands under William I of the house of Orange: an artificial aggregation of territories and populations that endured for scarcely two decades.

England's main interest on the European continent was the restoration and preservation of the "balance of power" and in this policy she could count on the full support of the Austrian State chancellor. With the defeat of France the danger of Russian hegemony in Europe loomed as a new and equally formidable threat. It was the tsar's intention to create a national and constitutional Polish State under his own supremacy. Alexander's position was greatly strengthened by Prussia's proposal to annex the entire kingdom of Saxony and the Austro-Prussian tension that resulted from these immoderate demands. Austria, Great Britain, and France were equally opposed to the Prussian plans and were willing to prevent the annexation of Saxony, if necessary, by force of arms. Finally, in view of the Russian danger, a compromise was worked out that gave Prussia approximately two fifths of Saxony. While she agreed to surrender the greater part of Prussian Poland to the tsar, she received substantial compensations on the left bank of the Rhine that practically restored the Prussian boundaries of 1806. Thus Prussia emerged from these political deals once more as one of the leading powers of Europe, and by the surrender of her Polish possessions to the tsar she had freed herself from the liability of having alien populations within her boundaries. Tsar Alexander proclaimed himself king of a united Poland and rounded off Russia's European frontiers by taking Finland from Sweden and Bessarabia from Turkey. He antagonized Metternich by his admonition to the European rulers to grant liberal constitutions to their subjects. All the territorial transactions were carried out with utter disregard for the wishes and aspirations of the populations, whereby the principle of "legitimacy" served as a convenient ruse and excuse.

g) *The German Question and the "Act of Confederation."* The most important result of the deliberations at Vienna was the creation of the "German Confederation," signalizing a provisional settlement of the complex "German question." From the beginning of the War of Liberation it had been generally recognized that some definite form of political organization must eventually supersede the defunct Empire. Many still believed in the possibility of resurrecting the "Holy Roman Empire of the German Nation" in a modernized and liberalized form. There was hardly any difference of opinion among the patriotic leaders as to the legitimate claims of the house of Hapsburg to leadership in such a reorganized and revitalized realm. When, in 1813, Baron vom Stein had called for the restoration of the imperial rule of the Hapsburgs, it was Metternich's keen political insight that had realized the incompatibility of the Austro-Prussian dualism with the idea of a centralized national monarchy. He was convinced that a durable political structure could only be erected in the form of a confederation of states that was sufficiently balanced and at the same time elastic enough to allow the coexistence of several autonomous national units, including the two great sovereign powers, Austria and Prussia. Only in such a decentralized union, welded together by a community of certain vital interests, but avoiding all unnecessary infringements on the sovereign rights of the member states, could the "peaceful dualism" of Prussia and Austria prove itself fruitful and creative.

But Metternich's plan of a "perpetual federation" (*foedus perpetuum*) among equals did not meet with the approval of the representatives of Prussia, Hardenberg and Humboldt. They, too, wanted to adhere to the system of a "peaceful dualism," but they demanded absolute supremacy for Prussia in the north and for Austria in the south, calling for the subjection of the smaller central states to the rule of their powerful neighbors. The negotiations of a committee of five, consisting of the representatives of Austria, Prussia, Hanover, Bavaria, and Wurtemberg, finally resulted in the passing of the "Act of Confederation" (1815), which designated Austria as the presiding power in the new Confederation and stipulated the creation of a Federal Diet (*Bundestag*), that was to meet in Frankfurt-on-the-Main.

The defined purpose of the "German Confederation" (*Deutscher Bund*) was "the preservation of the external and internal security of Germany, and the independence and inviolability of the individual German states." The Confederation consisted of thirty-nine sovereign states and included the king of Denmark (representing Holstein), the king of England (who was also king of Hanover), and the king of the Netherlands (representing the Grand Duchy of Luxembourg). A complicated electoral system was devised to prevent the larger states from outvoting the smaller ones and to make it impossible for any combination of the small states to force their will upon the larger ones. Each of the eleven large states had one vote, while the twenty-eight small states were divided up into six groups, each group commanding one vote. This total of seventeen votes made up the "Inner Council." Despite its many shortcomings this confederation of states acted as a check on the practically unlimited particularism that had prevailed in the Empire before 1806. Though still handicapped in its internal policies by too many conflicting interests, the new Confederation was able to present a united front when foreign affairs were concerned.

h) The "Hundred Days" and the End of Napoleon. In the same month of June, 1815, when the new order of Europe was sealed by the decrees of the Congress of Vienna, the dramatic episode of Napoleon's escape from Elba and his short-lived return to power — the rule of the "Hundred Days" — came to an end. Encouraged by the dissensions among the great powers and by the news of France's intense dislike of the Bourbon Restoration, Napoleon had landed on the French Riviera on March 1, 1815, accompanied by his loyal guard which he had been permitted to retain in exile. The French troops who had been dispatched to arrest him, and whom he encountered on his way to Paris, enthusiastically joined the banners of their old commander. The French people, apprehensive of the probability of renewed suffering and bloodshed, observed an attitude of watchful waiting. Although Napoleon in his proclamations declared himself willing to establish a strictly constitutional rule, the powers whose representatives were assembled in Vienna and on whose decisions the fate of his *coup d'état* depended, immediately forgot their quarrels and closed their ranks. They refused to receive the emperor's envoys and, on March 13, solemnly declared Napoleon an outlaw: an "enemy and destroyer of the peace of the world."

Four armies, commanded by Wellington, Blücher, Schwarzenberg, and Tsar Alexander, were hurriedly put into the field and made ready to invade France. Blücher was named commander in chief of the allied armies and Gneisenau was appointed chief of staff. The Prussians marched into the Netherlands but were thrown back by Napoleon who, using his customary strategy, had attacked before the armies of the enemy should have time to rally and unite their forces. The Prussian retreat might have developed into a rout if the superior strategic genius of Gneisenau had not recognized that the Prussians and the British must join their forces at any cost. Thus Gneisenau commanded his troops to relinquish their bases of operation and to withdraw in the direction of the village of Waterloo, south of Brussels. While Napoleon's Marshal Grouchy, assuming that the Prussians were retreating toward the Rhine, discovered too late that he was on the wrong track and had lost contact with the enemy, Napoleon himself turned against Wellington, unaware of the possibility of a joint English-Prussian opposition.

Wellington had moved into a defensive position near Waterloo, after he had received word from Blücher that the entire Prussian army was about

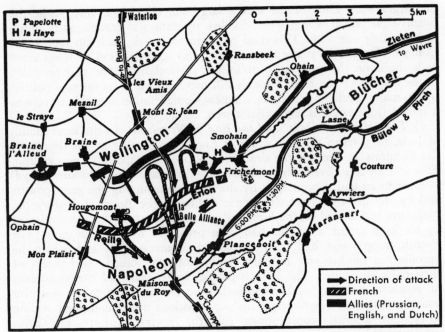

From *Der Grosse Herder*, Herder, Freiburg i. Br.

Battle of Waterloo.

to join the English mercenary troops. Wellington, who combined tenacity
with cool circumspection, was eminently fitted to direct and employ the
minutely calculated methods of defensive operations. While countless French
attacks spent their force on the massive wall of Wellington's army, the duke
calmly gave out the "order of the day": "Our strategy is quite simple: the
Prussians — or night!" When at last the Prussians advanced upon the right
flank of the French army, the British immediately joined in the forward
movement, taking possession of the field of battle. The French retreat became
an irregular flight, and while Wellington stopped and hesitated, the
Prussians followed the enemy, inspired by Gneisenau's "order of the day":
"We have shown how to win a victory; now let us demonstrate how to
chase an enemy!"

After six days the whole campaign was over. In Blücher's headquarters
there was general agreement that the new peace must be dictated in Paris
and that this time the military and national aspirations of Germany must
be given due consideration. Wellington and the English government, too,
wanted the march on Paris, but only to proclaim once more the restoration
of the Bourbons. When the Prussians, attacking the capital of France from
the south, had broken the resistance of the enemy, Fouché, Napoleon's
former minister of police, surrendered the city in the name of the provisional

government. Gneisenau demanded that the emperor of the French be handed over to the Prussians to face a court-martial. Napoleon abdicated a second time and, in order to avoid his being captured by the Prussians, asked his archenemies, the English, for asylum.

In the second Peace of Paris (November 20, 1815) the conservative point of view of the British government prevailed and the Prussian demands for reparations and securities were only partly fulfilled. France, under a restored Bourbon monarchy, retained the boundaries of the year 1792, but she had to pay an indemnity, and the greater part of the stolen art treasures were restored to the various capitals of Europe. An army of occupation under the command of the duke of Wellington was stationed in the northern provinces of France to see that the peace terms would be carried out in good faith.

Napoleon was given the asylum he had asked for: the lonely island of St. Helena in the South Atlantic became his prison for the remaining years of his life (1815–1821). Here he wrote his political testament, the *Memorial of St. Helena* (*Mémorial de Sainte Hélène*), in which he pronounced judgment over past and future and posed as the great pioneer of freedom and universal peace: "I have closed the crater of anarchy and untangled chaos. I have cleansed the revolution, ennobled the nations, strengthened the rulers. I have stimulated competition, rewarded every merit, enlarged the boundaries of fame. That is something. . . . I wanted to give peace to the world, but they have made me into a demon of war." He spoke of his dream of seeing free and creative peoples in a unified Europe, ruled by a constitutional monarch and protected by a citizen army, no longer subjected to the dictates of nobles and priests, but united in the idea of the great occidental commonwealth, the social and democratic Empire of the future. And, truly, with all his failings and unhealthy ambitions, there was dimly alive in this "executor of the revolution" the realization of the significance of the two major social forces of the nineteenth century: liberalism and nationalism. He started Europe's nations on their way to the new liberal economy, the new concepts of constitutional and democratic law, and the new glorification and deification of national destiny.*

Europe and the "Holy Alliance." The leaders of the four great powers which shared in the overthrow of Napoleon and were responsible for the new Europe that took shape at the Congress of Vienna were united in their will to lay the foundations for a lasting peace. Austria, Russia, Prussia, and England were resolved to establish themselves as a permanent council of a League of Nations, to which France was conditionally admitted in 1818, and which was to assume a kind of guardianship over European affairs,

---

* One of the lasting achievements of Napoleon was the creation of the *Code civil des Français*, better known as the *Code Napoléon* (1804). The historical significance of this law code lies in the fact that it incorporated some of the positive accomplishments of the French Revolution in the concepts of *civil law*. It was adopted and retained for shorter or longer periods in the Netherlands, in Luxembourg, in Belgium, in the later Prussian *Rheinprovinz* (in the *Pfalz*, in *Rheinhessen, Baden, Westfalen, Berg*, and *Hanover*), in some Swiss cantons, in Italy, and in Poland. It exerted decisive influence on the contemporary civil law codes of Switzerland, Mexico, and Central and South America.

by means of frequent consultation and mutual co-operation. To further this aim, congresses were held at Aachen (1818), Troppau (1820), Leibach (1821), and Verona (1822). The first rift in this "Concert of Europe" occurred when Great Britain reclaimed her freedom of action and resumed a policy of "splendid isolation." In 1825, Canning, the British prime minister, stated without misgivings that Europe was "once more back to the situation in which every nation is for itself, and God for all."

By reviving the spirit of isolationism England dealt a deathblow to the manifold attempts at international co-operation that were backed by an illustrious tradition, having found speculative expression in the thought of Leibniz, Kant, and others, and having become part of the theory of international law, a creation of the seventeenth and eighteenth centuries.

It was a reborn European solidarity that had vanquished Napoleon, and it was this new Europe that acted collectively in Vienna to defend this solidarity against disturbances from within and without. In the circles of the monarchs, diplomats, and intellectuals assembled at Vienna the idea of a "Christian State" was seriously discussed and finally translated into political actuality by the formation of the "Holy Alliance" (1815). It was Tsar Alexander who first proposed that the monarchs of Europe should act as the "Delegates of Providence" in pledging themselves "to take for their sole guide the precepts of Sacred Religion, namely the precepts of Justice, Christian Charity, and Peace," and to base international relations as well as national and social administration "upon the sublime truths which the Holy Religion of our Saviour teaches. . . . "

The "Holy Alliance," to which all the princes of Europe, with the exception of the pope, the Turkish sultan, and the prince regent of Great Britain, subscribed, was an outgrowth of the pietistic and romantic leanings of the restoration period and of the personal mysticism of the tsar. The monarchs declared that their governments and their peoples were members of one great Christian commonwealth whose only true sovereign was Christ. In three articles they summarized in a programmatic form the leading ideas of the restoration movement: the subjection of political life to the principles of Christian ethics, the adherence to the patriarchal form of government, the belief in the divine origin of all rulership, and the proposal to secure eternal peace by the creation of a League of Nations.

Despite the fact that many of the European princes signed this moral pledge halfheartedly, with mental reservations or even with cynical hypocrisy, the settlement of Vienna and the conclusion of the "Holy Alliance" were followed by forty years of relative calm in the political relations between the great powers. Castlereagh, the British minister of foreign affairs, spoke the mind of the skeptics when he called the pledge of the princes "a sublime piece of mysticism and nonsense," and Metternich's political realism saw in the document an expression of one of Tsar Alexander's pietistic moods, a "high-sounding nothing" that was "useless, to say the least." The pope, on the other hand, objected to the proclamation of the "unity of the great Christian Church in its three branches" (Catholic, Protestant, and Greek-Orthodox), and to the idea of a theocracy of secular monarchs, considering themselves as delegates of Christ.

Metternich and the Principle of Legitimism. Some of the monarchs who pledged adherence to the principles espoused by the originators of the "Holy Alliance" were the same who had based their claims to their hereditary titles and territories on the principle of "legitimacy." They forgot that their ancestors had established their absolute monarchical rule with callous disregard of the traditional rights of the Estates of their realms, and that there was hardly a throne in Europe that had been gained by other means than brute force and illegal encroachments upon the rights of individuals and groups. Nevertheless, the principle of "legitimacy" in itself was an attempt to combat the lawlessness of international relations by relating politics to moral norms, to overcome the Machiavellian separation of political action from moral sanctions by subjecting political rule to the laws of reason and justice. This was, despite its many shortcomings, the inherent tendency and significance of the "Metternich System" that impressed its stamp on the entire period between 1815 and 1848.

Prince Metternich himself was the truest personification of the European counterrevolution. In theory and practice he represented the ideas of conservation, order, and stability and opposed them to the doctrines of social and political revolution. His cool and systematically calculated diplomacy was inspired and strengthened by an almost grotesque vanity and the conviction of his own infallibility. He was averse to any kind of emotionalism, and his dispassionate aloofness made him a stranger to the life and thought of the people and incapable of the self-abandon and personal fervor that characterize the truly great statesman. He felt at home and moved with perfect ease only in the glittering atmosphere of the "salon" and the royal cabinet, but was unwilling to expose himself to the political storms that were brewing in the world at large and especially in the growing revolutionary sentiment of the middle classes. The restoration of the European balance of power appeared to him the surest guarantee for the preservation of the graduated feudal structure of Western civilization. It was for this reason that he made the continuation of this historic order the quintessence of his "system" and his "legitimism." His closest confidant and associate was Frederick von Gentz (1764–1832), a publicist of extraordinary talent and dubious morality. He popularized Metternich's reactionary ideas and aided his friend and superior in the development of an ingenious system of political censorship that held Austria and part of Germany in intellectual bondage from the end of the War of Liberation to the days of the "March Revolution" of 1848 (cf. p. 527 sqq.).

In the name of the "reason of state" the organs of Metternich's police organization waged a relentless war against both nationalism and liberalism. Metternich had to carry on this struggle to the bitter end if he wanted to remain true to himself and his deepest convictions. But he was not unaware that the end would spell defeat for him and his entire system of values. Yet his opposition to what he considered the diabolic spirit of the age admitted of no compromise. In his diary of 1820 we read the following words: "I have to live my life in an abominable period. I was either born too early or too late; as it is, I am of little use for anything. Had I lived in an earlier period, I could have enjoyed the spirit of the times, and if I had lived in a later period, I could have served the work of reconstruction. But today I am spending my life in supporting decaying structures. I ought to have been born in the year 1900, with the twentieth century before me. . . . It is my most secret thought that the old Europe is at the beginning of its end. Resolved to perish with it, I shall know how to do my duty. The new Europe, on the other hand, is still in the process of becoming, but there will be chaos between the end and the new beginning."

Restoration in State and Church. The major theme of the political and social struggles of the nineteenth century was the antagonism between monarchical rule and the sovereignty of the people. After France had been readmitted to the "Concert" of the great powers of Europe (1818), the five leading monarchs (of Prussia, Austria, Russia, England, and France) established themselves as a new aristocracy of legislators and administrators. They considered it their principal task to preserve the newly gained stability and to suppress any and all political trends which threatened a resurgence of the revolutionary sentiments of 1789. In their attempt to restore the political and social structure of the *ancien régime* the monarchs welcomed the aid of religion as a handmaid of absolutism, and a reunion of "throne and altar" was to act as a check on the growing popular demand for democratic and constitutional representation.

To justify their antirevolutionary measures the politicians of the restoration movement made use of the arguments that the English statesman Edmund Burke (1729-1797) had advanced in his *Reflections on the French Revolution* (1790). He had distinguished between a legitimate struggle for the inalienable rights of man, as evidenced by the British Revolution of 1688 and the American War of Independence (1774-1783) — a struggle which in the Anglo-Saxon world extended from Magna Charta to the Declaration of Independence and the "Bill of Rights" — and the nihilistic tendencies of the French Revolution of 1789. Frederick von Gentz translated and commentated Burke's *Reflections* and thereby popularized Burke's ideas in the circles of the French emigrants in Germany and Austria. Men like Joseph de Maistre or the poet Chateaubriand (1768-1848) had experienced the Jacobin reign of terror and, in exile and destitution, they had preserved their reverence for the traditional values of home, family, political authority, and religion. They acted as the vanguard of counterrevolution, social restoration, and political reaction. For De Maistre Royalism and Catholicism were natural allies, and in his work on the papacy (1819) he called upon the princes and peoples to overcome anarchy and dissolution by recognizing the universal mission of the Roman pontiff, and by accepting the guidance of the ancient authorities of State and Church. De Maistre's theory of the "organic" and "corporative" nature of State and society was adopted and further developed by the German spokesmen of the restoration period, by statesmen and historians as well as by the representatives of arts and letters. The Congress of Vienna restored Pope Pius VII to his temporal possessions in Italy, and the Jesuit Order (cf. p. 254 sqq.) that had been suppressed in 1773 was re-established and reorganized in 1814.

The "German Movement." In Prussia the War of Liberation had been fought as a crusade of the people, who had been promised by their leaders that victory would carry with it both national independence and a more just social order. The king of Prussia had promised his people a constitution, but as soon as victory was assured he had let himself be dissuaded by Metternich from carrying out the provisions of his pledge. The only German states in which constitutions were granted in the years after the close of the war were Bavaria, Baden, Weimar, Wurtemberg, Hanover, Nassau, and Hesse-Darmstadt. The disillusionment of the war-weary populations was aggravated by a catastrophic failure of crops in 1816–1817 and by a severe economic crisis that was caused by the flooding of German markets with English goods, following the lifting of the continental blockade. The middle classes were utterly discouraged and fell back into their former lethargy and political indifference. Under Hardenberg's chancellorship Stein's political and social reforms were gradually deprived of their meaning and finally completely nullified.

The apathy of the middle classes was not shared by the academic youth, by those young men who had readily offered their lives for the liberation of their country. Those who returned from the battlefields were unable to resign themselves to the idea that their faith and idealism should go unrewarded and that the drab routine of political and social bureaucracy should again settle down on the German lands and stifle the élan of the national awakening. They demanded to have a voice and a share in the molding of their own and their people's future destiny.

Thus the beginnings of the liberal and democratic movement in Germany was in the truest sense a "youth movement." The first important step was the reform of student life, the education of youth for an active and intelligent participation in the political life of a nation in the making. It was only a start but as such it was vigorous though at times ill balanced and prone to overstep its bounds. The way was hard and wearisome, beset with dangers, humiliations, and repressions: the first phase in the slow process of the emancipation of the German middle classes, whose habitual inertia could only be overcome several decades later when the new technological and scientific evolution had provided the requisite social and economic bases for complete success.

In the course of the seventeenth and eighteenth centuries the original groups of "nations" of the medieval universities (cf. p. 137 sqq.) had developed into student corporations (*Verbindungen, Landsmannschaften*) whose members had nominally retained their regional character (Westphalians, Franks, Saxons, etc.), but whose lives and ideas had been influenced by the cosmopolitanism and humanitarianism of the age of Enlightenment. As to social behavior, the students had developed their own code of morals, based on a collective opposition to the well-tempered morality of the bourgeois "philistine." They spoke their own conspicuous lingo, set their own standards in fashion and custom, displayed a supreme disdain of the social conventions of the middle classes, and spent altogether too much time on carousing, dueling, and gambling.

The events at the turn of the century and the changing outlook on life of the generation of the War of Liberation had their profound effects on the thought and habits of the German students. While their associations persisted in their loyalty to the inherited forms of the convivial academic style (the *Komment*), they imparted a new meaning to these external forms. Men like Schiller and Fichte set a living example that acted as a powerful stimulus in the impending reform of academic life. The University of Jena, which for some years had counted both Schiller and Fichte among the members of its faculty, became the model institution of higher learning in the early period of the romantic movement (cf. p. 470 sqq.). In his lectures *On the Idea of Our Universities* the romantic nature philosopher, H. Steffen (1773–1845), described these institutions as "the guardians of the national spirit and the creators of moral freedom." During and following the War of Liberation the corporative students' unions (*Corps*) in all German universities were organized in the "Association of Senior Members" (*Seniorenconvent, S.C.*), acting as the representatives and spokesmen of incorporated and unincorporated students alike. The *Corps* furnished the largest contingents of volunteers, and the common cause made them forget all regional differences and petty factional disputes.

A new plan for the "Order and Institution of the German *Burschenschaft*" had been submitted by Ludwig Jahn (cf. p. 442 sq.) as early as 1811, with the avowed purpose of putting an end to all particularistic tendencies among the academic youth and to enlist all students in Jahn's program of physical education and moral reform. The idea bore fruit in 1818, when the German *Burschenschaften* pledged allegiance to the common ideals of "freedom, honor, and fatherland," and adopted black, red, and gold, the colors of Major von Lützow's heroic "Free Corps," as a symbolic manifestation of their convictions. In proclaiming black, red, and gold as the ancient imperial colors of Germany, the *Burschenschaften* were referring to the imperial standard of the old "Holy Empire" that showed the emblem of a black eagle with red talons, set off against a background of gold.

It was in the circles of the *Burschenschaft* that the idealism of the War of Liberation was kept alive. The only German regions that remained, on the whole, unaffected by the new academic spirit were Catholic Bavaria and Austria, where a patriarchal and paternal relationship between teachers and students still prevailed and where the original affiliation between monastic school and university was still essentially unimpaired.

The year 1817, the year of the third centennial of the Lutheran Reformation and the fourth anniversary of the battle of Leipzig, was chosen by the *Burschenschaften* to manifest publicly their unity and the ideals by which it was inspired. A mammoth demonstration was staged at the Wartburg, the famous castle near Eisenach where Luther had translated the New Testament (cf. p. 226). One of the speakers linked the Protestant Reformation with the struggle for political independence and eulogized "the dual feast of the rebirth of free thought and the liberation of the fatherland." The entire celebration presented an unusual combination of divine service and political demonstration, and it was concluded with prayer, benediction, and the singing of one of the old Protestant hymns.

If this had been all, the meeting at the Wartburg would probably never have acquired its great historic fame. What gave it a spectacular and wholly unexpected prominence was the sequel to the main proceedings, enacted by some radical Berliners, after most of the participants had already left. Imitating Luther's burning of the papal bull in Wittenberg (cf. p. 224), these high-spirited young men built a bonfire and committed to the flames several books by reactionary authors as well as some of the despised symbols of benighted absolutism and political conservatism, among them a pigtail and a corporal's staff. After having defiantly shouted their *"Pereat!"* ("Let it be destroyed forever!"), they went home in peace, proud of having done a day's work.

But Metternich and with him the German princes saw in the Wartburg Festival a serious threat to the monarchical and authoritarian principles of government. They were strengthened in their conviction that revolution was about to raise its ugly head and that something must be done about it when the liberal press praised the student demonstration as an event of great political significance. There followed a diplomatic exchange of opinions between the courts of Berlin and Vienna, the outcome of which was a joint *démarche* with the Grand Duke Charles Augustus of Saxe-Weimar, on whose territory the offense had been committed and who, having granted his people a constitution in the same year, was strongly and rightly suspected as a friend of democratic reforms. But Charles Augustus, who was also the friend of Goethe and the promoter and protector of German Classicism and Humanism, could not be intimidated. He lent further encouragement to the members of the *Burschenschaft* and made it possible for a general student gathering, composed of delegations from fourteen German universities, to meet at Jena (1818) and to draft and adopt a constitution. It was an important document that emphasized the German-Christian character of the *Burschenschaft* and made membership dependent on the profession of an exclusive nationalism, on devotion to "Luther's German God," and on the acceptance of a standardized academic code of honor.

The members of this German youth movement were motivated in their deliberations and actions by a deep-seated resentment against the feudal aristocrats, whose influence still dominated the petty principalities of Germany, whose ideas on culture and education were borrowed from France, and who were separated from their subjects by the barriers of social prejudice and distrust. Their sons began to flock to the fashionable students' *Corps* in increasing numbers and were taught by their elders to look down upon the *Burschenschaften* as the *rendez-vous* of the academic rabble.

The majority of the academic youth, on the other hand, came from the German middle classes. They were proudly conscious of the moral and cultural virtues that they had inherited from the tradition of the Lutheran parsonage. They were joined by those young noblemen who had fought the battle of liberation shoulder to shoulder with them and who shared their contempt of class privilege, sloth, complacency, bureaucracy, the idolization of material possessions and the fecundity of money. And yet, the effects of the academic reform were not very far reaching. After the original élan of the new movement had subsided, the dividing lines between *Corps* and *Burschenschaft* were largely obliterated and pharisaic bigotry and an affected cult of the sophisticated and the unconventional became a characteristic mark of most of the members of the German student fraternities.

The one distinguishing character trait that was retained by the members of the *Burschenschaft* and that made them the standard-bearers of the national movement was their abiding interest in the political destinies of Germany. Practically all the pioneers of German unification grew up under the influence of the *Burschenschaft* and owed to it the pattern of their lives. From the ranks of the more radical of its members the party of the so-called "unconditionals" (*die Unbedingten*) was recruited, aiming at a thorough reform of the governmental system of Germany, with the ultimate establishment of a German republic as their goal. The "unconditionals" were inspired by the glowing fanaticism of Karl Follen (1795-1840) who, together with Karl Schurz (1829-1906) and Franz Lieber (1800-1872), is counted among the early leaders of German Liberalism and who, like Schurz and Lieber, after having been expelled from Germany, found a ready response and a broader field for his activities in the United States.*

In Jena Karl Follen made the acquaintance of Karl Sand, a student of Protestant theology, an idealist whose mental equilibrium had been badly shaken by the emotional strain of the war and the anticlimax that was provided by the broken promises of the German princes. Sand knew no higher ambition than to become a martyr for the exalted cause of social freedom, and he decided that he could best prove himself a true disciple of the teachings of Karl Follen by assassinating the German playwright August von Kotzebue (1761-1819), whose *History of Prussia* had been burned on the occasion of the Wartburg Festival and who, because of his

---

* Karl Follen became one of the leaders of the antislavery movement in the United States. From 1824-1835 he was a member of the German faculty of Harvard University.

close relations with the Russian tsar, was hated by the students as "a paid spy of despotism."

Though Sand paid with his life for his sordid crime, he was hailed by his fellow students as well as by many others of his liberal-minded fellow countrymen as a martyred hero who had sacrificed his life for the honor and future greatness of Germany.

The case of Karl Sand was a real godsend for all those who had long advocated the sternest repressive measures against the liberal and democratic movement. Metternich in particular was firmly determined to make the most of this opportunity "provided by the splendid Sand at the expense of poor Kotzebue," as he caustically expressed his own reaction. The Austrian minister communicated immediately with the government of Prussia to effect, if possible, joint action on the part of both monarchies. Prussia declared her willingness to aid in crushing the spirit of social revolution and, after preliminary negotiations between Metternich and King Frederick William III, the ministers of Austria, Prussia, Bavaria, Wurtemberg, and some of the smaller German states met at the fashionable spa of Karlsbad in Bohemia to work out the famous "Karlsbad Decrees" of 1819, which were shortly afterward ratified by the *"Bundestag."*

Even before the publication of the decrees the persecution and incarceration of suspect persons had begun, and immediately after the document had been ratified a rigid censorship was imposed on all publications and the freedom of speech was radically curtailed. Red, black, and gold, the colors of the *Burschenschaft,* were banned as symbols of the spirit of revolt, and the *Burschenschaft* itself was dissolved. All teachers who were spreading "pernicious doctrines, hostile to public order or undermining existing political institutions" were to be dismissed, and in each university a government official was to supervise all lectures, so as to give them "a wholesome direction, calculated to prepare the studying youth for their future destination."

On May 15, 1820, the "Vienna Final Act" (*Wiener Schlussakte*) was adopted by the *"Bundestag,"* signalizing the triumph of the forces of reaction and putting the final stamp of approval on the repressive measures of the individual governments. The "Karlsbad Decrees" were the most authentic documentation of the "Metternich System." By their ruthless infringements on human rights they arrested a development whose dynamic force, however, could not be permanently halted. It only gathered strength and momentum for the inevitable radical outburst that was to tear apart Metternich's carefully woven web of prohibitions.

Chapter 14

GERMAN ROMANTICISM

Classicism and Romanticism. The world of ideas which inspired the generation that lived through the Wars of Liberation and the ensuing period of political restoration was in many ways a logical outgrowth and culmination of that cult of personality that had been the creed and ideal goal of the leaders of German Classicism (cf. Chap. 12) and the New Humanism (cf. p. 403 sq.). But whereas Goethe and Schiller had sought and achieved a happy balance of human faculties and their expression in literature and society, the Romantic movement of the early nineteenth century dissolved again into its constituent parts the unity and harmony that had been achieved by the classical thinkers and writers. While German Classicism had succeeded in fusing the irrationalism and sentimentalism of "Storm and Stress" with the rationalism of the period of Enlightenment, and had been able to integrate form and content in their works and moral freedom and constraint in their lives, German Romanticism restored to the fullest extent the polarity of these antagonistic forces. The German romanticists believed that the classical synthesis had been achieved at the expense of the depth and breadth of human experience and that an actual unification of the individual and the universal, of personal freedom and objective law, of content and form — nonexistent in the world of appearances — could only be realized in that ideal world to which their yearning aspired.

The proposed classical solution appeared to the romantic authors as merely one solution, but by no means the best and the most desirable. It was their contention that in the attempt to achieve harmonious beauty and formal perfection the classical writers had neglected or suppressed certain vital aspects of reality. For the sake of clarity and intelligibility they had excluded from their abstract speculation and their concrete literary accomplishments the mysterious realms of the preternatural and supernatural, the occult borderland of dreams, visions, and mystical intuitions.

It would be erroneous to designate German Romanticism as a flight from reality. It is more correct to say that Classicism and Romanticism differ in their concept and definition of reality. The classicist experiences with Aristotle the ideal in the contemplation of the individual and concrete, while the romanticist considers with Plato the realm of ideas and universals as supremely real, attributing to the individual object only a borrowed, shadowy, or at best symbolic form of existence. In its endeavor to span all the heights and depths of being, German Romanticism is engaged in a restless search for a wished-for totality, moving from one extreme to the other, always suffering from the fault of excess, always overstating its case, always on the way but never at rest. Life thus reveals itself in its aspects of boundlessness rather than in its limitations, in its dynamism rather than in its static repose and permanence. The "longing infinite" becomes an end in itself, a longing that falls eternally short of its fruition, and all the endeavors and adventures of the human soul are seen as "hieroglyphics of the one eternal love" for the supreme realities of absolute truth, goodness, and beauty. Whereas the classical writer and thinker is concerned with immediate personal values and their realization, the romanticist is always preoccupied with distant goals whose realization transcends and defies the limitations of time and space. Romanticism at its best offers the sublime spectacle of a prodigious quest of the religious and metaphysical meaning of life, nature, and art. At its worst it plunges its protagonists into a chaotic world of shapeless phantasms and hapless imaginings.

Some literary historians have described Classicism and Romanticism as two polar and ever recurrent attitudes of human nature, related and at the same time opposed to each other, as are light and darkness, clarity and formlessness, or male and female. Mme. de Staël (1766–1817) was the first author who dwelt upon the contrast between the "romantic North" and the "classical South," and others have gone further, viewing Romanticism as the truest and fullest manifestation of the northern, Germanic mind.

Historic evidence seems to reveal such rigid classifications as short cuts which fail to do justice to very complex phenomena. One would certainly miss the mark if one were to consider the classical thinkers and writers of Germany as less "Germanic" than those of the romantic age. It is quite obvious, on the other hand, that Germany at certain stages of her cultural evolution has shown decided preference for romantic forms and concepts and that the ideal of classical beauty and perfection has figured historically as a more remote possibility. We feel justified therefore in saying that Classicism and Romanticism reflect a dual aspect of German mentality as perhaps of human nature in general, but that Romanticism as an intellectual pattern and as a medium of literary and artistic expression seems to recommend itself more readily to the Germans.

It is likewise a matter of historical record that just as there are different non-Germanic forms of Classicism so also the romantic movement flourished in the other countries of Europe as well as in the United States of America. The eighteenth-century romanticism of Young's "Night Thoughts" (1742–1745), Macpherson's "Ossian" (cf. p. 393), and Sterne's sentimental novels (cf. p. 392) exerted a strong influence on the German romanticists, as did Walter Scott's novels and Byron's poetry in the early nineteenth century. But even stronger was the impetus that English and American nineteenth-century Romanticism received from Germany, especially during the decades that followed the Napoleonic wars (Carlyle, Poe, Longfellow, Margaret Fuller, and the New England "Transcendentalists"). Italy, France, Spain, the Scandinavian and Slavic nations had romantic movements of their own, more or less remotely related to the contemporary intellectual trends in Germany. French romanticism broke with the classico-rationalistic national tradition, while Italian Romanticism ushered in the literary and political *risorgimento* (national unification, *c.* 1815–1870), and Scandinavian Romanticism marked the "golden age" of the literatures of the northernmost European countries. The general adoption of the term "romanticism" points, to be sure, to a number of common characteristics, but this should not obscure the fact that these several romantic movements carry a widely different meaning within the framework of different national cultures.

"The Romantic School." German Romanticism constituted itself in a literary "school" whose members worked out a new set of aesthetic rules which they opposed to those of the classical authors. But despite this seeming opposition they were still under the spell of Classicism to such an extent that they gave their first periodical a Greek name (*Athenäum,* 1798–1800) and considered Goethe's classical novel *Wilhelm Meister* as the incarnation of everything truly artistic and poetic.

a) *Representative Authors.* The members of the so-called "older" and "younger" romantic school, though actually belonging to the same generation, represent two distinct phases in the development of the movement. The former laid out the general program and provided the aesthetic theory, the latter translated the romantic ideology into the language of poetry and creative artistic accomplishment.

Jena, Heidelberg, Berlin, and Dresden were the intellectual centers of the movement as a whole, which included among its "older" members: August Wilhelm Schlegel (1767–1845); Friedrich Schlegel (A. W.'s younger brother, 1772–1829); Friedrich von Hardenberg ("Novalis," 1772–1801); Wilhelm Wackenroder (1773–1798); Ludwig Tieck (1773–1853).

Among its "younger" members are: Clemens Brentano (1778–1842); Achim von Arnim (1781–1831); Jakob Grimm (1785–1863); Wilhelm Grimm (J.'s younger brother, 1786–1859); Joseph Görres (1776–1848); Ernst Theodor Amadeus Hoffmann (1776–1822); Joseph von Eichendorff (1788–1857).

More or less loosely related to the "romantic school" were the patriotic romanticists who in prose and poetry glorified the War of Liberation: Ernst Moritz Arndt (1769–1860), Max von Schenkendorf (1783–1817), Theodor Körner (1791–1813); the Swabian romanticists: Ludwig Uhland (1787–1862), Eduard Mörike (1804–1875); the romantic playwrights: Heinrich von Kleist (1777–1811), Franz Grillparzer (1791–1872), and a number of *epigoni* (imitators) who adopted some of the romantic paraphernalia without understanding the romantic spirit as such.

In the process of welding together the different romantic individuals and groups, in establishing bonds of friendship and love, in stimulating enthusiasm and inspiring literary production, the part played by the leading women of the romantic circle and their aesthetic *salons* can hardly be over-estimated. Dorothea, the daughter of the philosopher Moses Mendelssohn (cf. p. 369), who married Friedrich Schlegel, and August Wilhelm Schlegel's wife Carolina were the most prominent among a group of highly cultured, intellectually sophisticated, and morally "emancipated" women. It was their influence that kindled the early romanticists' intense interest in the problems of marriage and sexual relations and gave new impetus to their speculations on the interrelation of art, religion, and love.

b) *Translators and Historians.* It was the feminine element in German Romanticism and the significant role that it played in social life and culture that imparted to romantic thought much of its intuitional character and without doubt contributed its share to making the romanticists masters in the art of translation. In the pages of the *Athenäum* the brothers Schlegel laid down definite rules for the translation of literary masterpieces, stressing the importance of inspirational empathy (*Einfühlung*), whereby the trans-lator was to become "the poet of the poet." He was to transpose himself into a foreign tongue and mentality and, having become one with it, was to re-create the spirit of the work in his vernacular language. By following this advice the romantic translators appropriated for their own nation the poetic treasures of foreign cultures and literatures (Shakespeare, Dante, Tasso, Ariosto, Cervantes, Calderón, Lope de Vega, Camoēs, etc.). Thus they brought nearer to realization Herder's and Goethe's idea of a "world-literature" that was to be the common property of all civilized peoples.

Friedrich Schlegel, who described the historian as a "retrospective prophet," exemplified in his own critical works the romanticists' innate and highly cultivated historical sense. It was this sense that enabled them to delve into the cultural deposits of the past and, aided by inner kinship, to redis-cover the German and European Middle Ages. They re-evaluated the achievements of the past in art and literature as well as in the fields of political and social endeavor, thereby inspiring their contemporaries with a new love for certain indigenous qualities of German thought, life, and culture. This love for the timeless qualities of the German mind was alive in the fervor of German nationalism in the days of the War of Liberation. And this nationalism was replenished by the poetic glorification of the Holy Empire of the Hohenstaufens and enhanced by the magic charm of a reborn world of quaint medieval cities, of proud castles overlooking the vales and plains and silvery rivers, and of towering cathedrals whose princely majesty stood guard over a sturdy people of valiant nobles, prosperous burghers, and deft and devout artisans. And past and present were linked and enveloped by the same nature in which the spirit of the changing times lived an en-chanted life, in which a multitude of voices united in the enduring trans-figuration of the mystery of creation.

c) *"Longing Infinite" and "Romantic Irony."* The endeavor of the romantic writers to embody in their works the entire breadth of life, its lofty heights and dark abysses, the secrets of heaven, earth, and hell, found its expression in Friedrich Schlegel's definition of poetry: "Romantic poetry is progressive universal poetry. It is destined not only to reunite all the separate branches of poetry and to relate poetry with philosophy and rhetoric, but also to fuse and bind together poetry and prose, creative and critical ingenuity, to vitalize and socialize poetry, and to poetize society . . ." (*Athenäum*). For August Wilhelm Schlegel "the poetry of the ancients was that of possession: ours is a poetry of longing; the one rests firmly on the ground of the present, while the other sways to and fro between recollection and presentiment." Thus German Romanticism, at its best, strove for the realization of absolute truth, goodness, and beauty, ever conscious, nevertheless, that infinite and absolute perfection can be approximated only in the form of finite symbols and "hieroglyphics." It was this consciousness of the relative and fragmentary character of artistic and literary forms that became the source of "romantic irony": the supreme effort on the part of the author to overcome the necessary limitations of human accomplishments by the sovereignty of the human spirit which rises above the contingencies of its own creations and ironically contrasts the absolute idea with the frailty of its symbolic representation.

d) The New Medievalism. Despite the fact, however, that the romanticists were most vitally concerned with problems and experiences that had their dynamic center in their own personalities, they aspired to a superindividual realm of ideas and to a communal culture that was to impart added significance to their individual lives and works. They seized upon philosophy and religion in their attempt to unify and integrate personal experiences in a transcendent sphere of values. Living in an age that was witnessing the gradual dissolution of the universal religious and social structures of the past, their yearning for a total view of life attached itself retrospectively to an idealized image of the Catholic Middle Ages, their religion, their thought, and their culture.

Novalis (cf. p. 476), in his essay *Christendom or Europe,* solemnly and passionately sounded the call "back to the Middle Ages!" Himself a Lutheran with pietistic and mystical leanings, he described in glowing colors the unified civilization of medieval Europe as it had emerged from a dark and chaotic world: "Those were beautiful, splendid times, when Europe was one Christian country, when one Christendom inhabited this . . . continent. One great common interest united the most remote provinces of this broad spiritual realm. . . . One sovereign guided and united the great political forces. . . . And how agreeable and well adapted to the inner nature of man this governance and this institution was, is proven by the . . . harmonious development of all human faculties, by the greatness that was achieved by individuals in all the branches of those sciences that constitute art and life, and by the flourishing trade with spiritual and material wares, inside Europe and even extending to the remotest regions of India." The author pictures the Lutheran Reformation as the first phase of the incipient anarchy of Europe, culminating in the rule of Absolutism and the disasters of the French Revolution. He is convinced that Europe's wounds can only be healed and Europe's peace and unity restored by a spiritual power which will be strong and respected enough to lay the foundations for a true League of Nations (*Staatenverein*): "No peace can be concluded among the warring powers . . . , all so-called peace is merely an armistice as long as the point of view of political cabinets prevails. . . . Blood will continue to flow over Europe, until the nations become aware of the horrible insanity which drives them about in a circle, until . . . they again approach their former altars, performing the works of peace and celebrating upon the smoking ruins the great brotherly feast of reconciliation. . . . Religion only can reawaken Europe, provide security for its peoples, and reestablish Christianity in new splendor. . . ."

Like Novalis the early romanticists visualized the "invisible" universal Church of the future and like him they were fascinated by the kindred spiritualistic philosophy and theosophy of Jacob Böhme (cf. p. 270) and the pantheistic speculation of Spinoza and Goethe. They became more and more interested in the mysterious borderlands of the human soul, and by aesthetic considerations as well as by their desire for new metaphysical bearings they were led into the fold of the Catholic Church. While Tieck and Novalis professed a sentimental attachment to Catholicism, Friedrich Schlegel, F. von Stolberg, Zacharias Werner, and others actually embraced the Catholic faith, and Görres and Brentano returned in the end to the abandoned creed of their youth.

e) *From Classicism to Romanticism: Jean Paul and Hölderlin.* Turning from a general analysis of the romantic movement to a brief consideration of individual authors, the first to demand attention are two precursors of German Romanticism whose works single them out as pioneers, standing on the threshold of a new literary age.

In an obituary speech the poet Ludwig Börne (cf. p. 580 sq.) eulogized *Jean Paul* (Johann Paul Friedrich Richter, 1763–1825) in these words: "A star has gone down, and the eyes of the century will be closed before another of the same magnitude will appear. . . . There will be a time, however, when he will be reborn for all, and they all will then mourn his departure. But he stands patiently at the gate of the twentieth century, waiting with a smile on his lips, until his creeping people will have caught up with him." Jean Paul, a parson's son of a small Franconian town, was both a child of his age and the representative of ideas that heralded the spirit of a liberal and democratic society. One of the greatest stylists of the German tongue, his prose is saturated with a rich and childlike humor, with which he softens and dissolves the tragic dissonances of human life. A born educator, he advocates in both his pedagogical and literary works the ideal of the harmonious development of the faculties of intellect, will, and emotions. As an author he is more interested in standards of truth and righteousness than in formal beauty and artistic perfection. His loving human heart, ever devoted to the woes of his fellow men, makes him an ardent champion of the poor, the weak, and the humble in their defensive struggle against their oppressors and exploiters.

Jean Paul, the writer, is greatest in the literary form of the idyl, in which he encloses a glittering world of quaint characters and occurrences, of princes and fools, eccentric geniuses and pedantic schoolmasters, an abridged universe in which life and death, joy and pain, love and iniquity rest in the embrace of his golden humor. The melodiousness of his style points forward to the rhythmical musicality of romantic prose and sets him apart from the plastic-formal classicism of Goethe and Schiller.

Jean Paul, the moralist and political theorist, expects social and cultural regeneration from a highly developed sense of personal responsibility: "When I read of wars and other calamities . . . I do not curse or whine or remain inactive: rather, since all this misery results from the immorality of some individuals—, I try to extirpate and avoid any and all immorality within myself, well knowing that my own immorality must strike ever new wounds in others." This deep sense of personal accountability, having its roots in the author's virile Protestant faith, made Jean Paul aware of the social significance of his work and made him strive for the reunion of life and literature. Leading art and poetry back from their lofty isolation to the great current of popular tradition, Jean Paul anticipated the ideals of an art that was determined by the ethical motives of social and national consciousness.

Friedrich Hölderlin (1770–1843), a Swabian poet and the second of the great precursors of the Romantic School, shares with Jean Paul the fate of having been rescued from prolonged oblivion by the authors and literary critics of our own century. Although in his youth he associated with Schiller, Schelling, and Hegel, he stands even more apart from his contemporaries than Jean Paul. His life and his poetry were inseparably intertwined. Like the hero of his one and only novel (*Hyperion,* 1797–1799) he lived as a "hermit" in the midst of a society which could offer no satisfactory answer to his longing for a unified world view. In tragic isolation and burdened with a typically Swabian inclination to brooding introspection, he sought in vain to bridge the chasm between subjective experience and objective reality. In vain he tried to find refuge and consolation in nature, in art, and in love, the three symbols and sublimations of his frustrated quest of the divine and its realization in a community of beautiful souls. In the idealized forms and figures of ancient Greece he had visualized the serene harmony of body and mind that seemed denied to him and his generation. And then, quite miraculously, and for the duration of one blessed moment that bore the weight of eternity, the ideal seemed to have assumed human shape in Susette Gontard, the wife of a Frankfurt banker, in whose house he had been engaged as a private tutor. But even this happy idyl was clouded with the hues of impending resignation and profound melancholy. When the hour of parting came, the poet's fate was sealed.

From a brief sojourn in Spain he returned as an aimless wanderer, spending the remaining thirty-seven years of his life in incurable mental derangement.

To Hölderlin's love for Susette Gontard, the "Diotima" of his *Hyperion* and his poems, we owe not only some of the greatest literary documents of the German tongue but also an exchange of letters that rank with the most sublime specimens of epistolary literature. As a poet Hölderlin proved himself a great master of style and artistic form who from inner affinity clothed his experiences in complex Greek meters. In the dynamically moving force of his free rhythms he resuscitated the strong religious individualism of Pindar's (*c.* 520–446 B.C.) Greek odes and anticipated the hymnic language of Friedrich Nietzsche (cf. p. 695 sq.).

f) Leaders of the "Older School." The critical theories of the Romantic School owe their precise formulation to *August Wilhelm Schlegel* and his younger brother Friedrich. August Wilhelm's cultivated sense of literary form and the supple flexibility of his mind made him the master translator of his age. His Shakespeare translation (completed by Tieck's daughter Dorothea and her husband, Count Wolf Baudissin) as well as his translations of Spanish, Italian, and Portuguese masterpieces are contributions of lasting value to German literature. He actually succeeded in making Shakespeare one of the most universally known and revered authors in German lands and one of the most popular ones on the German stage. In his aesthetic and critical works he systematically explored the literary documents of the German past and demanded the reformation of German life and culture in conformity with the ancient indigenous forces of the German mind. For several years the author was the faithful travel companion of Mme. de Staël who with her book *De l'Allemagne* (1810) had been the first to arouse intense interest in her native France in the achievements of classical and romantic German literature. As professor of literature and art history at the newly founded University of Bonn on the Rhine, A. W. Schlegel devoted the years of his mature life to an extensive study of Sanskrit (Hindoo) language and literature.

Friedrich Schlegel, more so than his brother, was given to a passion for rational analysis, evidenced as much in his literary and historical criticism as in the poetic paraphrases of his own self. He interpreted history in terms of personal needs and experiences. In vain he tried to master the discordant urges of his own nature from a focal point in his own personality and, failing in this, he found the desired unity in the "universalism" of the Catholic Church. In the three great works of his later life (*Philosophy of Life; Philosophy of History; Philosophy of Language*) he endeavored to demonstrate the unity of knowledge and faith and "to make manifest to this dissipated age the divine power of the Church in all the sciences and in all human relations." His linguistic and literary studies, especially in the field of Sanskrit and other Oriental languages, have earned him a prominent place in the history of philology and in the newly developing disciplines of systematic literary history and literary criticism.

More creative as a poet and more unified in his world view than the Schlegels was *Friedrich von Hardenberg,* better known by his pen name *Novalis.* His short life was filled to the brim with the romantic "longing infinite," burning within him as a living spiritual flame and sapping his physical strength. To his friends he appeared as a stranger from another planet, but he nevertheless combined with the ethereal and otherworldly qualities of a romantic poet a remarkably developed practical sense that enabled him to distinguish himself as a student of law and as a mining engineer. One of the numerous modern disciples of Plato and the Platonic mystics and theosophists, he described the human soul as imprisoned in an earthly body, striving for liberation and longing to return to its divine source.

The poet more than other human beings has remained conscious of this exalted dignity of the human soul, and he alone knows of the secret paths that lead to the spiritual truth that underlies all sense appearances. It is the task of the poet, therefore, to lead mankind from reason to faith, from philosophy to religion, through true self-knowledge to the mastery of the material and spiritual worlds whose motley forms and forces are mere hieroglyphics of the divine spirit. This "magic idealism" furnishes the key to the understanding of Novalis' unfinished novel, *Heinrich von Ofterdingen,* in which the broad realms of nature and history yield their secrets to the clairvoyant intuition of the poet. The theme of the *Hymns to the Night,* on the other hand, wherein Death appears as the great liberator and the longing for Death as the driving force of life, was suggested by the premature death of Sophie von Kühn, the young girl to whom the author had become engaged. This bittersweet experience confirmed in Novalis the conviction that an intercourse of the living with the souls of the departed was possible, and it caused to ripen within him the determination to cut short his own life and hasten the actual reunion with Sophie by the magic force of his will.

Wilhelm Heinrich Wackenroder and *Ludwig Tieck,* both natives of Berlin, were united by bonds of friendship but differed greatly in their attitude toward life and poetry. As young university students they traveled together throughout Germany and became the enthusiastic discoverers of the romantic charms of the old German towns and the soulful beauty of the native countryside. They were deeply moved by the monuments of the past that met their admiring eye and mind. Nuremberg, the city of Albrecht Dürer (cf. p. 197) and Hans Sachs (cf. p. 202), cast its spell over them, and in breathless admiration they succumbed to the magic enchantment of ruined medieval castles, overgrown with ivy and bathed in moonlight, the solemn contours of mountain ranges and lonely forests, bearing witness that both art and nature were as resplendent and praiseworthy in the inclement North as under the azure skies of sunny Italy. One of the fruits of these youthful wanderings was Wackenroder's *Confessions of an Art-Loving Friar* (1797), one of the earliest documents of German Romanticism and a source of inspiration for the romantic painters of several generations.

Wackenroder died before the romantic movement had really come into its own, but Tieck lived to an advanced age and turned out to be the most flexible and versatile of all German romanticists. Though a prolific writer who tried his skillful hand at every established literary form, many of his works lack the inner necessity and singleness of purpose that we admire in some of the less finished products of his contemporaries. He began with narratives in the mood and style of eighteenth-century Enlightenment but soon paid his tribute to Romanticism in ironic-satirical comedies as well as in dramatizations of legends and folk books with elaborate medieval pageantry, in his paraphrases of the old German folk tales and fairy stories, and in romantic-phantastic novels and short stories of his own invention. Yet he outlived the romantic period and in his later years became a writer of realistic fiction and historical narrative.*

g) *Leaders of the "Younger School."* The names of *Clemens Brentano* and *Achim von Arnim* who married Brentano's sister *Bettina,* the authoress of the widely read but partly fictitious *Goethe's Correspondence with a Child,* are as inseparable as the names of Tieck and Wackenroder. Both poets were members of the younger Romantic School, and together they collected the precious forgotten documents of old German folklore and edited *Des Knaben Wunderhorn* (*The Boy's Magic Horn*), the most renowned anthology of German folk songs.

Brentano was the son of a Frankfurt merchant of Italian ancestry and of Goethe's friend, Maximiliane de Laroche. He was one of Germany's most richly gifted poets but at the same time the most discordant and least balanced character of the entire romantic generation. While the musicality of his lyrics is unsurpassed, the incidental beauty of his prose works (the novel *Godwi*) and his dramatic attempts (*Ponce de Leon*) is marred by an utter lack of logical coherence and aesthetic form. He is at his best in his romantic fairy tales, among which the tragic story of *Casper and Fair Annie* has achieved lasting fame. After having spent four years of his mature life in the company of Katharina Emmerick, a stigmatized nun of Dülmen in Westphalia, he published his recorded observations of her visions, dealing with certain aspects and phases of the life of Christ. He finally found peace of mind and soul in the abandoned Catholic faith of his youth. He will always be remembered as the inventor of the *Lorelay* legend (cf. Violetta's song in *Godwi*) which inspired Heine's (cf. p. 580 sqq.) better known poem of the mysterious maid whose charms lure the skippers to their doom in the watery grave of the Rhine.

Achim von Arnim is known as the author of romantic novels (*Countess*

---

* Representative of the different phases of Tieck's literary development are the following works: *William Lovell* (1794–1796), a psychological novel; *Franz Sternbald's Travels* (1798), a novel depicting the character development of an artist; *Puss in Boots* (1797), a satirical fairy comedy; *Emperor Octavianus* (1804), a romantic drama of partly legendary, partly historical character; *Vittoria Accorombona* (1840), a historical novel; the translation of Cervantes' *Don Quixote* (1799–1804).

Dolores; The Guardians of the Crown) and dramas (*Halle and Jerusalem*) which are carefully planned but poorly executed. A native of the Mark of Brandenburg and the descendant of old Prussian nobility, his heart beat for the cause of the liberation of his homeland from French oppression.

The most talented among the romantic storytellers was *Ernst Theodor Amadeus Hoffmann*, whose versatile genius comprised a strange mixture of seemingly opposite qualities of character and occupation. He was not only a romantic writer, composer, painter, and critic of note but simultaneously an eminent legal expert and an almost pedantic state official. The same mixture of heterogeneous elements is a conspicuous mark of his literary creations and especially of the fragmentary and partly autobiographical novel, *Murr, the Tom-Cat's Reflections on Life* (*Kater Murr*), in which the romantic narrative of Kapellmeister Kreisler's life is grotesquely interwoven with fragments of the tomcat's autobiography. The resulting confusion serves to set off in sharpest contrast Kreisler's idealism and Murr's platitudinous philistinism. Most of Hoffmann's stories present a factual, everyday world, casually and nonchalantly populated with specters and spooks, split personalities, sleepwalkers, and visionaries, a motley array of creatures of a gruesome imagination and a keenly penetrating and realistic observation. The *Tales of Hoffmann* have not only inspired Jacques Offenbach's fantastic opera of the same title, but exerted considerable influence on English and American authors, notably on the fertile genius of Edgar Allen Poe.

Joseph von Eichendorff has been called "the last knight of Romanticism." In his poetry and prose the best that the Romantic School had to offer appears once more collected as in a focus. God, nature, folk, and fatherland are the basic realities that motivate Eichendorff's life and work, and around them his poetic fancy wove a garland of ripe and serene beauty. With Arnim, Brentano, and Görres, who like himself were members of the Heidelberg group of romantic writers, he shares the fondness for folk song and folk tradition. His lyrics, on the other hand, are wider in scope, lending voice to the entire range of human emotions and making nature a symbol and mirror of personal moods and experiences. Eichendorff's love for the Middle Ages and the ideals of chivalry, like that of Novalis, grew out of his longing for a spiritual unification of mankind, and for him, too, the true poet is at once a singer, a seer, a knight, and a priest.

"He who wants to understand a poet thoroughly, must know his homeland," Eichendorff wrote, thus explaining the secret and inimitable charm of his own poetry. It was the radiance of a happy and sheltered childhood and youth, spent in the ancestral castle of Lubowitz in Upper Silesia, that provided the dominant note for Eichendorff's works and that filled them with an unspeakable yearning for a paradise lost and never to be regained on this earth.

After happy student years in Halle and Heidelberg Eichendorff followed the call of his king to the colors and, as a chasseur in the Free Corps of

Major von Lützow, he took part in the war against Napoleon. After the liberation of Prussia he became a conscientious government official, first in Danzig and later on in Berlin.

Among his many works in prose and poetry the tale *Pages from the Life of a Good-for-Nothing* stands out as a real gem of romantic fiction and as one of the most genuine expressions of a thoroughly Germanic poetic temper. All the "leitmotifs" of the Romantic School seem combined and fused in this simple narrative: the glorification and transfiguration of nature with its changing moods and aspects; the scintillating richness of the human heart, its unending cravings, venturing far out and yearning for the home-coming (*"Fernweh," "Heimweh,"* and *"Wanderlust"*); the sweetness and sadness of human love; and the realization that all our striving is in many disguises nothing but the unquenchable quest for our eternal home, and everything transitory only a symbol of eternity.

While a student at the University of Heidelberg Eichendorff was especially attracted by the vigorous personality of a young *Privatdozent* by the name of *Joseph Görres*. Görres had declared himself emphatically in sympathy with the aims of the Romantic School which by that time had overcome the libertinistic and anarchical rantings of its earliest protagonists and had affirmed its loyalty to the political and social ideas of the reborn Prussian State. Joseph Görres and *Ernst Moritz Arndt* became the two most militant exponents of a political romanticism that was born of their passionately held religious convictions. Although he was no poet Görres ranks among the most prominent members of the Romantic School. He was a native of Coblenz and had been brought up in the crisp atmosphere of eighteenth-century Enlightenment, in the shadow of the speculation of Kant (cf. p. 371 sqq.) and the French *philosophes* (cf. p. 368). His moral rigorism had welcomed the French Revolution of 1789 as the grand fulfill-ment of the hopes and dreams of the defenders of true progress. In *Results of My Mission to Paris* (1800) he tells of the disillusionment that followed upon observation at close range of the political conditions in the France of the Revolution and of Napoleon. He felt all the heavier the yoke of the French emperor that had crushed the spirit of freedom in his native Rhine-land, and both his hatred for the foreign conqueror and his longing for German national unity prescribed for him his true mission as an author. In the service of the German Idea he found himself and became the most important political writer and publicist of his time. He was admired by his friends and fellow countrymen, and both feared and respected by the not easily impressed French emperor. In his essays and editorials Görres fought relentlessly against the spirit of State absolutism and imperialism and for the idea of a national and constitutional democracy, the hoped-for creation of a powerful union of the German people.

In his youth Görres had been chiefly interested in the natural sciences. In his Heidelberg period (1806–1808) he devoted himself to linguistic, aesthetic, and mythological studies and made valuable contributions to the revival of old German art and literature and to the knowledge of Oriental languages. In the period of political reaction that followed the Wars of Liberation Görres barely escaped arrest by his flight to Strasbourg (1819–1827). As professor of history at the University of Munich (1827–1848), where he had been called by King Louis I of Bavaria, Görres became the champion of the new medievalism and of a virile political Catholicism.

The historic significance of *Ernst Moritz Arndt,* the militant Protestant publicist and poet from the Island of Rügen (a Swedish possession at the time of his birth), may well be compared with that of Görres, the Rhenish Catholic. With *Theodor Körner* and *Max von Schenkendorf,* Arndt was one of the "Poets of the Wars of Liberation," but he surpasses them by the wider range of his experience and the more enduring quality of his ideas. Although there was little or nothing of the ethereal and dreamlike in his nature, Arndt concurred with the romantic writers in their glorification of the *Volksgeist* and their vindication of medieval political and social theories and institutions. In his *History of Serfdom in Pomerania and on the Island of Rügen* he deplores the gradual deterioration of the economic, legal, and social status of the peasantry since medieval times and accuses the secularism of the territorial princes and the mechanism of the absolutistic State of having caused this disintegration. He criticizes courageously the totalitarian political maxims of Frederick the Great (cf. p. 316 sqq.) and points out the identical faults in the political system of Napoleon. Like Stein and Görres he advances the idea of the national State against the idea of world imperialism. And again like Stein and Görres he suffers denunciation and persecution, spending many precious years of his life in exile or condemned to involuntary silence.

After having spent the year of 1812 with Stein at the court of Tsar Alexander of Russia, he returned to Prussia in the following year and fanned the enthusiasm of the German youth with his patriotic songs and pamphlets. In 1818 he accepted a position as professor of history at the University of Bonn, but was shortly afterward dismissed because of his active participation in the movement of the *Burschenschaft* (cf. p. 464 sqq.). He was reinstated by King Frederick William IV in 1840 and gained a seat in the First National Assembly of Frankfurt in 1848 (cf. p. 530 sqq.), where he worked for the unification of Germany under Prussia's leadership.

h) German Philology: The Grimm Brothers. As J. J. Winckelmann (cf. p. 399) had established systematic archaeology as an independent discipline, so the brothers *Jakob* and *Wilhelm Grimm* became the founders of the science of Germanistics. From their childhood days they lived together in an intimate communion of thought and work. Both began their academic career as librarians in Kassel, later on accepted professorships in the University of Göttingen, were dismissed in 1837 because of their democratic leanings, and both died as members of the Academy of Sciences in Berlin. Under the influence of the romantic writers they began to study the literary and cultural documents of the German past and systematically endeavored to understand and interpret the German *Volksgeist* in its various mani-festations. Following Herder's (cf. p. 396 sq.) profound intuitions they con-sidered the history of language and literature as an inexhaustible treasury of human thought, revealing definite character traits of individual national cultures.

The Grimm brothers started out with the collection of fairy tales that established their fame internationally: *Deutsche Kinder- und Hausmärchen* (1812-1814). They had listened to these tales as they were told by the common people in the intimate atmosphere of their hearths and homes, and they retold them with an unembellished simplicity that preserved their original and natural charm. Once again the tales of "Little Red Riding Hood" (*Rotkäppchen*), "Cinderella" (*Aschenbrödel*), the "Sleeping Beauty" (*Dornröschen*), "Snow White" (*Schneewittchen*), and many others became the property of the entire people, children and grownups alike.

Like Herder and Humboldt the Grimm brothers speculated on the origin of language, and in 1819 the first volume of Jakob's *German Grammar* was published. This is a historic and comparative study of all Germanic dialects that revealed the general structure and morphology of the Germanic languages and was based on painstaking research and personal observation. Here for the first time all those laws of syntax and grammar — *Umlaut, Ablaut,* weak and strong declension and conjugation, sound shift, the rules of phonology, etymology — were developed which today form part of the basic equipment of the German philologist. For Jakob Grimm the history of the German language and grammar was a true mirror of the nature, mentality, and cultural history of the German people. In his *Mythology* (1819) and the *Antiquities of German Law* (1828) he laid bare the common roots of legal and poetic concepts, using as his chief source the judicial case material of the medieval Germanic village communities (*Weistümer*).

After their dismissal from Göttingen the brothers began their last great philological enterprise, the *German Dictionary* (*Deutsches Wörterbuch*), a word encyclopedia of monumental scope which remained unfinished (four volumes) in their lifetime and to which committees of scholars added many volumes after their death.

Reverence for tradition and a sensitive organ for real progress, the two qualities that they most admired in their Germanic forebears, were con-spicuous in the life and thought of the Grimm brothers. In past and present they found comfort and encouragement and lovingly understood both as resulting from an unfathomable providential design. They transmitted the fruits of their labors and the high scholarly standard of their work to a number of German linguists of their time, among whom Karl Lachmann (1793-1851) and Karl Müllenhoff (1818-1884) deserve special mention. Their efforts in the field of scientific philology culminated in an un-completed history of German antiquities, entitled *Deutsche Altertumskunde,* a work that gives clear evidence of the novelty of their methods which were appropriated by several successive generations of German philologists.

The Swabians: Uhland and Mörike. From the same region that had largely contributed to the greatness of German poetry in the golden age of *Minnesang* (cf. p. 155 sq.) came two authors who represented the more sober and conventional aspects of German Romanticism. The chief member of the so-called Swabian School was *Ludwig Uhland,* a poet, a scholar, and a champion of the constitutional rights of the people. His poetry is rooted in the soil and the historic traditions of his homeland and includes romances, ballads, political lyrics, and simple nature songs. All of his poems strive for impersonal objectivity and most of them achieve an admirable clarity and simplicity of form and content. Documents of a healthy mind and a noble and gentle human heart, they approach the artless and sturdy integrity of folk song and folk ballad.

Uhland wrote poetry only in his youth. After having served for three years as professor of German language and literature at the University of Tübingen, his interest in his country's constitutional struggles prompted him to enter the political arena and to take an active part in the fight for liberalism and democracy. His early legal studies in Tübingen and Paris made him well qualified to fulfill the legislative functions connected with his membership in the parliament of the kingdom of Wurtemberg and later on (1848) in the first German parliament at Frankfurt. The bases of his political creed were his profound respect for natural and moral law and his implicit faith in the dignity of man.

In his scholarly contributions to the history of literature and civilization Uhland appears as one of the cofounders of the sciences of Germanistics and Romanistics (Germanic and Romanic philology). In his monographic work on *Walther von der Vogelweide* (1822) he professes his admiration for the greatest lyric poet of the German Middle Ages and makes Walther's voice audible again for modern ears. In the *Myth of Thor* (1830) he lays down the basic principles of mythological research, and in his *Collection of Folk Songs* (1844) he continues and perfects the work of Herder and Arnim-Brentano.

Eduard Mörike, in contrast to his fellow countryman, was one of those quiet and introspective Swabians who are by nature averse to any involvement in political or social controversies, whose intense inner life absorbs all their interest, thus making them strangers to the noisy conflicts and cataclysms of the external world. As a student of Protestant theology in Tübingen, in the quietude of a country parsonage, as a teacher in Stuttgart, the capital of the kingdom, Mörike remained in all these different environments essentially unchanged, faithful to the soft and gentle rhythm of his life, in love with nature's minute and intimate secrets and miracles. In calm detachment he witnessed the death of Romanticism and the rise of new literary fashions, while he himself continued to live in his self-contained poetic realm, the heir of Classicism and of Romanticism, whose sensitive soul combined psychological intuition with formative genius.

In subject matter and metrical form Mörike's lyrics and ballads span a wide range of possibilities, reaching from the simple and direct expression of folk poetry to the classical patterns of antiquity. While in his novel *Maler Nolten* he seems unable to reconcile the classical and romantic, the realistic and phantastic elements, thus falling short of his model *Wilhelm Meister* (cf. p. 412), his story of *Mozart's Journey from Vienna to Prague* is a perfect example of the fusion of romantic fancy, realistic description, and classical mastery of form.

The Dramatists: Kleist and Grillparzer. The romantic mind and temperament expressed themselves most naturally in the subjective literary language of lyric poetry and the lyrically instrumented prose narrative. The members of the Romantic School found it difficult if not impossible to attain to that plastic objectivity and dialectic acuteness that are some of the necessary requisites of dramatic art. While some members of the School exhibited profound and expert knowlédge of dramatic theory, their own dramatic attempts, paying no heed to or being unaware of the requirements of the stage, rarely progressed beyond the experimental phase.

Kleist and Grillparzer, the two great dramatists of the romantic age, can only with certain reservations be classified as romantic authors. They shared with the romanticists the fertility and flexibility of mind, their intense idealism, and their opposition to Classicism, but their more realistic appraisal of the possibilities and necessities of the stage and their fuller and firmer grip on life made them succeed where the romanticists failed. The element of tragic frustration that is conspicuous in the life of both authors was due to the fact that both felt the pressing need for the creation of a new dramatic style that was to unite modern individual and psychological characterization with the traditional classical idealization, an undertaking that would have required the combined genius of a Sophocles and a Shakespeare.

Heinrich von Kleist, the descendant of an ancient family of noblemen and army officials of the Mark Brandenburg, was by nature endowed with a morbid and melancholy temper which made him all the more sensitive to his unhappy personal circumstances and to the national disaster that befell his Prussian fatherland under the yoke of the Corsican conqueror. After having taken part in the Coalition War of 1795 (cf. p. 324 sq.) as an ensign, he resigned his army commission and devoted himself to the study of literature and philosophy. His acquaintance with Kant's *Critique of Pure Reason* (cf. p. 372) plunged him into utter confusion and despair, resulting in a complete breakdown, caused by the fearful thought of finding the gateways to the attainment of absolute certitude of knowledge closed once and for all. Partially recovered, his restless mind urged him to find the much-needed relaxation in travels that led him into France, Switzerland, and Italy. In vain he tried, in compliance with the wishes of his family, to earn a living as a petty state official. His failure to conquer the German stage and the German public with his plays, his clashes with the

Prussian censors, the complete fiasco of several ambitious journalistic enterprises, and the ever widening rift with his family finally seemed to leave no avenue open to him but self-destruction. Kleist was thirty-four years of age when he and Henriette Vogel, a casual acquaintance who was suffering from an incurable disease, decided to commit a double-suicide.

The characters of Kleist's plays are magnified symbols of his own urges and ideals. These characters are haunted by the same demonic forces that played havoc with Kleist's own life. They are romantic in that they, too, suffer from the fault of excess. In *Schroffenstein,* his first tragedy, written under the influence of Shakespeare's *Romeo and Juliet* and Schiller's *Bride of Messina* (cf. p. 425 sq.), two families are destroyed as much by the unruly passions of the individuals as by the inscrutable decrees of Fate. *Robert Guiscard,* leader of the Norman conquerors of Sicily, the hero of Kleist's monumental fragment of the same title, falls a victim to his excessive will to power. *Penthesilea,* the queen of the Amazons, the heroine of Kleist's most dynamic play, is destroyed by her boundless love for Achilles. Her love turns into hatred when she believes herself betrayed by the valiant Greek and, joining the maddened pack of her hounds, she mutilates the body of her lover, only to follow him in death in the anguish and agony of unspeakable remorse. It was in *Penthesilea* that Kleist revealed himself as the antipode of Goethe, for whom he nourished a mixed emotion of "love-hatred," similar to Penthesilea's feelings for Achilles. Of *Penthesilea* he said himself: "My innermost being is embodied in it . . . the entire anguish and splendor of my soul," and he felt hurt and humiliated beyond all measure when Goethe coolly described this work and its main character as ill proportioned and bordering on the pathological.

When Goethe, in connection with Penthesilea, spoke of "confused emotions" (*Gefühlsverwirrung*), he named the main deficiency of most of Kleist's characters: they lack balance, proportion, and therewith the prerequisites for unerring and resolute action. *Käthchen of Heilbronn,* the romantic heroine of Kleist's "Great Historical Drama of Chivalry," seems to be the one exception. Kleist describes her as "the reverse of Penthesilea, her opposite pole, a human being that is as great by her passive devotion as Penthesilea is by her action." This drama, Kleist's most genuine contribution to the romantic movement, makes use of the widespread interest in somnambulism and the mysterious forces of nature and mind. Käthchen's unfailing instinct makes her pursue the object of her love and devotion with unfaltering step, so that all the miraculous events and roundabout ways converge quite plausibly in the predestined union of Käthchen and her beloved Count Wetter vom Strahl.

This fairy play and the following realistic comedy *The Broken Jug* are like breathing spells before Kleist's final dramatic effort. The story of Adam, the village judge, who by an overdose of his own cunning and deceit becomes more and more entangled in his self-spun web of lies, is rightly considered as the healthiest and sprightliest of German comedies. It is at the same time the first great example of dramatic realism, embodying in its characters, its plot, and its setting the intimate charm, sparkling vitality, and brisk humor of a Dutch genre picture.

The two remaining dramas of Kleist are affirmations of his fervent patriotism. The *Hermannsschlacht* presents the plight of the Prussian State by means of a portrayal of the analogical struggle of the great Cheruscan leader Arminius (Hermann), "Germany's liberator," against the might of the ancient Roman Empire, ending in the decisive victory of the united Germanic tribes over the Roman legions in the Teutoburg Forest (A.D. 9, cf. p. 20). It is a scarcely disguised call to arms against Napoleon, an outcry of passionate hatred and a document of excessive nationalism. The second patriotic drama, *The Prince of Homburg*, is a more positive presentation of a similar problem. The disguise is even more transparent, the plot dealing with an episode in the military career of the Great Elector of Brandenburg-Prussia (cf. p. 310 sq.) and involving some of the other leading figures in the more recent history of the Prussian State. The theme is the moral education of a Prussian prince who, under the guidance of the Elector's pedagogical wisdom, turns from youthful irresponsibility to a free recognition of the just claims of the State, which confronts the individual as the moral law incarnate, demanding unselfish obedience and supreme sacrifice.

Heinrich von Kleist's prose narratives resemble his dramas in their terse, chroniclelike style, moving inexorably toward a tragic climax. In *Michael Kohlhaas* the author presented Germany with a work of which Friedrich Hebbel, another one of the great playwrights of the nineteenth century (cf. p. 586 sqq.), has well said: "I maintain that in no other German narrative does the horrifying depth of life . . . appear as vividly as in this work, in which the theft . . . of two horses is the first link in a chain that stretches from the horse-dealer Kohlhaas to the German Emperor. . . ." Kohlhaas, a contemporary of Martin Luther, is characterized by Kleist as "the most upright and at the same time the most frightful individual of his time," a man whose violated sense of justice causes him to become a highway robber and murderer. And, like Michael Kohlhaas, Kleist himself was headstrong, self-willed, and determined not to compromise with conventional tastes and norms. This explains in part his failure to find during his lifetime the response which would have mitigated the tragedy of his personal fate.

Franz Grillparzer, despite his egocentered philosophy of life and his lack of self-harmony, has even less claim than Kleist to be classified as a genuine romanticist. His personality and his works are related to all the great literary styles of the eighteenth and nineteenth centuries, owing as much to the influence of Enlightenment (cf. p. 368 sqq.) and Baroque (cf. p. 330 sqq.) as to that of Classicism and Romanticism, and even foreshadowing some of the essential elements of the realistic modes of the generations of writers that succeeded him.

A true child of his native Vienna, Austria's greatest playwright continues his country's literary traditions and forcefully expresses the positive and negative implications of this cultural heritage. In his searching self-analysis he experienced the weight of his Austrian temperament as a bane rather than a blessing, attributing to it his morbidity, his dissecting criticism, and the lack of concentrated will power which prevented him from mastering the adverse circumstances of his life.

Condemned to spend the greater part of his youth and manhood in the shadow of the Metternich regime, continually vexed and severely handicapped by an arbitrary system of political censorship, he ceased writing for publication at the very height of his literary development. The remainder of his dramatic production, hidden away in his desk, had to wait for the author's death to meet the eye and gain the belated favor of the public.

Personal bitterness, caused by disappointment, frustration, and disillusionment, made Grillparzer preach a doctrine of melancholy resignation and made him seek contentment in a simple and unproblematic life. This aspiration was fulfilled in his old age when, in addition to the gift of peace of heart and mind, the long-coveted universal recognition was granted to him. When he died he was mourned and celebrated as Austria's great "classical" dramatist.

Grillparzer's first important play, *Die Ahnfrau* (the "Ancestress," i.e., the ancestral family ghost), was a distinctive contribution to a peculiar species of romantic drama, the so-called "Fate-Tragedy," of which the East Prussian, Zacharias Werner (1768–1823), was the most talented exponent.* *Die Ahnfrau* is a combination of spook and fate-tragedy, in which motifs of the popular Austrian stage (*Volksdrama*) and the classical rhetoric of Schiller are fused to produce a sweeping melodramatic effect. *Sappho,* conceived in the classical vein under the influence of Goethe's *Iphigenia* (cf. p. 411) and *"Tasso"* (cf. p. 411), is a drama of unrequited love and final renunciation, in which Grillparzer portrays his own disheartening experiences in the guise of the tragic life and death of the great Greek poetess (*c.* 600 B.C.).

The classical setting is retained in two other works of Grillparzer, of which the trilogy *The Golden Fleece* presents a modern version of the Greek legend of Jason and Medea and the expedition of the fifty Greek Argonauts to the Black Sea. The dramatically moving story of the recovery of the "Golden Fleece," of the love and gradual estrangement of Jason and Medea, the effective confrontation of Greeks and Barbarians and their surrounding worlds reveal the author as a master of individual characterization and psychological motivation. In conceiving the Golden Fleece as a symbol of human greed and in portraying its dehumanizing effects

---

* The romantic "Fate-Tragedy" (*Schicksalsdrama*) was born of a misunderstanding of the significance of "Fate" in ancient Greek tragedy. The religious and metaphysical motivation in the dramas of Sophocles, Aeschylos, etc., is here replaced by a "Fate" that attaches itself to external tools or symbols, such as fateful days, weapons, etc.

Grillparzer approaches a synthesis of classical fate-tragedy and modern character drama.

Waves of Love and the Sea is a dramatization and modernization of the legendary account of the unhappy love of Hero, the priestess of Aphrodite, and Leander, the gallant Greek youth, who braves the nightly tempest and the waves of the Hellespontus and whose shattered body becomes a messenger of death for his beloved also.

All of Grillparzer's dramatic works are more or less didactic: they have an ax to grind or a lesson to teach. This is especially true of his historical dramas which deal with certain leading personalities of the ruling dynasty of Austria and are conspicuously pro-Hapsburg. The one comedy he wrote (*Woe to Him Who Lies*) is no exception to this rule: it preaches a humorous and gentle sermon against the fanatics of truth and rectitude, making an eloquent plea for the toleration of the imperfection of all human and earthly things.

Among Grillparzer's posthumous works the most interesting is the psychological character tragedy *The Jewess of Toledo,* whose plot was suggested by Lope de Vega (1562–1635), the great Spanish playwright. King Alfonso, who has become forgetful of his royal duties as a result of his infatuation for Rahel, a seductive but heartless Jewess, regains his true moral stature after Rahel has been put to death at the behest of the queen. While this work marks a further step on the way to dramatic realism, Grillparzer's last and ripest contributions to German Romanticism are his fairy play *The Dream that is Life* (*Der Traum ein Leben*), and his mythological play *Libussa.* *The Dream that is Life* is a counterpart of Calderón's Spanish drama, *Life is a Dream.* In it Rustan, the hero, foresees in a dream all the dangers and vicissitudes of his contemplated journey to the Court of Samarkand. He derives from this experience a more sober view of reality and a clearer insight into human relations, resigning himself to the moderate amount of happiness that is found within the narrow confines of man's immediate environment and in the tranquillity of his soul. *Libussa,* the dramatized legend of the foundation of Prague, is the story of a mythological fairy queen of the same name. She sacrifices her royal dignity and descends from her unreal world to be united with her beloved Primislaus, the representative of a new realistic order of practical and creative activity. But, remaining a stranger in this new environment, she withers away and is lost in the ever widening chasm between dream and reality, memory and love, past and present.

Romantic Art. Although the German romanticists were deeply interested in the philosophy of art and the principles of art appreciation, only the arts of painting and interior decoration showed the influence of the romantic modes of thought.

a) *Individual Romantic Painters.* The preoccupation of the romanticists with the art and civilization of the German past suggested much of the subject matter of the romantic painters. Many of their works were the result of historical retrospection. In the attempt to cultivate an art that was typically and exclusively German they often were too much concerned with the ideal content and neglected the requirements of artistic form. They wanted to tell stories and thus made their works illustrative complements of historical and literary contexts. In this way much of the immediacy and the spontaneous expressiveness of the great German art of the past was lost. Unable to offer a tangible substitute for the discarded formal values of the Italian Renaissance, they either created in accordance with pedantically observed academic rules or abandoned themselves to personal moods, but did not succeed in anchoring their works in the universal consciousness of an artistic style.

Ludwig Richter (1803–1844) and *Moritz von Schwind* (1804–1871) were chiefly illustrators of fairy tales, legends, and the intimate charms of German domestic life. Their works provide a perfect accompaniment of the restrained and self-contained philistinism of the *"Biedermeier,"* the style of family culture and complacent middle class comfort. Both painters, however, deserve the highest praise for their share in the discovery and poetic glorification of the German landscape. Freeing their pictorial compositions from the artificially calculated designs of the Neo-Classicists (cf. p. 400 sqq.), they made nature the sensitive medium of romantic moods.

It was in the field of landscape painting that some of the romantic masters achieved real greatness. Looking at nature they felt, in the words of *Philipp Otto Runge* (1777–1810), "ever more distinctly that in every tree and flower there is hidden a certain human spirit, idea, or feeling." Runge, the friend of Ludwig Tieck, was the most talented of the early romantic painters. His dream of a "synaesthetic" fusion of all the arts points forward to Richard Wagner's *Gesamtkunstwerk* (cf. p. 495), while his theoretical studies on the symbolic values of color and his understanding of the significance of light, atmosphere, and movement place him in the immediate neighborhood of the impressionists (cf. p. 715 sq.) of the later nineteenth century. Characteristic of the symbolic-allegorical tendency of some of his works are his unfinished *Four Seasons* which he had conceived as a romantic "musical poem." The picture of his parents shows Runge's ability as a portraitist and is at the same time a lovable document of German middle-class life and culture at the turn of the century.

The greatest of the romantic landscapists is *Caspar David Friedrich* (1774–1840) who endows the romantic scene with distant horizons and the mysterious sheen of unearthly luminance. His paintings are spiritually alive with the rhythmical breath of almost imperceptible nuances of light and color. His moods are sweet, gentle, and softly melancholy, always truly romantic and never sentimental.

Somewhat apart from the afore-mentioned artists stands *Karl Spitzweg* (1808–1885), whose remarkable genius expresses itself in paintings of miniature size. The warmth and vehement brilliance of his colors and the irresistible charm of his wit and satire make him impart a rare quality

Feast of St. John, by Ludwig Richter

of persuasive actuality to his genrelike descriptions of small-town life and characters. No one knew better than Spitzweg the tender emotions, inclinations, and habits that animate a philistine world of the smallest proportions, and he enhanced this petty world by an aura of human greatness and everlasting significance. In his treatment of light and color Spitzweg, like Runge, anticipated some of the innovations of the impressionistic school of painting.

  b) *The "Nazarenes."* The nationalism as well as the medievalism of the romantic movement was expressed in the ideals of a small band of painters who at the beginning of the nineteenth century called for the restoration of an art that was both German and Christian. These "Nazarenes," as they were half ironically called because of their ascetic-pietistic retirement from the world, gathered together in an abandoned monastery in Rome and, like the Pre-Raphaelites in England, tried to imitate the life and work of the religiously inspired schools of painting of the later Middle Ages and the early Renaissance. Their exquisite draftsmanship is best evidenced in their sketches and cartoons, while the completed fresco paintings for the Casa Bartholdy in Rome (now in the National Gallery in Berlin) reveal their insufficient mastery of coloristic patterns. Nevertheless, it remains their great merit to have revived understanding for the tasks of monumental mural design and the almost forgotten technique of alfresco painting.

  The leader of the "Friars of St. Luke," as the Nazarenes called themselves, was *Friedrich Overbeck* (1789–1869), a devout Roman Catholic, to whom art was "like a harp on which I would always hear sounding hymns in praise of God." *Peter Cornelius* (1783–1867), another member of the group, more widely known by his illustrations to Goethe's *Faust* than by his series of fresco paintings, became in his advanced age director of the art academy of his native Düsseldorf and worked in Munich in the service of the Bavarian court.

  c) *Biedermeier.* The period between the Congress of Vienna and the March Revolution of 1848 (*"Vormärz,"* cf. p. 461 sqq.) was characterized by a mode of living and an artistic taste which derived their peculiar traits from the philistinism of the middle classes. The "philistine" is the "Biedermeier," a name which is sometimes applied to the entire *"Vormärz"* but more specifically refers to the then prevailing fashion of interior decoration. This fashion reflects the homely frugality of life, a culture of small proportions and limited possibilities, which had developed under the influence of the political pressure of the Napoleonic era, the economic depression that followed the Wars of Liberation, and the restrictive measures of the restoration period. As it favored soberness and simple comfort in the style of living, so it encouraged deft and solid craftsmanship and smooth and harmonious design in home furnishings as well as quite generally in the applied arts and crafts.

  Romantic Music. All romantic art and literature contained an element of musicality and secretly or openly betrayed a tendency to approximate and imitate the effects of music, the most unplastic of all the arts. Wackenroder, in his essay on *The Miracles of Musical Art,* considers music the most sublime of the arts, because it interprets human feelings in a superhuman way, "because it makes manifest all the movements of the human mind . . . because it speaks a language unknown to us in ordinary life, a tongue which we have learned we know not where and how and which one feels tempted to describe as the language of the angels." Tieck asks: "Should it not be permissible to think in sounds and to compose musically in words and thoughts?" And the philosopher Schopenhauer (cf. p. 505 sq.) sees in the art of music the most immediate realization of the universal "world-will." We are therefore not surprised to find in the works of musical romanticism a genuine and condensed expression of romantic ideas and experiences.

a) *"Lied" and Instrumental Music.* The earliest of the romantic com-posers was *Franz Schubert* (1797–1828), the youngest of the fourteen chil-dren of a Viennese schoolmaster. While he did not break with the musical tradition as established by Haydn, Mozart, and Beethoven, he enriched this heritage by cultivating the style of lyrical music on a grand scale and became the creator of the universally known and loved species of the German *Lied.* When he was sixteen years of age Schubert composed the beautiful musical setting for Gretchen's *Song at the Spinning Wheel* from Goethe's *Faust* and one year later the immortal melody to Goethe's *Erl-King.* Inexhaustible in his melodious resourcefulness, he wrote over six hundred *Lieder* in all, among them such gems as *The Heather Rose, Mignon's Song* (from Goethe's *Wilhelm Meister*), *The Trout, Death and the Maiden,* and the song cycle of *A Winter's Journey.* Schubert's larger instrumental works, including fourteen string quartets and eight symphonies, of which the *Unfinished* (1882) is the best known, are highly picturesque and of great lyrical beauty but suffer at times from various defects of composition. Among his many choral works are six Masses and a number of smaller works of a religious nature. Franz Schubert was a largely self-taught artist, whose short life was fraught with much bitterness and disappointment, but who valiantly prevailed over a multitude of adversities.

The second phase of musical romanticism in Germany is represented by *Felix Mendelssohn-Bartholdy* (1809–1847) and *Robert Schumann* (1810–1856). The former was the grandson of Lessing's friend, the popular philos-opher Moses Mendelssohn (cf. p. 369). The son of a Jewish banker of the city of Hamburg, Mendelssohn was financially independent and able to satisfy his urge for travel in foreign lands. A citizen of the world, he lacked the distinctive national character traits of other exponents of German Romanticism. His several trips to England and Scotland earned him great popularity in the British Isles and bore fruit in the composition of the *Hebrides* overture and the Scotch Symphony. The romantic fluency of his melodies blends happily with a classical formal equilibrium and his music on the whole is scarcely touched by the complexities of the romantic temperament.

By the time he was fifteen Mendelssohn had already composed twelve symphonies and a large number of other instrumental and vocal works. He paid his tribute to the spirit of the age by the creation of a kind of "elfish romanticism" (*Elfenromantik*) which is best exemplified by his incidental music to Shakespeare's *A Midsummer Night's Dream*, while his *Songs without Words* mark a new departure in the style of romantic pianoforte composition. In his overtures and symphonies Mendelssohn develops his themes and melodies around a definite "program,"* and in his oratorios and choral works he revives and continues the tradition of Bach and Händel (cf. p. 350 sqq.). As director and conductor of the famous "Gewandhaus Concerts" in Leipzig and as cofounder of the Leipzig Conservatory Mendelssohn's judgment carried great weight and he used his influence to bring about a new appreciation of Bach's musical genius.

Robert Schumann was a child prodigy and only six years old when he made his first attempts at musical composition. He grew up to become not only the most astute of the romantic composers of his day but one of the first and greatest of modern music critics as well. As the founder and editor (1834–1844) of the *Neue Zeitschrift für Musik* he laid down the basic principles of the appreciation of music. In 1840 Schumann married *Clara Wieck,* the daughter of his piano teacher in Leipzig, who herself became a noted pianist and a composer of songs and music for the pianoforte. In his later years Schumann showed symptoms of progressive mental derangement; he died in a private asylum which he had entered at his own request.

The fervent subjectivity of Schumann's musical style was held in check by the transparent clarity of musical patterns deriving from an iron discipline of technique and a mature artistic intellect. Equipped with such splendid mastery of musical form and content, Schumann developed a new epigrammatic and miniature style of pianoforte music and became the most distinguished lyrical composer of the second major phase of German romantic music. While the best of his 248 *Lieder* vie in melodiousness and popularity with those of Schubert, his four symphonies and numerous choral works, rich as they are in lyrical and pictorial beauty, suffer not infrequently from the typically romantic faults of antithetical disjointedness and short-winded abruptness.

b) Symphonic Poem and Opera. The third and final major phase of romantic music in Germany has as its chief protagonists *Franz von Liszt* (1811–1886) and *Richard Wagner* (1813–1883). While the earlier romantic

---

* The term "program music," in contrast to "absolute music," is applied to any kind of music which tries to reproduce in musical form certain observed data, events, or images in nature or definite psychological moods and experiences. "Program music" in one form or another was a familiar mode of musical composition in all musical epochs, but it acquires an unprecedented prominence in the second half of the nineteenth century (Liszt, Richard Strauss, etc.).

composers had continued and further developed the traditional classical forms of sonata and symphony and had added as their own major contribution the glories of the German *Lied,* the inventive genius of Liszt and Wagner created the indigenous style of the symphonic poem and the romantic opera. The symphonic poem was an intermediate form between symphony and opera, utilizing the possibilities of both and adapting the symphony to the requirements of descriptive "program music." In this way the symphonic poem becomes capable of expressing poetic values without requiring either actors or a stage setting. The metamorphoses of the musical theme were a further development of the classical "variation" and represent the connecting link between the latter and Richard Wagner's *"Leitmotiv."*

Liszt was above all a brilliant technician and musical improviser, with a decided leaning toward the theatrical and spectacular. As composer he is at his best in his most unpretentious works, such as the Hungarian rhapsodies (19), in which he finds a natural outlet for his forceful musical temperament. In his ecclesiastical compositions he tries to combine the austere melodic structure of Gregorian Chant (cf. p. 83 sq.) with the musical sentiment of modern harmony. His symphonic poems include musical paraphrases of *Tasso, Faust,* and various operatic motifs.

Liszt was born in Hungary of a German mother. He made his first public appearance in Vienna. From the year 1842 dates his association with Weimar, where he stayed for twelve years after having received an appointment as "Court Kapellmeister" in 1849. It was his ambition to make Weimar once again the center of art and culture that it had been in Goethe's and Schiller's time, and even if that dream fell short of its realization, he did succeed in making the city a musical metropolis in which his own warmhearted personality and unselfish endeavors provided guidance and encouragement to a large number of younger composers. In Weimar Wagner's acquaintance with Liszt grew into a solid friendship, and it was in the same city that the foundations were laid for Wagner's future fame.

In *Richard Wagner* the romantic movement in German music reached its culminating point. The "music drama," his most distinctive achievement, had been anticipated in its general idea in the earlier romantic operas of *Carl Maria von Weber* (1786–1826), whose *Freischütz* (1820) had marked the victory of the German over the Italian style of the opera. Weber's romantic nature feeling, the elegance and nobility of his musical sentiment, and his fervent patriotism made him one of the most popular composers in the period of literary romanticism and in the years of the national uprising against Napoleon. Although the texts underlying his operas were hardly less stereotyped than the cheap and conventional libretti of the Italian operas, his clear understanding of the interrelation of text and music, singers and orchestra, helped him overcome to a large extent the handicap of an unsuitable literary form. His fairy opera *Oberon* became almost a symbol of German musical romanticism.

Weber's highest aspirations, however, were realized by Richard Wagner, who established the desired balance of music and dramatic action. Wagner thus emancipated the German opera once and for all from the tyranny of the Italian *"recitativo"* style which had subjected the musical instrumentation to the requirements of the libretto and of which even Mozart (cf. p. 353 sq.) had not been able to free himself. With Wagner, however, the music was allowed to fulfill its legitimate functions and both music and text were duly balanced and proportioned to each other. The orchestra, assuming the significance of the chorus in ancient Greek tragedy, demonstrated its almost unlimited possibilities in interpreting the secret motivations of the characters and in uncovering the mythological and spiritual background of the action. This was mainly achieved by the introduction and ingenious manipulation of the *"Leitmotiv,"* a device that had been used with great effect by the French composer Hector Berlioz (1803–1869) but that was perfected by Richard Wagner. It consists essentially in the association of short, rhythmically characteristic musical phrases with specific characters and situations; their frequent repetition serves to intensify the effect of identical emotional reactions and also aids in the clarification of the thematic structure of the composition.

It seems that Wagner's task in carrying out these innovations was simplified but at the same time made more exacting by the fact that he was a playwright as well as a composer and therefore his own librettist. But Wagner was not satisfied with achieving fame in the fields of music and drama: it was his ambition to create "the art-work of the future," the *Gesamtkunstwerk* (the total work of art). This was to result from a union and fusion of all the arts, including poetry, song, instrumental music, painting, acting, dance and festival play, and even the arts of the stage machinist and technician. If any man could dare to strive for such a goal without bringing upon himself the lasting odium of wayward presumption, that man was Richard Wagner who, by virtue of his astounding catholicity of tastes and talents, appeared to Nietzsche (cf. p. 695 sq.) as "a great cultural force."

Wagner attained to artistic greatness as well as to public recognition relatively late, after he had been unsuccessful in many early attempts at musical expression. He was born and educated in Leipzig and achieved professional prominence first as a choir director in Würzburg (1833) and an orchestra conductor in Magdeburg (1834) and Königsberg (1836). It was in the latter city that he married the actress Minna Planer, from whom he separated in 1861. From Riga, where he had spent a short time as director of the local opera, he fled to London and Paris to escape his creditors, and before his return to Dresden in 1842 and his appointment as "Court Kapellmeister" of the king of Saxony (1843–1849) he had completed the operas *Rienzi* and *The Flying Dutchman*. These were followed by *Tannhäuser* (1845) and *Lohengrin* (1847), which were both produced by Liszt on the

Weimar stage in Wagner's absence. The composer in the meantime had arrived in the Swiss city of Zurich, on his flight from Dresden, where he had taken part in the revolutionary uprisings of the year 1849.

The period of Wagner's mature creations begins with his "exile" in Zurich (1849–1859). It was during these years that the idea of the Wagnerian "music drama" and the "art-work of the future" assumed its final shape. The plan of the tetralogy *The Ring of the Nibelungs,* textually based on the Scandinavian saga cycle of the *Older Edda,** was first conceived in 1848. The completed *Ring,* comprising the operas *Rheingold, Die Walküre, Siegfried,* and *Götterdämmerung (Twilight of the Gods),* was first produced in its entirety in the Wagner *Festspielhaus* in Bayreuth, August 13–17, 1876. In the same year this new and unique Bayreuth Opera House had opened its doors to the public.

In the *Ring* Wagner had definitely broken with the existing theater, and the new playhouse had been especially designed to fit the requirements of his tetralogy. The seats for the audience were arranged in rising semi-circular rows, following the model of the ancient amphitheater. The space that intervened between the proscenium and the first row of seats had been conceived by Wagner as a "mystic abyss" that was to separate the real from the ideal and was to make the dramatic personages appear on the stage at a mythical distance and in superhuman proportions.

Wagner had of course several collaborators who aided him in the practical execution of his ideas, but he was himself intimately familiar with the artistic and technical possibilities and requirements of the stage: he actually lived, worked, wrote, composed, and conducted for the stage and from the point of view of the stage. The *Festspielhaus* was designed by him in close co-operation with Gottfried Semper, a famous Neo-Classical architect. The style of opera developed on this newly created stage marks a definite and significant phase in the history of European music as well as in the evolution of modern stagecraft and stage production.

As a stage director Wagner fostered a kind of romantic historicism that had become popular in the age of Walter Scott and the era of the historical novel and which in the field of the theater had become associated with the efforts of Duke George II of Meiningen (1826–1914). In his court theater the duke had encouraged the trend toward historically accurate and artistically integrated stage productions. This growing interest in historical verisimilitude was in itself a deviation from the indiscriminate medley of styles that was characteristic of the romantic stage proper, with its veritable craze for picturesqueness. In Wagner's operas the stage setting acquires more than historical or archaeological significance: it takes part in the

---

*The *Older Edda* or *Saemundar-Edda* contains next to the *Nibelungenlied* (cf. p. 154) the most important source material of the Nibelungen saga. It is an Icelandic collection of thirty-five songs, compiled in the thirteenth century and consisting of two major divisions: (a) the mythological songs of Odin, Thor, etc.; (b) the heroic songs of Helgi and the Nibelungs.

dramatic action and becomes a medium for a parallel expression of those voices and forces of nature and spirit that are alive in the musical score.

The realization of Wagner's artistic dream would never have come about without the generous aid and encouragement that he received from Louis II, the "mad" king of Bavaria (1864–1886), who built those phantastic dream castles that adorn some of the most beautiful sites in the Bavarian Alps. He sensed in Wagner's music a world in which his lonely soul could be exalted and soothed in an atmosphere of spiritual kinship. Louis came to Wagner's rescue in the hard and unhappy years that followed the "exile" in Zurich. Wagner was invited to Munich and commissioned to complete the composition of the *Ring*. *Tristan und Isolde* was produced in Munich in 1865, *Die Meistersinger* in 1868. The first performance of *Parsifal* took place in the Bayreuth *Festspielhaus* in 1882. From 1865–1872 Wagner lived in Triebschen near the Swiss city of Lucerne. In 1870 he had married Liszt's daughter, Cosima, the divorced wife of his friend and pupil, the famous conductor Hans von Bülow. The final years of his life Wagner spent in the palatial "Villa Wahnfried" in Bayreuth.

Richard Wagner's philosophy of life was closely linked with the ideological structure of his works. As his own art grew out of the problems of his life, so he demanded of all art that it be humanly and socially significant. He complained of the art of his time that it was nothing but a hothouse plant, that it had no roots in the natural and national soil, and that because of its separation from reality it did not and could not exert a formative influence on social and public life.

With the romanticists Wagner concurred in their high esteem of philosophy, mythology, and religion. Like them he was in love with the Germanic past, intensely interested in the national destiny of Germany, and convinced of the cultural fertility of the German mind. Philosophically he was torn between the opposing influences and urges of Ludwig Feuerbach's (cf. p. 556 sq.) sensualistic materialism and Arthur Schopenhauer's (cf. p. 505 sq.) doctrine of resignation and universal compassion. His friendship with Friedrich Nietzsche (1869–1876) ended with a shrill discord when Wagner in his *Parsifal* paid a glowing tribute to the creative and regenerative forces of Christianity. Nietzsche complained that Wagner, at the end of his life, had "helplessly broken down at the foot of the Christian Cross."

Wagner, in point of fact, expected the renascence of modern mankind from a synthesis of Germanism and Christianity, a line of thought that is followed with a fair amount of consistency from *Tannhäuser* to *Parsifal*. The Christian virtues of self-denial, sacrifice, and compassion are motifs that are interwoven in the dramatic plots of most of Wagner's operas. Those who infringe upon this code of ethics — Tannhäuser, Siegfried, Tristan, Amfortas — atone by suffering retribution and death. Even Siegfried, the nearest personification of Nietzsche's "Superman" (*Übermensch*), the embodiment of the triumphant instincts of strength and power, cannot escape the sanctions of retributive justice and is therefore no exception to the general rule. The complexity of Wagner's heroes and heroines reflects on the whole the composer's own complex personality. As a man Richard Wagner was impelled by the burning ambition to fulfill his mission as an artist. Of this mission he was conscious from the time of his earliest artistic endeavors, and his vanity and naïve egotism were merely outward manifestations of his singular determination to sacrifice everything, including every human loyalty and friendship, to what he considered his supreme task in life.

Political Romanticism. The political and social ideas of most of the leading romantic writers in Germany were as much opposed to eighteenth-century Absolutism as to nineteenth-century Liberalism. They affirmed the value and dignity of the human person but denied the equality of all human beings. As against economic competition, based on the law of supply and demand, they advanced the solidarity of medieval society, with its "divinely willed" inequalities, its pyramidal system of interdependent rights and duties, functions and services, "offices" and "callings," that had been the constitutive principle of the pre-absolutistic social order of Europe.

In accordance with these ideas the three major concerns of political romanticism were: (1) the reawakening of a sense of historic continuity; (2) the re-establishment of social and national unity; (3) the restoration of a society that was inspired by Christian impulses. In formulating their program the political romanticists made use of Herder's doctrine of the enduring characteristics of the "folk spirit" (cf. p. 396 sq.) and of Edmund Burke's (cf. p. 386) conservative and counterrevolutionary ideology which had been partially realized in the political system of Metternich and Gentz.

The State was no longer considered as a mechanical aggregation of individuals but as an organic whole whose functions were not confined to the maintenance of law and order but included the political, social, moral, and religious education of its citizens. Human society in its concrete historic manifestations was to be strictly delimited by a community of linguistic, moral, and racial characteristics.

The most influential spokesman of political romanticism was *Adam Müller* (1779–1829), the friend of Friedrich Schlegel and Heinrich von Kleist and one of the first romanticists to embrace the Catholic Church. For him the State is even more than an organic society: it is a moral personality; it is the "eternal alliance of men among themselves." He disregarded entirely the historic significance of Absolutism and Revolution and set up the corporative society of medieval Feudalism as an absolute ideal, as "the eternal scheme of all true state government, the safeguard of permanence and power." As a partisan of the prerogatives of the nobility who was himself knighted by Metternich, he praised the warlike and knightly spirit of the German race. Giving the lie to his own professed ideal of a restoration of the unity and universality of Western Christian civilization, he visualized a final triumphant rule of Germanic warriors and noblemen over all the "inferior" races of Europe. Although it is certainly true that the nationalism of Adam Müller and his friends was still checked by ethical and religious considerations, and that they were entirely sincere in proclaiming a "holy war" against Napoleon's dream of world conquest, it cannot be denied that the ruthless *Machtpolitik* of the nineteenth century was partially carried through with the intellectual armor borrowed from the arsenal of the political romanticists.

Romanticism and Jurisprudence: Savigny and Eichhorn. The political romanticists' emphasis on the principles of organic growth and historic continuity bore fruit in the work of some of the leading jurists of the early nineteenth century. *Friedrich Karl von Savigny* (1779–1861) and *Karl Friedrich Eichhorn* (1781–1854) became the founders of the so-called "historical school" of law as opposed to the rationalistic legal concepts of the eighteenth century. For both men all human law is the product of organic growth and as such firmly rooted in the "folk spirit" and one of the integral and vital elements of national culture. "All law grows and develops in harmony with the life of the people and it dies as soon as the people lose their distinctive character traits" (Savigny). If, however, the people and their culture are the ultimate source of law, there is little room left for any arbitrary interference with the organic processes of evolution, and the legal changes and innovations introduced by absolutistic rulers must be summarily rejected. Thus Savigny's historical method results in an almost quietistic attitude of *"laissez-aller,"* resenting any progressive and positive legislation as an interference with the principle of "organic growth" and as a "break with the laws of history." Such an attitude was obviously determined by romantic influences, although in other respects, and especially in his capacity as a scholar and teacher, Savigny was a model of classical calm and balanced dignity.

To Savigny belongs the merit of having restored the venerable tradition of "Roman Law" from its original sources to its original purity and in its historic growth. K. F. Eichhorn, Savigny's colleague in the University of Berlin, can claim a similar title for the regeneration of "Germanic Law." The two heads of the "historic school" of law in its "Romanic" and "Germanic" branches voiced their convictions in the *Zeitschrift für geschichtliche Rechtswissenschaft* which they founded in 1815. When in the early years of his academic career Savigny lectured at the University of Marburg, the brothers Grimm were among his most responsive listeners. They were greatly impressed by his doctrine of the organic evolution of the "folk spirit" and successfully applied the "historical method" to the fields of language and literature.

Romantic Philosophy. The philosophical speculation of the romantic age, and in fact most of the philosophy of the nineteenth century, is determined by its relationship to Kant (cf. p. 371 sqq.). As far as romantic philosophy as such is concerned, it culminates in the three great "idealistic"*

---

* Philosophical "idealism" means first of all the affirmation of spiritual principles in the explanation of reality. In its Platonic form it considers the world of visible objects as represen-

systems of Fichte, Schelling, and Hegel. Schopenhauer's philosophico-religious system may be added to this list, if we disregard his personal antipathy for the leading philosophers of his time, and overlook the fact that his own philosophy went unrecognized until the middle of the century.

a) Johann Gottlieb Fichte (*1762–1814*).   It had been Kant's contention that things can never be known by us as they are "in themselves" but only as they appear to us in our subjective consciousness. The mind receives certain sense data as its raw material, so to speak, and out of these data it constructs its conceptual knowledge. But Kant's followers and idealistic critics, more radically and perhaps more consistently, argued that since it was the mind that made the distinction between the mental and the non-mental, between what is objectively given and what is subjectively apprehended, these sense data themselves were no less mental than the concepts the mind forms of them. For this reason Fichte called the distinction between "things in themselves" and appearances an arbitrary assumption, asserting that in human knowledge both object and subject were mental or spiritual realities. For Fichte the form as well as the content of knowledge is derived from the sovereignty of the creative Ego, the spiritual Self which, finding itself confronted with the manifold limitations and restrictions of the "Non-Ego," demonstrates its capacity for spiritual freedom and self-realization by gradually overcoming all that renders it finite. Such a moral and creative evolution of the Ego will eventually result in the submersion of the individual Self in the infinite reality of the universal or "transcendental" Self. Therefore this Universal Ego was for Fichte the supreme reality and the moral force that was capable of transforming and elevating individual and social life. In his *Wissenschaftslehre* (theory of knowledge and learning) he describes the activity of the Transcendental Ego in typically romantic terminology as an "infinite striving," whose goal is an ever increasing clarity of consciousness.

Accused of teaching atheistic doctrines, Fichte had to resign from his professorship in Jena in 1799. He moved to Berlin, where he was enthusiastically received by the members of the Romantic School and where, in 1810, he became the first *Rector* of the newly founded university. His *Address to the German Warriors,* delivered in 1806, at the beginning of the Napoleonic wars, was followed after Prussia's defeat by the *Addresses to*

---

tations or images of eternal ideas. In the epistemological sense "idealism" maintains that the human mind is the basic reality and the main source of the knowledge, comprehension, and structure of the extramental world. For the "subjective idealist" (e.g., Berkeley) this extramental world is merely an idea of the individual ego, while for the "objective idealist" (Fichte, Schelling, Hegel, Schopenhauer) the world is the representation and realization of the Absolute, Universal, or Transcendental Ego or the Absolute Spirit. Almost all philosophical idealists are also pantheists. The idealistic German philosophers of the romantic period have in common an unshakable belief in the constructive power of human thought, coupled with a more or less pronounced disregard for experience and experimental science as sources of knowledge. They all endeavor to reduce the sum total of reality to one fundamental principle (Fichte: the "Transcendental Ego"; Schelling: the "World-Soul"; Hegel: the "World-Spirit"; Schopenhauer: the "World-Will").

the German Nation (1807–1808, cf. p. 439). It was a stirring appeal, citing the faults and neglects that had caused the downfall of Prussia, and it was directed to all social groups. Fichte castigated the complacency of the old and the inertia and indifference of the young, the cowardice and effeminacy of the ruling classes, and the social injustice that had wrought the oppression and exploitation of the poor. Calling for "national education" (*National-erziehung*) as an absolute prerequisite for the rebirth of his country, he maintained that the creation of a perfect State could only be accomplished by "a nation which first of all must have fulfilled the task of educating perfect human beings." And yet he believes that despite the many symptoms of decadence the German people as a racial unity are still best qualified for political and moral leadership.

Fichte constantly stressed the primacy of the moral law as the regulative norm of action for nations and individuals, but he also demanded that individual happiness be at all times subordinated to the welfare of the nation. Thus his *Kulturstaat* was to be a composite of nationalist and socialist incentives, containing in its structure the seeds of State socialism and a new State omnipotence.

b) Friedrich Wilhelm von Schelling (*1775–1854*). German "nature philosophy" (*Naturphilosophie*), as represented by Schelling and some of his romantic friends, was a protest on the part of philosophy against the encroachments of the natural sciences and their mechanistic concepts of nature on the prerogatives of the human spirit. Where the natural sciences seemed to have failed, namely in supplying a satisfactory explanation of the ultimate moving force of the universe, and in offering a solution of the riddle of life, of biological and morphological growth, the German nature philosophers hoped to succeed.

Fichte had approached nature from the point of view of the mind, but Schelling tried to go the opposite way and to explain mental phenomena from the point of view of nature. By starting from the data and observations of the exact sciences and following the forces of nature on their path from the inorganic to the organic forms of existence, he tried to develop a harmonious and all-inclusive philosophico-theological system. For him all the phenomena of nature and mind, of the real and the ideal, are manifestations of an aboriginal force which he calls the "World-Soul" and whose living incarnation is the universe, composed of a graduated series of self-developing and organized forms of being. All being, on both the inorganic and the organic levels, tends toward the fullest realization of the immanent spiritual-ity of the "World-Soul." In the unity of the "World-Soul" nature and spirit are one, but they are separated in the duality of the worlds of nature and mind, and they incessantly strive to become one again by returning to the original source of their unity.

Schelling's speculation, though partly influenced by Fichte's moral ideal-ism, was even more indebted to Spinoza's (cf. p. 355 sq.) pantheistic philos-ophy and to Jacob Böhme's theosophy (cf. p. 270). The same intuitive trans-

port of mind that caused him to consider art as the highest manifestation of
the Absolute, and aesthetic contemplation as the highest form of knowledge,
made him anticipate some of Lamarck's and Darwin's discoveries concerning
the evolution of organic life, at the same time preserving him from laying
too much stress on abstract speculation at the expense of concrete observation.

   c) *Georg Wilhelm Friedrich Hegel* (*1770–1831*). How can the freedom
of the individual be reconciled with the demands of an all-powerful "World-
Spirit" (*Weltgeist*)? This question constituted the major problem and the
starting point of the philosophical speculation of Hegel, who undoubtedly
was the greatest and most influential of the romantic philosophers. Up to
this day his ideas are recognizable in many standard works of political and
social philosophy, in the philosophy of history and civilization, in aesthetic
theory, and to no lesser degree in political ideologies and their attempted
realizations.*

   It may be said that Hegel exhausted all the possibilities of idealistic
philosophy, carrying it to its extreme conclusions and establishing a metaphysical edifice that rested on the mastery of an immense mass of factual
data. While as a metaphysician he created the crowning philosophical
synthesis of the nineteenth century, as an observer of reality he prepared the
way for the staggering triumphs of the empirical sciences. He absorbed
and digested the influences of European Enlightenment and of German
Classicism and Romanticism and constructed his own imposing system of
thought out of the ingredients of all these intellectual movements.

   A rationalist at heart, Hegel proclaimed the identity of thinking and being:
"Whatever is rational is real, and whatever is real is rational." Therefore it
becomes the task of philosophy to use the data of history and of science
to demonstrate the rationality of everything that is real. The world is for
Hegel a universe of varying and changing forms in which the gradual
evolution of the "World-Spirit" manifests itself. The philosopher is called
upon to comprehend these multiform phenomena as aspects and phases of
a logical and necessary development. This development follows the scheme
of the dialectical triad of "thesis, antithesis, and synthesis": ideas and
phenomena cannot be comprehended unless we think and know their
opposites. We cannot, for example, define the nature of the good unless we
know the nature of evil; we do not know what is rational unless we know
what is real. The dialectical thinking and understanding of opposites (theses
and antitheses) leads to a synthetic comprehension of the nature of reality.

---

   *In 1806, the year of Prussia's defeat, Hegel had finished his first important work, *The
Phenomenology of the Spirit*. Between 1812 and 1816 he completed his *Logic*. From 1816–
1818 he was professor of philosophy at the University of Heidelberg. In 1818 he took over
the chair of philosophy at the University of Berlin, which position he held until his death.
Seven of his pupils published a posthumous edition of his works in 17 volumes, arranged
in the following order: Vol. 1, Philosophical Treatises; Vol. 2, The Phenomenology of the
Spirit; Vols. 3–5, Logic; Vols. 6, 7, Encyclopedia of Sciences; Vol. 8, The Philosophy of
Right; Vol. 9, Lectures on the Philosophy of History; Vol. 10, Lectures on Aesthetics; Vols. 11,
12, Lectures on the Philosophy of Religion; Vols. 13–15, The History of Philosophy; Vols. 16,
17, Miscellaneous Writings.

The romantic concept of the organic evolution of an eternally becoming world furnished Hegel the tools with which to explain and justify the necessity and rationality of the individual within the general workings of the "World-Spirit": all things in nature and human life evolve consciously and rationally, but their rationality becomes visible only as they reach the higher stages of consciousness and intelligibility. For Hegel philosophy and religion are identical in that the explications of thought are at the same time the explications of the "Absolute Spirit."

The process of a becoming world is most clearly noticeable in the history of civilization and particularly in the organism of the State, the truest "objectivation" of the "World-Spirit." The "Absolute Spirit" is manifested in ever changing forms in the "folk spirit" itself as much as in its leading exponents; it is incarnate in State and society, in art and religion, in science and economics. But while all these cultural forms are perishable and while one historic epoch gives way to another, the "World-Spirit" as such proceeds unperturbed on its progressive march through history.

All individual life must be understood as being part and parcel of the comprehensive totality of life. Individuality and society are correlated and interdependent, both partakers of the supreme reality of the "Objective Spirit." Individuality becomes real and acquires the attributes of spirituality and morality only as it consciously comprehends itself as determined by and embedded in the universal dynamic movement of the "World-Spirit." For this reason individual freedom and historic necessity are merged by a law of pre-established harmony: the individual may believe he follows his own urges and pursues his own ends, while in reality he serves the higher and still hidden designs of the ruling spirit of the universe. The great political leaders of the past and present may think of themselves as freely moving forces and self-acting agents of world history: in reality they are only the "clerks" of the "World-Spirit" and, after having served its ulterior purpose, they are cast away "like empty shells."

Among the many manifestations of the Universal Reason the State is the highest and the most perfect. It is the realization of the idea of morality, reason, and spirit incarnate, and as such it is partly human and partly divine. The State, in short, is "God walking upon the earth," and therefore the dignity and worth of the human person is ultimately derived from the State.

It was only logical that this political theory should make Hegel an advocate of State omnipotence and a passionate opponent of German Liberalism (cf. p. 523 sqq.). No longer was the State to serve the well-being of the individual, but the individual existed and acted for the aggrandizement of the State. Hegel was consistent, too, in that he placed the State above religion, because religion was concerned with "beliefs," but the State was the possessor of infallible "knowledge." Luther's subservience to all legally constituted authority was transformed by Hegel into the self-sufficiency and moral supremacy of the State, and tolerance henceforth became a "criminal weakness."

This, then, was the ideological framework of the Hegelian *Kulturstaat,* whose essential features the philosopher believed he recognized in the Prussian State of his time and whose structure proved equally suited for the political philosophies of extreme nationalism and of State socialism. There was no room in this scheme of ideas for either moral or international law, the State being no longer the servant of the law but its infallible creator, interpreter, and master. The most powerful State at any given historic epoch was entitled to consider itself as the mouthpiece of the "World-Spirit" and therefore its own advantage was its supreme law. A peaceful society of nations on the basis of equality became an impossibility, the ideal of "eternal peace" was termed an empty abstraction or an idle dream, and the dialectic of history had to justify ever recurring waves of warfare, while international agreements became mere "scraps of paper," whenever practical political considerations made it advisable to disregard them.

Hegel's *political philosophy* was in one respect an ingenious attempt to justify philosophically the theories of Machiavelli (cf. p. 247 sq.). Might and force were identified with Spirit and Right, and the revolting human conscience was soothed by shifting the responsibility for political crimes to the inexorable laws of the "World-Spirit." Success and failure became the ultimate criteria of the right and wrong involved in political action.

There was a strange contrast between Hegel's comfortable bourgeois existence and the revolutionary implications of his ideas. The same man who in his youth had been a student of Protestant theology in Tübingen and had been associated there in thought and feeling with Hölderlin and Schelling, the romantic enthusiast who in the political confusion of the Napoleonic wars had made no secret of his admiration of the French emperor, whose personality he reverently compared with the dynamic force of the "World-Soul" — he became after the Wars of Liberation the official "State Philosopher of Prussia" and a defender of some of the more dubious aspects of the hegemony of Prussia. The same Hegel who in his youth had declared himself in sympathy with the ideas that inspired the French Revolution of 1789 — he became the spokesman of political reaction. He was clearly satisfied with the belief that his age and his nation had achieved the heights of human and cultural perfectibility and that it was therefore no longer necessary to build actively and creatively for the future but that the time for retrospection and a comprehensive digest of the past had finally arrived.

As Hegel was convinced that in the history of the world today's error might be tomorrow's truth, he was much more interested in the dynamism of historical forces than in their shades of true or false, right or wrong. While on the one hand he encouraged abstract metaphysical speculation to go far beyond the limits of the empirically knowable, his genuine interest in every type of reality made his mentality akin to that of the postromantic "realists" (cf. p. 583 sq.), whose novel ways of thought and life were to supplant the idealistic philosophies of the early nineteenth century.

When Hegel died in 1831, he left behind a band of faithful disciples, well versed in the intricacies of the master's dialectical method and applying it rather indiscriminately to the fields of history, law, natural philosophy, aesthetics, and religion. It was due to Hegel's influence that from now on to the very end of the century the history of philosophy became the leading philosophical discipline and professors of the history of philosophy occupied the most important philosophical chairs.

The Hegelian School was divided into the opposing camps of a Christian-conservative right wing (Old Hegelians) and a radically anti-Christian and materialist left wing (Young Hegelians). This division in itself reflects the ambiguity of Hegel's system and of the dialectical method which lent itself to diametrically contradictory conclusions. The phrase, for instance, "everything that is real is rational," could be used as a strong argument for the preservation of the existing social and political order. But the same phrase, in the negative formulation: "everything that is not rational is not real," contained in it the seeds of utter radicalism and a call for revolutionary action, to make reality comply with the demands of reason. The Young Hegelian radicals made the latter interpretation their own and believed themselves as much justified in referring to Hegel as their teacher as the Old Hegelian conservatives.

The most astonishing and, historically speaking, the most consequential fate, however, befell the dialectical method at the hands of Karl Marx (cf. p. 556 sqq.), who claimed that Hegelian philosophy, which "had stood on its head," had been put by him "on its legs again." He used the dialectical method, not to explain objective and material reality by referring it back to ideas, but conversely, to explain ideas as resulting from basic material realities. Hegel's dialectical idealism thus provided the methodical foundation for Marx's dialectical materialism. By taking over Hegel's concept of the State and by filling this ready-made mold with a different content, Marx developed "scientifically" the pattern of the classless society and the dictatorship of the proletariat.

d) Arthur Schopenhauer (1788–1860). Seeing in the universe a wonderfully designed organism, in which each member held its proper place and fulfilled its God-given function by virtue of a "pre-established harmony," Leibniz (cf. p. 358 sq.) had designated the world we know as "the best of all possible worlds." Schopenhauer, on the other hand, weighing the actual amount of good and evil in the world against each other, arrived at the pessimistic conclusion that life was "a business whose profits do not nearly cover its expenses" and that therefore this world of ours was "the worst of all possible worlds." For him the prevalence of evil was the most obvious of facts and he considered the supposed rationality of the universe as an assumption and a product of the wishful thinking of armchair philosophers.

With Schopenhauer the incongruity between thought and life, theory and practice was even more striking than in Hegel's case. The greatest pessimist among philosophers was personally fond of life and good living, fond of good food and drink, and fond of sensual pleasures. His unsociability and his contempt of women were largely the result of the experiences of a lonely childhood, of the premature death of his father and the estrangement from his mother, Johanna Schopenhauer, who was much more interested in writing (worthless) novels and in mixing in literary and social affairs than in the education of her son.

Schopenhauer was a native of Danzig. He traveled in France, England, and Italy for some time to acquire cosmopolitan tastes and to perfect his natural ability in the command of foreign languages. He was a great admirer of Lord Byron, but envied the English poet his luck with women and therefore refused to make his personal acquaintance. As a student of philosophy he attended Fichte's and Schleiermacher's lectures in Berlin and was so unfavorably impressed that he developed a lifelong antagonism against all the representatives of idealistic philosophy. When he temporarily settled down in Berlin as a *Privatdozent,* Hegel and Schleiermacher had become the favorites of the academic world, while Schopenhauer's lectures and writings found no response. He gave vent to his disappointment in bitter attacks against "the professorial philosophy of the philosophy professors" (*die Professorenphilosophie der Philosophieprofessoren*) in general and against Hegel in particular, whom he dubbed a quack, a charlatan, and a servile creature of the Prussian government. The cholera epidemic of the year 1831, which claimed Hegel as one of its victims, caused Schopenhauer to move to Frankfurt, where he spent the rest of his solitary life, with his faithful black poodle as his only companion.

Schopenhauer's philosophy was romantic in that it magnified inner experiences and personal moods into a system of thought which he superimposed on external reality. With Kant (cf. p. 371 sq.) he maintained the subjective origin of time, space, and the categories of pure reason, but against Kant he claimed that the reality (the "thing in itself") that underlies all appearances was knowable. In inner perception and self-knowledge, reality can be recognized as a "World-Will" or a "will to live" that manifests itself in the forms of both unconscious instinct and conscious desire. It is this universal "Will" that causes disease, suffering, and death, that forges the endless chain of souls, migrating from birth to death and rebirth, in different bodies and on different levels of existence.

While in this metaphysical speculation Schopenhauer was chiefly influenced by his profound knowledge of Buddhist philosophy and religion, his ethical convictions represent a blend of Buddhist and Christian ideas. Sympathy with all suffering creatures and mortification he considered as the two pillars of morality. The fatal cycle of births and rebirths can be brought to a halt, the chain of pain and suffering can be broken by an integral asceticism or the absolute negation of the "will to live," whereby all individual wills become one in the universal life stream of the "World-Will," and all restlessness ceases in the eternal quiescence of the great "Nirvana." Suicide, on the other hand, or the self-destruction of the individual "will to live," offers no way out, because it leaves the universal "will to live" untouched.

Schopenhauer describes, however, an intermediate realm between the universal will and its refractions in individuals: in the realm of Ideas the "World-Will" appears "objectified" in the various forms of artistic creation and most poignantly and directly in the world of music. In the contemplation of art human beings may experience a temporary escape from the curse of pain and suffering, but lasting salvation can only be obtained by overcoming desire and in attaining the bliss of "Nirvana."

Schopenhauer, who had a very high opinion of his own works and was fully conscious of his extraordinary qualities as a thinker and a stylist, designated as his *opus maximum* the book entitled *Die Welt als Wille und Vorstellung* (*The World as Will and Mental Representation*). This work was first published in 1818 and republished in 1844, when its author had at last been given the recognition that was his due. It contains his main ideas in a masterly presentation and combines philosophical depth with poetic intuition and a brilliant literary form.

Romantic Theology: Schleiermacher (1768–1834). The greatest Protestant theologian of Germany since the days of the Reformation and one of the most influential religious writers of the nineteenth century was *Friedrich Daniel Schleiermacher*. He was the contemporary and friend of the leaders of the Romantic School, who in his own intellectual and spiritual development had successively experienced the influences of Pietism (cf. p. 364 sqq.), Enlightenment (cf. p. 368 sqq.), Classicism (cf. Chap. 12), and Romanticism. His versatility, his striving for a total view of life, and his religious subjectivism mark him as a romantic character. The central concept of his philosophy of religion was the idea of individuality, and like Hegel he wrestled with the problem of how the claims of the individual could be reconciled with the demands of superindividual realities, be they State, society, a visible ecclesiastical community, or the Deity itself.

A true synthesis of the particular and the universal, according to Schleiermacher, can only be achieved in contemplation and personal "feeling" (*Gefühl*). In his earlier period he defines religion as "the contemplation of the infinite in the finite, of the eternal in the temporal"; later on, as a presence of the infinite in a personal "feeling of absolute dependence." Religion, then, has its roots in human personality, and in taking this position Schleiermacher was as much opposed to the orthodox defenders of "revealed religion" as to the representatives of the "natural religion" of the period of Enlightenment. His concept of religion was most closely related to the ideas of the New Humanists (cf. p. 000) and their religious exaltation of human personality. For them as for Schleiermacher man is a finite incarnation of the infinite spirit, and by consciously developing the divine likeness within him he prepares himself for moral action and emerges as a human character.

The religious community and the organized Church represent for

Schleiermacher the living form and force of the moral law, in whose embrace the individual experiences an awakening of his mind, a strengthening of his will, and an enlargement of his soul. Schleiermacher's *Discourses on Religion, Addressed to the Educated among its Despisers* (*Reden über die Religion an die Gebildeten unter ihren Verächtern*) picture Christ as the most perfect specimen of humanity, the creative inaugurator of a new and unique destiny of the human race. Christ was the great exemplar, challenging and stimulating the moral courage of men to follow his spiritual leadership. In Church dogmas and cultic observances Schleiermacher saw symbolic expressions of subjective truths and personal religious experiences. As a modern theologian of the "historical school" he was no longer concerned with revelations of supernatural truths that claimed objective validity but rather with the historically conditioned religious contents of the changing individual consciousness. This was a novel approach to the phenomena of religion, favoring the development of the new disciplines of the psychology and comparative history of religion.

Schleiermacher's most unfriendly critic and opponent was Hegel, whose intellectualism and rationalism rose up in revolt against Schleiermacher's vindication of religious feeling. For Hegel religion was an expression of reason, and as such an inferior kind of philosophy. "If religion," he said, "is essentially based on the feeling of dependence . . . then the dog is the finest Christian, for he . . . lives pre-eminently in such a feeling. He even experiences feelings of redemption, at the moment when his hunger is satisfied with a bone."

Chapter 15

LIBERALISM, NATIONALISM, AND THE UNIFICATION OF GERMANY

A. *POLITICAL AND ECONOMIC TRENDS*

The Policy of Intervention. The period of the "Vormärz" (1815–1848) is marked by a latent or open struggle of ideas in practically all European countries. The old Absolutism has to defend itself against the new Liberalism; the principle of "legitimism" (cf. p. 461 sq.) finds itself threatened by the principle of "national self-determination." At the Congress of Troppau (1820) the reactionary governments of Prussia, Austria, and Russia had pledged themselves to intervene, if necessary by force of arms, in the affairs of any country in which the authoritarian regime was endangered by revolution. Thus Austria received the mandate to suppress the liberal movements in Naples and Sardinia (1820), and France, under the restored Bourbon monarchy, was commissioned to execute the "Will of Europe" by crushing the liberal rebellion in Spain (1822). The British government, on the other hand, had shown itself steadily opposed to the policy of armed intervention, and Canning (1770–1827), the British foreign secretary and future prime minister, had proclaimed for the first time the right of the "self-determination of the people."

Both Great Britain and the United States were equally interested in keeping the Metternich System confined to continental Europe and in preventing a reactionary Spain from regaining her Central and South American colonies, which had severed their ties with the mother country during the Napoleonic wars. Canning informed the French government that England would consider the sending of a French expeditionary force to the Americas as a warlike act, and President James Monroe declared in a message to Congress that any attempt made by European powers to extend their political system to any part of the Western hemisphere would be considered as endangering the peace and security of the United States (Monroe Doctrine, 1823).

Thus the policies of Metternich's European "Concert" of powers were shattered by the combined forces of Liberalism and Nationalism. The principle of "legitimacy" received its deathblow when Metternich, in the course of the Greek War of Independence (1821–1829), expressed his sympathies for the cause of the Turkish sultan, condemning the Greeks for their rebellion against their "legitimate" ruler. By the joint action of Russia, France, and England, Greek independence was finally secured. In helping Greece to achieve her goal, the mercantile and political interests of the three great powers mingled with idealistic motives, but Metternich's principle of European solidarity no longer played a part in their considerations and actions.

The enthusiasm of Lord Canning for the cause of Greek independence was as sincere as that of Lord Byron, who sacrificed his life for it. In a famous speech of the year 1826 Canning assured all the suppressed peoples of the world of British sympathy and designated the protection of freedom and human rights as the great task of the British empire. It is true that this moral idealism ran parallel with Great Britain's commercial interests. It is equally true that English foreign policy could be just as ruthless as that of any autocratic government whenever British interests were in conflict with the interests of the suppressed peoples (e.g., Ireland, India, the Boer War). By contributing to the liberation of the smaller European peoples England earned their gratitude together with their trade and willingly assumed the role of their protector and guardian. While Gentz (cf. p. 461) spoke of Great Britain as the "source of rebellion" and Metternich had nothing but contempt for Canning's foreign policy, the latter forged an enduring alliance between British Nationalism and the forces of Liberalism. This tradition, once established, was consistently adhered to by Canning's successors, "Lord Firebrand" Palmerston (1784–1865) and Gladstone (1809–1898). The peculiar genius of British statesmanship knew how to enlist the human love of freedom and the popular desire for national independence in the cause of her own aggrandizement. These mixed incentives of British politics provided a temporary bulwark against the increasing amoralism, opportunism, and cynicism that invaded the field of international relations in the course of the nineteenth century.

The Goals of Constitutional Liberty and National Unity. The German people fought as bravely and enthusiastically for their civil liberties and for national unity as any other nation, but a long period of political repression and the historically conditioned particularistic tendencies of the several German states rendered this struggle especially hard and prolonged. The eventual unification of Germany under Bismarck's leadership (cf. p. 546) was an event of such magnitude that it completely overshadowed the issue of constitutional liberty, for which the German Liberals had fought and suffered persecution during the earlier part of the nineteenth century.

Germany Under the Rule of the "German Confederation." The political organization of Germany that had been created by the "Act of Confederation" of 1815 (cf. p. 456 sq.) was the result of a compromise that tried to please everybody but in reality satisfied no one. It was an attempt to deal with a complex situation without disturbing the existing "peaceful dualism" of Prusso-Austrian relations. As a system of government the "German Confederation" was much too unwieldy to function efficiently and to give voice and weight to a national will. It offered conclusive evidence that Germany was not yet a nation in the same sense in which France, England, or Russia were sovereign and relatively homogeneous states.

The "German Confederation" was dominated by the Holy Alliance (cf. p. 459 sq.), which in turn was the instrument of Metternich's political designs. Its endeavors were paralyzed by the selfish interests of the member states and by the latent antagonism between the two largest of them — Austria and Prussia. The fifty years that followed the passage of the "Act of Confederation" witnessed various attempts on the part of the German people to break the political deadlock that was preventing Germany from reaching the goal of her national aspirations.

Political and Social Reaction in Prussia. Frederick William III was fundamentally a cautious conservative who dreaded all revolutionary changes and who was sentimentally attached to the political institutions of the prerevolutionary *"ancien régime."* The events of the years of Prussia's humiliation had forced his hand, and much against his will he had tolerated the work of the reformers who had rescued and liberated the State from foreign oppression. After 1815 the king was glad to join the forces of restoration and reaction and to follow the lead of Metternich and the Russian tsar. Without misgivings he submitted to Austria's growing influence in the "German Confederation," convinced that in the close collaboration with Metternich lay the surest guarantee for the peace and stability of Prussia. In 1815, following the trend of the times, Frederick William III had promised in a proclamation the establishment of representative government in Prussia, but eight years elapsed before the provincial estates were convoked for the first time, and more than forty years before some form of constitutional and representative government was forced upon the State by the will of the people.

In the meantime, Prussia's failure to keep abreast of the changing political and social conditions caused further cleavages in the social structure of the State and contributed to the growing antagonism between Prussia and the more progressive southern German states. The king surrounded himself with bureaucrats of the old school and seized upon every opportunity to restore the former privileges of the nobility as a ruling class. The eight Provincial Diets of Prussia were dominated by the members of the nobility and lacked the most elementary forms of parliamentary rights. They were merely advisory bodies without legislative powers and were subject to the absolute sovereignty of the king. The rural reforms of Stein and Hardenberg were largely undone, and the attempt to liberate the peasants ended with the victory of the manorial lords and the restoration of serfdom or semi-serfdom. The result was a huge expansion of the large estates and the creation of a peasant-proletariat. Whereas formerly the peasants had been unfree but socially more or less secure, they now became day laborers without either property or social security, their pay depending on the fluctuations of the markets. This rural proletariat provided the "industrial army of reserves" (Karl Marx), from which the growing industrial civilization recruited its workers: broken existences that doubled and trebled the population figures of the industrial centers by their migration from the rural districts to the big cities. These conditions prevailed above all in the regions east of the Elbe river, while in the Rhineland the influence of the French Revolution and the social reforms of the Napoleonic era aided in creating and preserving a well-to-do and healthy peasantry.

Austria, Prussia, and the "German Confederation." When Francis II had abdicated as German emperor in 1806 (cf. p. 325), it had not been his intention to weaken the ancient prestige of the Hapsburg dynasty or to renounce its claims to political and cultural leadership in the German lands. However, as far as common partnership in the "German Confederation" was concerned, the interests of Prussia and Austria were not identical but contradictory. While Austria's interests lay largely outside the Germanies, in Italy, in Galicia, in the Balkans, and in the Adriatic region, Prussia's interests in all important issues were in harmony with those of all the minor German states. Accordingly, Metternich had devised the "German Confederation" as a large buffer state that was to protect Austria from French attack. This purpose was best served by a loose federation that could rally to a defensive war against foreign encroachments, without being sufficiently consolidated in itself to challenge Austrian leadership.

The Congress of Vienna had returned to Prussia the Polish province of Posnania (*Posen*) in the East and the Rhenish provinces (*Rheinlande*) in the West. Prussia, the immediate neighbor of the Slavs and the French, had thus to assume the responsibilities of a frontier guard on two exposed fronts and had to prepare itself for the risks and dangers involved in a two-front war. As far as Germany as a whole was concerned, this problem was not a new one. Germany's central position on the European continent had compelled German military strategists in the past to take into account the possibility of a dual or triple attack from different directions, and, conversely, French foreign policy from the time of Louis XIV on attempted to threaten and intimidate Germany by means of an encirclement by hostile powers or to force her to fight simultaneously on two or three fronts. But Prussia had not faced this danger since the days of Frederick the Great, and only slowly and hesitatingly did she grow into her new tasks and responsibilities. When she was finally ready to assume the role that destiny seemed to have assigned to her, she had begun to realize that her own existence was inseparably linked with the fate of all the German lands and that she was entitled to consider herself as the champion of a united German nation. In the meantime, however, Prussia tried to ease the burden imposed upon her by the decrees of the Congress of Vienna, advocating a military reorganization and consolidation of the "German Confederation" in order to increase its striking power and make it a more effective instrument for national defense.

Economic Unification: The German "Zollverein." The "German Confederation" proved as inefficient in dealing with the divergent economic interests in the German lands as it had shown itself in solving the political problems. The Empire that had died in 1806 had been burdened with an extreme economic as well as political particularism. All earlier demands for the creation of a uniform currency and the abolition of trade barriers in the form of inland customs duties between the different states and principalities had been foiled by the selfish policies of the territorial princes. Here again the interests of the new Prussia coincided with the economic advantage of the smaller German states in the north and south, while Austria, on the other hand, as an economically self-sufficient unit with favorably located ports and outlets for her markets could not be expected to consider the economic unification of Germany as one of her vital concerns.

While in the rest of Germany the conviction was gaining ground that the creation of a unified German economy was overdue, it remained still doubtful whether the "German Confederation" or the state of Prussia would take the lead in solving this vital problem. The answer to this question of leadership involved much more than a mere matter of priority or even prestige. When Prussia, in 1818, abolished the sixty-seven different tariff schedules in her territories and replaced them by a uniform tariff, thereby making the entire state a single marketing unit, she did it primarily for the economic interests of the big landowners and noblemen (*Junker*) east of the Elbe river. While it is true that this benefited the Rhenish industrialists in the West as much as the *Junkers* in the East, the extremely low export and import duties, as established by the customs law of 1818, were devised to meet the demands of the manorial lords, who were thus enabled to export large quantities of grain, timber, and wool and to import English machines. The Free Trade tendencies of the new customs law worked, however, to the disadvantage of the growing German industry, which found it more and more difficult to compete with England without the benefit of a protective tariff.

It was apprehensions such as these that prompted Friedrich List (cf. p. 514 sqq.) to submit in 1819 to the Federal Diet (*Bundestag*) in Frankfurt as well as to the Diets of the individual German states a memorandum that called upon the "German Confederation" to create by its own initiative a unified German economy and a uniform tariff schedule. Thus the choice between the "German Confederation" and the Prussian State involved, as far as the economic problems were concerned, the choice between a policy of protective tariffs and the principles of Free Trade. But this choice had already been made, not by the German people and their governments, but by Prussia, who imposed her will on the rest of Germany, while the "Confederation" remained a passive spectator. The subservience of the Prussian crown to Austrian political leadership and the endorsement of the policy of "peaceful dualism" did not prevent the allied economic interests of the Prussian monarchy and the landed nobility from gaining a decisive influence on the German markets. Favored by her geographical position, Prussia exerted heavy economic pressure on the other German states by imposing high transit duties on all imports from Holland and England.

Prussia was respected but also feared and distrusted by the non-Prussian governments, and they hesitated to enter into a customs union with such a powerful and ambitious neighbor. But their own disunity and mutual distrust worked slowly yet inevitably into the hands of Prussia. The "South-German Customs Union" between Bavaria and Wurtemberg (1828) was a temporary device that could not halt the logical sequence of events.

The actual economic unification of Germany under Prussian leadership was essentially the work of the Prussian minister of finance, Friedrich von Motz (1775-1830). In 1828 he concluded a customs treaty with Hesse-Darmstadt, thereby extending the Prussian customs policy into the German South. Motz was one of the younger and more progressive members of the Prussian cabinet, a man who had grown up in the era of the Prussian reforms and for whom the political ideas of Frederick the Great were a living legacy. He knew and appreciated the significance of the rising middle class and of the Industrial Revolution (cf. p. 548 sqq.), and as an adherent of Adam Smith's economy of Free Trade and unlimited competitive enterprise he enjoyed the sympathies of the Prussian *Junkers*. In his memorandum of 1829 he explained to the Prussian king the "significance of the tariff and trade treaties concluded with the South German States," adding that "a unification of these States in a tariff and trade association implies an eventual unification in one and the same political system," and that "a truly united . . . and free Germany under the protection of Prussia" would be the final result of a unified economy.

Friedrich von Motz did not live to witness the realization of either of these hopes. The economic unification of Germany was largely achieved by 1834, four years after his death, but the political unification did not come about until 1871. In 1834 the tariff and trade barriers between eighteen of the German states were eliminated, and by the middle of the century all German states with the exception of Austria had joined the Customs Union.

Friedrich List's Doctrine of Economic Nationalism. The Prussian officialdom of the *Vormärz*, indoctrinated with the economic liberalism of Adam Smith, favored the principle of Free Trade, not only because it served best the interests of the *Junkers* but also because free competition seemed to them the most effective stimulus to economic activity. Adam Smith's ideas, as expressed in his masterpiece *The Wealth of Nations* (1776), were embodied in the so-called "classical school" of economy in Germany, early in the nineteenth century. Friedrich List's historic significance lies in the fact that he opposed to the theories of "economic liberalism" his own doctrine of national economy or economic nationalism. Though a liberal by training and inclination, an enemy of princely absolutism and official bureaucracy, he advocates in his *National System of Political Economy*

(1840) the introduction of protective tariffs and shows himself as a fore-runner of the "historical school" of national economy.

Persecuted and twice imprisoned by the reactionary government of his native Wurtemberg, because of his participation in the movement for national unity, he was pardoned in 1825 with the stipulation that he emigrate to North America. In the United States he took an active part in the industrial development of the New World, acquired a fortune by his mining operations, and returned to Leipzig in 1832 as consul of the federal government in Washington. "I feel toward my fatherland," he said during this American intermezzo, "as mothers do toward their crippled children: the more crippled they are, the more they love them. In the background of all my plans lies Germany and the return to Germany."

The experiences that he had gathered in the United States turned List against the "cosmopolitanism, materialism, and individualism" of the "classical" school of political economy and made him resume with deeper insight some of the principles of "mercantilism" (cf. p. 328 sq.). The United States, where the policy of protective tariffs was most firmly entrenched from the outset, taught him that a growing national industry in any part of the world depended largely on tariff protection. Free Trade was well adapted to the needs of Great Britain with her technical and industrial superiority and her domination of the world markets. But Free Trade was ruinous for Germany, whose economic conditions were still unstable and whose industry had to fight for its survival in the face of British competition.

These convictions led List to the conclusion that Adam Smith and his followers were wrong when they proclaimed that their teachings were merely an expression of eternally valid economic laws, a doctrine that benefited no one but the British merchants and manufacturers. List main-tained, on the contrary, that economic systems and theories were based on considerations of expediency and that it was therefore necessary to re-nounce the dogmatism of the "classical school" and to free the German mind from its Anglophile preoccupations. He accused the German intel-lectual and political leaders of lack of realism and practical experience. "It is possible for a nation," he wrote, "to have too many philosophers, philologists, and men of letters, and too few skilled workmen, merchants, and sailors. This is one of the results of a highly advanced and profound culture which is not balanced by a highly developed manufacturing power and a flourishing domestic and foreign trade." In such a nation "there is a surplus of useless books, subtle theoretical systems, and learned arguments, which detract the national mind from useful occupations."

Although List speaks here as the son of a new scientific era and as the teacher of a new nationalistic and capitalistic bourgeois society, it would not be quite correct to call him a materialist. Both he and Adam Smith were intellectually and emotionally influenced by the ideas of Christianity, of Humanism, and of Enlightenment. Adam Smith conceived economic life as a huge rational mechanism, in which egotistic and altruistic interests were harmonized by division of labor, free competition, and the law of supply and demand, and which, if only kept free from the arbitrary interference of states and individuals, proceeded on its predestined course to the goal of general human happiness. List, on the other hand, interposed between the individual human being and the idea of a united mankind the State and the Nation as the major promoters and guarantors of universal progress. According to Adam Smith, the law of supply and demand and the law of the division of labor applies as much to world economy as to an individual factory. If each nation produces those goods for whose manufacture it is best equipped by nature, then it will make its divinely apportioned contribution to the civilization of the entire race. Free trade and free competition, therefore, are the most efficient incentives for all to do their best and fulfill their God-given tasks. In this scheme of things England functioned as the nation which Providence had selected as the standard-bearer of world industry, while other nations were to continue in their agricultural pursuits and to supply the world markets with the produce of the soil.

To List this kind of reasoning appeared fallacious and detrimental when tested by the actual conditions of the world. He demanded that all the peoples of the West should have their share in the industrial evolution, and he declared that England owed her astounding industrial advances not to greater talents or any divine predestination but to more favorable historic circumstances. Furthermore, he was convinced that the natural egotism of all nations was far too great to make possible the free flow of spare products and spare capital from one region or one continent to another, so as to provide sufficient abundance for all. Therefore each nation must shape its own destiny with the resources at its disposal. With reference to Germany, he thought there should be no more talk of Free Trade and cosmopolitanism until Germany had achieved economic equality with England. Nevertheless, List was not concerned with the material development of Germany as an end in itself.

Adam Smith considered economic laws as autonomous mechanisms, pursuing their own ends, independent of the larger contexts and concerns of society and culture. List, however, maintained that all economic activity was interlinked with the different provinces of life and culture and had its vital center and final goal in the perfection of human personality. Thus he considered material power and prosperity as means to "spiritual" and "cultural" ends, to better education, a more just social order, and greater freedom of political institutions.

List wanted to see Adam Smith's principle of the division of labor applied first and foremost to a closed national economy, not to foster unlimited competition and cutthroat practices in national industries and on the labor market, but to unite all individual efforts into a unified national will. From these demands arose his criticism of the prevalence of agriculture over industry. To him the purely agricultural State appeared as a cripple with only one arm, whereas a State that had achieved equilibrium of production by the co-ordinated cultivation of agriculture, trade, and industry seemed "infinitely more perfect."

In all these considerations List never lost sight of the one supreme goal — the creation of a united German nation. He believed that a customs union was a necessary preliminary step toward that end. What he really had in mind was the idea of a "Greater Germany" that was to include Austria and whose territories were to extend from the Adriatic to the North Sea. The next immediate task was an education of the national consciousness for the realization of the great industrial future that lay ahead and for a general program of *Weltpolitik*. Colonies in different continents were to supplement the domestic resources of industry and commerce and to provide the necessary reservoirs of political and economic power. These same colonies were to furnish raw materials and unfinished products and to absorb the manufactured goods of the mother country. List also visualized the possibilities of land settlement and colonization on a large scale in the German East, in Mecklenburg and Prussia, where vast and thinly populated territories were offering invaluable opportunities to German farmers and agricultural workers. The proposed economic unification and reorganization of central Europe was in the last analysis aimed at the economic supremacy of England, whose great industrial genius List envied and admired. In the year of his death he paid a visit to the British Isles, and his last publication dealt with the "Value and Conditions of an Alliance between Great Britain and Germany."

List's ideas were so far in advance of the limited perspective of his contemporaries that the record of his life became an unbroken series of disappointments and failures. The land-owning nobility was opposed to his idea of an industrialized State. The leading economists were specialists in their fields and unable to understand the interrelation of political and economic developments. The practical businessmen were unwilling to follow List into the realm of his farseeing speculations, and the spokesmen of Liberalism were defenders of Free Trade and rejected any interference of the State in the economic sphere. In the very year in which List ended his life by his own hand, England adopted a policy of unlimited Free Trade and thereby decided the victory of economic liberalism in all European countries.

Growth of Population and German Emigration. The peaceful years that followed the Napoleonic wars witnessed a rapid increase of the German population. At the end of the eighteenth century the German-speaking lands counted approximately twenty million people, but by the end of the nineteenth century this figure had more than trebled. This astounding phenomenon is partly explained by the diminishing infant mortality and the prolongation of human life brought about by the advances in medicine, public and personal hygiene, technological science, and, generally speaking, by a much greater stability and security of living conditions.

The absolutistic State of the eighteenth century had looked with favor upon an increase in population and had used various means to encourage immigration from foreign lands. It had appreciated the working capacity of its subjects without being greatly concerned about their social well-being. This frequently resulted in growing destitution among large sections of the rural and urban populations, and this in turn led to occasional waves of mass emigrations to the New World.

Ever since William Penn (1644–1718), the founder of the Quaker State of Pennsylvania, had by his missionary efforts started the wave of German emigration on its westward trail, there followed an unending stream of German emigrants, continuing throughout the eighteenth and to the end of the nineteenth century. Between 1820 and 1870 2,368,483 Germans migrated to the United States. Between 1871 and 1880 the annual emigration amounted to an average of 62,500, and in the following decade even to an annual average of 134,100. Next to the English colonists these German immigrants played a major part in the construction and organization of the civilization of North America.

The gradual realization that this continued mass emigration constituted in the long run an irreparable loss for the mother country and a fatal drainage of its national energies led to legal enactments that placed certain restrictions on further emigration. A nationally planned emigration policy was designed to preserve and strengthen the ties between the German elements abroad and the culture and traditions of their homeland, by means of political, educational, and missionary agencies and activities. The conviction, in turn, that the emigration problem was an issue of great national importance furnished additional arguments for the acquisition of colonies. These colonies, it was argued, would be capable of absorbing the surplus population, without depriving the emigrants of their nationality and without depleting the German nation's creative and productive resources.

Construction of Railroads. Next to the tariff problem the issue of an improved and unified system of transportation played an important part in the considerations of those who worked for the creation of a national industrial State. The free movement of goods within the territories of the Customs Union became an actuality only with the construction of railroads. Friedrich List, by his relentless efforts in behalf of a "national railway system," inaugurated for Germany a revolutionary change in transportation methods. List had actively participated as a shareholder in the development of steam-propelled railway traffic in the United States, and he relates in his memoirs how "in the wilderness of the blue mountain-ridges" of America he dreamed of a German railway system: "It was perfectly clear to me that only in this way could the economic unification [of Germany] be made fully effective." He prophesied that by means of an ever increasing speeding-up process in transportation and economic and cultural exchange the German people would achieve national unity, and the peoples of Europe and the Americas would eventually create a world-embracing system of political and commercial economy.

List was personally responsible for the construction of the railroad that was to connect the Saxon cities of Leipzig and Dresden. However, before the execution of this project was actually undertaken (1839) the first German railroad, covering the short distance between the Frankish cities of Nuremberg and Fürth and propelled alternatingly by horses and steam locomotives, was thrown open to public traffic in 1835, one year after the establishment of the German Customs Union. The Berlin-Potsdam, Berlin-Anhalt, and Berlin-Stettin railroads were built by three different companies between 1838 and 1842. The same years witnessed the opening of several economically lucrative Austrian railway lines, financed by the Viennese branch of the Rothschild banking concern and designed by some of Germany's leading mechanical engineers.

Although these German railways were built with private capital, the State exercised a strict control by means of granting or withholding concessions and by obtaining membership in the administrative boards. The first German state railways were those built between Braunschweig and Wolfenbüttel in the north and between Mannheim-Heidelberg and Basel in the state of Baden in the south (1838). Owing to the spirit of enterprise that animated the German industrialists, the German net of railways soon became one of the most extensive on the European continent, second only to that of Belgium.*

Friedrich List had also been one of the first to point out the military significance of the railway and had frequently used this argument in his negotiations with the German state governments. "The day might come," he wrote, "when France and Russia will join hands, and if that should happen, the advantages of a German railway system are incalculable." The reluctance of the Prussian state to adapt its railway gauge to that of her eastern Russian neighbor was likewise due to military considerations. The real test came in the wars with Denmark (cf. p. 537 sq.), Austria (cf. p. 538 sq.), and France (cf. p. 542 sqq.), when Moltke as chief of the general staff utilized to the full the facilities of the railway system for the speedy mobilization of the armed forces and for the flexible conduct of the military campaigns.

The fact that only a few of the privately financed German railways turned out to be profit-yielding enterprises led to the gradual nationalization of practically the entire German railway system. The only European country in which the railroads were developed and are supported exclusively by private initiative is England. As early as 1814 George Stephenson had built the first steam locomotive in England, and the first railroads, between Stockton and Darlington and between Liverpool and Manchester, had been constructed during the following two decades. While the German railway system assumed a strictly authoritarian character, with an almost militarily organized and uniformed personnel and a rigid code of regulations and

---

* In 1932, Germany, with a railway net of 58,619 kilometers, ranked first in Europe; Russia second, with 57,500 km.; France third, with 53,561 km.

instructions, the English system preserved the character marks of a liberal institution, relying chiefly on expert training and personal responsibility.

To realize the truly revolutionary significance of the advent of the "railway age" we do well to remember that the means of transportation had not materially changed from the days of ancient Greece to the third decade of the nineteenth century A.D. As road builders the medieval and modern Europeans had never equaled the ancient Romans, and we learn from a vivid description by Moltke of the year 1815 that "the highways of the Middle Ages had come down to us virtually unchanged, the only difference being that the robber-knights have been supplanted by the legalized highway robbery of the customs house officials." The generation that had broken down the customs barriers was the same that created the railway, and it was felt that both innovations were interrelated in that they both were supposed to advance the causes of social progress, national unity, and growing international solidarity. It was still inconceivable to the progressive idealism of the pioneers of this age that the forces of the new technology could be used for evil as well as for good, for destructive as well as for constructive purposes.

Reorganization of the Civil Service. The economic and political unification of Germany owes a great debt of gratitude to the civil service organization in the German states. The territorial changes that had taken place during and after the Napoleonic wars made it necessary to adapt the entire administrative organism of the German states to the requirements of the new political and social constellations. This task was accomplished by the princes and statesmen of the *Vormärz* with such success that up to this day the German civil service is universally admired as a model of thoroughness and efficiency. This is especially true of Prussia, where the "reform period" had created the preliminary conditions for the unified State that grew out of the victoriously fought Wars of Liberation. The Congress of Vienna had added new provinces to the territories of Prussia, and Prussian officialdom, thanks to its excellent training, its moral integrity, and its unselfish devotion to the State, accomplished the difficult task of co-ordinating in its administration the politically and racially heterogeneous populations of Rhinelanders, Westphalians, Saxons,* and Poles.

The peaceful policies of King Frederick William III favored the consolidation of this administrative reform, permitting a gradual amalgamation of the Old Prussian military absolutism and a New Prussian State paternalism that extended its control over the political, economic, and moral activities of its subjects. These subjects as much as the ruling Protestant bureaucracy were determined in their mentality and in their ethical convictions by the religious doctrines of Martin Luther and by the moral philosophy of Kant. Both Luther and Kant had taught them an ethics of duty and discipline

---

* To punish Saxony for having sided with Napoleon in the Wars of Liberation, the Congress of Vienna gave more than half of her territories to Prussia.

("*Pflichtethik*"), making perseverance in one's God-given "calling" (*Beruf*) the test of moral qualification, and demanding unquestioning obedience to the voice of the moral law that issued from the divinely delegated authority of the State.

The New Militarism. The soldierly and warlike spirit was stronger and more inherent in the national temper and tradition in Prussia than in any other German state. Its rebirth in the nineteenth century was partly inspired by the same forces as the professional ethics of the Prussian civil service. The army bill that was introduced by Hermann von Boyen (1771–1848), the newly appointed Prussian minister of war, was framed in the spirit of Scharnhorst's (cf. p. 436 sq.) military reforms. It provided for universal conscription, retaining the already familiar distinction between the regular army of the line (standing army), the *Landwehr*, and the *Landsturm* (cf. p. 438). Its first paragraph proclaimed that "every individual who has reached the age of twenty is in duty bound to join in the defense of his country." But, "in order to interfere as little as possible with the physical and scientific education" of the young men, they were permitted to apply for military service at the age of seventeen. The forces of the standing army were to spend three years in continuous service and two more years in the army reserves. The two levies of *Landwehr* I and II, extending to the age limit of thirty-nine, included the army of trained reservists "on leave," to be drafted only in case of national emergency or actual war. The *Landsturm,* including the age classes between forty and fifty-five (later on changed to age limit of forty-five), could be called to the colors only in case of invasion and by a special summons of the king. In case of emergency this system of military conscription made available for the Prussian State a trained armed force of half a million men, not including the reserves of the *Landsturm.* The idea of the "people's army" (*Volksheer*) was thus legally incorporated in the structure of the Prussian State, and this Prussian system, which itself had originally borrowed the idea of universal conscription from the armies of the French Revolution, was copied by most of the other continental states in the course of the nineteenth century.*

The liberal idea of a "militia" with periodical short-term levies of the citizenry, that had still prominently figured in Scharnhorst's army reform, was now rejected as contrary to the spirit of professional military training. Nevertheless, a provision was adopted in 1822 that permitted those young men who had attended a secondary school for a certain number of years (four, later on six) and had obtained a qualifying certificate, to serve for one year only and to join an arm of the service of their own choice ("*Einjährig-Freiwilligen-Zeugnis*"). This was a concession to the spirit of an age that was convinced that a liberally or humanistically educated youth was necessarily so much ahead of his fellows in alertness and power of comprehension that his military training could be completed in one third of the

---

* Universal conscription was introduced in Austria-Hungary in 1868, in France in 1872, in Russia in 1874, in Italy in 1875 (in Japan in 1872).

ordinary time. The officers of the Landwehr and subsequently also those of the army reserves were largely recruited from the holders of such "One-Year-Certificates." The provision itself was later on adopted by the armed forces of all the German states that were united in the new German empire (1871) and was in force to the end of World War I.

When early in the second half of the nineteenth century Albrecht von Roon (1803–1879) took over the Ministry of War, the organization of the Prussian army underwent further important changes. A growing cleavage between the conservative professional officers of the standing army, most of them members of the nobility, and the more liberal-minded personnel of the *Landwehr* led to the complete subordination of the latter to the army of the line. This renewed antagonism between an arrogant and socially exclusive army clique and both the middle and working classes destroyed Scharnhorst's, Gneisenau's, and Boyen's idea of the *Volksheer*. The broad Humanism of these great military leaders and educators gave way to the professionalism of the class-conscious military expert and technician. Only the military genius of Moltke (cf. p. 534) was able even within these limitations to attain to a perfection of scientifically calculated military strategy that commands respect and admiration.

The spirit of the "military reform" of the era of the Wars of Liberation lived on, however, in the works of Karl von Clausewitz (1780–1831), the philosopher among the Prussian generals and the author of one of the great classics of military science (*Vom Kriege,* 1832–1834). One of Scharnhorst's most talented disciples, Clausewitz had resigned his commission in the Prussian army after the conclusion of the Prusso-French alliance of 1812. During the Wars of Liberation he had become an officer in the Russian army and had fought against Napoleon; after the war he was first appointed as chief of staff of one of Gneisenau's army corps, and in 1818 was made director of the Prussian Military Academy. This position in itself was rather meaningless, involving chiefly the routine tasks of administration and pedagogic discipline, but it offered Clausewitz sufficient leisure for meditation and writing.

Military strategy is treated by Clausewitz as an inductive science whose methods are dictated by experience and not predetermined by inflexible rules. The new scientific age with its experimental approach to facts and problems for the first time invades here the field of military strategy and supplants the mathematical and mechanical calculations of eighteenth-century rationalism. According to Clausewitz the great strategist has to take into consideration the peculiar circumstances of each individual situation, including the incalculable and unpredictable personal elements that are involved in any such set of conditions, requiring a personal, spontaneous response on the part of the military leader. For him the proper use of the psychological forces of intellect, emotion, and will are the decisive factors in successful warfare.

Clausewitz taught the advantages of a national defense that is ever on the alert and ready to be turned at any moment into a swiftly striking offensive warfare. The general staffs of the Prussian and German armies, however, were unwilling to follow these precepts. They placed the emphasis on attack rather than defense and began at an early date to train their troops for the tactics of the *Blitzkrieg*.

Nationalism and Political Liberalism. After the successful conclusion of the Wars of Liberation King Frederick William III of Prussia had declared: "It is I who shall determine at what time the promised constitutional representation will be granted. . . . It is the duty of the subjects to await patiently the moment that I shall find opportune." As nothing further happened and as the subjects, for the time being at least, were willing "to wait patiently," the political antagonism between those German states in the south, in which various forms of moderate constitutional government had been established, and the despotically ruled Prussian state in the north, became more and more pronounced and retarded the momentum of the movement toward national unity. Austria was ruled even more autocratically than Prussia and, considering her medley of nationalities, the attempt to introduce parliamentary forms of government would have seemed suicidal. For Prussia, on the other hand, constitutional government would have been possible and beneficial, but the fear of impending revolutionary changes made the king and his advisers follow the course of reaction and repression.

a) The Common Root of the National and Constitutional Movements. The constitutional agreements between medieval rulers and the estates of their realm, of which *Magna Charta* furnishes a characteristic example, were no constitutions in the modern sense of the term. They limited and controlled monarchical rule to a certain extent, but they established no national unity that originated with the people as a representative and sovereign power. The American Constitution of 1787 and the French Constitution of 1791, on the other hand, had each been drawn up and proclaimed by a "National Assembly" of the people and could therefore serve as the great models for the constitutional movements of the nineteenth century.

It has been mentioned (cf. p. 304) that medieval political philosophy derived the royal prerogatives from an original popular delegation of powers and that these prerogatives were theoretically limited by contract, custom, and the supremacy of the "moral law." The doctrine of the sovereignty of the people had then been further elaborated by and received additional support from the political theorists of the Jesuit Order in the sixteenth and seventeenth centuries (cf. p. 304 sq.) as well as the Scotch Calvinists, Puritans, and various independent sectarian movements in Europe and in the New World. Nineteenth-century Liberalism, linking these ancient rudiments of constitutional theory with Rousseau's optimistic belief in the unlimited perfectibility of human nature and popular institutions, made the people and their chosen representatives the sole originators and guarantors of legislation, subject only to the exactions of their own creation, the ideal National

State. The common root, therefore, of the national and constitutional movements was given in their common conviction that a nation or a state in the true sense cannot exist without a constitution that guarantees and protects the civic rights of all and thereby transforms a *Machtstaat* (autocratic State) into a *Rechtsstaat* (constitutional State).

b) The "Rechtsstaat" and National Liberalism. The civic and human rights to be guaranteed by the liberal *Rechtsstaat* included freedom and inviolability of person and home; the protection of private property; freedom of speech, press, and assembly; freedom of worship, equality of opportunity, equality before the law, and the universal, equal, and direct form of suffrage. These rights were conceived by the framers of the model constitutions of the American Union and of the French Republic as embodying the "absolute law of reason" and therefore as "eternal rights," existing prior to the State and thus "inalienable," and independent of the State in their validity.

The creation of the *Rechtsstaat* with its clearly defined guarantees of individual rights and the additional safeguard of the three independent branches of government (executive, legislative, and judicial), as originally demanded by Locke and Montesquieu, is the greatest and historically most significant achievement of political Liberalism. Its greatest theoretical proponent in Germany was the philosopher Kant, according to whom the meaning of "political freedom" is not that everyone should be permitted to do what he pleases, but rather that everyone should be free to do anything that is "right," and that no power on earth should ever compel anyone to do what is "wrong." When Kant defined "legal freedom" as the right of the citizen to obey only laws to which he had given his free consent, he thereby expressed the main principle of "government by the consent of the governed."

Kant and the entire political Liberalism of the eighteenth century still believed in absolute values, not necessarily derived from a divine revelation, but inherent in the God-given reason and moral sense of man. They believed in the truth and falsehood of the ideas that underlie social and political structures, and they were convinced that a *Rechtsstaat* was a good form of society precisely because it was based on intellectual and moral truths.

These ideal and rational bases of the older political Liberalism were gradually undermined by the historical and utilitarian spirit of the nineteenth century. While for Kant the purpose of the State was the realization of the idea of "Right," Jeremy Bentham (1748–1832) early in the nineteenth century considered "the greatest good of the greatest number" as the goal of all State legislation, thereby substituting the sociological motives of utility and expediency for the abstract demands of "Right" and "Equity." If the idea of the *Rechtsstaat* was to survive without surrendering its liberal tenets to the ideology of a new *Machtstaat,* it had to look for new norms and sanctions to fill the void created by the abandonment of the old religious and moral standards. Thus Liberalism entered into an alliance with modern

Nationalism, expecting from this union a revitalization of its own creed and the realization of the cultural, social, and political aspirations of modern mankind. If only, in accordance with the principles of Liberalism and Nationalism, Europe could be transformed into a continent of autonomous national and constitutional States, then at last universal peace would be assured!

German Liberalism in particular had not forgotten the teachings and convictions of the Lutheran Reformation and of the New Humanism. It constantly replenished its vigor and vitality with the inspiring thought of a personal freedom and autonomy that were to be used as instruments for individual perfection and the cultural advancement of the race. The idea of the National State was but another means to achieve the goal of a thoroughly personalized culture that could not become a reality as long as the efforts of the individual were not encouraged and aided by liberal political institutions and a national community of ideas and interests.

German Liberalism and Nationalism in Action. While in most of the continental European states the reactionary political system of Metternich seemed firmly entrenched, the liberal movement, carried forward by the awakened middle classes, had gathered sufficient momentum to make itself felt as a force that had to be reckoned with by the monarchical rulers.*

a) The French "July Revolution" and Its Sequel. The signal for the liberal revolt was given in France in 1830, when the reactionary regime of the restored Bourbon monarchy of Charles X (1824–1830) was overthrown and the "Bourgeois King," Louis Philippe of Orléans, was placed upon the throne. The French "July Revolution" marked the first victory of middle class Liberalism over the forces of political reaction on the one hand and over republican radicalism on the other. The parliamentary principle had won the day, with bankers, industrialists, and liberal-minded intellectuals seizing the reins of government. The working class and the Paris radicals had failed in their attempt to restore the Jacobin Republic of 1793, and the privilege of suffrage was still restricted to the "men of property."

The "July Revolution" in France was followed by similar uprisings in other European countries, in which Nationalism and Liberalism worked hand in hand. The Belgians, united with Holland by a decree of the Congress of Vienna, regained their national independence, the German Prince Leopold of Saxe-Coburg becoming the head of a liberal constitutional Belgian monarchy. In 1839, England, France, Prussia, Austria, and Russia agreed to respect and protect the "perpetual" independence and neutrality of the new Belgian State, a pledge that was used by England to justify her entry into the war in 1914, after Belgian neutrality had been violated by Germany.

Poland's attempt to free herself from Russian domination ended in tragic

---

* The term "liberal" was first adopted by the Spanish Cortes (Diet) of 1812 to distinguish the defenders of constitutional government from the representatives of Absolutism. In the following years it became a household word all over Europe.

failure. She lost the semiautonomy that she had possessed as a kingdom under the supremacy of the Russian tsar, and was incorporated into the Russian empire by Nicholas I (1825–1855). Polish Nationalism was crushed, the Constitution abrogated, and the liberal and patriotic leaders exiled. Revolutionary outbreaks in northern Italy and in the Papal States were likewise suppressed with the aid of Austrian troops.

The reverberations of the "July Revolution" were felt in several German states, and as a result some additional local constitutions were granted, but on the whole autocratic rule remained unbroken. Nevertheless, the efforts of Liberals and patriots were not lost. Liberalism and Nationalism had tested their strength and their cause had been consecrated by the blood of heroes and martyrs. In England the news of the successful French Revolution produced a cabinet crisis that brought about the defeat of the Tories and the accession to power of the Whigs. In 1832 the liberal "Reform Bill" was passed by both houses of Parliament, signalizing the victory of the manu-facturing interests of the middle class over the landed nobility.

b) The French "February Revolution," the "Second Republic," and the "Second Empire." The second wave of revolutionary movements in the nineteenth century again took its start in France. The rule of Louis Philippe had rapidly become unpopular, and by his attempts to compromise with both the conservative and progressive elements he had made enemies on all sides. In February, 1848, the Paris mob erected barricades in the streets once more and forced the "Bourgeois King's" abdication. A partly liberal, partly socialist government proclaimed the "Second Republic" of France. A radical socialist revolt of the same year was bloodily crushed, and soon afterward a democratic Constitution, providing for one legislative chamber and a president, elected by universal manhood suffrage, was adopted. But, surprisingly enough, the first general election returned to power a con-servative and royalist majority and placed in the president's chair Louis Napoleon, a nephew of Napoleon I and the legitimate pretender to the imperial succession. In a successful *coup d'état* (1851) he substituted a system of councils for the democratic Constitution and, in 1852, he assumed the title of Napoleon III and made himself the head of the "Second French Empire."

c) Revolts in Austria. Outside France the "February Revolution" of 1848 had repercussions that were more far reaching in their effects than the upheavals of 1830. The revolutionary movement spread rapidly to the Austrian crownlands, to Italy, and to the states of the "German Confederation."

The year 1848 marks the fall of the "Metternich System" and the end of Prince Metternich's political career. The veteran statesman, forced by an angry citizenry to abdicate, went into exile in England, and the liberal Austrian leaders received from Emperor Ferdinand I (1835–1848) the promise of a constitution. In the meantime, Austria had to strain all her forces to check three major rebellions, in Hungary, Bohemia, and in her

Italian provinces of Lombardy and Venetia. The Hapsburg monarchy mastered this difficult task with courage and skill. All the insurrections were quelled, and the armies of Sardinia, which had joined the rebellious Italian states, were routed by the Austrian General, Radetzky. Imperial troops under Prince Windischgrätz recaptured Prague, the capital of Bohemia, and crushed the rebellion in Vienna.

The fiercest rebels were the Hungarian Magyars, whose leader Kossuth had proclaimed an independent Hungarian republic. The Magyars were defeated only with the aid of Russian contingents dispatched by Tsar Nicholas I, who still adhered to the "policy of intervention" (cf. p. 509 sq.) in the interest of the principle of "legitimacy." Hungary was deprived of her constitutional privileges and became one of the several provinces of Austria.

In the midst of these revolutionary upheavals Emperor Ferdinand I decided to abdicate in favor of his nephew, Francis Joseph, who was then only eighteen years of age. Metternich was succeeded in office by Prince Felix von Schwarzenberg, a man of similar political convictions but of much smaller caliber. Metternich himself returned to Vienna, satisfied that once more his system seemed to have weathered a major storm.

In 1849 Emperor Francis Joseph I (1848–1916) promulgated a new Constitution for all the Austrian lands, providing for a centralized administration and leaving the power of autocratic government virtually unimpaired. Her victory over the forces of Liberalism and Nationalism had greatly increased the prestige of Austria as a champion of conservatism and made her a powerful contestant in the bid for political leadership in the "German Confederation."

d) The "March Revolution" in Prussia. When Frederick William IV succeeded his father on the Prussian throne in 1840, the hopes of the Prussian Liberals for constitutional reforms were revived. Those who visualized Prussia as the future leader of the German nation felt that the sympathies of the German South could only be won if Prussia were no longer looked upon as the champion of political and social reaction. The new king seemed at first not disinclined to listen to the arguments of the Liberals, and he began his reign with a proclamation of political amnesty and with the exoneration or reinstatement in office of some of the exiled liberal professors. However, the high expectations of the Liberals were soon turned into bitter disappointment. Frederick William IV was at heart a romanticist whose mind lived in the past rather than in the present, and he looked with growing horror and disgust upon the advancing wave of revolutionary sentiment at home and abroad. Wavering between the desire to redeem his father's and his own promises to give his people a constitutional government and his unwillingness to compromise the exalted dignity and supremacy of the royal crown, he contented himself with half-measures that satisfied no one.

By a royal patent of the year 1847 the king summoned the "United Diet"

(*Vereinigter Landtag*), composed of the eight Provincial Diets of the Prussian State. In his opening address he made it perfectly clear that he felt himself unable to make any substantial concessions to the liberal demands. It seemed inconceivable to him that the natural relationship between the ruler and his people might be transformed into a constitutional contract: "No written sheet of paper," he declared, "shall ever interpose itself like a second Providence between God in Heaven and this land." Sharing in the faith of absolutistic rulers in government by divine right and delegation, Frederick William wanted to rule "in accordance with the law of God and the State," not in accordance with the arbitrary decisions of "so-called representatives of the people" and their shifting majorities.

Thus the deliberations of the "United Diet" led nowhere. The delegates, brusquely rebuffed in their demands for definite constitutional rights, proved obstinate on their part in their refusal to co-operate with the crown and in particular rejected the government's request for a loan. As the opposite points of view of the crown and the delegates appeared irreconcilable, the Diet was finally dismissed without having achieved any tangible objective.

In the meantime, the news of the French "February Revolution" had caused the Diet of the "German Confederation" in Frankfurt to revoke a number of reactionary measures and to announce its eagerness to enter upon a process of reorganization and modernization. As an outward symbol of its change of heart this ultraconservative body adopted the revolutionary colors of black, red, and gold and the emblem of a golden eagle on a black background.

In all the smaller German states the fall of the Bourbon monarchy in France frightened the governments and advanced the cause of Liberalism. New, liberal ministries were recruited from the members of the liberal opposition in the local state chambers, and thus without bloodshed the revolutionary movement had gained a number of important victories.

With the struggle for liberty near its goal, the voices that called for national unity likewise became louder and louder. In the forties, shortly after the accession of Frederick William IV to the Prussian throne, some threatening gestures on the part of France had aroused the national feeling to a high pitch. All eyes instinctively turned toward Prussia, which alone among the German states seemed strong enough to offer organized resistance to a foreign invader. It was at that time that Hoffmann von Fallersleben (1798–1874) wrote the stirring verses of the future national anthem, *"Deutschland, Deutschland über alles, über alles in der Welt."**

With Austria engaged in putting down rebellions in her crownlands, it would have been relatively easy for Prussia to seize upon the opportunities that were offered to her by the events of the stormy year of 1848 and to assume leadership in German affairs. But Frederick William IV proved

---

* The opening lines of this German national anthem are often misinterpreted: The phrase "Germany above everything else in the world" does not imply any desire for world domination but simply means that, for every German, Germany ranks foremost.

unequal to the great task. What he abhorred more than anything else occurred under his very eyes: on March 18 the revolution flared up in Berlin and for half a year terrorized and humiliated the king and his cabinet. Prince William of Prussia, the king's brother and the later German emperor (1871, cf. p. 546), wrongly suspected of having given orders to fire on the excited crowds in the castle yard, had to flee to England. The king, in order to save his life and his crown, was compelled to ride on horse-back through the streets of his capital, surrounded by waving banners of black, red, and gold.

But while the prestige of the crown had suffered some damage, the State and its backbone, the army, remained unshaken. The people were averse to revolutionary violence, and in November, 1848, the Prussian troops marched unopposed into Berlin. In December of the same year Frederick William IV proclaimed a Constitution for Prussia that satisfied at least some of the demands of the Liberals. It was adopted in its complete and final form in 1850, providing for a House of Representatives, elected by universal (yet indirect and open) manhood suffrage, but limiting these constitutional gains by dividing the voters into three classes, in accordance with their tax-paying capacity. By means of this *Dreiklassenwahlrecht* (three-class suffrage) the wealthy and propertied classes were always assured a majority over the representatives of rural and industrial labor and other groups of small wage earners.* The democratic features of this constitutional

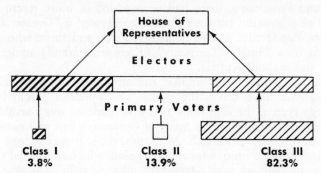

(Each class of the "Primary Voters" chooses one third of the "Electors." The "Electors," in turn, choose the deputies of the House of Representatives.)

system were further weakened by the creation of a House of Lords (*Herrenhaus*) in 1854, composed of noblemen and manorial lords who were appointed for life and whose offices were made hereditary. Despite an ever growing opposition the Prussian *Dreiklassenwahlrecht* continued in existence until the revolution of 1918.

On the whole, Prussia emerged from the revolutionary tempest of 1848

---

* The inserted graph may serve to illustrate the electoral system of the *Dreiklassenwahlrecht*.

as a civil and military State whose authoritarian character was scarcely touched. The few concessions to liberal sentiment had been made reluctantly and halfheartedly, and the king, in a secret political testament, recommended to his successors that they discredit the Constitution by withholding their oath of allegiance.

The Frankfurt Assembly (1848–1849). Shortly after the violent outbreaks in Berlin had occurred, five hundred men, delegated by a self-appointed committee of fifty-one representatives from the different German states, met in St. Paul's Church in Frankfurt. They deliberated about the most suitable ways and means to give Germany both national unity and constitutional liberty. All were agreed that a German Parliament must be created that was worthy of the name and that was to take the place of the unwieldy and inefficient *Bundestag* (Federal Diet).

The liberal leaders, assembled in Frankfurt, constituted themselves as a "Preliminary Parliament" (*Vorparlament*) and immediately took in hand the preparations for the election of a National Assembly, composed of deputies from all German states.

The National Assembly actually convened on May 18, 1848, but the delegates had hardly begun their deliberations when all the controversial issues that had divided the German lands and peoples for centuries presented themselves with renewed vigor. To the old religious and cultural antagonisms and rivalries between North and South, Prussia and Austria, Catholics and Protestants, there had been added in more recent years the differences of conviction between those who favored a "Greater Germany" (*Grossdeutschland*) that was to include Austria, and those who advocated the creation of a "Smaller Germany" (*Kleindeutschland*) under Prussian leadership and without Austria.

It was a foregone conclusion that the attainment of a workable compromise between these conflicting wishes and opinions would be beyond the ingenuity even of the illustrious men who made up this assembly, among whose almost 600 members were many of Germany's best and noblest minds (Jahn, Uhland, Jakob Grimm, E. M. Arndt, etc.). It was indeed a "Parliament of Professors," a unique forum of scholars who had learned the lessons of German Humanism and Classicism, who as politicians displayed the wisdom of philosophers and the vision of poets, and who unreservedly devoted their knowledge, their strength, and their very lives to the service of their nation. If they failed to translate their ideas into practical political reality, it was certainly not due to lack of enthusiasm and good will but to a combination of adverse circumstances and a series of well-nigh insuperable obstacles.

The National Assembly elected as its president Heinrich von Gagern (1799–1880), a government official of Hesse-Darmstadt, a former member of the *Burschenschaft* (cf. p. 464 sq.), and the leading advocate of a united Germany under Prussian leadership. In his opening address he outlined the aims of the Frankfurt Parliament: "We have to frame a Constitution for

Germany, and we derive our authority for this purpose from the sovereignty of the nation. . . . Germany desires to be one, a single State, ruled by the will of the people. . . . "

Upon the recommendation of von Gagern the assembly elected Archduke John of Austria as *Reichsverweser* or imperial administrator and executive head of the German nation. The archduke had married a commoner and was generally known as a man of liberal sympathies. Thus far the transactions of the legislators made a fairly impressive showing on paper, but it was a hard and cruel fact that the Constitution of the "German Confederation," dating from 1815, could not be changed without the consent of both Austria and Prussia. Neither of these powers showed any inclination to recognize the legislative authority of the Frankfurt Assembly.

While the debates on the nature of the proposed Constitution were dragging on and the difficulties increased, the sudden uprising of the two Elbe duchies of Schleswig-Holstein against Denmark injected a further distracting and controversial issue into the proceedings. The duchies were united with Denmark by a "personal union" with the Danish king. This arrangement dated back to the year 1460, when the estates of Schleswig-Holstein had elected the king of Denmark as their duke and when, together with the provision of this dynastic union with Denmark, the duchies had received a pledge that they should "permanently remain free and undivided." Thus the king of Denmark was also duke of Schleswig-Holstein, although the Congress of Vienna had made Holstein a member of the "German Confederation," which had thereby been given the right to interfere in the political affairs of the southern duchy. While the language spoken in Holstein and southern Schleswig was German and the sympathies of the population were with Germany, the people of northern Schleswig spoke Danish, and many of them considered Denmark's cause as their own. The Danish nationalists wanted to make both duchies part of the kingdom of Denmark, and the growing national sentiment in Germany was equally desirous of seeing them both incorporated in the "German Confederation."

In 1848 the two duchies rose in revolt against Denmark's repeated attempts to deprive them of their independence. The "German Confederation" expressed its sympathies for the cause of the insurgents, and Prussian troops under General Wrangel stormed the "Danewerk," Denmark's ancient frontier wall, and penetrated into Jutland. After the temporary truce of Malmö, brought about by English and Russian pressure, the fight was resumed by Denmark in 1849, with Bavarian, Saxon, and Austrian troops joining the Prussian contingents. Although the war ended with a Danish victory, the Treaty of London (1852) decreed that Schleswig-Holstein should retain its semiautonomous political organization in continued personal union with the king of Denmark. The treaty tried to counteract future complications by stipulating that Prince Christian of Glücksburg, the heir to the Danish crown, should also be made the reigning duke in Schleswig-Holstein.

The struggle for Schleswig-Holstein had demonstrated that the Frankfurt Parliament was unable to make its influence felt in foreign affairs. Its members were without power and authority, and their envoy was not even admitted to the negotiations that led to the Truce of Malmö. Nevertheless, swallowing their pride, they continued their labors and, in March, 1849, completed the draft of a Constitution; two months later they sent a deputation to Berlin to offer the hereditary imperial crown to King Frederick William IV of Prussia.

The Constitution drawn up by the Frankfurt Parliament was a skillful compromise that might have provided a practical basis for conciliating the differing points of view, if all parties concerned had been animated by the same earnest desire for a just and impartial solution as were the members of the assembly. The draft provided for a constitutional monarchy, a "mixed" form of government, in which, as its framers believed, all the good features of monarchical, aristocratic, and democratic rule were combined. The representatives of the people were to be chosen by universal, equal, direct, and secret ballot. In all fundamental principles and in many minor details the German Liberals had drawn freely upon the experiences and political beliefs of France, England, Switzerland, and the American Union, countries which were considered as models of political wisdom, progressive legislation, and free institutions.

It was especially the structure of a federal state, combining the idea of national unity with the interests of particularism and regionalism, that seemed to recommend the American Constitution as worthy of imitation. German Liberalism therefore looked upon the United States as the country that had succeeded in creating the most liberal and most perfect system of government that the world had ever seen. And with all its deficiencies the German Constitution of 1849 was the first attempted realization of the idea of a German Nation, united and organized on the basis of the guiding principles of modern democracy.

Frederick William IV refused to accept the proffered imperial crown from the hands of the people, declaring that such a dignity could be conferred upon him only by the German princes. Austria, on her part, had already recalled her delegates from Frankfurt, offended by the compromise proposal which provided that only the German provinces of the Hapsburg monarchy be included in the German Union.

And so this work, undertaken with such sincerity of conviction and from the noblest of motives, ended in disappointment and failure. Once more revolts broke out, in Saxony, in the Palatinate, and in Baden, giving vent to the resentment of the people, who saw their fondest hopes betrayed by princely whims and dynastic interests. The king of Prussia had to send two army corps under the command of his brother, Prince William, to the German South, to aid in putting down the rebellion.

After thirteen months of deliberations the Frankfurt Parliament was finally dissolved. The restoration of the "German Confederation" and the

"Federal Diet" in 1851 signified another victory of Conservatism over Liberalism. Prussia had made up her mind to follow the reactionary course of Austria, and in the Treaty of Olmütz (1851), usually referred to as the "Humiliation of Olmütz," she formally agreed to relinquish all plans for a German Union under her own leadership.

A New Era in Prussia. The dismal failure of the Frankfurt Parliament was the severest setback that the German liberal and national movement had yet experienced. The decade from 1850 to 1860 found the patriots in silent or open despair. A new wave of censorship and persecution forced many to leave their native land, to continue the struggle for the ideals of freedom and national unity in the New World. Many of these emigrants dedicated their lives to the defense of the American Union during the American Civil War and fought for the liberation of the American Negro slaves. Among them was Karl Schurz (1829–1906), a native of the Rhineland who, having taken part in the revolutionary movement of 1848, had evaded the death sentence imposed upon him by escaping to America in 1852. He devoted his gifts as an orator and publicist to the cause of the Republican party, commanded an army corps in the Civil War, and became a prominent political figure as a United States senator (1869–1875) and Secretary of the Interior (1877–1881).

For those who remained in the home country it seemed to be proven beyond a doubt that their idealism had been misspent. They were slowly getting ready to view the political and national scene with a sober and unsentimental realism. In the light of incontrovertible facts many of the influential leaders in the smaller German states were driven to the conclusion that of the two interdependent issues that had been debated and defeated at Frankfurt, the cause of national unity took precedence over the cause of political liberty. If the former could be achieved, Liberalism might still have a chance, whereas it was doubtful whether political liberty without national unity was even worth fighting for. But it also had been demonstrated that national unity could not be attained unless it was possible to find a solution for the problem of the Austro-Prussian dualism.

As far as their governmental systems were concerned, Austria and Prussia were both committed to a course of political reaction, but Prussia was at least an integral German state, while part of Austria's interests lay outside Germany. Furthermore, there was a slight encouragement in the fact that Frederick William IV, yielding to continuous pressure, had finally promulgated a Constitution, and had done so at the risk of incurring the displeasure of Austria. Finally, as the leading state in the German *Zollverein* (cf. p. 513 sq.), from which Austria was excluded, Prussia seemed to be in a logical position to build up a political leadership that rested on a solidarity of economic interests. Considering all these factors, the smaller German states became more and more reconciled to the thought of accepting the solution of a "Smaller Germany," headed by Prussia, as the most promising compromise under the given circumstances.

Those who nourished such hopes were greatly encouraged by the changes in Prussian administration brought about by the appointment of Prince William, the brother of the childless Frederick William IV, to the regency of Prussia (1857), after the king had become mentally incapacitated by several paralytic strokes. Upon Frederick William IV's death in 1861 the prince regent succeeded to the Prussian throne as King William I (1861–1888; "German emperor" after 1871). These events marked the opening of a new era for Prussia as well as for Germany.

The new king, already sixty-three years of age when he formally took office, was a soldier by training and inclination, and the army ranked foremost among his interests and loyalties. The appointment of *Count Helmuth von Moltke* (1800–1891) as chief of the general staff and of *Count Albrecht von Roon* (1803–1879) as minister of war — two men who combined with the best Prussian military training an intimate acquaintance with modern problems of military science, strategy, and organization — indicated the intention of the monarch to build up the Prussian army to a maximum of strength and efficiency and to make it the most up-to-date military force in the world.

The request for the necessary appropriations to carry out this military program involved the king in a bitter feud with the lower chamber of the Prussian Diet. A majority of the members, having twice reluctantly granted the requested credits, obstinately refused to pass the new army bill of the year 1862.

This defeat of the government was in part due to the newly acquired strength of the "Liberal-Progressive Party," which had been founded in 1861 and had twice gained a majority in Parliament. Its presiding chairman and cofounder was the famous physician and anthropologist Rudolf Virchow (1821–1902). The party program called for the unification of Germany under Prussian leadership, for liberal legislation, and for the reduction of the period of compulsory military training from three to two years. It was a matter of conviction and principle with the "Progressive Party" to oppose every one of the moves of Otto von Bismarck (cf. p. 535 sqq.) from the moment the latter assumed responsibility for the governance of the domestic and foreign affairs of Prussia.

The clash between king and Parliament precipitated a major crisis, in which the rival claims of authoritarian and constitutional government were once more put to a decisive test. The king felt that the prestige of the royal crown itself was at stake, and he was determined to renounce his throne rather than to undergo what seemed to him ignominious surrender to parliamentary pressure.

The document of abdication had already been drawn up when, through the intervention of Albrecht von Roon, the course of events took an entirely different turn and one that was of momentous import for the future destiny not only of Germany but of all Europe. Roon himself had promised to stand by his king, at a moment when even the queen and the crown prince had added their voices to those of the parliamentary opposition. And Roon knew still another man who was willing to come to the support of the king and who had been kept informed by the minister of war of the critical state of affairs. He was an old friend of Roon's and at the time Prussian ambassador in Paris. His name was Otto von Bismarck-Schönhausen.

William I let himself be persuaded by his minister of war to receive Bismarck in private audience before making his decision final. On September 22, 1862, the memorable interview took place that marked the beginning of a new epoch in the history of modern Europe. Without hesitation Bismarck declared his willingness to complete the reorganization of the army against the will of the majority in the Diet. The king decided to continue the struggle with the aid of his newly appointed prime minister who, a few days after the fateful conversation with William I, declared in the Budget Committee of the Chamber of Deputies: "Germany does not look to Prussia's Liberalism but to her power. . . . The great questions of the time will be decided not by speeches and the resolutions of majorities — that was the mistake of 1848 and 1849 — but by blood and iron."

The Policy of "Blood and Iron." Otto von Bismarck (1815–1898), the man who from 1862 to 1890 directed the domestic and foreign policies of Prussia and, after 1871, also those of the Second German Empire, was a descendant of the ancient nobility of the Mark Brandenburg. The future "Iron Chancellor" was born at Schönhausen in the Prussian province of Saxony and had inherited from his forefathers a strong faith in military discipline and in the principles of autocratic government. In 1839 he had retired from the Prussian civil service to devote himself to the management of his father's Pomeranian estate of Kniephof. The historical studies which he pursued in his leisure time deepened his insight into the political problems of his own day, and the intercourse with the families of the neighboring manorial estates served to strengthen his conservative views. At the same time it brought him into renewed contact with the orthodox Lutheran form of piety, from which he had become estranged in his gay and carefree student days at Göttingen, where he had been a member of one of the aristocratic students' corporations (the *Corps* Hannovera).

Bismarck first stepped into the limelight of political life as leader of the conservative right wing in the United Prussian Diet of 1847, pleading for the prerogatives of the crown, for the privileges of the nobility, and for the preservation of the feudal order of society. He had no sympathy with the liberal ideology of the Frankfurt Assembly and had approved Frederick William IV's refusal to accept the imperial crown from the hands of the people's representatives. Prussia's "humiliation" at Olmütz (cf. p. 533) had cured him of his initial admiration of the conservative regime of Austria and confirmed in him the conviction that sooner or later the "German Question" must be settled by force of arms. As Prussian envoy (1851–1858) to the restored "Federal Diet" at Frankfurt he mapped his plans for a

Prussian *Realpolitik* that had as its goal the gradual weakening and final elimination of Austria from an anticipated German Union under Prussian supremacy.

a) Bismarck's Attitude in the Crimean War (1853-1856). When in 1853 Turkey, in alliance with England, France, Austria, and Sardinia, started its campaign against Russian domination in the Black Sea and against the assumed right of Tsar Nicholas I to act as the protector of all Christian denominations in Turkey, it was Bismarck's counsel that prevented Prussia from joining in the war. He knew that Russia's gratitude and friendship were indispensable for the consummation of his political scheme.

The "Crimean War" was concluded by the Treaty of Paris (1856), in which Tsar Alexander II (1855-1881) renounced Russia's protectorate of the Christians in Turkey and the Russian sphere of influence in the Danubian principalities of Walachia and Moldavia, and agreed to the closing of the Black Sea to the warships of all nations. Turkey was formally admitted to the Concert of European Powers on an equal footing. In a special "declaration" the Congress of Paris adopted a number of new rules of naval warfare, outlawing privateering and revising the rights of naval blockade by prohibiting the seizure on the high seas of neutral as well as enemy goods of nonmilitary character (noncontraband goods). In 1861 the principalities of Walachia and Moldavia agreed to unite and together established the independent principality of Rumania.

b) Prussia's Attitude in the Austro-Sardinian War (1859). The struggle for the unification of Germany had its counterpart in Italy, where the kingdom of Sardinia, under the leadership of the great Italian statesman Cavour (1810-1861), played a role similar to that assumed by Prussia in the North. By aiding France in the Crimean War Cavour had managed to gain the support of Napoleon III in his attempt to force Austria out of northern Italy. In 1859 Austria answered the intentional provocations of Sardinia with a declaration of war, and the French emperor sent an army across the Alps to assist in the conquest of the provinces of Lombardy and Venetia. Austria, in launching her Italian campaign, had counted heavily on Prussian support, but Prussia remained aloof and thus further aggravated the strained relations between the two powers. Napoleon III, on the other hand, acutely aware of the power of Prussia and surprised at the unexpected strength of the Italian national movement, that seemed to leave little chance for France's taking over the Austrian sphere of influence in northern Italy, suddenly reversed his policy and concluded the armistice of Villafranca. Nevertheless, in the Treaty of Turin (1860), France received Savoy and Nice as rewards for her intervention on the side of Italy, while the Italian provinces of Lombardy, Tuscany, Parma, Modena, and part of the Papal States were united with the kingdom of Sardinia. Thus Austria lost Lombardy but retained Venetia, and Emperor Francis Joseph declared in a manifesto to the European powers that he had been forced to agree to the peace terms by the desertion of Prussia, his nearest and natural ally.

c) *Parliamentary Struggles and Diplomatic Moves.* While Europe found itself embroiled in this complex game of political intrigues and rival bids for power, Bismarck followed with ever increasing self-assurance a political course that had become a fixed pattern in his mind. He remained undismayed by lack of understanding and support, by personal vilifications, by threats of impeachment, and by several attempts on his life. The blunt and vehement frankness with which he expressed his opinions had partly been responsible for his appointment as Prussian ambassador to St. Petersburg (1859) and to Paris (1862). It was felt that his presence in the Prussian capital was in itself provocative and a constant source of political friction and diplomatic embarrassments.

When he was finally called back to save the prestige of the crown and to face the hostile majority in the Prussian Chamber, he was prepared for a fight to the finish. For four years (1862–1866) he administered the affairs of the State with a complete defiance of popular and parliamentary opinion. He drew on the treasury without constitutional authorization and without submitting an account of his expenditures; used the powers at his command to enlist the services of censorship, police, and armed force for the suppression of free speech and a free opposition press; and even disregarded the immunity of the members of the Prussian Chamber. Bismarck achieved his objectives systematically one by one, but to many of his contemporaries he appeared either as a ruthless Prussian *Junker* or as a reckless political gambler.

In 1863 Emperor Francis Joseph presided over a Diet of the German princes (*Fürstentag*) at Frankfurt, which had been convoked by Austria to bring about a reorganization of the "German Confederation." Bismarck suspected that the real purpose of the *Fürstentag* was to gain for Austria a predominant position in the German *Bund* and to curb Prussia's increasing influence. On the advice of his prime minister the king of Prussia declined to participate in the deliberations. The only real reform of the *Bund* that Bismarck envisaged was a unified Germany, headed by Prussia. This, however, required first of all the expulsion of Austria, and everything that fell short of this radical solution could only retard the inevitable course of events.

In the same year in which the *Fürstentag* met at Frankfurt (1863) the Poles had staged another revolt against Russia. The liberal sentiment in England, France, and Germany favored the cause of Polish independence and called for strong diplomatic representations in St. Petersburg, even at the risk of becoming involved in war with Russia. But Bismarck, contrary to the general trend of public opinion, decided to give diplomatic support to Russia and thus strengthened the ties of friendship between the tsar and the king of Prussia.

d) *The Danish War (1864).* While Bismarck was still wrangling with the opposition in the Prussian Chamber, the Schleswig-Holstein question, which was believed to have been settled by the Treaty of London (cf.

p. 531), was revived again. This gave Bismarck the desired opportunity to test the political and military strength of Prussia in the foreign field.

The Treaty of London that had been signed by all the great European powers, including both Prussia and Austria, had declared that, despite the "personal union" of the duchies with the king of Denmark, they were to retain their separate political organization and that the rights of their German population must be respected. However, in 1863, King Christian IX of Denmark published a new Constitution for all Danish territories, including the duchies, and this was considered as a breach of the London agreements. At the same time Duke Frederick of Augustenburg, whose father had renounced his rights of succession in Schleswig-Holstein in favor of the king of Denmark, revived the claims of his line and was supported by the German Confederation.

But Bismarck had his own ideas on the Schleswig-Holstein question. He was neither interested in the claims of the duke of Augustenburg nor in the political independence of the two duchies. From the outset he had made up his mind to incorporate Schleswig-Holstein into the Prussian state, and he used every kind of dissimulation and subterfuge to hide his real aims, until the opportune moment for decisive action had arrived.

The first step in the execution of Bismarck's bold scheme was to persuade Austria to ignore the "German Confederation" and to work hand in hand with Prussia, while he pretended that he himself was as much interested in upholding the terms of the London Treaty as the emperor of Austria. Both powers then agreed that the Schleswig-Holstein question must be decided by force of arms and that the future of the duchies should be determined by the friendly understanding and mutual consent of Prussia and Austria!

In 1864 Prussian and Austrian troops under the command of the octogenarian General Wrangel invaded Schleswig, captured the *Danewerk,* stormed the redoubts of Düppel, and occupied the greater part of Jutland. This first phase of the war was followed by a truce and by subsequent negotiations in London. Bismarck now declared that while Prussia and Austria considered the London Protocol of 1852 invalidated by the actions of the Danish king, the two German powers were still willing to concede political autonomy to Schleswig-Holstein, including a continued personal union with the Danish crown. Upon the refusal of Denmark to accept these proposals, hostilities were resumed and the allied armies advanced deeply into the continental and island territories of the northern kingdom. Then a new Danish ministry asked for a truce, and in the Peace of Vienna Denmark agreed to cede the duchies of Schleswig-Holstein unconditionally to Prussia and Austria. The Danish campaign, whose strategic details had been worked out by Moltke, had lasted from February to October.

e) The "Seven Weeks' War" Between Prussia and Austria (1866). With the handing over of the Elbe duchies to Prussia and Austria the Schleswig-Holstein question was far from settled. The dispute as to what was to become of the spoils of the Danish War occupied the cabinets in Berlin and Vienna and soon brought about a renewed tension in Austro-Prussian relations. There is no doubt that both the emperor of Austria and the king of Prussia honestly wanted peace and mutual understanding, but Bismarck's mind was set on the outright annexation of Schleswig-Holstein and also on a final settling of accounts with Austria. To please his sovereign the Prussian prime minister declared himself willing to agree to the temporary compromise of the Treaty of Gastein (1865), according to which Prussia was to take over the administration of Schleswig and Austria that of Holstein.

But this compromise had hardly been agreed upon when the relations between Prussia and Austria reached a critical stage with the revival of the Augustenburg claims to the two duchies. Austria openly backed the demands of the prince of Augustenburg, chiefly because she found it rather burdensome to administer a distant northern province and would therefore have preferred the establishment of an independent German state of Schleswig-Holstein. The intransigent attitude of Prussia finally caused Austria to carry out her previously announced threat of submitting the Schleswig-Holstein question to the Federal Diet in Frankfurt which, at the request of Austria and by a majority of votes, decreed the mobilization of the federal army. As the Prussian contingents were not included in the mobilization order, it was clear that the measure was directed against Prussia. Bismarck thereupon declared that the Treaty of Gastein had been violated by Austria and that the mobilization also was a breach of the Federal Constitution. As a countermeasure, directed against Austria, Prussia then proposed a new German Confederation without Austria and called for the election of a German Parliament. These proposals were flatly rejected by the majority of the states represented at the Federal Diet.

Thus it seemed that an armed conflict between Prussia, on the one hand, and a majority of the German states, led by Austria, on the other, had become inevitable. But this development contained no element of surprise for Bismarck. Although he had possibly hoped for a certain measure of support from the smaller states, he was prepared for every eventuality.

The international scene seemed favorable for decisive action: Bismarck's previous diplomatic moves had gained him the friendship and secured the neutrality of Russia. England, interested as much as ever in the European balance of power, considered a strong Prussian state as a desirable counterpoise against the continental hegemony of France. Napoleon III, hoping to share in the spoils of the fratricidal German war, intimated that France's friendly neutrality could be bought, and Italy, eager to wrest Venetia from Austria, entered into a secret alliance with Prussia. From a military point of view the stage was likewise carefully set. While in numbers the opposing armies were almost evenly matched, the Prussians were able to rely on their superior discipline, equipment, and leadership.

Crown Prince Frederick and Prince Frederick Charles, commanding the main forces of the Prussian armies, executed their moves in perfect coordination with the carefully planned tactics of von Moltke, the chief of the general staff. In Austria, meanwhile, Ludwig von Benedek (1804-1881), a general of proven courage and ability in the Italian theater of war, only reluctantly accepted the supreme command of the northern armies. His unfamiliarity with the terrain and an ever present presentiment of impending doom contributed materially to the outcome of the struggle.

The essence of Moltke's strategy was lightning speed, aided by perfect teamwork. A union of the armed forces of the minor states aligned with Austria against Prussia had to be prevented. In June, 1866, after having quickly overrun Saxony, Hesse, and Hanover, the Prussian armies marched against Bavaria and the other states of the German South. The Bavarians and their allies were defeated and the cities of Frankfurt, Würzburg, and Nuremberg were taken.

Now the main Austrian forces, stationed in Bohemia, were simultaneously attacked by three Prussian armies that struck from Saxony, Lusatia, and Silesia. The Austrians lost the entire war in the decisive defeat at Königgrätz (July 3), and the victorious Prussians advanced simultaneously toward the Hungarian border and upon Vienna.

In the meantime, however, the Italians, attacking Austria from the south and attempting to seize Venetia, were defeated both on land and on the sea by vastly inferior Austrian forces. But these Austrian victories over Italy had no influence on the outcome of the struggle. The "German War," after having lasted for only seven weeks, was brought to a conclusion by the Truce of Nikolsburg and the subsequent Peace of Prague (August 23). Hostilities were ended just in time to prevent France and Russia from active intervention, as both powers began to show growing uneasiness in view of the amazing efficiency of the Prussian armies.

Bismarck's goal, the elimination of Austria from the affairs of Germany, had been achieved. He wanted no more and vigorously opposed the plan of King William to humiliate Austria by severe peace terms and to annex some of the Saxon provinces. It was the first time that Bismarck demonstrated the wisdom of moderation in victory, carefully refraining from engendering unnecessary bitterness and a desire for revenge in the heart of the enemy. We know from his memoirs that the nervous strain resulting from his heated arguments with the king made him think of retirement from the political scene and, for a brief moment, even of suicide. Only the generously offered moral support of the crown prince gave him the strength to persist in his efforts to make the king amenable to his own point of view.

In the Peace of Prague Austria acknowledged the dissolution of the "German Confederation" and consented to the reorganization of Germany under Prussian leadership. Italy, despite her military blunders, received Venetia as a reward for her participation in the war against Austria, and Prussia rounded out her frontiers and unified her territories by the annexation of Schleswig-Holstein, Hanover, Hesse-Cassel, Nassau, and the city of Frankfurt. The remaining states of northern Germany including Saxony formed with Prussia the North German Confederation (*Norddeutscher*

Bund). The southern German states — Bavaria, Wurtemberg, Baden, and Hesse-Darmstadt — were persuaded by Bismarck to enter into secret alliances with Prussia.

Austria, now strictly confined to her own German and non-German territorial possessions, adopted at last a number of liberal reforms which actually strengthened her internal and international position. In 1867 Emperor Francis Joseph granted his seventeen provinces a constitution that provided for a bicameral parliamentary system of government. Hungary became a semiautonomous kingdom within the dual empire of Austro-Hungary, the Austrian emperor retaining his title of King of Hungary.

The victorious war of 1866 seemed to have vindicated also Bismarck's domestic policies. He persuaded the king to conciliate the opposition in the Prussian Diet. In a solemn speech from the throne William I admitted that for several years the government had conducted the affairs of state in an unconstitutional manner and asked for a parliamentary "indemnification" of the public expenditures of the past four years. This "act of indemnity" was passed by a substantial majority of votes. The split votes of the members of the "Progressive Party" subsequently led to the secession of the right wing

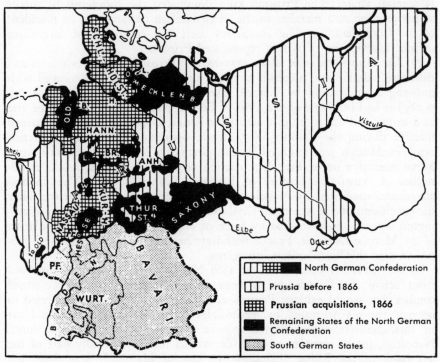

	North German Confederation
	Prussia before 1866
	Prussian acquisitions, 1866
	Remaining States of the North German Confederation
	South German States

From *Der Grosse Herder*, Herder, Freiburg i. Br.

The North German Confederation.

Liberals, who formed the "National-Liberal" Party, from the intransigent left wing Liberals, who continued their opposition to Bismarck.

f) *The North German Confederation.* The twenty-one states of northern Germany that had joined the newly created North German Confederation recognized Prussia as their self-chosen leader. In the Federal Constitution, which in its essentials was framed by Bismarck himself and which was published in 1867, the king of Prussia held the hereditary office of president of the Federation. The executive power was vested in the federal chancellor and, to a limited degree, in a *"Reichstag"* (Federal Diet), representing the people and elected by universal manhood suffrage, and in a *Bundesrat* (Federal Council), representing the princes of the different member states. The *Staatenbund* (Federation of States) of the "German Confederation" of 1815 was thus transformed into a *Bundesstaat* (a unified and centralized "Federal State"). The king of Prussia, as president of the Confederation, was commander in chief of the federal army and appointed the federal chancellor, but he had no legislative and no veto power. Bismarck, the prime minister of Prussia, occupied also the post of the federal chancellor.

In this way Prussia had secured for herself the control of the army and of foreign affairs. The Prussian king dominated the *Bundesrat* by virtue of his prestige as a member of the Hohenzollern dynasty and as president of the Confederation. The *Bundesrat* itself was composed of forty-three members, seventeen of whom represented Prussia.

g) *The Franco-Prussian War (1870–1871).* Prussia's military victories and Bismarck's diplomatic successes at home and abroad had been viewed with growing apprehension by France. Ever since the time of Richelieu (cf. p. 289) it had been one of the aims of French politicians to prevent the rise of a strong and united empire across the Rhine. Napoleon III had remained inactive during the Danish War, chiefly because at that time a French army in Mexico was engaged in the phantastic scheme of establishing a Mexican empire under French protection, to be headed by Archduke Maximilian of Austria, a brother of Emperor Francis Joseph. This farcical adventure, sponsored by Napoleon III, had ended in tragedy when, after the conclusion of the American Civil War, the federal government in Washington seemed ready to deal by force of arms with this flagrant violation of the Monroe Doctrine. France withdrew her troops, and Archduke Maximilian was shot by Mexican insurgents.

In the "Seven Weeks' War" of 1866 Napoleon III again had abstained from active interference, partly because he had hoped for a prolonged conflict that would exhaust Prussia, and partly because he had expected to be paid for his neutrality by territorial compensations. Some broad hints in this connection had drawn evasive responses from Bismarck, until Napoleon, in the summer of 1866, demanded more specifically part of the left bank of the Rhine, including the city of Mainz. It was then that Bismarck categorically refused to cede even one inch of German territory, using simultaneously Napoleon's demands for territorial compensations to arouse the southern German states against France. Napoleon had no better luck when he tried in 1867 to purchase Luxembourg from the Netherlands and to extend French influence into Belgium by a proposal to buy up the Belgian railroad system. Both states were backed in their resistance to these demands not only by Bismarck but also by the governments of England and Russia.

These repeated setbacks in his foreign undertakings added to the growing unpopularity of Napoleon's regime at home. The French Liberals and Republicans had never forgotten the *coup d'état* to which the Second Empire owed its existence, and their opposition in Parliament and in the country at large became more and more vociferous. The monarchists, on the other hand, felt that the waning prestige of the Empire could only be retrieved by a striking success in the field of foreign affairs. And they were convinced that nothing could do more to regain for the emperor the sympathies of the French people than the humiliation and diplomatic defeat of Prussia.

Napoleon, with his armies newly equipped and brought up to full striking power, believed himself equal to the task of checking any further ambitions of the Prussian upstart, by means of intimidation and an impressive show of France's armed strength. Although he had no doubt that the French army was superior to that of Prussia, Napoleon was on the lookout for possible allies in the eventuality of an armed conflict. But secret negotiations with Austria and Italy yielded no positive results. Austria certainly remembered the day of Königgrätz but neither had she forgotten that Napoleon had been instrumental in depriving her of Lombardy. The Italians still resented the way in which Napoleon had acquired Savoy and Nice and the part played more recently (1867) by the French garrison in Rome, where the French had prevented Italian nationalists from wresting the Eternal City from the hands of the papacy. There still remained to Napoleon the hope for the sympathies and possibly the active support of the German South, whose anti-Prussian sentiments had manifested themselves in the past and were still taken for granted, Napoleon naturally being unaware of the secret commitments of these states to come to the aid of Prussia.

Bismarck knew that he held most of the trump cards in his own hands. In a war with France, which he believed unavoidable and for which he therefore worked deliberately, he could count on the armed support of the German South and on the neutrality of the European powers. He foresaw that such a war would irresistibly draw together all the provinces and peoples of Germany and that the anticipated victory would be crowned by the achievement of national unity.

Relations between Prussia and Russia were still friendly, and the dynasties of England and Prussia had aided a rapprochement of their two nations by the marriage of the daughter of Queen Victoria to the crown prince of Prussia. Furthermore, England intensely disliked Napoleon's attempted meddling in the affairs of Belgium.

The Prussian general staff had worked out its strategic plans in every detail and with the utmost precision. The armed forces, including the trained reserves, could be brought to full war strength at the shortest notice, and thus diplomatically and militarily Prussia had reached a state of complete preparedness.

Sooner than he had expected an opportunity seemed to present itself to Napoleon to earn some inexpensive laurels by administering to Prussia a diplomatic rebuff and thus putting her in her place. In 1869 the Spanish throne had been vacated by revolution and the Spaniards had offered the crown to Prince Leopold of the house of Hohenzollern-Sigmaringen, a member of the Catholic branch of the Hohenzollerns and a distant relative of the king of Prussia. Immediately the French government raised a great hue and cry, conjuring up the ghosts of the Austrian-Spanish Hapsburgs and painting all the horrors of a prospective dual Spanish-Prussian monarchy of the Hohenzollerns. For Bismarck the knowledge that the candidature of Prince Leopold was disagreeable to France was a good enough reason to support it, and while King William, anxious to preserve the peace, tried to persuade the prince to decline the Spanish offer, the prime minister behind the scenes used all his influence to secure the acceptance of the candidacy.

When Prince Leopold finally announced that he did not consider himself a candidate for the Spanish throne, the international tension relaxed considerably and Napoleon could have cherished an important diplomatic success. But by listening to the advice of the imperialist extremists in the French cabinet, the French emperor committed the greatest folly of his political career and worked directly into the hands of Bismarck.

In July, 1870, it became known that Napoleon, through the French ambassador to Prussia, had demanded of King William a formal pledge that never in the future would he give his consent to a revival of the Hohenzollern claims to the Spanish throne. The king of Prussia, in an angry mood, asked that Bismarck be informed by wire of the French demands and of William's negative answer. The message was sent to Bismarck from the spa of Ems, where the king was taking the waters, and the Prussian prime minister did not fail to make the most of this incident. He re-edited the dispatch, and made it, by means of several condensations and omissions, to use Moltke's approving words, "sound like a fanfare." In this revised version the "Ems Dispatch" appeared to the Prussians as a gross insult to their king and to the French as an intentional slight of their ambassador. Napoleon's answer was a declaration of war (July 19). Four days earlier, Emile Ollivier, the French prime minister, had declared in the Chamber of Deputies that the French government viewed the imminence of an armed conflict with Prussia "with a light heart."

Bismarck's foresight now reaped its rewards: the German princes immediately rallied to the support of Prussia, placing their armies under the command of the Prussian general staff. Napoleon faced a united Germany whose peoples had forgotten all their political, social, and tribal differences.

Almost overnight Germany had acquired a national will and a national physiognomy.

The nominal commander in chief of the German armies was the king of Prussia, but all military movements and operations were directed by the strategic genius of Helmuth von Moltke. He had divided his forces into three large sectors: a central army under the command of Prince Frederick Charles, a northern right wing under General von Steinmetz, and a southern left wing, consisting of South German contingents, under the crown prince of Prussia.

Six weeks after the start of hostilities a French army of 86,000 men, with the emperor in their midst, were forced to surrender at Sedan (September 2). Two days later the Second Empire of France collapsed and a republican provisional government of National Defense, headed by the French lawyer Gambetta, was proclaimed in Paris. A second French army of almost 200,000 men under the command of Marshal Bazaine was compelled to withdraw to the Moselle fortress of Metz and surrendered after a short siege (October 27). In the meantime, the German armies had marched into the heart of France and had encircled the French capital. Paris offered heroic resistance, but after four months the beleaguered city was finally forced to surrender on January 28, 1871.

A newly elected French National Assembly, convening at Bordeaux, chose Adolphe Thiers, a veteran French statesman and twice prime minister under Louis Philippe, as executive head of the French Republic (1871–1873). He crushed an attempt of the radical "Commune" to establish a socialist regime in France and conducted the negotiations that led to the preliminary peace agreements of February 26. Thirty thousand German troops had staged a symbolic occupation of part of the French capital but were withdrawn after the French National Assembly had accepted the preliminary peace terms.

The final peace treaty was signed at Frankfurt on May 10, 1871. If Bismarck's counsel had prevailed in the peace settlement with France as it had in 1866 in the peace treaty with Austria, the terms would have been severe but would have inflicted no incurable wounds to French pride and self-esteem. He would have been satisfied with a substantial indemnity and the cession of Alsace, the majority of whose population was German in language and cultural tradition. But this time Bismarck was overruled by the men of the army. Without consulting the wishes of their populations the provinces of Alsace and part of Lorraine were annexed by Germany and incorporated into the Prussian system of administration. Administrative autonomy was withheld from both provinces until 1918, and during all these years the Prussian government by a series of psychological mistakes kept alive popular resentment and tried to whip the provinces into line by coercion and intimidation. In addition to these territorial losses France had to agree to German occupation of her key fortresses, until the war indemnity of five billion francs (about one billion dollars) were paid in full. French thrift succeeded in paying off this debt in the surprisingly short time of two years, and in autumn, 1873, the German army of occupation was withdrawn.

The Creation of the Second German Empire. With the defeat of France Bismarck's "policy of blood and iron" had achieved its final triumph. Even before the surrender of Paris the political unification of Germany had become an accomplished fact. In the Peace of Frankfurt France dealt not with Prussia alone but with a resurrected German empire.

The negotiations with the southern states had begun soon after the battle of Sedan. To overcome the hesitations of Bavaria and Wurtemberg, Bismarck declared himself willing to grant these two largest states of the south certain constitutional privileges, chief among which were independent military administration in time of peace and a partially independent railroad, postal, telegraph, and telephone system. The treaties concerning the admission of the southern states into the united empire were signed in November and December, 1870. On behalf of the German princes King Louis II of Bavaria asked King William I of Prussia to accept the hereditary imperial title and therewith the leadership of the German nation. A delegation of the North German *Reichstag* presented the same request on behalf of the people. Before his final acceptance the king had to be persuaded by Bismarck to desist from his original demand of becoming "Emperor of Germany" and to be satisfied with the title of "German Emperor." It was Bismarck's calculation that this latter title was less provocative to the susceptibilities of the minor German princes and might make it easier for them to relinquish part of their sovereignty.

The solemn proclamation of King William I of Prussia as "German Emperor" took place in the Hall of Mirrors of Louis XIV's palace of Versailles, on January 18, 1871. The king's declaration of acceptance was read by Bismarck and contained the following memorable passage: "We accept the imperial dignity, hoping that the German people will be allowed to enjoy the reward of their enthusiastic and unselfish fight in a lasting peace. . . . But to us and our successors may God grant that we be at all times augmenters of the German Empire, not by war and conquest, but by the blessings and gifts of peace, the welfare and moral greatness of the nation."

The Imperial Constitution ("Reichsverfassung"). The second German Empire was a centralized *Bundesstaat,* dominated by Prussia, which occupied by far the largest territory with almost two thirds of the population of the new Germany. The Empire comprised four kingdoms (Prussia, Bavaria, Wurtemberg, Saxony), six grand duchies, five duchies, seven principalities, three free cities (Hamburg, Bremen, Lübeck), and the territories (*Reichslande*) of Alsace-Lorraine.

The political structure of the Empire rested juridically on the new *Reichsverfassung* which, with few alterations, followed the pattern of the Constitution proposed by the Frankfurt Parliament in 1849 (cf. p. 530 sq.) and the Constitution of the North German Confederation (cf. p. 542). The sovereign rulers of the different states were represented in the *Bundesrat* (Federal Council), a kind of imperial senate, whose members held their offices by princely appointment, not by popular election. In this body Prussia had seventeen votes out of a total of fifty-eight. The representatives of the people, chosen by universal manhood suffrage, formed the *Reichstag,* whose legislative powers, however, were limited by the prerogatives of the *Kaiser,* the *Reichskanzler,* and the *Bundesrat.* The *Reichskanzler,* the appointee of the *Kaiser,* appointed in turn his collaborators in the different governmental offices. The chancellor was responsible only to the emperor and could be removed from office only by imperial decree. Thus it is quite evident that while the governmental system of the Second German Empire was constitutional and representative it was not parliamentary. The *Reichsverfassung* was not as reactionary as the Constitution of Prussia, but it differed even more widely from the democratic parliamentary rule in France, England, or the United States of America, with their far-reaching control of the legislative and executive branches of government.

The political parties in the new *Reichstag* were the same that had functioned before in the individual states and in the North German Confederation. The "Conservatives" were recruited chiefly from state officials and the holders of landed property. The "Liberals," comprising the "national-liberal" monarchists and the "progressive" democrats, were advocates of *"laissez-faire"* and unlimited competition in economics and of "secularism" (freedom from church influence) in politics, culture, and education. The "Center-Party" (seated in the center of the chamber, between Conservatives and Liberals) was originally founded in Prussia (1852) and was reorganized on a national basis by Ludwig Windthorst in 1871. A politico-religious party, it proclaimed the defense of Christian principles in political and social life as well as in education, and it represented especially the interests of the organizations and institutions of German Catholics. The seats on the extreme left of the *Reichstag* were occupied by the "Social-Democrats," the more or less radical disciples of Karl Marx, Friedrich Engels, and Ferdinand Lassalle. Their anticapitalist, pacifist, and internationalist creed as well as their adherence to materialism and atheism placed them in opposition to all the other parties of the Diet, but their gospel of social compassion and of the redemption of the masses from want and social degradation, together with the ability of some of their leaders, gained many converts to their cause and, fortified in their determination by persecution and repression, their party experienced a phenomenal growth during the following decades.

The political unification of Germany was followed by the adoption of a uniform criminal and civil law code (*Strafgesetzbuch, StGB,* 1871) and uniform commercial and industrial legislation, while the administration of justice and the judiciary, with the exception of the Supreme Court (*Reichsgericht,* 1879) in Leipzig, were relegated to the authority of the individual states. The introduction of uniform weights and measures, based on the decimal and metric system, and of a uniform system of currency (the German "Mark," 1871–1924) based on the gold standard, were among the lasting achievements of the reorganized *Zollverein* (cf. p. 513 sq.) of 1868.

B. *INDUSTRIAL REVOLUTION, TECHNOLOGY, AND THE NATURAL SCIENCES*

Men and Machines. In the course of the nineteenth century the European mind experienced an evolution so far reaching in its effects that it left its indelible mark on all modern nations and their cultures. The dynamic activism inherent in the Western belief in cultural and scientific progress had been greatly strengthened by both the rationalist and empiricist trends of the preceding centuries, as also by the neo-humanist cult of the human personality and its self-sufficiency. Lord Bacon's (1561–1626) slogan, "Knowledge is Power," provided the cue for the unprecedented and unparalleled development of industry, technology, and science which characterizes the civilization of the "machine age."

The machine seemed to promise an ardently desired enlargement of the human ego, permitting an extension of human forces into the external world of matter and leading at last to a complete sovereignty of man over inorganic and organic nature. The machine was expected to create more favorable living conditions for all by overcoming the limitations of space and time and by placing within the reach of everyone a multitude of material goods and unheard-of satisfactions.

a) England and the "Industrial Revolution." The country in which the spirit of the new age achieved its first triumphs was England. Here several historic circumstances worked together to lay the foundations for the development of modern industrialism. In the second half of the eighteenth century Great Britain began to reap the fruits of the flourishing colonial empire which she had acquired by the exploits of war and diplomacy. The parliamentary system of government had prevented the establishment of princely absolutism and militarism in the British Isles and had strengthened in the ruling classes the spirit of personal initiative and free commercial enterprise. While the continental states went through a series of destructive wars and economic crises, England's insular position made her practically invulnerable to foreign attack and enabled her to live through the era of the French Revolution and the Napoleonic wars (1789–1815) in relative political and economic stability and thus to prepare herself to become the great arsenal of the industrial capitalism of the nineteenth century. Hence, the decisive changes in the methods of production, in the technical exploitation of the forces of nature, and in the utilization and evaluation of human labor that are commonly associated with the "Industrial Revolution" were first made effective on English soil.

b) Capitalist Industrialism. Up to the latter part of the eighteenth century the technical mastery of nature and its resources had hardly progressed beyond the conditions prevailing from the days of antiquity, and correspondingly the general standards of human life, of comfort, occupation, and recreation were essentially unchanged. The peasantry still comprised by far the largest aggregate number of workers and producers. The majority of the townspeople were still artisans engaged in their home industries and handicrafts, and the chief means of transportation and commercial communication were still the stagecoach and the sailing ship. Life in general was characterized by a relative economic stability resulting from the limitation of both needs and satisfactions.

All this changed almost overnight with the invention of machines and the concomitant advent of capitalist industrialism. Capitalism as such, to be sure, was much older than the industrial system, dating back in its beginnings to the later Middle Ages. But the combination of capital and mechanized industry, favoring the growth of a new money aristocracy on the one hand, and of a propertyless class of wage earners or proletarians on the other, was new. A huge concentration of wealth in the hands of a class of individual owners or of shareholders in various industrial enterprises tended to enthrone the industrial entrepreneurs as leaders of men and states. The labor-displacing machinery made for an increasing insecurity in the life of the workingman, for sharp and ruthless practices in the labor market, and the accompanying evils of unemployment and destitution.

c) The Factory System. Crowded together in the impersonal and unhealthy atmosphere of the factory, the laborers lost the artisans' pride in the quality of their work and became mere "hands" in the big mechanism of industrial mass production. Long working hours, starvation wages, and the employment of women and children added to the wretchedness of living conditions in the factory, frequently reducing human existence to a subhuman level. Various laws were passed in England and in some continental countries to mitigate the hardships and hazards of factory labor, until by the middle of the nineteenth century the worst abuses had been checked. But even these moderate improvements in the factory system were not achieved without violence. The workers, driven to desperation by hunger and destitution, tried to take their revenge on the despised machines that had brought ruin to their homes and families. Early in the nineteenth century the "machine wreckers" in England smashed the weaving frames and power looms in the factories, and in the forties the weavers in Prussian Silesia rose in revolt against their capitalist exploiters.*

The employers found comfort and a moral alibi for their ruthlessness in the *"laissez-faire"* doctrine of economic liberalism, especially in its contention that business and morality don't mix, and that the "survival

---

* For a dramatic account of these tragic events in Silesia, cf. Gerhart Hauptmann's moving play *The Weavers;* Ernst Toller's (cf. p. 729) expressionistic drama *The Machine Wreckers* treats of the revolt in the English factories.

of the fittest" is no less a law of economics than a law of nature. The factory owners were plainly not interested in the lot of their workers as persons but merely in their labor, which they bought, like any other commodity, at the lowest possible rate. When his labor was no longer needed, the workingman joined the ranks of the unemployed, and he and his family faced starvation. Those employers, moreover, who were imbued with the Calvinist teaching of "predestination" and "divine election," felt inclined to look upon poverty as a sign of God's disfavor and upon riches as an infallible proof of a person's being predestined for salvation.

The ideas of economic liberalism found their most formidable expression in such industrial centers as Manchester and Liverpool. Within a short span of time industrial production in these two cities experienced an almost fabulous expansion and the factory owners felt themselves as the executors of a historic and national mission. "Manchesterdom" (*Manchestertum*) became in all European countries a symbol of unlimited industrial competition and of the principle of Free Trade.

d) Flight From the Land. The industrial civilization of the nineteenth and early twentieth century developed into a civilization of city dwellers, marked by the rapid and unnatural growth of big urban centers and a general flight from the land. The big city, with its factories, its educational, cultural, and recreational facilities, and its social and economic opportunities, promised work, advancement, and increasing personal independence. But relatively few of those who were attracted by these allurements were able to enjoy any of the privileges and advantages of city life. The vast majority were forced to spend their lives in overcrowded tenements, in hovels and slums, divorced not only from nature and the soil but shut off from air and sunlight as well. The big city of the nineteenth century was a motley agglomeration of buildings, hastily constructed for reasons of commercial profit, without planning and due regard for the exigencies of nature and the needs of man. It was without beauty and utterly devoid of any distinctive personal or national physiognomy. Many of the new industrial settlements arose in the immediate neighborhood of coalpits, ore deposits, or canals, and the beauty of many historical sites and landmarks was marred or destroyed forever by the tyrannical forces of industry and technology.

In Germany the movement of population into the large industrial centers began about the middle of the nineteenth century. It was indicative of the transformation of the country from an agricultural into an industrial nation. In 1871, 63.9 per cent of the German population were still living in rural districts; in 1895 the percentage had dropped to 50.1; in 1910, to 39.98; and in 1925, to 35.6.

Before long, however, the migration to the city was followed by a flight back to nature. Out of disillusionment and disappointment was born the protest against the artificiality of city life and against the inhumanity of its soulless industrialism. From John Ruskin (1819–1900) and William Morris (1834–1896) to Leo Tolstoi (1828–1910), Eric Gill (1882–1940), and

Mahatma Gandhi (1869–1948) the call for a return to the simple and natural modes of life, for the lost virtues of the artisan, and for a revival of the home industries, as voiced by sensitive artists, writers, and astute reformers, steadily gained in passionate intensity. The German *Wandervogel* and Youth Movement (cf. p. 708 sq.) of the early twentieth century as well as the attempts to revive the folk arts and folk traditions owe their origin to a generally felt impulse to rediscover the beauty of nature and the sanity of natural habits in a seemingly disenchanted and barren world. In the form of *Schrebergärten* (so named after Daniel Schreber [1808–1861], a German orthopedic physician), located at the outskirts of industrial cities and providing small patches of arable land for the laboring and middle classes, or in the form of artistically planned labor colonies, the "back to the land movement" entered the very precincts of the city itself.

e) The Age of Coal and Iron. The "Industrial Revolution" began in England in the latter part of the eighteenth century with the invention of improved methods for the mechanical production of cotton fabrics, for the weaving of silks and woolens, and the knitting of hosiery and lace. A spinning machine, for example, as constructed by Samuel Crompton in 1779, was capable of equaling the work of two hundred manual laborers. As a result England's imports of raw cotton had reached in 1810 the staggering amount of 120 million pounds a year, four times as much as she had imported in 1790. In the relatively peaceful years of the *Vormärz* (1815–1848) the new textile machinery gradually gained a foothold on the European continent, notably in France and Belgium. But the most decisive innovations in machine construction were brought about in those industries that worked with iron and coal, the two most important raw materials of the industrial era. By freeing iron from its ore, and by subjecting it to the processes of smelting and casting, the Industrial Revolution won some of its greatest victories. The traditional building materials of wood, leather, and hemp were replaced by iron, steel, and wire. Similarly the new coal industry revolutionized the older methods of generating heat, light, and power: coke and coal were henceforth used in place of wood, peat, fat, and wax.

Transportation and Communication. Among the nations of the Old and New World only Germany and the United States had accessible coal and iron deposits comparable with those of Great Britain. Germany, however, was prevented by unfavorable political and economic conditions from competing with the industrial development of England, and the United States remained in part dependent on European industry as long as the exploitation of her vast resources was retarded by the sparseness of her population. In England the year 1769, in which James Watt (1736–1819) obtained the patent for his newly invented steam engine, is usually regarded as the beginning date of her Industrial Revolution, though it took nearly half a century until the epochal significance of this invention was fully realized and its productive capacity utilized. The use of this new mechanized source of power supply for railroad and steamship transportation transcended eventually in its effects all national boundary lines and created in the modern world a slowly growing consciousness of the economic interdependence of all nations.

a) Steamships. When the American engineer Robert Fulton (1765–1815) demonstrated on the river Seine his experimental steamboat to Napoleon I, the French emperor showed great enthusiasm and expressed his conviction that this invention would "change the face of the earth." In 1807 Fulton's paddle-wheeled steamboat *Claremont,* equipped with one of Watt's steam engines, successfully completed its first cruise on the Hudson River. In 1819 the steamboat *Savannah* crossed the Atlantic Ocean from New York to Liverpool. The first cruise in 1816 of an English steam-propelled ship without masts, sails, and rudders to the Rhenish city of Cologne caused a great sensation on the European continent. A few years later a regular weekly steamship traffic was established between Rotterdam and Cologne. In 1825 several steamship companies were organized in the Rhineland, and in 1829 the shipbuilding yard of Ruhrort was founded. Regular steamship traffic on the Danube was inaugurated by the "Danubian Steamship Company" (*Donau-Dampfschiffahrts-Gesellschaft*) in 1831. The *Kölner Dampfschleppschiffahrtsgesellschaft* (Steam-Towage Company of Cologne), founded in 1841, specialized in the construction of huge tugboats made of sheet iron and handling most of the goods traffic on the Rhine. Two new trade routes from the Rhine to the Atlantic Ocean were created by the construction of the French Rhine-Rhone Canal and the Rhine-Marne Canal, linking the Rhenish lowlands with the French ports of Marseille and Le Havre.

In the forties of the nineteenth century the paddle steamer was replaced by the screw steamer, an innovation that aided in speeding up the development of overseas steamship traffic. The first steamship line between Bremen and the New World, financed with American capital, was established in 1847, and in the same year the Hamburg-America line (*Hapag*) was founded. The Congress of Vienna had restored Hamburg's privileges as a "Free City" and had thereby greatly stimulated the commercial initiative and the pioneering spirit of the patrician merchants of this proud city-republic, which from then on contributed more than its share to the expanding world trade of the industrial era.

Ever since the rise of England as a colonial power both Hamburg and Bremen had served as the German entrance gates of British commerce and British ideas, and the Hamburg merchants in particular were among the most outspoken advocates of Free Trade policies. In the twenties of the nineteenth century the city of Bremen succeeded in obtaining a strip of land from the neighboring state of Hanover, and in 1827 it established the new port of Bremerhaven at the mouth of the Geeste River. In 1857 the North German Lloyd was founded, the second of the great German transocean lines. Its central administrative offices were located in Bremen, and both Bremen and Bremerhaven offered their port facilities to the in-coming and outgoing steamship traffic.

b) *Telegraph and Telephone*. The revolutionary changes brought about by steam-propelled traffic on land and on the sea were supplemented and completed by the invention of telegraph and telephone, the new means of communication. The so-called "optical telegraph" had been constructed as early as 1793 by the Frenchman Claude Chappe and had proven its useful-ness in the service of the revolutionary "National Convent" as well as in the campaigns of Napoleon I. The "optical telegraph" was used for the transmission of messages by means of light signals, and it served almost exclusively the purposes of governmental administration and military strategy.

In 1809 the German physician and mathematician *von Sömmering* (1775-1830) demonstrated before the Bavarian Academy of Sciences "a new little telegraphic machine," which for the first time used electricity for long-distance communication. Sömmering's invention was further developed and improved by the mathematician *Karl Friedrich Gauss* (1777-1855) and the physicist *Wilhelm Eduard Weber* (1804-1891), two German scholars who in 1833 established electrical telegraphic communication between the physical institute and the observatory of the University of Göttingen. The transposition of telegraphic signals into alphabetic symbols was first at-tempted in 1837 by the German physicist and industrialist *August von Steinheil* and by the English physicist *Charles Wheatstone*. One year later the American inventor *Samuel Morse* obtained a patent for an improved system of electrical telegraphy, the practical value of which was increased by the creation of the "Morse Alphabet." These inventions made it possible for *Werner von Siemens* (1816-1892), a German industrialist and electrical engineer, to build the important state telegraph systems connecting Berlin with the cities of Frankfurt and Cologne, to develop the technics of electrical weak currents, and to become the leading electro-technical industrialist of Europe.

The invention of the telephone (German: *Fernsprecher*) was first con-ceived of in a rudimentary form by the German schoolteacher *Philipp Reis* in 1861 and was afterward (1872) developed into a practical system of long-distance communication by the English physiologist *Alexander Graham Bell* (1847-1922).

German Industry. In 1765 the Italian popular philosopher Antonio Genovesi, a disciple of Christian Wolff (cf. p. 360), had ventured the pre-diction that the productive capacity of German trade and commerce would never equal that of England and France. This remained true until the middle of the nineteenth century. But as soon as Germany began to com-prehend realistically the new problems presented by the Industrial Revolu-tion, she pushed ahead with typical Germanic thoroughness and tenacity. Germany was rich in ore and coal deposits and her people had learned discipline of thought and work in the schools and in the army. These acquired habits were complemented by an inborn talent for organization and administration.

The first German industrialist who succeeded in competing successfully with England in the field of machine construction was *August Borsig,* who opened his Berlin railway plant in 1837. Only a few years later Borsig's locomotives not only matched the English machines in speed and power but were actually superior to them. Similar advances were made in the textile industries. The trade of the ancient weaver guilds of Augsburg, for instance, which could take just pride in a long and honored tradition, experienced a revival on the basis of modern capitalist industrialism, a development that carried with it, however, the extinction of the trade and labor concepts of the guilds as such.

The rapidly increasing manufacture of cotton, superseding the time-honored production of linen and woolen goods, was partly responsible for the impoverishment of the linen weavers in Silesia and in other German provinces. It was the linen industry that suffered most severely from the effects of the Industrial Revolution in Germany, and both spinners and weavers felt the full impact of the advancing machine age.

The most impressive accomplishments of the German iron and steel industries are associated with the name of *Friedrich Krupp* (1787–1826) in Essen in the Rhineland and with the work of his son *Alfred* (1812–1887) and his grandson *Friedrich Alfred* (1854–1902). It had been Friedrich's ambition to manufacture a type of cast steel that was to equal if not to surpass in quality the English product. He succeeded at the cost of great personal sacrifices, but lack of funds forced him to close down his newly acquired iron foundry in Altenessen. When he died at the age of 39, his widow and four children were left on the verge of starvation. But on his deathbed he had bequeathed the secret of the production of cast steel to his eldest son Alfred, who was then fourteen years of age. The younger Krupp, confronted with the task of supporting his family and of settling his father's debts, worked his way to success through untold hardships and privations.

Banking and Big Business. With the increasing emphasis on the profit motive in production and business and with the expansion of the capitalist credit system, banking acquired a new significance in financial transactions. The big banking or moneylending institutions date back in their origins to the later Middle Ages and the Renaissance (cf. p. 244 sqq.), but their development in the nineteenth century is characterized by a new factor, namely, the fusion of banking and industrial interests.

The wars of the seventeenth and eighteenth centuries had played into the hands of the Jewish money-changers and moneylenders, who had made themselves indispensable to the absolutistic princes. Even in the first half of the nineteenth century the rulers of states and principalities were depending in their financial enterprises on their "court Jews" (*Hofjuden*) or "court bankers." In the age of Metternich most of the Jewish court bankers of Austria were baronized, although they were still deprived of citizenship.

The most influential of these Jewish banking concerns was the House of Rothschild, whose founder, Meyer Amschel Rothschild (1743-1812), a petty moneylender of the city of Frankfurt, had made his fortune by obtaining government contracts for war supplies during the "Coalition Wars" that followed the French Revolution of 1789. Meyer Amschel's five sons represented the firm in its branch offices in Frankfurt, Vienna, London, Paris, and Naples. During the Napoleonic wars one of the brothers acted as adviser to the French emperor, while the one in charge of the house in London worked hand in hand with the British. When Meyer Amschel died in 1812 he knew that the financial power of his firm had become equally indispensable to both sides in the armed conflict. The founder of the House of Rothschild had regarded it as absolutely essential for financial success to remain politically detached but at the same time to back financially the prevailing sentiments and the political course of the most powerful groups in the different states. Thus when Napoleon's downfall appeared unavoidable, the Rothschild brothers immediately shifted their allegiance to the cause of the Allies and took charge of the shipment of English subsidies to the European continent. After 1815 they lent their financial support to the policies of Metternich and to the forces of the Restoration movement.

Within a bare two decades the family of an obscure moneylender of the Frankfurt Ghetto had risen to a position of international prominence. In 1822 the Austrian Rothschilds were given a patent of nobility. In the early years of the machine age the Viennese and Paris branches financed the Austrian, French, and Belgian railroad systems, but otherwise the Rothschilds refrained from engaging in industrial enterprise.

The first German banks with large capital investments in industrial concerns were the *Schaafhausensche Bankverein* in Cologne (founded in 1848) and the *Bank für Handel und Industrie* (Bank for Trade and Industry) in Darmstadt (founded in 1853). In the second half of the nineteenth century the union of capital and industry led to the formation of large concerns, in which several individual enterprises were collectively organized in the form of huge impersonal corporations, syndicates, and trusts with divided responsibility and limited liability, the individual shareholders hiding under the name of a corporative firm. The capital amassed in some big banking or industrial concerns soon began to wield a power that was all the greater as it was exercised by those who controlled the allotment of credit and therewith the very life source of production. This concentration of money power in the hands of small groups of financial and industrial wizards tended to extend the influence of economic interests over the entire state, its domestic and foreign policies, and into the broad field of international relations, resulting alternately in extreme economic nationalism and international economic imperialism.

In the course of time the multifarious interrelations of industrial and financial interests began to form an intricate web of mutual technico-economic dependencies, superimposing themselves on the traditional manners and customs of life and work and threatening the preservation of the inherited types of national culture. Countless millions in all countries became more and more dependent on the fluctuating price levels of the world market, and the masses began to curse an economic system which produced want in the midst of plenty. The increasing social unrest called for an antidote, and the unbridled ambitions of capitalist industrialism found themselves challenged by the militant forces of socialism and the incipient "revolt of the masses."

Capitalism and Socialism. The fact that the ownership of the means of production and the accumulation of capital provided the employer class with both economic security and political power, while at the same time it forced the masses of wage earners into economic and political servitude, created a growing class consciousness among the dispossessed and led first to the formation of defensive organizations and finally to a violent counterthrust of the aroused "proletariat"* against capitalist exploitation.

a) *Trade Unionism.* The earliest manifestation of these combinations of labor groups was the movement of trade unionism, which originated as a direct sequel of the Industrial Revolution and which fought for the right of labor to organize for the purpose of obtaining shorter working hours, improved working conditions, and higher wages. The struggle of the trade unions for recognition was hard and prolonged. They were first fully legalized in England in 1871, while in Germany they were at best reluctantly tolerated but not officially recognized as representative workers' organizations until 1918.**

b) *The Socialist and Communist Movement.* The majority of trade unionists entered into an ideological and practical alliance with the socialist doctrines of *Karl Marx* (1818–1883), and *Friedrich Engels* (1820–1895). Marx was a German-Jewish economist who, after having joined in the revolutionary movements of 1849, and after having been expelled from continental Europe, had settled in London. There he continued his activities as a publicist, in close collaboration with Friedrich Engels, who had gone through similar experiences and had likewise found refuge in England. Both men were strongly influenced by the dialectical philosophy of Hegel (cf. p. 502 sqq.) and the anthropological materialism of Ludwig Feuerbach (1804–1872), who was himself a member of the "Young Hegelian" school (cf. p. 505). Marx and Engels had subjected the capitalist system of economy to a keen and penetrating analysis and published their conclusions in programmatic form in the *Communist Manifesto* (1848).

---

* The term "proletariat" (from Latin, *proles* = "progeny") was originally used in ancient Rome to designate those citizens who had no money with which to pay taxes and therefore had to place the working capacity of their children at the disposal of the state.

** The socialistic *"Hirsch-Duncker"* and "Free" trade unions of Germany were organized in the sixties of the nineteenth century. The foundation of the interdenominational "Christian Trade Unions" was prompted by the desire to counteract the antireligious tendencies of the Marxist unions. The first German "Christian Trade Union" was founded in 1894.

In 1841 Feuerbach had published his *Essence of Christianity* (*Das Wesen des Christentums*), followed by the *Essence of Religion* (*Das Wesen der Religion*) in 1845. In both works the erstwhile student of theology had maintained that God and the entire realm of the supernatural were a creation of man's hopes and fears: man was not created in the image and likeness of God, but God was created in the image and likeness of man. If man would achieve happiness, Feuerbach claimed, he must not search for it above himself but within himself: theology must be transformed into anthropology.

Marx and Engels greeted this materialistic anthropologism as a sort of revelation, and their trained historical sense traced the beginnings of modern materialism back to the philosophy of Nominalism (cf. p. 142). "Materialism," wrote Engels, "is the natural-born son of Great Britain. . . . Nominalism, the first form of materialism, is chiefly found among the English schoolmen [of the Middle Ages]." And Lenin, the leader of the communist revolution in Russia, described Marxism as a synthesis of German philosophy, English political economy, and French socialism.

The quintessence of the socialist-materialist doctrines as developed by Marx and Engels and presented first in the *Communist Manifesto,* and later on in Marx's *Das Kapital* (1867), is the conviction that "it is not consciousness that determines life, but life that determines consciousness," that "the mode of production . . . conditions the social, political, and spiritual life in general," and that "the history of society is the history of the class struggle." The new materialistic philosophy of history implied in these statements visualized historic evolution as a series of civil wars, culminating in the Industrial Revolution of the nineteenth century. The modern class struggle between capital and labor, employers and wage earners, "bourgeoisie" and "proletariat," was a process of social evolution and interaction that followed the laws of material and biological evolution. Modern mankind was divided by Karl Marx into capitalist "proprietors" and "expropriated" proletarians, and the warfare between these two groups was to end with the "expropriation of the exproprietors."

The class struggle, therefore, was seen by Marx not as an end in itself but as a means to the elimination of classes and class privileges, leading eventually to the abolition of national boundaries and the establishment of the universal co-operative State. There was no doubt in the mind of Karl Marx as to the inevitability of this immanent movement of the "dialectic" of economic forces toward the desired goal. On the day when the means of production would be concentrated in the hands of a few capitalist owners, capitalism would have dug its own grave, and a class-conscious international proletariat would stand ready to take over the system of industrial production and organize the redistribution of wealth with a view to the welfare of all.

While the socialistic theory of Marx and Engels describes the ultimate realization of the ideal proletarian commonwealth as resulting from a necessary evolutionary process, it is admitted that the dictatorial assumption of political power by the workers and the armed repulsion of the forces of counterrevolution might become mandatory during the period of transition and readjustment. The violent overthrow of governments and of the established social order was not compatible with the teachings of historical and dialectical materialism and was consequently not explicitly advocated by Marx and Engels themselves. It was rather advocated by some of their more radical and less philosophically minded disciples and by the protagonists of syndicalism and anarchism of the later nineteenth and early twentieth centuries.

Socialism and communism were united in their antagonism to the institution of private property, in their demand for the socialization of the means of production, and in their protest against the enslavement of human beings by the misuse of the privileges of ownership. In the writings of Marx and Engels the two terms were used almost synonymously. Gradually, however, the term communism came to be generally understood as an extreme form of Marxian socialism. It denoted the increasing emphasis on the more violent aspects of the class struggle and the clamor for the dictatorship of the proletariat, including the demand for the general socialization of economic goods, of articles of production as well as of articles of consumption. In the perfect communistic society the welfare of the individual was to be subordinated to the thoroughly rationalized economic and political mechanism of the proletarian Society, in which economic and social forces claimed such absolute supremacy as to leave little room for the cultivation of moral and cultural values.

Socialization or communization of property had been advocated many times before the advent of the machine age, either in political blueprints for the establishment of an ideal State, such as Plato's *Republic* or Thomas More's *Utopia,* or in communistically organized religious sects (Waldenses, Albigenses, Anabaptists, etc.) and monastic orders. It will also be remembered that common ownership of the soil was the rule in early Germanic times (cf. p. 8). But most of these communistic schemes of an earlier age were limited to one state or region or they were proposed and executed on a religious and voluntary basis, whereas Marxist communism called for a compulsory and world-wide system of socialization. It was to be brought about by a society that had first to be thoroughly secularized and whose social outlook was to be determined by the adoption of the materialistic creed.*

---

* A redistribution of property to combat the evils and social injustices of both communist and capitalistic systems has been advocated by the so-called "distributists" (Chesterton, Belloc, etc.), who reject the idea of State ownership and on the contrary demand the widest possible distribution of privately owned property, restoring the means of production to the individual workers. This program seems to be in essential agreement with the social ideas advanced by the French "Jacobins" as well as with those of Thomas Jefferson, who envisaged a solution of the social problem by the creation of a community of landowning small farmers. The British artist and writer Eric Gill cites the following reasons for the restoration of property to individuals:

Small, voluntary social communities, based on the principle of co-operation, somewhat analogous to the religious communist organizations of the past and present, were favored by the French school of social reformers (Cabet, Fourier, Saint-Simon, etc.) in the early nineteenth century. Some of the socialistic ideas of the highly talented and romantically inclined *Ferdinand Lassalle* (1825–1864), German-Jewish social philosopher and political agitator, were well received even by such conservative leaders as Bishop von Ketteler (cf. p. 600 sq.) and Otto von Bismarck (cf. p. 535). Lassalle formulated the program of the "German Workers' Union" (*Allgemeiner deutscher Arbeiterverein*) and thus became the founder of the first German socialist party (1863). His proposed "productive associations" of workers under the protectorship of the State amounted to a moderate form of State socialism. Although Lassalle's theories were rejected by the orthodox Marxists, the merger of his "Workers' Union" with the radical Marxist party organization of *Wilhelm Liebknecht* in 1875 resulted in the formation of the united Social Democratic Party in Germany.

c) The "International." The common international aims of the socialist workers of Europe found their constitutional and organizational representation in the "First International" (London, 1864), whose statutes had been drawn up by Karl Marx himself. After factional disputes had led to its dissolution in 1876, the "Second International" was founded in 1889. In 1907 a radical minority, advocating the instigation of civil wars and headed by Lenin and Rosa Luxemburg (cf. p. 646), seceded from the more moderate majority. World War I brought about further factional and regional divisions, but after the conclusion of the war (1919) the "Third International" was created in Moscow, following a strictly communistic pattern.

A Generation of German Scientists. The philosophy of Hegel and his school (cf. p. 502 sqq.) and the abstract speculations of the "nature philosophers" (cf. p. 501) dominated the intellectual scene in Germany during the early decades of the nineteenth century, and while their intuitions stimulated the spirit of scientific research, their poetico-romantic leanings retarded at the same time the progress of experimental science. The scientifically minded nineteenth century was turning rather sharply from generalization to specialization, from rational speculation to empirical observation. Germany had first to free herself from the spell of Hegelianism before she could make her own vital contributions to the great discoveries and advances in the several fields of the natural sciences.

On the threshold of the age of modern empirical science in Germany stands *Alexander von Humboldt* (1769–1859), Wilhelm von Humboldt's

---

" . . . because property is natural to man; because it is a bulwark against the exploitation of man by man; because unless you own the means of production you cannot control production; because unless you control you cannot be responsible; because responsibility for his deeds . . . is the very mark of man. . . . The injustices of property owners in the past have only been possible because the few owned too much and the many nothing at all. The law therefore should favor ownership, whereas at present it favors exploitation" (Autobiography, Devin-Adair Co., New York, 1941, p. 296 sq.).

(cf. p. 439 sqq.) younger brother, one of the greatest exponents of natural science and a prominent humanist scholar besides. In him the universalistic-philosophical and the empirico-scientific tendencies were equally strong, but he was able to reconcile them by virtue of the synthetic faculty of his mind. Like some of the romantic "nature philosophers" Humboldt had attended in his youth the famous Mining Academy of Freiberg in Saxony, and later on at the University of Göttingen he had undergone a thorough training in scientific method. Nevertheless he did not escape the censure of the contemporary scientific specialists on the one hand and of the philosophers and poets on the other. The former objected to his universalism, the latter to his empiricism.

Humboldt's special field of research was scientific geography, understood as a comprehensive analysis of climate, vegetation, and fauna in their relation to human activities. He collected an inexhaustible wealth of material on his many travels to foreign lands and continents, and of all these expeditions the trip to the Spanish colonies of South America (1799–1804) yielded the richest scientific reward. On his homeward journey he visited Mexico and the United States.

Humboldt's peculiar gift of seeing the interrelations between different branches of science enabled him to make important discoveries in several scientific fields. The sciences of meteorology, geology, and physics are indebted to him for the invention of isotherms, for his research on volcanic formations, and for his investigation of the nature of terrestrial magnetism. In his herbarium he had assembled 5000 newly discovered plant species, and his collection of rare butterflies was unique in its kind. At his own expense, and unafraid of difficulties and dangers, this model research worker accumulated countless specimens of plants, animals, and minerals, of coins, ornaments, weapons, and art objects of various kinds, gathered from many parts of the world. In Paris, in close association with the scientists of the French Academy and the *Ecole Polytechnique,* he organized his treasures and his notes and published the results of his American journey in the French language (*Voyage aux régions équinoxiales du nouveau continent, fait en 1799–1804;* 30 vols., 1834). During the final years of his long life Humboldt completed his *Kosmos,* a monumental compendium of the physical structure of the universe that was soon translated into all the languages of the civilized world. The United States paid tribute to Humboldt's genius by the erection of the Humboldt monuments in St. Louis and Philadelphia.

Another outstanding representative of the first generation of German inductive scientists was *Justus von Liebig* (1803–1873), an eminent chemist, who owed his professorship in the University of Giessen to the recommendation of Alexander von Humboldt. As a young man he had studied in Paris and had received his training in experimental methodology from the leading scientists in the field of physico-chemistry. In his own laboratory he trained several generations of future scientists, teaching them the methods of determining the chemical composition of organic substances and laying the foundations for the development of organic chemistry. By linking chemistry with the physiology of animals and plants Liebig made important contributions to the knowledge of metabolic processes and became the founder of agricultural chemistry. A lifelong friendship bound him to his teacher, the famous French chemist Gay-Lussac, and to Friedrich Wöhler, his most distinguished pupil, together with whom he had experimentally worked out the principles of the new organic chemistry.

After Liebig had been called to the University of Munich by King Louis I of Bavaria (1852), he devoted himself almost exclusively to the problems of agricultural chemistry. By the discovery of new methods of soil conservation and fertilization he became the first great representative of scientific "technical chemistry." In his *Chemical Letters* he popularized his findings, attributing the decay of races and nations to the exhaustion of the soil, brought about by the unmethodical waste of its chemical substance.

A scientist and scholar of the highest rank, equally proficient in the disciplines of mathematics and physics, was *Karl Friedrich Gauss* (1777–1855). His scientific research and his writings are distinguished by their originality and many-sidedness. After having spent his early youth in his native Brunswick, Gauss completed his studies at the University of Göttingen, where from 1807 to his death he was professor of mathematics and director of the local observatory, which he himself had planned and designed.

Regarding arithmetic as the queen of the sciences, Gauss applied his new methods not only to the different branches of higher mathematics but to experimental and mathematical physics, to theoretical and practical astronomy, to geodetics and the science of terrestrial magnetism. Together with the physicist *Wilhelm Weber,* his colleague in the University of Göttingen, he constructed the first electromagnetic telegraph.

Despite his many contributions to applied science, Gauss regarded the practical aspects of his research as of minor significance: "There is for my mind a satisfaction of a higher kind, in regard to which material things are irrelevant. I don't care whether I apply mathematics to some clumps of dirt, called planets, or to purely arithmetic problems; I must confess that the latter have a greater charm for me." His great love and knowledge of nature served only to increase Gauss's humility and his admiration for an all-pervading divine intelligence.

On a vacation trip Gauss made the acquaintance of *Joseph von Fraunhofer* (1787–1826), the greatest optician of the age, who had founded an optical institute of world fame in the Bavarian town of Benediktbeuren. Like Gauss, Fraunhofer had gone through the hard school of poverty and privation, but with inborn genius, industry, and perseverance he had familiarized himself at an early age with the most intricate problems of the science of optics. Together with *Georg Reichenbach* (1772–1826), whom he met in Munich, Fraunhofer had begun to manufacture scientific instruments. It was due to the work of these two men that Munich soon was to step into the place of Paris and London as the leading production center for precision tools. The construction of the leviathan telescope and the so-called "Königsberg Heliometer" were also among the fruits of their combined labors. Fraunhofer's name in particular will always remain associated with the discovery of the "dark lines" ("Fraunhofer Absorption Lines") in the sun's spectrum and with the experiments that first established the exact length of light waves. Fraunhofer's new methods of spectrum analysis were afterward perfected by *Gustav R. Kirchhoff* (1824–1887) and *Robert Bunsen* (1811–1899). The wealth of new information concerning the chemical composition of celestial bodies, derived from the analysis of the spectra of sun, stars, and comets, led in turn to new discoveries in the field of astronomy. Fraunhofer's construction of microscopic instruments was continued with greatly improved methods by the *Carl Zeiss Works* in Jena, founded in 1846. The perfection of scientific methods and instruments was the necessary prerequisite for the phenomenal progress of the sciences dealing with plant and animal organisms, of biology, physiology, botany, zoology, and medicine.

The principle of the "conservation of energy," one of the most fundamental laws of physical and physiological science, was first discovered and formulated in 1842 by *Robert Mayer* (1814–1878), an obscure Swabian country doctor. One year later the English physicist *James Joule* arrived at the same conclusions, and in 1847 the eminent German physicist and physiologist *Hermann von Helmholtz* (1821–1894) demonstrated the validity of the law of the *"Erhaltung der Kraft"* for every branch of the physical sciences. Helmholtz claimed and received all the credit for this discovery, while Robert Mayer was suspected of megalomania and even temporarily confined to an insane asylum. In the sixties of the nineteenth century the English physicist *John Tyndall* rendered a service to the cause of justice and decency when he revealed the tragic fate of Robert Mayer and called attention to his scientific accomplishments. The entire system of modern physics is based on the fact that heat is generated by mechanical forces and that there exists a definite and constant relationship between heat and energy. Robert Mayer's law therefore is as essential to modern physical science as are the discoveries of Galilei and Newton.

In *medicine* as in the other sciences Germany lagged behind France and England in the early nineteenth century but rose to a position of world leadership within a few decades. And, as was the case in the other sciences, the first generation of physicians had to emancipate themselves from the unrealistic theorems of "nature philosophy" in order to be able to transform medicine into an experimental science.

Scientific medicine in the strict sense began in Germany with the anatomical research of *Johann Schönlein* (1793–1864), the inaugurator of modern clinical methodology, whose laboratory at the University of Würzburg became a veritable shrine for the medical students of all European countries. In 1840 Schönlein founded the "German Clinic" in Berlin and thus became the first of a long series of celebrated clinical physicians in Germany.

The great genius, however, in this first generation of German medical scientists was *Johannes Müller* (1801–1858), a shoemaker's son of Coblenz on the Rhine, among whose pupils were some of the most illustrious scientists of modern times, such as Emil Du Bois-Reymond, Helmholtz, and Virchow. Müller taught anatomy, physiology, and pathology, and felt at home in every branch of the biological sciences. In his synthetic approach to scientific problems he followed the lead of Goethe's scientific studies, opposing specialization and endeavoring to comprehend and interpret the vast complex of scientific phenomena in their totality. An adherent of biological "vitalism," he defended the idea of design and purpose in the growth of organic structures against the biological theories of mechanism and materialism. The life force that informs the organism appeared to him as a manifestation of a purposive and creative power.

In the following generation German medical science followed the general trend of the age toward specialization and accepted the mechanistic explanation of inorganic and organic nature. Berlin became the center of inductive medical research in the field of internal medicine as well as in the new science of surgery. As the latter was traditionally associated with the barber's trade, it had to carry on a long fight before being granted recognition as an academic discipline.

Another landmark in the development of modern medical science was reached with the publication of *Rudolf Virchow's* (1821–1902) *Cellular Pathology* (1858). The great pathologist succeeded in linking disease with certain processes of morbid growth or disintegration of cellular structures. For the first time Virchow described the organism as a system of cells subject to various kinds of transformation. Thus the individual cell was recognized as an active agent in the production of disease. *Jakob Henle* (1809–1885), Johannes Müller's oldest and dearest pupil, likewise contributed to cellular research, and in his *Investigations on Pathology* of 1840 he anticipated intuitively the later discoveries of *Pasteur* and *Robert Koch* (cf. p. 565) concerning the microbic nature of certain diseases. He was the first to recognize that some infections of the organism were caused by "parasitical beings, which are among the lowliest and smallest but at the same time most prolific varieties of organisms."

Biological Evolution and Heredity. The new geological evidence of the great antiquity of the earth, produced early in the nineteenth century, vastly changed the ideas on man's function and position in the universe and stimulated scientific inquiry into the origins of life and into the relations that exist between its different manifestations. A new answer was given to these questions by the theory of biological evolution, also known as the theory of "transformism," or, in Germany, as *Abstammungslehre*. The idea as such was not new, and the principle of evolution had been advanced in one form or another by such thinkers as Empedocles (495–435 B.C.), Aristotle (384–321 B.C.), and St. Augustine (A.D. 354–430) in antiquity, by St. Thomas Aquinas in the Middle Ages, and by Leibniz, Lessing, Herder, Kant, and Schelling in modern times. The partly rationalistic and partly intuitive approach of these philosophers gave way in the nineteenth century to the new methods of scientific observation. While this modern research supplemented the older theories by offering a wealth of factual evidence, the materialistic premises of the modern philosophy of science suggested at the same time a set of new and far-reaching conclusions concerning the origin and nature of man. Thus many Darwinists maintained that the theory of evolution exposed the scriptural account of man's creation as a poetic myth and that man was descended both in body and mind from the lower and lowest animal organisms. It might be well to keep in mind, however, that such conclusions have no essential relation to the factuality of biological evolution as such and that, strictly speaking, they rest on a philosophical rather than a scientific basis.

The first two scientists to advance the theory of evolution in the nineteenth century were the Frenchman *Lamarck* (1744–1829) and the German *Treviranus* (1776–1837). They claimed that new needs produced by environmental changes were responsible for organic transformations in the plant and animal kingdom, and that these newly acquired characteristics were transmitted to the descendants of the species.

But these preliminary speculations were almost thrown into oblivion by the appearance of *Charles Darwin's* (1809–1882) *The Origin of Species* (1859) and *The Descent of Man* (1871). The English scientist, adding the theory of "natural selection" to the theory of evolution, demonstrated by a vast accumulation of factual data that organic species are subject to indefinite change. He asserted that in the struggle for existence the fittest individuals of a species have a better chance for survival and adaptation to changing environments than the weaker members, and that this principle of the "survival of the fittest" is the ulterior cause of the biological evolution of infinite varieties of species. If carried to extreme (and logically as well as scientifically unwarranted) conclusions, such a theory might well be used to justify the cruelties and injustices in social and economic life as well as the Machiavellian thesis of "Might is Right" and the idea of a "master race" of "supermen" in international relations. Darwinism was interpreted in this way by the Young Hegelian materialist *Max Stirner* (1806–1856), by the French diplomat and philosopher *Count Gobineau* (1816–1882), by Richard Wagner's son-in-law, the English-born but naturalized German popular philosopher *Houston Stewart Chamberlain* (1855–1927), and most of all by *Friedrich Nietzsche* (cf. p. 695 sq.). It is one of the ironical twists of history that Charles Darwin should thus have unwittingly become the ancestor of the myth of the intrinsic superiority of the "Aryan race." Darwin, however, repeatedly emphasized that the applicability of the theory of "natural selection" was limited in scope, and that the principle of the "survival of the fittest" must take into account the co-operative as well as the competitive, the social as well as the antisocial instincts and reactions of the species.

The most enthusiastic of the German Darwinists was *Ernst Haeckel* (1834–1919), one of Johannes Müller's pupils, who popularized the theory of evolution in his best seller, *Die Welträtsel* (*The Riddles of the Universe*). In Jena, where he held the position of professor of zoology at the local university, he founded a museum whose contents were to elucidate the problems of biological evolution. The results of Haeckel's scientific expeditions were made accessible to the public in several illustrated works, revealing the author's brilliance of style and the artistic qualities of his mind.

With the name of the Austrian-Czech botanist and Augustinian abbot *Gregor Mendel* (1822–1884) is associated the discovery of the law of the transmission of hereditary characteristics of the organism. By carrying on over 10,000 individual experiments with specimens of hybrid sweet peas Mendel worked out a method that made it possible to determine with mathematical exactitude the frequency of the reappearance of inherited "unit characters" in the line of descent. However, the significance of Mendel's contribution to the science of biological evolution was not recognized until after his death.

Bacteriology. The greatest progress in the treatment of infectious and epidemic diseases was due to the research of the French scientist *Louis Pasteur* (1822–1895) and the German physician *Robert Koch* (1843–1910). Pasteur proved conclusively that many infections of plants and animals were caused by micro-organisms and that therefore certain diseases might be prevented if these microbes could be either destroyed or antagonized by inoculating the organism with a weakened germ culture of the disease. By the process of "pasteurization" the temperature of the environment of the deadly microbes was raised to a degree that made it impossible for them to survive.

Robert Koch is generally regarded as the founder of the science of bacteriology. His research on anthrax, cholera, and tuberculosis resulted in the isolation of the anthrax bacterium and in the discovery of the micro-organic agents of Asiatic cholera and tubercular diseases.

In 1886 the French Academy of Sciences founded the *Institut Pasteur* which in the early years of its existence devoted all its efforts to the treatment of rabies. In 1899 Pasteur himself was appointed as director of the Institute. The "Robert Koch Institute for the Treatment of Infectious Diseases" was founded in Berlin in 1891 with Robert Koch as its director. *Emil von Behring* (1854–1917), one of Koch's assistants, discovered a serum for the successful treatment of diphtheria in 1894, and both he and Koch were awarded the Nobel Prize.

Experimental Psychology. The methods of psychological research in the nineteenth century were developed in harmony with the spirit of the age of inductive science. Thus psychology, which formerly had been a chiefly rational and speculative science attached to metaphysics and ethics, now became an experimental laboratory science, whose major tools were tests and quantitative measurements of sensations, perceptions, reflex actions, and other mental and emotional processes. With growing insight into the correlation of mental phenomena and brain processes, biological and psychological research became closely linked, and the study of animal behavior was regarded as providing most of the clues for the understanding of human thought and action. Once more the materialistic premises and biases of the contemporary philosophy are clearly recognizable in these attempts to measure thought or to precondition human behavior by the perfection of the new laboratory methods.

In Germany Johannes Müller was the first to establish definite laws relating to a "specific energy of the senses" that makes them respond in certain ways to different kinds of stimuli. *Helmholtz* measured the velocity of nerve messages in 1851, and *Gustav Fechner* (1801–1887) founded the science of psychophysics, which regards material phenomena as physical manifestations of an underlying spiritual reality. The credit for having brought together the many isolated data of experimental psychology to form a consistent scientific system belongs to Fechner's successor in the University of Leipzig, the German philosopher and psychologist *Wilhelm Wundt* (1832–1920), who, in 1879, founded the first psychological laboratory.

Sociology and Social Science. Just as psychology had formerly been treated as a branch of theoretical and practical philosophy, so too had sociology. The works of Plato and Aristotle, of the leading medieval schoolmen, and of many philosophers of the postmedieval centuries abound in sociological speculation. But it was not until the nineteenth century that the attempt was made to convert sociology into an empirical and inductive science.

Sociology in the form of a "social physics" was first developed by the French philosopher *Auguste Comte* (1798–1857). Comte's so-called "positivistic" system of social science was philosophically broadened by *Herbert Spencer* (1820–1903), an English engineer, journalist, and scholar, who in his *System of Synthetic Philosophy* made social science part of a naturalistic and utilitaristic metaphysics.

Comte's endeavor to build up an integral system of social science based on a system of "positive philosophy" was motivated by the breakdown of the *ancien régime* and of the Empire of Napoleon on the one hand, and by his admiration for the great achievements of the natural sciences on the other. In Comte's opinion the past was irrevocably dead, and the future was uncertain. To avoid growing confusion and disintegration of thought and culture he regarded it as necessary to create a new social order anchored in a new system of thought. To bring this about he first of all proclaimed sociology as the standard science, displacing metaphysics, mathematics, and physics, which at various times had held that exalted position.

Comte's "law of the three states" contended that the human mind of necessity passes successively through a theological and a metaphysical phase, to arrive in the end at the mature and "positive" knowledge of the age of science. This third and final state, he claimed, was reached in the nineteenth century, when the inquiry into causes was rendered meaningless and the description and explanation of facts became all important. The modern social scientist is called upon to establish definite laws that are derived from the observation of social facts and that may be used to create a new and better social order. In short, Comte demanded that social science be made the servant of social needs and a tool for the promotion of human happiness and contentment.

It is interesting to note that in order to complete his system Comte felt compelled by the implications of his own thought to streamline the concept of science by arbitrarily excluding all those sciences that would not fit into his theoretical scheme. Then it seemed necessary to formulate a dogmatic "scientism" that had all the earmarks of a substitute religion, including an organized clergy, a supreme object of cultic worship ("Humanity"), and the solemn excommunication of all dissenters — Catholics, Protestants, and Deists alike. "In the name of the Past and of the Future, the servants of Humanity . . . come forward to claim . . . the general leadership of this world. Their object is to constitute a real Providence in all departments — moral, intellectual, and material" (*Catechism of Positivism;* trans. by R. Congreve, London, 1858; Preface, p. 19). Thus, as Etienne Gilson aptly remarks, "the science of sociology gave rise to sociolatry, with love as the principle, order as the basis, and progress as the end" (*The Unity of Philosophical Experience;* Scribner's, New York, 1937, p. 266).

C. *CULTURAL TRENDS*

The Arts. What appeared evident from the analyses of the artistic styles of the past remains true also in the nineteenth century: artistic expression depends in its form and subject matter to a large extent on the spirit of the age, its religious, philosophical, social, and economic standards and forces. The Baroque Age (cf. pp. 330–354) had witnessed a final demonstration of the formative cultural power of the Church and its princes, a power which it was forced to share with the splendor-loving secular rulers. In the nineteenth century, however, Church and State have to yield their leadership in the arts to the "third estate," the *bourgeois* class. The rise, in turn, of the "fourth estate," the proletariat, after the middle of the century exerts a gradually increasing influence on aesthetic concepts and on artistic creation. In the twentieth century and especially after the upheavals of World War I and the subsequent revolution the collectivist tendencies of society are clearly reflected in both the plastic and literary arts.

a) Art in the Service of the State. Napoleon I in France and King Louis I of Bavaria (1825–1848) were the last secular princes in Europe who pressed the arts into the service of the State and carried on a systematic dynastic art policy on a grand scale. Monumental works of architecture in Munich, among them churches, palaces, and other public and private buildings (Ludwigskirche, Palais Wittelsbach, Feldherrnhalle, Propyläen, the state university and library, etc.) bore witness to Louis' initiative and excellent taste.* The noble neo-classical style of these buildings, which was most conspicuous in the stately structures flanking the Ludwigstrasse and in the palatial beauty of the architectural monuments enclosing the spacious *Königsplatz* (Royal Square), gave Munich its distinguishing mark. By the time the king's grandson, Louis II (1864–1886), succeeded to the throne of Bavaria the vitality of neo-classicism was exhausted, and the king's extravagant taste delighted in a pseudoromantic revival of the palace style of the eighteenth century. In the German North the well-intentioned attempt of Emperor William II (1888–1918, cf. p. 617 sqq.) to promote and direct the arts in his realm by his personal protectorship revealed in its dismal failure the extent to which the truly creative artistic forces had become estranged from the ideals of the ruling dynasty.

b) Museum, "Kunstverein," and Academy. With the waning significance of Church, State, and nobility as standard-bearers of artistic fashions, the individual artists found themselves deprived of their traditional financial protectors and employers. To establish a closer contact between the artists and the representatives of the new *bourgeoisie* and in order to spread aesthetic education among the members of the now leading social groups, the nineteenth century gave new prominence to the internationally established "art museums" and created a new type of art forum in the *Kunstverein* (art association).

The "museum" owes its origin to the princely collectors of Renaissance and Baroque (cf. p. 330 sqq.). In 1793 the French "National Convent" created the first modern type of a national museum by making the treasures of the Louvre accessible to the public. In Germany the demand for the creation of a national center that was to house the art treasures of the past led to the foundation of the Germanic Museum in Nuremberg in 1852 and of the Berlin National Gallery in the seventies of the nineteenth century. Art collection and art appreciation were linked by *Alfred Lichtwark* (1852–1914) who as director of the Hamburg art gallery succeeded in devising a systematic educational program that included serial lectures, conducted gallery tours, and periodically changing exhibits of art works of the past and present. Lichtwark's pedagogic ideas were adopted by the directors of other municipal museums in Germany and met with the liveliest response in the artistic and educational circles of the United States.

While the art museum was primarily engaged in the preservation and presentation of the values and documents of the past, it became the special concern of the *Kunstverein* to encourage the activity of living artists, to

---

* Most of these buildings were destroyed during World War II.

cultivate contemporary art, and to educate the public for its appreciation. The earliest of these German art associations was founded in Karlsruhe (Baden) in 1818. In 1932 they numbered well over one hundred and exercised a power that has unfortunately worked as often to the detriment as to the advantage of art and artists. Especially after the middle of the nineteenth century the *Kunstverein* came to represent more and more the taste and temper of a *bourgeoisie* which intolerantly took its stand against anything that would not submit to its set of aesthetic rules and conventions. Thus many an artist of strong-willed and extraordinary genius found himself ostracized by commercial or artistic cliques and condemned to a solitary struggle against the current of organized public opinion, cut off as it were from those social forces that might have vitalized his artistic style. The lack of such fruitful give-and-take between artist and society was largely responsible for the rise of successive movements and fads that characterized the late nineteenth and early twentieth century, the creations of eccentric minds which, having lost their social and moral bearings, indulged in frantic and often sterile experimentation.

Similar critical reservations apply to the third of the institutions by means of which the nineteenth century had hoped to bring about a revival of the arts and crafts — the Academy. When the first German art academies were founded in the seventeenth and eighteenth centuries, they fulfilled a vital function in supplying the princely employers with a sufficient number of uniformly trained and thoroughly qualified artists and craftsmen.* But with the breakdown of the *ancien régime,* its social ideals and their stylistic manifestation in the arts, the academies lost their *raison d'être,* and the greatest of modern artists actually grew up and achieved their pre-eminence in opposition to and in perpetual struggle with the conventional rules of the academies. This is as much true of the "Nazarenes" (cf. p. 491) and their romantic contemporaries of the early nineteenth century as of the impressionists (cf. p. 715 sq.) in its closing decades. The State-supported academies turned out an overplus of technically well-trained but mediocre artists, the majority of whom were left to shift for themselves, with little chance of steady employment, an artistic proletariat that was forced to commercialize its talents or to submerge in an irresponsible "bohemianism."

National and international "art exhibitions" were held originally in connection with the academies, in order to give a public accounting of the progress of artistic endeavor and to foster more intimate relations between artists and connoisseurs. *Kunstvereine* as well as individual art dealers played a prominent part in organizing such art exhibits all over Germany, and at the end of the nineteenth century permanent "exhibition palaces" were erected in several German cities to provide a dignified setting and a sort of social center for the artists and an art-loving public.

---

* The Academy of Vienna was founded in 1694, that of Berlin in 1764. In 1932 the German academies numbered 24, including several industrial schools for applied arts and crafts.

An important innovation in the methods of art education was achieved in the second half of the nineteenth century. "Master studios" (*Meister-ateliers*) were created for especially talented art students and separate art schools were established for different branches of craftsmanship, such as the arts of goldsmithing (Hanau), lacemaking (Plauen), book printing (Leipzig), and so forth.

The so-called "secessions" of the end of the nineteenth century (*Münche-ner Sezession,* 1892; *Berliner Sezession,* 1893) were associations of artists who were resolved to fight collectively for their progressive ideas, using commercial organization and periodical exhibitions as major instruments to achieve their goal. But as the members of the original "secessions" grew old, their artistic style became ossified, and they found themselves challenged by new "secessions" of the younger generation, whose right to live and work in accordance with the changing spirit of the age they had intolerantly denied.

c) *Architecture.* It has been pointed out that German Romanticism (cf. p. 487 sqq.) was artistically creative chiefly in the arts of painting and music, but on the whole unproductive in architecture and sculpture. This statement may be enlarged so as to include much of the development of these arts throughout the nineteenth century. The abdication of Church and State as protectors of the arts made it difficult for architecture in particular to achieve that social and communal expressiveness that is of its very essence. While the more personal arts of sculpture and painting found ways and means to convey a vital message, architecture remained chiefly eclectic and retrospective, dabbling in various styles of the past, without being able to present an integrated artistic interpretation of the cultural forces of the present.

The historical reception of past architectural styles began with the pseudoromantic "Gothic revival." In the latter part of the eighteenth century the English nobility began sentimentally to appreciate the hitherto ignored but still extant monuments of medieval Gothic architecture. The "Gothic revival" in England went hand in hand with the development of the new "English" style of garden architecture. Irregular design and intimate natural charm supplanted the rigid formality of the representative gardens of Renaissance, Baroque, and Rococo and remained in all European countries the prevailing style of landscape gardening to the present day.

With the exception of *Leo von Klenze* (cf. p. 400) even the leading neo-classical architects of Germany submitted to a smaller or larger degree to the influence of the "Gothic revival." To the very end of the nineteenth century neo-Gothic forms of building can be traced in all parts of Germany. The chief impetus for the renewed preoccupation with German Gothic architecture was provided by the German romanticists' intense interest in medieval forms of life and culture. Long after German Romanticism as such had died down the medievalist tendency in architecture held sway over much of the building activity in German lands.

The Cathedral in Cologne

Interior of Cologne Cathedral

A culturally significant by-product of the "Gothic revival" in Germany was the restoration of medieval monuments of ecclesiastic and secular architecture. Between 1842 and 1880 the great Cathedral of Cologne, which had come down from the Middle Ages as a monumental fragment, was completed in accordance with the original plans, and the days of its consecration were celebrated as symbolizing the unity of the reborn German empire (1880). The restoration of the Cathedrals of Bamberg and Spires (Speyer) and Ratisbon (Regensburg) was carried out under the protectorate of King Louis I of Bavaria. Besides the churches a large number of medieval castles, among them the Wartburg and the *Heidelberger Schloss,* owed their total or partial restoration to the "Gothic revival."

By far the most important of the historical-minded German architects of the nineteenth century was *Gottfried Semper* (1803-1879), a native of Hamburg. As artist and scholar he exemplifies the dangers that threaten a creative genius in an age of cumulative historical and technical knowledge. Semper was fully aware of the fact that an overdose of theoretical knowledge hampered his best efforts, depriving him of the spontaneity of his artistic vision and making him an imitator of the past rather than a molder of the present. In his critical masterpiece on *Style** he followed the materialistic trend of the age in relating the origins and transformations of art forms to the contingencies of technical and material possibilities and requirements. He had studied the monuments of antiquity and of Renaissance and Baroque in Italy and France, and among the several styles from which his historically trained sense drew inspiration he gave decided preference to the Renaissance. His fruitful building activity in Dresden, which included the construction of the Opera House and the Palais Oppenheim, was cut short by his involvement in the May revolts of 1849. But his years of exile in Paris and London gave him a welcome opportunity to continue his theoretical studies. At the behest of Queen Victoria's husband, the Prince Consort Albert of Saxe-Coburg-Gotha, Semper served as one of the chief advisers in preparing the London International Exposition of 1851 and in designing the plans for the South Kensington Museum. In Switzerland he was commissioned with the construction of the Polytechnical Institute and the observatory in Zurich and of the city hall in Winterthur. In 1871 he was called to Vienna to assume the post of director of building for the *Burgtheater* and the Imperial Museums of Art History and Natural History, together with the Viennese architect *Karl von Hasenauer.* Semper gave evidence of his clear realization of the problematic situation of architecture in his own epoch when he wrote in 1854: "Our architecture is without originality and has lost its pre-eminence among the arts. It will recover it only when modern architects begin to give more attention to the present state of our industrial arts. The impulse for such a happy change will come from the handicrafts."

d) *Art and Technology.* The possibilities of a "functional" artistic style

---

* *Der Stil in den technischen und tektonischen Künsten,* 2 vols. (Munich, 1860-1863).

that would have suited the new building materials (iron, steel, concrete) and construction methods of the machine age were not recognized by the generation of artists who were contemporaries of the Industrial Revolution. Their love for the decorative design of historically sanctioned art forms prompted them to adorn the architectural façades and the interiors of factory buildings, industrial plants, and railroad depots indiscriminately with meaningless and wholly inappropriate ornamentation. However, the fanciful yet outmoded decorations that were thus pasted on the structural frame satisfied the luxurious but uncultivated taste of the ruling bourgeois plutocracy.

The only positive and direct influence of the new techniques of the machine age on artistic creation is recognizable in the revival of the ancient German craft of bronze casting, a revival that was again due to the initiative of King Louis I of Bavaria. The Munich Foundry produced a large number of sculptural monuments of international fame, among which the symbolic colossal statue of the "Bavaria" ranks foremost. It was the work of *Ludwig Schwanthaler* (1802–1848), the descendant of an old Bavarian family of wood carvers, who completed this unique masterpiece after six years of unremitting labor. *Ferdinand Miller* (1813–1887), the director and ultimate owner of the Munich Foundry, was likewise the heir of several generations of skilled craftsmen. He succeeded in combining the new industrial methods with the co-operative spirit of the medieval craft guilds and thus fulfilled Gottfried Semper's demand of a reunion of art and handicraft.

e) Painting. Whereas architecture and sculpture during the greater part of the nineteenth century remained attached to styles of the past and therefore lacked true originality, the art of painting became the medium of expression for several representative geniuses of the age of liberal individualism and nineteenth-century realism.

In the so-called "Düsseldorf" school the romantic style of historical painting in the "Nazarene" manner (cf. p. 491) lived on as a mere convention, until the Rhinelander *Alfred Rethel* (1816–1851) gave it a new meaning and a strikingly original and realistic note. The new style, combining the indigenous psychological qualities of Albrecht Dürer's graphic art with the figural composition of the Italian Renaissance, became first apparent in Rethel's illustrations of the *Lay of the Nibelungs* and achieved its greatest triumphs in the monumental fresco paintings of the city hall in Aix-la-Chapelle (Aachen). Before Rethel's brilliant mind was destroyed by the ravages of an incurable brain disease he had completed his *Dance of Death*. This realistic sequence of woodcuts is a dramatically moving interpretation of the revolutionary tendencies of his age, and an accomplishment that fully holds its own when compared with Holbein's treatment of an identical theme (cf. p. 198). Rethel's conservatism viewed the revolution of 1848 as a personal and national tragedy brought about by political demagogues. The lamentations and exhortations of his woodcuts move

Dance of Death, by Alfred Rethel

Three Women in Church, by Wilhelm Leibl

inexorably to a grand finale: the pathetic figure of Death, crowned with a laurel wreath, his banner unfurled, mounting the top of the barricades.

The most representative realistic painter of Germany in the nineteenth century, however, is *Adolf von Menzel* (1815–1905), a native of Silesia but domiciled in Berlin from boyhood on. He grew up in the forced and unnatural calm of the *Vormärz* (cf. p. 461 sqq.) and experienced the revolution of 1848 as a rough but wholesome awakening from the sleep of philistinism. From his earliest to his latest works he recognized in nature his unfailing guide, and while he never relinquished entirely the romantic inclinations of his youth, he willingly accepted the challenge of the machine age and was one of the first to discover aesthetic values in its sober and matter-of-fact approach to reality.

Menzel was equally proficient in the techniques of lithography and oil painting, and his sympathetic pictorial interpretation of the age of Frederick the Great (cf. p. 316 sqq.), his personality, his court, and his army, striking a timely note of nationalism and patriotism, endeared him to the German people and its rulers alike. Although dividing his attention between the past and the present, he remained ever alert in anticipation of new goals. His long life extended well into the period of impressionistic *plein-air* painting (cf. p. 715 sq.), and early in his artistic career he developed a luminous brilliance of coloristic pattern and composition that was impressionistic in everything but name.

Menzel's greatness towered far above the work of a host of painters of historical subjects and battle scenes, glorifying the military exploits of the German armies and their leaders. The most popular among these politically minded artists was *Anton von Werner* (1843–1915), whose honest but arid naturalism gave a reliable documentary account of Prussia's more recent political and military triumphs. As director of the Berlin Academy, Werner did his best to harness the talents of the younger generation of painters. The limitations of his own aesthetic concepts are evidenced by the fact that he seriously doubted whether the art of painting would be able to compete with the newly developed technique of photography.

In the second half of the nineteenth century Munich began to take the lead in painting as in the other arts. Here *Karl von Piloty* (1826–1886) continued the tradition of Cornelius and Kaulbach in historical paintings whose subject matter was taken chiefly from the Roman and German past. One of his pupils, *Gabriel Max* (1840–1915), a talented colorist and an adherent of spiritism, softened Piloty's naturalism by a touch of reflective sentiment. Another pupil, *Franz Defregger* (1835–1921), the son of a Tyrolese peasant, depicted with deft accuracy and a cultivated sense of form the natural beauty of his homeland and genrelike episodes of his countrymen's struggle for liberation from French oppression (cf. p. 444).

The graphic arts are indebted to *Wilhelm Busch* (1832–1908) and *Adolf Oberländer* (1845–1923), both of whom were gifted humorists and achieved great popularity as illustrators and clever cartoonists. Busch's humor, saturated with a generous dose of Schopenhauer's pessimism, found pointed expression in the textual frames with which he surrounded his graphic narratives and in which he satirized and castigated human weaknesses. His illustrated character sketches, composed in the form of serial sequences and mostly published in the comic weekly *Fliegende Blätter* and in the *Münchener Bilderbogen* (*Max und Moritz, Die fromme Helene, Maler Klecksel,* etc.), became popular classics and served as models for the "comic strips" of American newspapers.

Classicism in painting, which had produced only mediocre talents at the end of the eighteenth century, experienced a revival of more enduring significance in the work of some of the most promising artists of the nineteenth century. *Anselm Feuerbach* (1829–1880) was the grandson of the famous jurist Paul Anselm von Feuerbach, the creator of the criminal law code of Bavaria (1813); his father was an outstanding classical archaeologist, and his uncle the Young Hegelian philosopher Ludwig Feuerbach (cf. p. 556 sq.). By inheritance he was an aristocrat who developed a classical style of painting that bore his personal stamp, although he had been influenced successively by nineteenth-century French realism (Couture, Courbet) and by Venetian, Florentine, and Roman Renaissance and Baroque. In Rome he met Nanna Risi, who became his wife and inspired the ripe classical beauty of some of his masterly portraits (*Medea, Iphigenia,* etc.). When Nanna left him, both his life and his art suffered an irretrievable loss, and the grayish hues of his coloring assumed an ever increasing air of cool detachment and quiet resignation.

The second great master of the classical form in the second half of the nineteenth century was *Hans von Marées* (1837–1887), a native of the Rhineland, whose nobility of character is reflected in the placid beauty and flawless integrity of his works. Aided by the unfaltering devotion of his friend *Conrad Fiedler* (1841–1895), the famous art critic whose understanding and generosity compensated Marées for the indifference or hostility of his contemporaries, he followed the dictates of his artistic conscience with undeviating determination and succeeded in freeing his art from the shackles of a sterile historicism. On his travels in Spain, France, Holland, and Italy Marées experienced the influence of the great masters of the past without ever losing the sturdy independence of his own artistic idiom. The monumental frescoes in the Library of the International Zoological Station in Naples (1873), depicting in the timeless frame of the southern landscape the everlasting vitality of the Neapolitan fishermen and farmers, marked the crowning achievement of Marées' life.

Romantic painting, which had flourished early in the nineteenth century (cf. p. 487 sqq.), likewise came to life again in its second half. In the Swiss master *Arnold Böcklin* (1827–1901) the melodious musicality and brooding symbolism of German thought appeared clothed in the garb of romantic and historically inspired allegory. Endowed with the poet's vision and imagination, Böcklin discovered in nature the many secret voices that bespeak the riddle of life and death and reveal their magic charm in myths and legends. In most of his works the moods of nature appear symbolically condensed in human forms, and the luminosity of local colors is ingeniously used to accentuate the mysterious and phantastic aspects of nature and human life. Böcklin's landscapes and figures are as timeless as those of Marées but more unreal, creations of dream and fancy, even though on the surface the scenery presents reminiscences of the master's beloved Italy. With the greatest German painters of the past Böcklin shares the conspicuously German genius for descriptive illustration and metaphysical interpretation.

A romantic painter of a different type was the Austrian *Hans Makart* (1840–1884), a pupil of Piloty and a protégé of Emperor Francis Joseph. His works reflect his own exuberant temper and extravagant taste as well as the immoderate craving for spectacular display that was characteristic of a Germany thrown off her spiritual balance by the dazzling prospects of a newly acquired political power and economic abundance. The romantic fireworks of Makart's huge historic tableaux, lacking the formal restraint of a disciplined and cultured mind, issued from the frenzy of an aimless enthusiasm. The artist's autointoxication was nourished by the universal acclamation of his public, whose admiration found peculiar forms of expression in the creation of "Makart hats," "Makart bouquets," and so forth.

In an age of science and technology both classicistic and romantic leanings appear out of tune with the basic cultural trends. They were largely born of the isolation, the protest, or the maladjustment of individual artists whose sensitivity, shrinking from the harsh factualness of the present, sought refuge in the shelter of a more or less remote past. Those artists, therefore, who more accurately represented the spirit of the second half of the nineteenth century were masters of realistic observation and factual description. They had nothing but scorn for the dreams and historic revelries of the classical and romantic narrators in the pictorial arts, and they proudly proclaimed themselves as the disciples of nature and life.

One of the first and by far the greatest of these modern German "realists" in the art of painting was *Wilhelm Leibl* (1844–1900), born in Cologne but of Bavarian ancestry, who bade farewell to the fashions of historical retrospection and made man and nature the objects of his aesthetic devotion. In the simple forms of everyday life he discovered a beauty that was entirely of the earth and a spirituality that was inherent in nature itself. "If we paint man as he is," he wrote, "his soul is included as a matter of course." Originally destined to become a mechanical engineer, Leibl soon turned to painting and at the age of twenty entered the Munich Academy. When he found out that his teachers had nothing to offer that he regarded as of vital importance, and that he was on strange soil in the Bohemian atmosphere of the studios, he retired to the Bavarian countryside, pursuing his artistic goals with the singular determination of the old masters. The *Three Women in Church,* his most popular painting, is also his best. It is the work of an artist whose genius derived its enduring greatness from the fact that it was in love with life. Despite his opposition to the Academy and his disinclination to teach, the style of his paintings was eloquent and suggestive enough to attract a number of talented pupils and to give rise to a realistic school of modern German painting.

Literature. The political, social, and economic transformations of the nineteenth century found a more direct response in German literature than in the plastic and pictorial arts. After the "July Revolution" of 1830 (cf. p. 525 sq.) had temporarily strengthened the increasing opposition to literary romanticism, the new wave of political reaction that followed the political uprisings silenced the leaders of liberal thought and gave rise to a mood of pessimism and melancholy resignation. It was the time when Schopenhauer's philosophy (cf. p. 505 sq.) was at last given an enthusiastic reception.

The "March Revolution" of 1848 (cf. p. 527 sq.), marking the end of the reactionary period of the *Vormärz,* brought definitely to the fore the younger generation of writers and poets, whose political and social radicalism was resolutely bent on the destruction of the ideological heritage of German Classicism and Romanticism. All humanistic emphasis on the values of personality was henceforth overshadowed by the ideas of democratic liberation that had been imported from France, England, and the United States, above all the idea of social equality and the demand for political representation and the active participation of the masses in national affairs. In the name of the people and their liberties, literature was drawn from its pedestal. The cult of personality was denounced as a sort of idolatry, and the poet was required to serve the political and social needs of the day and the hour.

a) *"Young Germany."* The dictatorship of the *Zeitgeist* was openly proclaimed by the members of a literary clique united by the conviction that the technical advances of the machine age ascertained a progressive satisfaction of all human and social needs and that it was the duty of artists and writers to play their part in bringing about the corresponding political and social changes. Whoever excluded himself from this collective effort was regarded as a sterile aesthete or an antisocial reactionary. Thus the movement known as "Young Germany" laid down the rules for German writers and readers, and the predominant influence of its members as publicists and critics condemned to tragic isolation some of the greatest literary talents of the age.

The intellectual leaders of "Young Germany" were Löw Baruch, who adopted the pen name *Ludwig Börne* (1786–1837) and *Heinrich Heine* (1799–1856),[*] both of German-Jewish ancestry and both embracing Protestantism for reasons of expediency. Both had smarted under the stigma that attached to their race, and Börne in particular worked incessantly for

---

[*] Other representatives of "Young Germany" were *Laube, Gutzkow,* and *Wienbarg;* the latter, in his *Aesthetische Feldzüge* (1834), coined the name "Young Germany," which was then applied to the entire movement. A decree of the *Bundesrat* of 1835 banned the writings of all the members of the group.

the "emancipation" of the Jews, demanding that they be given full equality of civic rights and complete freedom in choosing their calling.*

Börne, Heine, and their companions, regarding themselves as the authentic spokesmen of the *Zeitgeist,* used the weapons of wit, irony, and scathing satire to arouse their contemporaries and to launch a concerted attack on everything that seemed to retard the march of progress. They were masters in the art of "debunking," but their stylistic finesse and journalistic adroitness exhausted itself in defamation and negation, and their massive materialism and cold intellectualism marred even their best intentions and made them skeptics and cynics against their will. They disdained a world that did not measure up to their ideas and they scoffed at ideals because they despaired of their realization. A good deal of their vaunting melancholy was an empty show and self-parody, and much of their "Byronism" was a mixture of clever play acting and vain pretense. When the novelist *Karl Immermann* (1796–1840) portrayed in his *Baron Münchhausen* (1838) the great master of lying, he created a symbol that exposed the moral instability and rootlessness of an entire generation which had succumbed too readily to the spell of "Young Germany." Immermann's *Münchhausen* novel embodies two distinct styles, the one indicative of the frivolity of the *Zeitgeist,* the other (condensed in the inserted village epic *Der Oberhof*) presenting as an utter contrast a world of lasting values, a saga of the "immortal folk" (*unsterbliches Volk*), firmly rooted in its maternal soil.

As a poet *Heine* towers far above the rest of the Young German writers. And yet Eichendorff's (cf. p. 478 sq.) severe criticism of some typical aspects of the movement applies also to Heine: "Some of them have shielded themselves with the sombre mask of Lord Byron. But Byron's melancholy discordance was real and therefore capable of producing a tragic effect, whereas these poets childishly dissect themselves or rather allow themselves to be dismembered by the imaginary monsters of their own fancy, so that an astonished public may see them bleed to death in picturesque poses. . . ."

Heine was born in the Rhenish city of Düsseldorf. Having spent several years as an apprentice in the business of a wealthy uncle in Hamburg, he subsequently studied law at the University of Göttingen. He traveled for some time in Germany, England, and Italy, and finally settled down in Paris, attracted by the glitter of Bohemian life and the promises of the French revolution of 1830. He lived on the proceeds of his journalistic writings and on a pension granted him by the French government. His marriage to Eugenie (Mathilde) Mirat turned out a failure and became a source of mental torture and self-accusation. In 1847 Heine was afflicted with a progressive spinal disease which made the nine remaining years of his life a prolonged agony. The gloom of these years of suffering was somewhat brightened by his love for Elise Krinitz (Camilla Senden, the *"Mouche"*),

---

* The Jews were granted equality of civic rights in France in 1791, in Prussia in 1812, in the rest of Germany between 1848 and 1869, in England in 1847, in Italy in 1858.

who appeared to the ailing poet as an angel of mercy and who stayed with him through the darkest hours. His deadly disease caused his body to die literally limb by limb.

Heine's most famous collection of lyrics, the *Book of Songs* (*Buch der Lieder*, 1827), was chiefly inspired by his unrequited love for his uncle's daughter Amalie. The natural rhythm and melodic charm of this early poetry was marred only by the author's ever watchful and wistful intellect, which maliciously delighted in turning its mockery and bitter satire against his own self and against the creations of his love and devotion. Many of the poems contained in the *Book of Songs* and in several collections of later date reveal Heine's indebtedness to the Romantic School (cf. p. 470 sqq.). Some of them achieved the simplicity and depth of folk poetry (*Die Lorelei*), while others owe their fame to the fact that they served as texts for some of the greatest of German song composers (Schubert, Schumann, Mendelssohn). The sincerest and artistically most mature poems are contained in the collection *Romanzero* (1853), in which Heine paid his debt of gratitude to Elise Krinitz. These last poems speak at times with the immediacy and passionate fervor of a great confession, revealing in tragic undertones a self-knowledge ripened by suffering and rising to the grand style of biblical lamentation.

Heine's prose* mastered all the nuances of wit and esprit, from subtle irony to bitter sarcasm, combining the plastic imagery of the poet with the sparkling lightness and versatility of the born journalist, but lacking the positive metaphysical qualifications of the genuine satirist.

In December, 1834, while in Paris, Heine wrote a series of essays on the *History of Religion and Philosophy in Germany*. In a penetrating analysis of the philosophy of Kant and his followers the author arrived at the conclusion that "transcendental idealism" constituted a revolution in the realm of thought which was bound to make itself felt in the arena of political action. In almost prophetic words he predicted a sequence of events that would logically follow from the adoption of the philosophical premises of Kant, Fichte, Hegel, and Schelling: "There will be followers of Kant," he wrote at the end of the third book, "who will forsake piety and reverence even in the world of phenomena. Pitilessly they will ransack the foundations of Europe. . . . Followers of Fichte will appear on the scene in full armor. The fanaticism of their will-power can be checked neither by fear nor by selfishness, for like the early Christians they live in a world of the spirit and defy matter. . . . But more horrible than all these will be the 'nature philosophers.' . . . They will re-establish contact with the telluric forces of nature, conjuring up the satanic powers of old-Germanic pantheism. Within their breast there will come to life a war-lust . . . which does not wish to

---

* Heine's major prose works include the *Reisebilder* (*Travel Pictures*, especially *Die Harzreise*, 1826) and *Die romantische Schule* (*The Romantic School*, but with antiromantic tendency); outstanding among his satires are *Atta Troll* (1843) and *Deutschland, ein Wintermärchen* (*Germany: A Winter's Fairy Tale*, 1844).

fight in order to destroy nor in order to vanquish, but which makes fighting an end in itself. . . . If the time should ever come when the Christian Cross will break down, then the savagery of the ancient warriors will reappear . . . ; the ancient gods of stone will rise from their graves. . . . Thor with his hammer will rise and destroy the Gothic cathedrals. We must expect the same revolution in the world of phenomena that we have witnessed in the realm of the spirit. Thought precedes action as lightning precedes thunder. . . . And when you hear it crash as it has never crashed before in the history of the world, then you will know that the German thunder has reached its mark. There will be such a commotion that the eagles will drop dead to the ground, and the lions in the distant deserts of Africa will put their tails between their legs and withdraw to their royal dens. Germany will then offer a spectacle which will make the great French Revolution appear as a harmless idyl. . . ."

b) *Literary Neo-Classicism.* In literature as in painting the victory of realism was preceded by a brief revival of classicism that was intended as a protest against the sentimentalities of a false romanticism on the one hand and against the uncouth informality of the Young Germans on the other. As painters, sculptors, and architects had been attracted to the court of King Louis I of Bavaria, so poets, scholars, and writers gathered at the court of his successor, Maximilian II (1848–1864). The members of the royal "Symposium," convening at regular intervals in the presence of the king, were united in their conviction that smoothness of form and purity of verse were more important than intensity of feeling or, generally speaking, vitality of content. The prose and verse compositions of the two leading neo-classicists of Munich, *Emanuel Geibel* (1815–1884) and *Paul Heyse* (1830–1914), suffered accordingly from defects which resulted from an aesthetic ideal that was unrelated to life: though sometimes rich in formal beauty, their works were cool and academic, carefully excluding all shrill discords and everything that was disorderly or in any way repugnant to sensitive minds.

c) *Poetic Realism.* The generation of the Industrial Revolution, of the early machine age, and of the great advances in the sciences was most adequately represented by a literature that was neither romantic and otherworldly nor in the service of social polemics and political propaganda but rather concerned with the realistic observation and description of life in all its aspects. The authors who were thus the spokesmen of the *Zeitgeist* in a more profound sense than the Young Germans may therefore best be characterized as "poetic realists." They were realists in that they were interested in giving an unvarnished account of contemporary life, and they were poets in that they knew how to discriminate between the essential and the trivial, how to select and how to condense, so as to impart to their works both the breath of reality and the shimmer of poetry.

Annette von Droste-Hülshoff (1797–1848), the first of the great nineteenth-century realists in Germany and one of the greatest poetesses of modern times, was a descendant of ancient Westphalian aristocracy. Until 1840 she lived mostly on the secluded estates of her family, but then she moved southward to spend the last eight years of her life in the old castle of Meersburg on the shores of Lake Constance. The unusual qualities of her poetry derive from an equally unusual personality, which was dominated by two steadying influences, the Catholic faith of her ancestors and the austere moorland scenery of her native Westphalia. Calling upon a masculine will to overcome the frail femininity of her physical constitution, she found in religion and nature the sources of her strength of character and of the clarity of her literary form. Her senses were wide awake, registering acutely the wonders of creation and experiencing cosmic order and fruitful abundance in its greatest and smallest manifestations. Her poetic vision penetrated through the physical contours of individuals, objects, and scenes, giving voice, shape, and atmosphere to the hidden creative forces of nature.

Annette von Droste's writings were true to herself, to her spiritual heritage, and to the traditions and local customs of her homeland. She is at her best in her nature poetry and in her verse epics and historical ballads, whose setting suggests the brooding melancholy and somber beauty of the Westphalian heath. Her cycle of religious poems entitled *Das geistliche Jahr* (*The Spiritual Year*), comparable to John Keble's (1792–1866) *Christian Year,* provides poetic paraphrases of the Sunday and feast-day Gospels (*Pericopes*) of the ecclesiastical year. In her village novelette, *Die Judenbuche* (*The Jew's Beech Tree*), she makes Nature herself the avenger of a secretly committed crime and therewith the guardian of moral law and the restorer of the violated cosmic order.

The Silesian *Gustav Freytag* (1816–1895), in his lengthy and ambitious historical novels, was a historian in disguise, like some of the painters of the same period. In *Soll und Haben* (Debet and Credit), however, he made use of his intimate acquaintance with contemporary social and economic trends in presenting a vivid realistic picture of the life of the commercial middle class. In his exuberant comedy *Die Journalisten* he portrays with kindly humor the representatives of the daily press and satirizes the methods of politicians and party bosses. Freytag's most endearing qualities live on in his *Bilder aus der deutschen Vergangenheit* (*Pictures From the German Past*), which in scope and literary form still ranks high among the standard works on German cultural history.

In *Adalbert Stifter* (1805–1868) the genius of Austria made one of its ripest contributions to German literature. Temporarily forgotten or unappreciated, this great novelist was rediscovered by Friedrich Nietzsche (cf. p. 695 sq.), who found in Stifter's works "a world of beauty" and who counted the novel *Nachsommer* (*Mellow Autumn*) among his favorite books.

In Stifter's life and work Austrian Catholicism and German Classical Idealism (cf. Chap. 12) fused. He was instructed in his early youth by monks of the Benedictine Order, and the sense of proportion and harmony embodied in the Benedictine pattern of life and thought became one of the precious assets of Stifter's literary art. His most admired models among modern German authors were Goethe, Herder, and Jean Paul. Contentment, however, he found neither in classical grandeur nor in romantic exuberance, but only in quiet communication with nature, in the great stillness that was born in him when he contemplated the humble forms of minerals, plants, and animals. He looked at nature with the sentiment of a religious devotee and with the eyes of an artist, thus discovering in its varying shapes and nuances "a visible incarnation of the Godhead."

Stifter was a great "poetic" realist, precisely because he was more interested in the moral norm incarnate in reality than in a mere counterfeit or literary double of life. His art was strong enough not to be affected by the innate pedagogical bent of his mind. The characters of his two long novels and of his many short stories* are symbols of a divinely consecrated life and of a human destiny that is shaped by the incentives of will and reason. God's providence extends throughout the universe in all directions, through past, present, and future. God reveals Himself, His designs, and His judgments no less in nature than in history, and the portrayal of the past as much as the description of the present become thus symbolic images of eternal verities.

Realists of an entirely different temper were *Otto Ludwig* (1813–1865) and *Friedrich Hebbel* (1813–1863) who, like Richard Wagner, were born in the year of the "Battle of the Nations" and whose minds reflected an experience of reality that was not unified and harmonized but dialectically broken by the impact of conflicting ideas. It was for this reason that both authors regarded the *drama* as their most suitable means of expression, although Ludwig at first wavered between music and literature and attained to greater artistic perfection in his realistic novels than in his two completed dramas** and his many dramatic fragments.

In accordance with the epico-musical propensities of his talent it was Ludwig's ambition to create an artistic form and technique which in theory at least may be compared with Richard Wagner's idea of the "music drama" (cf. p. 493 sqq.). The epical style of his novels, especially of the tragic village romance *Zwischen Himmel und Erde* (*Between Heaven and Earth,* 1856), comes closest to a combination of the elements of narrative and musical composition. The detailed realistic description of environment and the profound and exhaustive character analyses unite to bring out the dual

---

* The novel *Der Nachsommer* (1857) has as its cultural background the period of the Austrian *Vormärz;* the historical novel *Witiko* tells of the national aspirations of southern Bohemia in the twelfth century. The most accomplished of his novelettes are contained in the two collections *Studien* (6 vols.) and *Bunte Steine* (2 vols.).

** *Der Erbförster* (*The Hereditary Forester*), "a forest tragedy" (1850), whose plot is laid in Ludwig's homeland of Thuringia, and *Die Makkabäer,* the dramatization of an episode recorded in some (partly apocryphal) Old Testament texts, dealing with the persecution of the Jews under King Antioch of Syria, and their successful struggle for liberation (second century B.C.).

characteristics of plasticity and musicality. Ludwig's knowledge of the human soul, its conflicts, its delusions and aberrations, makes him one of the masters of the psychological novel. The stress laid on the conditioning influences of environment and heredity makes him anticipate some of the pet theories of the foremost naturalistic writers of the later nineteenth century (Zola, Ibsen, Hauptmann, etc.). Ludwig's interest in psychology as well as his antagonism to Schiller's idealistic type of drama caused him to delve deeply into the nature of Shakespearean tragedy, and as the fruit of these endeavors he composed two volumes of *Shakespeare-Studien*.

Ludwig's pronounced dislike of Schiller was shared by *Friedrich Hebbel*. This strong-willed playwright and lyricist was born in the North German lowlands of Dithmarschen (Holstein). He had several characteristics in common with his sensitive and introspective contemporary from the Thuringian mountains: both writers were stimulated as well as handicapped by a pungent intellect which in Hebbel's case frequently got the better of his poetic impulses. Both were masters of psychological analysis, both viewed their characters as in part determined by environmental influences, and Hebbel as much as Ludwig was given to philosophical speculation and rationalistic reflection. To this extent their "dialectical" realism appeared to be nourished by identical sources, but aside from such general similarities in their mental constitution they were far apart in their artistic will, in their basic ideological tenets, and in their literary technique.

Friedrich Hebbel, though he wrote lyric and epic poems, never doubted that he was predestined to be a dramatist. He adhered to this conviction with a rare singleness of purpose, undismayed by obstacles, setbacks, and disappointments of many kinds, until at last he achieved not only a high degree of perfection as a playwright but public recognition and also personal happiness in his marital union with the Viennese actress Christine Enghaus.

The son of a poor stonemason, Hebbel went through dark years of privation and humiliating human bondage. Maturing gradually in combat with adversities, he finally attained a philosophy of life which was consistent enough in itself, but whose pessimism reflected the disheartening experiences of his apprenticeship as man and author.

A letter addressed to the seamstress Elise Lensing dates from the years of Hebbel's dismal struggle for his material and spiritual existence. He felt bound to her not by love but by a weighty debt of gratitude, for she was not only the mother of his child, but by her unrelenting toil and sacrifice she had made it possible for the playwright to remain loyal to his literary calling. "You ask me," Hebbel writes, "what deadly disease had me in its grip? My dear child, there is only one death and only one deadly disease, but it is impossible to give it a name. . . . It is the experience of the absolute contradiction in everything. . . . Whether there is a remedy for this disease, I know not, but this I know, that the physician who would cure me (whether he reside above the stars or in the center of my own self), must first of all cure the entire world. . . ."

Hebbel's "pan-tragic" philosophy of life, which seems condensed in this passage as in an outcry of despair and to which the author later on gave forceful speculative and dramatic expression, was clearly suggested by Hegel's dialectics (cf. p. 502 sqq.). The philosophical elaboration of the theory of Hebbel's *"Pantragismus"* we find in his *Diaries,* its dramatic exemplification in his tragedies.

The "pan-tragic" view holds that there is an incurable cleavage in all life, manifesting itself in such antithetical contradictions as life and death, time and eternity, natural inclination and moral obligation, male and female, individual claims and social demands. Thus an irreconcilable dualism cuts straight through the entire realm of creation, inevitably carrying in its wake the seeds of conflict and tragedy. The tragic fate of individuals therefore does not result from personal guilt but rather from some primordial metaphysical guilt inherent in the texture of life itself and necessitated by the very fact of individuation. "In God alone is harmony," says Hebbel, contending that by his individuation man has set up himself against the universe and its Creator. Individuation implies guilt and suffering, because by asserting his individuality the individual clashes of necessity with the laws and conventions of superindividual realities, such as the State, Society, and Religion. The greater the individual personality, the stronger will be his self-assertion or his revolt against the "sleep of the world," the more devastating his encounter with the inexorable decrees of universal laws, and the more tragic his ultimate self-destruction.

By proclaiming that the happiness of the individual must be sacrificed on the altar of the "world spirit," Hebbel reveals his indebtedness to Hegelian metaphysics. The individual, in pursuing his own ends, serves in reality only the higher ends of this Hegelian Deity: while the individual tragically succumbs, the "world spirit" marches victoriously on.

The dialectical method influences also Hebbel's choice of the historical theme and *milieu:* his heroes find themselves placed in the midst of waning and rising cultural forces, and they find themselves involved in and eventually crushed by the impact of the elements of change and progress upon the inert strength of tradition. These heroes and heroines are "supermen" and "superwomen" who by virtue of their keener vision and their greater ambition are foredoomed to personal tragedy. But they were also predestined to be bold leaders in eras of transition (*Schwellenzeiten*), releasing the most vital ideological forces and pointing the way to cultural progress.

Thus Hebbel's most significant dramas are variations of an almost identical theme. In *Judith* the biblical heroine of the same name sets out to free her Jewish homeland from the danger of Assyrian invasion by killing Holofernes, the victorious general of King Nabuchodonosor (sixth century B.C.). Impressed by the commanding vigor of this barbarian chieftain she momentarily forgets her exalted mission. When she beheads the sleeping Holofernes she realizes with horror that her deed was not inspired by heroic patriotism but by the desire to avenge her violated womanhood. What she does not realize is that by an act of personal revenge she has been instrumental in assuring the victory of Judaism over heathen barbarism.

In the preface to the "middle-class tragedy" (*bürgerliches Trauerspiel*) *Maria Magdalene,* Hebbel reproaches his predecessors in this dramatic genre (Lessing, Schiller) for having evolved the tragic conflict from a clash between the middle class and the aristocracy. He proposes to demonstrate in his drama that "crushing tragedy is possible even within the most limited social circle." The result of this attempt fully justified the author's claim: *Maria Magdalene* became the unsurpassed model of modern realistic drama. The tragic conflict derives from the conventional middle-class concepts of honor and morality which seem unable to cope with the elemental emotions of the human heart and with the deepest and truest essence of human personality. "Meister Anton," who by his petrified code of ethics drives his daughter Clara into self-destruction, must confess in the end that he no longer understands a world that has outgrown the limited horizons of his bourgeois mentality.

Returning to the biblical setting of *Judith,* Hebbel develops in *Herodes und Mariamne* the pattern of Hegel's dialectical triad — thesis, antithesis, synthesis — almost in form of a spiral movement: the antithetical opposition between Judaism and Romanism presses irresistibly onward to the dawn of the Christian era. Herod, the representative of an egocentered individualism, is confronted with the progressive forces of Roman collectivism and the new Christian humanism, in which both the individual and social claims find themselves affirmed on a higher plane. Herod's love for Mariamne lacks the element of respect for the rights of human personality, and by violating her spiritual self through distrust and by the use of despotic force he invites the inevitable tragic conflict between the worlds which they both represent: a clash of ideas in which the "world spirit" once more demonstrates symbolically the doom of the one and the victory of the other.

The historic background of the tragedy *Agnes Bernauer* is the German duchy of Bavaria in the period of the early Renaissance (fifteenth century). Again the argument runs along Hegelian lines. Agnes, the "angel of Augsburg," the beautiful daughter of an Augsburg barber, happily married to Albrecht, the son of Duke Ernst of Bavaria, is drowned in the Danube at the behest of the old duke and in the name of the "reason of State." The ultimate approval of this dastardly crime on the part of Duke Albrecht is justified by Hebbel on the ground that, in the case of conflicting interests of the individual and the State, even the noblest individual is to be sacrificed for the greater glory of the State, since the individual is only a fragmentary expression of Morality and Humanity "writ large," as they are embodied in the State.

Gyges und sein Ring (*The Ring of Gyges*) resumes the thesis of *Herodes und Mariamne,* this time in a partly historical, partly mythological Greek setting. The Lydian King Kandaules, presented by his Greek friend Gyges

with a magic ring that makes its bearer invisible, tries to gain through another's testimony the reassurance of his wife Rhodope's matchless beauty
by persuading Gyges to enter the queen's chamber, protected by the ring's
magic power. The accidental discovery of the truth leads to the destruction
of both Kandaules and Rhodope: the king is killed by Gyges in single
combat, and Rhodope dies by her own hand. Kandaules and Rhodope are
both tragic characters: the former violating the narrowly circumscribed
sphere of the moral standards prescribed by Oriental custom, yet seizing
upon the wrong means to demonstrate his freedom from meaningless traditions and conventional prejudice; the latter falling a victim to her un-
thinking abidance by the rigid moral code of her ancestors.

Hebbel's last completed dramatic work, the trilogy of the *Nibelungen*
(*Horny Siegfried; Siegfried's Death; Kriemhild's Revenge*), was the first
of his plays to be enthusiastically acclaimed by the public. Following closely
the sequence of events as recorded in the *Nibelungenlied* (cf. p. 154), the
author tries to motivate psychologically the actions of the main characters. The tragic end of the Nibelungen appears as the necessary fate of
a world that has to die, so that a new creed may arise from the shattered
pagan ethics of revenge and brute force: Dietrich von Bern proclaims the
new message of mercy and forgiveness, "in the name of Him who died
on the Cross."

The panorama of literary Realism in the nineteenth century is rounded
out by the work of five authors, each of whom represents a very definite
milieu and a clearly circumscribed set of social and literary motifs. Three
of these writers are of German-Swiss nationality (Gotthelf, Keller, Meyer)
and two are North Germans (Raabe, Storm).

The one who is most significant as an epic poet and as a national educator, but least known outside the narrow circle of his immediate environment, is *Jeremias Gotthelf* (pen name for Albert Bitzius, 1797–1854), by
vocation a pastor of the Reformed (Zwinglian) Church of Switzerland.
His epic style is marked by a pithy humor, and the characters of his social
and pedagogical novels are robust and full of vitality. That Gotthelf's gifts
as a writer of the highest rank remained unappreciated by the critics and the
reading public of Europe was due not only to his frequent use of the Swiss
dialect but even more to his opposition to the liberal *Zeitgeist*.*

The distinctive qualities of Gotthelf's literary art lived on, however, in
the works of his younger countryman *Gottfried Keller* (1819–1890). Undecided in his early youth as to whether to turn to landscape painting or
literature, Keller became the most popular storyteller and lyricist of his
native country. Spending fifteen years of his mature life (1861–1876) as a
clerk in the civil service of his home Canton of Zurich, he embodied in his
novels, short stories, and poems the indigenous virtues of a solid bourgeois
culture and its democratic-liberal ideology. His sturdy humor derives its

---

* Gotthelf's two outstanding novels are *Uli der Knecht* (the farm hand) and its continuation *Uli der Pächter* (the farmer).

amiable naïveté and natural freshness from its closeness to the soil and to popular and national tradition.

Keller's "poetic realism" develops from the subjective immediacy of his early lyrics and narratives to the even flow and contemplative epic temper of his mature style. This important change is illustrated by the two versions of his partly autobiographical masterpiece *Der grüne Heinrich* (*Green Henry*, 1855 and 1879), one of the outstanding examples of the German *Entwicklungsroman* (novel of character development), which as a human document and as an artistic achievement may be said to be on a par with Goethe's *Wilhelm Meister* (cf. p. 412). In several cycles of novelettes, interwoven and united with each other by a common theme or "frame" (*Rahmenerzählung*),* Keller shows himself a master of the short story (*Novelle*). He reaches the heights of Shakespearean or Kleistian tragedy in the simple and austere contours of the village epic *Romeo und Julia auf dem Dorfe* (*A Village Romeo and Juliet*).

The prose and poetry of Keller's contemporary and fellow countryman, *Conrad Ferdinand Meyer* (1825–1898), represent a type of realism which is in some respects directly opposed to the human and cultural values embodied in Keller's art. Meyer, like Keller a native of the city of Zurich, was an aristocrat both by descent and personal taste. The nervously sensitive heir of past ages of daring and doing, he mourned his fate of being born in an era that seemed willing to sacrifice distinctions of character to egalitarian democratic ideals. He turned to the past for inspiration and found models for the main characters of his novels in the age of the Renaissance and Reformation, an age in which the forces of antidemocratic individualism had discovered new forms of passionate self-expression. Pouring the liquid fire of his emotional life into a classically chiseled stylistic mold, Meyer's literary creations linked the cultural and artistic traditions of the Romanic South with those of the Germanic North. Wavering for a considerable length of time between French and German as an adequate medium of his literary expression, Meyer's sympathy for Germany was aroused by the Franco-Prussian War, and in his epic poem *Huttens letzte Tage* he paid an enthusiastic tribute to both German nationalism and German Protestantism. Positively, in the glorification of the tendencies and characters of Renaissance and Reformation, and negatively, in his taunting of medieval institutions, his novels, short stories, and poems are flawless documents of his artistic and spiritual convictions.**

The realism of *Wilhelm Raabe* (1831–1910) is tinged with romantic longing and receives its pessimistic note from the author's abhorrence of the materialistic trends of his age. This north German novelist, a native of

---

* Keller's best known short stories are contained in the series *Die Leute von Seldwyla* (*The People of Seldwyla*), in which the human characters are portrayed in the native setting of a fictitious Swiss town, and in the *"Rahmenerzählung" Das Sinngedicht* (Epigram).

** Characteristic of Meyer's prose works are *Der Heilige* (*The Saint*), an account of the life and martyrdom of Thomas Becket († 1170), archbishop of Canterbury and chancellor of King Henry II of England, and *Jürg Jenatsch,* a novel of the Swiss past.

Brunswick (Braunschweig), whose style, philosophical outlook, and peculiarly melancholy humor are indebted to Dickens, Thackeray, Jean Paul, and Schopenhauer, went in his literary and spiritual development through several distinct phases. His early works were typical expressions of an intellectual crisis marked by the transition from romanticism to realism. The masterpieces of his second period (especially the trilogy, *Der Hungerpastor; Abu Telfan; Der Schüdderump*) portray with merciless realism the mortal combat between the powers of love and steadfast devotion and the demonic forces of sin, error, falsehood, and selfishness. In Raabe's third period a wisdom seasoned by manifold experience replaces his pessimism, and the author attains to a critically balanced and philosophically tempered understanding of human life (*Horacker, Stopfkuchen,* etc.).

Theodor Storm (1817–1888) is a bourgeois poet and novelist of romantic leanings, whose gentle melancholy lacks the dark strains of Raabe's pessimism. His realistic technique succeeds in making his narratives memoirs of the landscape of his beloved native Schleswig, of the vast north German plains, the heath, the marshlands, and the sea, and of the taciturn and sober Frisian people. An ardent German patriot, Storm, who had established himself as a lawyer in his home town of Husum, was forced to leave Schleswig in 1853. He entered the Prussian civil service in Potsdam but returned to his homeland after the Danish-Prussian War of 1864. With great versatility he cultivated every imaginable genre of the short story, at times taxing the reader's patience by the stereotyped repetition of identical motifs, but achieving occasionally a fusion of romantic mood, idyllic charm, and realistic animation which makes such tales as *Immensee* or *Renate* gems of rare beauty. In his lyric poetry Storm shows himself influenced by Eichendorff (cf. p. 478 sq.). Here as in his prose works the varying moods of nature and the emotions of love and longing figure prominently. In his lyrics the subdued gray and silvery hues of the north German landscape with its concomitant intimation of loneliness and ominous dread have found a deeply moving expression.

Historiography. The transition from romanticism to realism found the historians engaged in an endeavor to look at historic evolution from a "realistic" point of view. This implied first of all the narrowing down of the scope of history to include only the political structure of states and the material conditions of their growth, and secondly, the attempt to confine themselves to a strictly factual presentation of historical data. Wilhelm von Humboldt's demand that the historian disregard in his account the ultimate ends of life and history and be satisfied with factual observation and narration, was heeded by *Leopold von Ranke* (1795–1886), who tried in his great historical masterpieces* to understand historic events "as they

---

* The Roman Popes in the Sixteenth and Seventeenth Centuries (3 vols., 1834–1836); *German History in the Age of the Reformation* (5 vols., 1839–1847); *World History* (to the eleventh century, 9 vols., 1881–1888), etc. — Ranke's works comprise 54 volumes in all (new ed. of the German Academy, 1925 sqq.).

have actually occurred." In brilliant analyses Ranke describes the gradual emancipation of the modern national states from the universalism of the medieval empire. He found the idea of "Humanity" embodied in the history of individual nations, and in accordance with his theological convictions he maintained that "each epoch stands in an immediate relationship to God." He thus demanded a historiography that recognized the individuality of each epoch but with a view to its significance in the larger context of the universal history of the human race. "Historic epochs succeed each other," he wrote, "so that in their totality be fulfilled what is impossible of fulfillment in each of them individually and that thus the plenitude of the spiritual life infused into the human race by the Deity may become manifest in the sequence of the centuries." In the individual historic States he saw "original creations of the human mind, ideas of God, so to speak."

Ranke was the leading historian of this age of transition precisely because he was able to comprehend the conditioning factors in historical phenomena, without submitting to the materialistic dogmas of cultural determinism and historic relativism. As a historian who had the ambition "to extinguish his own ego," he differed from the eighteenth-century rationalists on the one hand and from the partisan political writers who succeeded him, on the other. As a devout Lutheran Ranke shared Hegel's unquestioning respect for the divinely willed authority of the State and was furthermore convinced of the providential mission of the German nation as the originator and standard-bearer of the Reformation.

Among the other great German "political historians" of the nineteenth century three stand out: *Gustav Droysen* (1808–1884), *Theodor Mommsen* (1817–1903), and *Heinrich von Treitschke* (1834–1896). As a member of the Frankfurt National Assembly (cf. p. 530 sqq.) as well as in his *History of Prussian Politics* (14 vols., 1855–1886) Droysen passionately advocated the idea of Prussian hegemony over all Germany. His studies of medieval history convinced him that the "Holy Roman Empire" was an ideological aberration and that Germany's greatness depended on Prussian leadership. The son of an army chaplain, Droysen had grown up in a military atmosphere in which the tradition of the Prussian soldier-kings blended with the ideals of nineteenth-century liberalism. Success he regarded as the infallible criterion of political action, and the shortest way to the goal of national power seemed to him the surest and therefore the best way.

Mommsen was a historian, jurist, and philologist of liberal-democratic convictions, whose *Roman History* is counted among the standard works of modern historiography. He taught at the Universities of Leipzig, Zurich, Breslau, and Berlin, and his political career included membership in the Prussian Diet and in the German *Reichstag*.

The one-sidedness of pro-Prussian political historiography found its most fanatical protagonist in Treitschke, whose *German History in the Nineteenth Century* (5 vols., 1879) became one of the most widely circulated and most effective documents of Pan-Prussianism and Pan-Germanism. His advocacy of Bismarck's "smaller Germany" under the leadership of Prussia made him a sworn enemy of the principle of federation* and a violent opponent of the supernational aims of Roman Catholicism.

Education. The practical tendencies of the machine age made themselves felt in corresponding changes and shifts of emphasis in the educational curriculum of secondary schools and universities. Training in "dead" languages, such as Greek and Latin, was regarded as unnecessary for the future captain of industry, factory executive, and public official. The new *Realgymnasium* tried to effect a compromise between the liberal arts curriculum of the humanistic *Gymnasium* (cf. p. 441) and the demand for due consideration of scientific and technical training and proficiency in modern languages. Special industrial and technical schools (*Gewerbeschulen*) were to prepare the students for specific practical occupations.

The abstract intellectualism firmly implanted and proudly adhered to in the humanistic *Gymnasium* was met by the educational "realists" with the creation of a new type of *Bürger-Gymnasium* (middle-class gymnasium) or *Realschule,* whose curriculum was made up chiefly of technical subjects, and which had as its object the preparatory training of specialists in commercial and industrial pursuits.

In the same degree in which the "realistic" secondary schools adjusted their curriculum to the practical requirements of the industrial age, the universities on their part submitted to the trend of specialization and assumed the character of professional training centers for scientists, physicians, jurists, educators, and theologians. The increasing demand for advanced technological training led to the creation of polytechnical institutes (*Technische Hochschulen*)** of university rank, open to those who had completed their prescribed course (9 years) of secondary education.

Education on a nationwide scale was thoroughly organized and monopolized, first by the individual state governments and afterward by the centralized national State. While this centralization and State control made possible great achievements in science and industry, it also tended in a steadily increasing measure to thwart true independence of thought. The schools came to function more and more as collective agencies for the propagation of certain governmental policies. Once the hegemony of Prussia over Germany was secured, the entire educational system was pressed into the service of Prussian nationalism and militarism. This important transformation was prepared during the period of the *Vormärz* (1815-1848) and received its systematic consolidation between 1848 and the closing decade

---

* Federalism (*Föderalismus*), as opposed to "unitarism" or centralization, advocates the autonomy or semiautonomy of individual states within the larger frame of a federal national State: it is diversity in unity. The "Holy Roman Empire" may be considered as a model of federalist organization. In modern times the United States and the republic of Switzerland are outstanding examples of federalist nations.

** The first polytechnical institutes in Germany were those of Beuth (1818), Karlsruhe (1825), Nuremberg (1827), Dresden (1828), Stuttgart (1832), and Darmstadt (1836). Later foundations are those of Munich (1867), Aachen (1870), and Breslau (1910).

of the century. While it is obvious that many of the larger and smaller German states contributed their share to educational theory and practice and that at no time the educational institutions of Germany accepted a pattern of mechanical uniformity, it is nevertheless true that the basic tenets adhered to by all German schools were those fostered by the political and intellectual leaders of Prussia. "When I look back upon the forty years during which I have been professor and examiner," wrote the famous anthropologist Rudolf Virchow (cf. p. 563) in 1890, " . . . I cannot say . . . that we have made material advance in training men with strength of character. . . . The number of 'characters' becomes smaller, and this is connected with the shrinkage in private and individual work performed during the pupil's school life."

Philosophy. Hegel's metaphysics (cf. p. 502 sqq.) represented a final attempt during the transitional period between romanticism and realism to unite science, philosophy, and religion in one all-embracing system of thought. We have pointed out (cf. p. 505) that Hegel's own dialectical method was seized upon by the "Young Hegelians" to attack and destroy the idealistic premises of their master's philosophical creed. Positivism (cf. p. 566 sq.) in the form of "historic materialism" no longer saw in history any issues involving truth or falsehood but merely facts and material forces. Even while Hegel was still alive the inductive methods of the empirical sciences began to replace the deductive rationalism of his own system, and metaphysical speculation suffered an almost total eclipse. Auguste Comte's (cf. p. 566) positivism became first a powerful rival of Hegelian thought and then its triumphant conqueror.

German positivism, following in Comte's footsteps, was nevertheless thoroughly German in that it recognized the intrinsic logical conclusions implied in Comte's positivistic premises and accordingly developed a consistent and integral materialism. In the course of the so-called *Materialismusstreit* (quarrel of the materialists), dating from the year 1854, the German Darwinist Karl Vogt published a widely read essay entitled *Köhlerglaube und Wissenschaft* (1855), in which he tried with cynical witticism to dispense with the problem of the human soul. According to Vogt, thought is a secretion of the brain just as the digestive juices are secretions of the stomach, bile a secretion of the liver, and urine a secretion of the kidneys. Three years earlier the physiologist Jakob Moleschott, in his *Kreislauf des Lebens (Cycle of Life)* had expressed similar views. At about the same time the physician Ludwig Büchner launched a violent attack against the "Kant-swindle" and against "Hegel and his accomplices," in a book entitled *Kraft und Stoff (Force and Matter)*, in which he likewise defended the theses

---

* *Superstition and Science.* The term *Köhlerglaube,* referring to the blind faith of the uneducated masses, is said to be derived from a sixteenth-century tale, according to which a *Köhler* (charcoal burner), when questioned by a theologian as to his faith, gives the answer: "I believe what the Church believes," and upon the further question: "What does the Church believe?" responds: "The Church believes what I believe."

of a crude materialism. These theories were in the main a rehash of the teachings espoused by some of the leaders of French Enlightenment in the eighteenth century, of Holbach's (1723–1789) naturalism and Condillac's (1715–1780) sensism. The monistic "energeticism" of Wilhelm Ostwald (1853–1932), on the other hand, reducing matter to the spontaneous movement of atomic structures, was an attempt to salvage cultural and spiritual values without sacrificing the basic convictions of secularism and naturalism.

The severest blow against Hegel, however, was struck not by the materialists but by a representative of the religious individualism of the Christian-Protestant tradition. The Danish religious philosopher Søren Kierkegaard (1813–1855) regarded Hegel's philosophy and the teachings of liberal Protestantism as the two most dangerous anti-Christian forces in modern times. Against Hegel's pantheistic identification of God and world, of human intellect and divine Mind, Kierkegaard emphasized the unbridgeable cleavage between nature and supernature. Against Hegel's and Schleiermacher's (cf. p. 507 sq.) humanization of dogma he preached a God who is the totally transcendent and absolute Ruler of the universe. Against Hegel's exaltation of the omnipotent State he proclaimed the "inwardness" of the individual, whose salvation he regarded as of infinitely greater importance than the self-realization of the "world spirit."

Kierkegaard's thinking was determined by Luther's contempt of reason on the one hand and by Hegel's exaltation of reason on the other. Because he was afraid that a positive evaluation of rational knowledge would of necessity lead to the obliteration of the distinctions between nature and spirit and ultimately to a Hegelian "philosophy of identity,"* he discarded reason for the sake of faith. Thus he contributed his share to the self-destruction of philosophy in the nineteenth century. Kierkegaard's epochal significance in the history of ideas was not recognized until more than half a century after his death, when, at the opening of the twentieth century, his numerous works and his *Journals* were not only widely read in his own country but became accessible in German translations.

More deeply and clearly than any other modern author, with the possible exception of Friedrich Nietzsche, Kierkegaard diagnosed the spiritual sickness of the modern age. Again and again he deplored the halfheartedness and intellectual slovenliness of his contemporaries, who lacked the courage and consistency to face the consequences of their own philosophical and religious convictions. He deplored that with the aid of Hegelian philosophy

---

* Kierkegaard's attack on Hegel was seconded from similar motives by Joseph Görres (cf. p. 479 sq.) who in 1842 parodied the "philosophy of identity" in these words: "In the beginning there was Nothingness, and Nothingness was with God, and God was Nothingness, and this Nothingness was with God from the beginning. Everything is made by the same, and without It nothing is made. In It was Life, and this Life was Death, which is the Light of Man, which out of non-existence stepped into existence, and which in Darkness and through Darkness begot individuality and consciousness. And Darkness shone into Light, but Light comprehended It not. There was a man sent forth from God. . . . His name was Hegel."

and liberal Protestant theology it had become an easy and comfortable thing to call oneself a Christian and actually be a pagan. And he drew a sharp dividing line between "Christianity" and "Christendom," maintaining that whereas the former was a spiritual reality, the latter was but an "optical illusion."

Thus Kierkegaard's thought culminated inevitably in the problem of "choice," in an all-decisive "either — or," as he formulated this alternative in the title of one of his best known works. "I want honesty," we read on one of the polemical statements written shortly before his death. "If that is what this race and generation wants, if it will uprightly, honestly, frankly, openly, directly rebel against Christianity and say to God: we can but we will not subject ourselves to this authority . . . , well then, strange as it may seem, I am for it; for honesty is what I want. . . . An honest rebellion against Christianity can only be made when we honestly admit what Christianity is and how we ourselves are related to it."

It is this refusal of compromise, this call for an intellectual honesty that emanates from the very roots of human existence, which constitutes the bases of Kierkegaard's influence on some of the most prominent philosophers and theologians of our own day. In the form of "existential" philosophy (cf. p. 694) and Protestant "Dialectical Theology" (cf. p. 700 sq.) Kierkegaard's speculation lives on as a challenge to the twentieth century.

Religion. The romantic movement had been instrumental in bringing about a revival of religious consciousness in Germany among both Protestants and Catholics. Schleiermacher (cf. p. 507 sq.) had developed his pietistic theology in opposition to the two prevalent religious trends, deistic rationalism and Lutheran orthodoxy. He in turn was attacked by Hegel, whose intellectualism had no use for any exaltation of religious "feeling." Hegel's philosophy of religion, which was an outgrowth of his philosophy of history, stimulated the theological speculation of Protestants and Catholics alike and served to revive the antagonism between the followers of the two creeds, which had been temporarily alleviated in the era of Enlightenment.

a) The School of Tübingen. The two opposing camps were entrenched side by side at the Swabian University of Tübingen, after a Catholic theological faculty had been attached to this ancient Lutheran stronghold in 1817. The leaders of the "School of Tübingen" were Friedrich Christian Baur (1792–1860), the earliest representative of liberal German Protestantism, and Johann Adam Möhler (1796–1838), one of the most influential Catholic theologians of the post-Reformation period. Baur was the first German theologian to apply Hegel's dialectical method to biblical history. His extended studies of the history of the Christian Church in the early Christian centuries and his implicit faith in the Hegelian method led him to the conclusion that the appearance and personal mission of Christ signified a historically conditioned phase in the dialectical evolution of the Christian idea, and that the Gospels were polemical pamphlets containing propagandistic falsifications. The Epistles of St. Paul he regarded as documents reflecting the ideological struggles in the early Christian communities. The Acts of the Apostles he described as the work of one of Paul's disciples who had attempted to effect a compromise by smoothing over the fundamental differences of conviction.* In the Catholic Church Baur saw the final result of this compromise and therefore an imperfect form of Christianity. Despite the revolutionary implications of his ideas Baur was at heart a conservative and personally convinced that Hegel's philosophy could be squared with a strictly theistic point of view. Thus he was far removed from subscribing to the radicalism of his pupil, David Friedrich Strauss.

Möhler contributed to the spiritual revival of German Catholicism in the nineteenth century by drawing on the rich treasury of thought enshrined in the literature and philosophy of German Classicism and Romanticism. He recognized the religious significance of the new ideas for the organic growth of cultural formations and for the principle of historic evolution, and he utilized them for a deeper understanding of the traditional content of faith and dogma. His thorough knowledge of Protestantism enabled him to write his *Symbolik* (1832), in which he presented the dogmatic differences of Catholics and Protestants on the basis of their "symbolic" books, i.e., the officially recognized documents and articles of faith. Möhler's scholarly research in the period of the early Church Fathers laid the foundations for the new theological discipline of "patristics" (from the Latin, *pater,* meaning "father"). In the visible and historic Church he saw the product of organic growth, the "objectivation and living representation of the Christian religion." While he placed strong emphasis throughout on the common heritage of all Christian denominations, he criticized those dogmatic convictions in which the Protestant Churches had laid themselves open to the inroads of naturalism and secularism.

b) The United Protestant Church. Shortly after the War of Liberation and under the emotional stress of the tercentenary celebration of the Reformation (*Reformationsfest,* 1817) a unification of the Lutheran and Reformed Churches was effected in most German states. The first decisive steps in this direction were taken by King Frederick William III of Prussia who, himself a Calvinist, declared in a proclamation that it would please him very much if the year of pious commemoration were to see the birth of a "Christian-Evangelical Church, revitalized in the spirit of its hallowed founder." The most serious obstacle to the contemplated unification was the opposition of the Old Lutheran Orthodoxy, whose spokesman, the Lutheran pastor Claus Harms of Kiel, vigorously stated the case for his coreligionists in ninety-five theses.

---

* According to the best authorities the Acts of the Apostles were written by Luke (*c.* A.D. 63), the collaborator and companion of Paul and the author of the synoptic Gospel that bears his name. In 28 chapters they relate the apostolic activities of Peter and Paul to the end of the latter's first imprisonment in the city of Rome. Cf. Giuseppe Ricciotti, *The Life of Christ* (trans. by Alba I. Zizzamia, Bruce Publishing Co., Milwaukee, 1947, Critical Introduction).

The United Protestant Church of Prussia, which was in the main the creation of the king and his chancellor, Altenstein, was a rigidly organized State Church and constituted a signal victory of the absolute monarchy. While the material contributions of the United Church to ecclesiastical training and discipline and to improved standards in general education will be readily admitted, it cannot be denied that the fusion of secular and ecclesiastical power in the person of the monarch made the Church an instrument of political power. Its splendid external organization was unable to stem the rising tide of religious indifferentism among the educated as well as among the masses.

Disregarding the profound doctrinal differences which had originally caused the cleavage between Lutherans and Calvinists, the Prussian State Church failed to offer a common doctrinal ground and was therefore united only by its opposition to "Roman errors and abuses" (Schleiermacher). As far as theological convictions were concerned, it was a loose federative union, which henceforth existed side by side with the established and unyielding Old Lutheran and Old Calvinist church communities. A full doctrinal unification was achieved in the state of Baden, where the ruling grand duke issued an ecclesiastical constitution and assumed the title of *Landesbischof*.

c) *The Churches and the Social Question.* The Industrial Revolution and the rise of the proletariat as a class, whose ideology was determined either by atheistic materialism or religious indifferentism, confronted the Christian Churches as a challenge, forcing them to revitalize their spiritual resources. The political revolts of 1830 and 1848 threw the social question into the limelight of public attention and made it incumbent on the Churches to think of ways and means to remedy the abuses of the capitalistic system, if they wanted to retain or regain the allegiance of the masses.

In the Protestant denominations the social impulses of Christianity were stressed and put to the practical test not so much by the orthodoxy as by the smaller Christian sects and groups in Germany, which in their social activities followed the example of the English and American Free Churches. About the middle of the nineteenth century a gradually increasing number of humane societies, poorhouses, nurseries, and other similar organizations for the care of the poor and the welfare of the young came into existence. The pietistic sects (cf. p. 362 sqq.) in particular, which had never ceased to teach and labor in the interests of a practical Christianity, assumed courageous leadership in the new social movement.

Among these Protestant-Pietist reformers of the nineteenth century two personalities stand out by their unselfish devotion to the ideas of social Christianity. Theodor Fliedner (1800–1864), a native of Hesse, had acquainted himself with the methods of organized Christian social endeavor in Holland and England, and he used his experiences in the "Evangelical Asylum," which he founded in the Rhenish town of Kaiserswerth in 1833. This institution was chiefly dedicated to the care and education of female ex-convicts. In 1836 a hospital was established in the same city as a training center for Protestant nurses (*Diakonissen*), the first Protestant institution of its kind and the cradle of an association that extended to every part of Germany. A printing press and a bookstore, attached to the mother house, served to spread the social ideas underlying the foundation. In 1854 Fliedner created in Berlin the first *Hospiz* for unemployed servant girls (*Marthahaus*). Florence Nightingale (1820–1910), the great organizer of the English system of nursing and hospitalization, received her early training in the institutions of Kaiserswerth.

The second great apostle of Protestant organized social work was Johann Heinrich Wichern (1808–1881), who was born in the city of Hamburg. Owing to its many contacts with English life and culture, Hamburg proved a favorable environment for the adoption and imitation of the methods of English charitable institutions. Wichern's *Rauhes Haus* (Tough House) on the outskirts of Hamburg owed its foundation to his own sordid experiences in the slums of his native city, which had strengthened in him the resolve to devote his life to the cause of the outcast and the downtrodden. This house of refuge was the birthplace of the Protestant "Home Missions" (*Innere Mission*), which in their nationwide organization comprised the three major fields of social charity, missionary activity, and constructive social work.

Das Rauhe Haus offered shelter and educational guidance to boys between the ages of five and fourteen, most of them picked from the Hamburg slums. The children were grouped into "families" of twelve or less, and each "family" was placed under the guardianship of a "helper" or "father." Workshops served to prepare the boys for their future trades, and a publishing house provided invaluable aid for the tasks of education and evangelization. Wichern was wholeheartedly attached to the patriarchal order of society with its high regard for the independent work of the craftsman and artisan, and accordingly he tried to kindle in his charges a love for the ancient handicrafts.

Theologically Wichern shared the irenic convictions of the leaders of the pietistic revival movement and their belief in "One True Catholic Church," of which all existing Churches partake. "We believe," he wrote, "in the kernel of Christian Truth that is incarnate in all denominations, because we believe in the presence of the living Christ in all of them." He blamed both the State and the official clergy for their failure to cope with the problems of modern civilization, and he recommended the creation of "free Christian associations" to act as intervening links between home and Church: "If the proletarians no longer seek the Church, then the Church must begin to seek the proletarians," he wrote.

The "Central Committee of the Home Missions" was founded in 1848, the year of the "March Revolution." It was to be a world-wide and supernational organization, but in contradistinction to the "foreign missions" for the conversion of heathens it was to confine its efforts to "baptized Christians, among whom in our days paganism is even more conspicuous than it ever was among devout heathens." The "Home Missions" regarded both the general priesthood of all the faithful and the official ministry as necessary ingredients of a true Christian *"Volkskirche."*

Within the Catholic Church in Germany, too, the Industrial Revolution caused a re-examination of Christian doctrine in the light of the social question. Even in the early decades of the nineteenth century some of the Catholic romanticists had raised their voices in protest against the degradation of manual labor and the displacement of the laborer by the machine. The romantic philosopher Franz von Baader (1765–1841) was the first to emphasize the original social function of the priestly office, thus reminding the clergy of their duties toward the laboring class.

The actual Catholic-social movement, however, had its beginnings in the thirties and forties of the century and received its main incentives from the teachings of the Church itself. The two pioneers of social Catholicism were Adolf Kolping (1813–1865) and Bishop Emanuel von Ketteler (1811–1877) of Mainz. Kolping, before his ordination to the priesthood, was a poor, migrant journeyman, while Ketteler, a Westphalian nobleman, had been active as a jurist in the Prussian civil service before the influence of Görres (cf. p. 479 sq.) and his friends made him turn to the study of theology. The *Gesellenverein* (Journeymen's Union), founded by Kolping in Elberfeld in 1845 and centralized in Cologne in 1851, was the first symbolic manifestation of a new type of "social ministry" which soon made its appearance in every part of Germany. The individual local *Gesellen-vereine,* each of them under the guidance of a priestly *Präses,* were destined to provide shelter for the young journeymen and opportunities for the improvement of their religious and vocational training as well as various recreational facilities.

A patriarchal family life served as the ideal pattern for each "Kolping-House." Kolping regarded it as one of the main objectives of his social endeavors to bring about a social regeneration by rebuilding "the crushed estate of craftsmen and artisans." Thereby he would render innocuous the two abuses of "rugged individualism" and listless collectivism: the society of the future was to rest as much on personal independence as on social responsibility, a combination of qualities that seemed to be prefigured in an exemplary way in the organism of the human family.

Bishop von Ketteler gained prominence as an outstanding leader of Christian-social thought and practical social policies in the stormy year of 1848, when he created a sensation with the social sermons delivered in the Cathedral of Mainz. He sided with the socialist doctrinaire Lassalle (cf. p. 559) in his fight against economic liberalism and took an active part in the trade-union movement among the workers. After an initial hesitation to endorse the enactment of State laws for the protection of the workingmen, fearing a fateful encroachment of the State on personal economic initiative, Ketteler became convinced in the end that private charitable and welfare organizations were unable to cope with the wide-spread distress of the proletariat, and that only an active and systematic social policy (*Sozialpolitik*) on the part of the State could check the abuses of economic power and protect the interests of the economically weaker members of modern society. Pope Leo XIII in his program of social reform specifically referred to the principles laid down in the writings and sermons of Bishop von Ketteler.*

* Cf. *Die Arbeiterfrage und das Christentum*, 1864; *Ausgewählte Schriften*, ed. J. Mumbauer, 3 vols., 1924.

PART VI. THE SECOND GERMAN EM-PIRE, WORLD WAR I, AND THE GERMAN REPUBLIC

1871–1887	*Kulturkampf*
1871–1888	William I, German emperor and king of Prussia, brother of Frederick William IV
1871–1890	Bismarck, *Reichskanzler*
1872	*Dreikaiserbund* (Three Emperors' League): peaceful understanding among William I of Germany, Francis Joseph I of Austria-Hungary, and Alexander II of Russia
1878	*Sozialistengesetz* (antisocialist law) — Congress of Berlin
1879	Protective alliance between Germany and Austria-Hungary — New protective tariffs ·
1882	The *Dreibund* (Triple Alliance) between Germany, Austria-Hungary, and Italy
1883	Enactment of health insurance legislation.
1884	Neutrality Treaty with Russia — Acquisition of German colonies in South West Africa, Togo, and Kamerun
1884–1887	Enactment of accident insurance legislation
1885	Acquisition of German colonies in East Africa and on South Sea Islands
1887	*Rücksicherungsvertrag* (Reinsurance Treaty) with Russia
1888	Frederick III, German emperor and king of Prussia, son of William I (March 9 to June 15)
1888–1918	William II, son of Frederick III, German emperor and king of Prussia
1889	Enactment of disability and old age insurance legislation
1890	Dismissal of Bismarck — England cedes Heligoland to Germany, in exchange for Zanzibar, Wituland, and Uganda (all in East Africa)
1890–1894	General von Caprivi, *Reichskanzler*
1891	*Arbeiterschutzgesetz* (law for the protection of labor) — Commercial treaties with several nations and lowering of protective tariffs
1894–1900	Prince Hohenlohe, *Reichskanzler*
1895	Completion of *Kaiser Wilhelm-Kanal* (North Sea-Baltic Canal)
1898	First naval building program — China leases Kiaochow to Germany (99 year lease)
1899	Germany purchases from Spain the Caroline, Marian, and Palau Islands in Pacific — Construction of Dortmund–Ems Canal
1900	Promulgation of *Bürgerliches Gesetzbuch* (Civil Law Code) — Acquisition of German-Samoa in the Pacific — Navy Bill
1900–1909	Count (later Prince) Bülow, *Reichskanzler*
1902	New Customs Tariff
1905	Wilhelm II's visit to Tangier (first Morocco crisis)
1906	Increased *Reichssteuern* (federal taxes) and program for larger navy — The Algeciras Conference on Morocco

1909	King Edward VII of England visits Berlin — German-French Morocco Treaty
1909–1917	Von Bethmann-Hollweg, *Reichskanzler*
1911	Germany sends the gunboat *Panther* to Agadir (second Morocco crisis) — Agreement with France on Morocco and Equatorial Africa — Promulgation of a unified *Reichsversicherungsordnung* (federal insurance legislation)
1912	The new navy bill — Renewal of *Dreibund*
1912–1913	Balkan Wars
1913	Adoption of new army bill
1914–1918	World War I
1917	The emperor promises reform of Prussian *Dreiklassenwahlrecht* (electoral law) — Annulment of *Jesuitengesetz* (law of 1872, excluding the Society of Jesus from German territory) — *Reichskanzler:* Michaelis (July to October); Count von Hertling (October, 1917, to October, 1918)
1918	Prince Max von Baden, *Reichskanzler* — Mutiny of the German fleet — Revolution — Armistice — Allied occupation of Rhineland — William II abdicates and flees to Holland — Abdication of all German monarchs
1919	*"Spartakisten"* uprisings — Opening of National Assembly in Weimar — *Reichspräsident:* Ebert; *Reichskanzler:* Scheidemann, afterward Bauer — Proclamation of Soviet Republic in Bavaria — Assassination of Eisner — Germany signs *Treaty of Versailles* — Germany adopts *Weimar Constitution*
1920	*"Kapp Putsch"* — Formation of Red army in Ruhr District — *Reichskanzler:* H. Müller, afterward Fehrenbach — Plebiscites in East Prussia, Schleswig, and in Eupen-Malmédy
1921	Plebiscite in Upper Silesia — Communist uprisings in central Germany, Hamburg, and Ruhr District — London Ultimatum on reparation payments — Assassination of Erzberger — Division of Upper Silesia — Wirth, *Reichskanzler*
1922	Conference of Cannes approves reduction of German reparation payments — Conference of Genoa — Treaty of Rapallo — Assassination of Rathenau — Promulgation of *Gesetz zum Schutz der Republik* (law for the protection of the Republic) — Inflation — Cuno, *Reichskanzler*
1923	French-Belgian march into the Ruhr District — Passive resistance movement — Stresemann, *Reichskanzler* — Separatist movements in Rhineland and Palatinate — *"Hitler Putsch"* in Munich — Creation of the *Rentenmark* — Marx, *Reichskanzler*
1924	Second Marx cabinet — Conference of London — Adoption of Dawes Plan
1925	Hans Luther, *Reichskanzler;* Hindenburg, *Reichspräsident* — Withdrawal of French-Belgian occupation forces from Ruhr District — Conference of Locarno and Locarno treaties
1926	Second Luther cabinet — Withdrawal of allied occupation forces from first Rhineland zone — Third Marx cabinet — Germany is admitted to League of Nations — End of allied military control

1927   Fourth Marx cabinet — Continuation of Locarno policy
1928   Second Müller cabinet — Germany signs Kellogg-Briand Pact
1929   Young Plan — Conference of the Hague
1930   Brüning, *Reichskanzler* — End of allied occupation of Rhineland —
        Germany's September elections (large increase of communist and
        national-socialist votes) — Reform program and emergency decrees
        of Brüning cabinet
1931   Second Brüning cabinet — German-Austrian proposal of Customs
        Union; rejected by Allies — Economic crisis and bank failures —
        Hoover Plan (reparations Moratorium) — Conferences of German
        and allied foreign ministers in London, Paris, Berlin, and Rome —
        Finance Conference of London — Further emergency decrees of
        Brüning cabinet
1932   Disarmament Conference of League of Nations — Reorganization of
        German banks — Hindenburg re-elected *Reichspräsident* — Fall of
        Brüning cabinet — Von Papen, *Reichskanzler* — Conferences on rep-
        arations (Basel and Lausanne) — National Socialists win 230 seats
        in *Reichstag* elections and become strongest political party — Fall
        of Papen cabinet — General von Schleicher, *Reichskanzler*
1933   Fall of Schleicher cabinet — Hitler-Papen-Hugenberg cabinet —
        Reichstag fire on eve of new elections; National Socialists gain 288
        seats in *Reichstag* and, with the aid of 52 deputies of *Deutsch-
        Nationale Volkspartei,* obtain absolute majority — Parties of the
        opposition are suppressed or dissolve "voluntarily" — Change of
        Constitution — Germany withdraws from League of Nations

Chapter 16

POLITICAL AND SOCIAL
DEVELOPMENTS

Two Concepts of Empire. As writing is resumed (May, 1946), after an interval of several years, another chapter in the history of Germany and of the human race has been brought to a tragic conclusion. But the destruction of the totalitarian regimes in Germany, Italy, and Japan has so far failed to bring the blessings of a durable peace and the "tranquillity of order" (Augustine) to the tormented peoples of the world. They are still haunted by greed, suspicion, and fear, and by the apocalyptic specters of famine and death. Internal unrest and social strife victimize the nations of victors and vanquished alike, and the burden of armaments is increased rather than diminished with the invention of new and ever more destructive weapons of warfare. National ambitions and international rivalries extend into the council chambers of the United Nations Organization, adding their prodigious weight to the multiple problems which face a confused and rapidly disintegrating civilization. Thus it seems that the words with which Leo XIII described the situation of Europe in 1894 have lost nothing of their prophetic import: "For many years," the pontiff wrote in an apostolic letter (*Praeclara Gratulationis*) addressed to all rulers and peoples, "peace has been rather an appearance than a reality. Possessed with mutual suspicions, almost all the nations are vying with one another in equipping themselves with military armaments. Inexperienced youths are removed from parental direction and control, to be thrown amid the dangers of the soldier's life; robust young men are taken from agriculture or ennobling studies or trade or the arts, to be put under arms. Hence, the treasures of States are exhausted by the enormous expenditures, the national resources are frittered away, and private fortunes impaired; and this armed peace cannot last much longer. . . . To repress ambition, greed, and envy — the chief instigators of war — nothing, however, is more fitted than the Christian virtues and, in particular, the virtue of justice; for, by its exercise, both the law of nations and the faith of treaties may be maintained inviolate, and the bonds of brotherhood continue unbroken. . . . And as in its external relations, so in the internal life of the State itself, the Christian virtues will provide a guarantee of the commonweal much more sure and far stronger than any which . . . armies can afford." Viewing with alarm the general contest for extended empire, the same pope had written in an allocution of 1889: "Since peace is based upon good order, it follows that, for empires as well as for individuals, concord should have its principal foundations in justice and charity."

The new German Empire, a latecomer among the great powers of Europe, was built on the national unity achieved in 1871, and its citizens, on the whole, accepted cheerfully Bismarck's "small-German" solution of the German Question (cf. p. 530). There were, however, dissenting groups, and one of their spokesmen was Konstantin Frantz (1817–1891). He was an astute political thinker and an uncompromising antagonist of Bismarck, who had advocated in his writings the idea of a federated "Greater Germany" (including Austria) which was to become the nucleus of a future world federation. Frantz, and with him all *grossdeutsche* conservative federalists, saw in Bismarck's Empire not a genuine union, but an artifact of Prussian nationalist statecraft and a deviation from the supranational universalist concept of the medieval "Holy Roman Empire of the German Nation." "Can it be the true vocation of the German people," asked Frantz, "to form a great centralized state when their entire history speaks out to the contrary? Can it be their vocation to break with their long historic past, to set up in its place an order dictated solely by utilitarian considerations?" Friedrich Wilhelm Foerster, one of the most severe contemporary critics of the iron chancellor who, according to his own testimony, "grew up in an atmosphere of loathing for Bismarck's work," finds in the writings of Frantz support for his contention that "autocracy superseded federation as the principle of unity. Force replaced the determination and establishment of law and legal rights. Bismarck thus founded that empire which Nietzsche denounced as the extirpation of the German spirit."* Because he excluded from his *Kleindeutschland* the Austrians and Sudeten Germans, Bismarck is for the Austrian historian Richard von Kralik "not the creator but the destroyer of German unity."

It is, then, the unshakable conviction of all these advocates of *Grossdeutschland* that Bismarck's Empire simply absorbed Germany into Prussia and, by dedicating the newly founded *Reich* to the ideas of Prussian *Realpolitik,* forced it into a dangerous and in the long run disastrous competition with the British empire.

Whatever may be the justification of such arguments, their weight was certainly not felt by the majority of those Germans who lived in the newly unified constitutional Empire; an empire which was not even a monarchy in the strict sense, but rather a commonwealth composed of princely (and some municipal) constitutional governments, the sovereignty being vested in the *Bundesrat* (cf. p. 542). The main prerogative of the emperor was

---

* Friedrich Wilhelm Foerster, *Europe and the German Question* (New York: Sheed and Ward, 1940), p. 20.

the appointment of the *Reichskanzler,* while he held no veto power over the legislative enactments of the *Reichstag* and the *Bundesrat.* In case of serious disagreements he could have recourse to the extreme measure of dissolving the *Reichstag* and of ordering new elections, but he could not do so without the consent of the *Bundesrat.* As the emperor became commander in chief of the armed forces only in time of war, his power was more restricted than that of the *Reichspräsident* of the Weimar Republic (cf. p. 649).

As the new empire — consolidated politically and economically by the decisive victory over France, the prompt payment of the French indemnity, and the ensuing expansion of industry, trade, and commerce — rapidly advanced to a leading and pivotal position in Europe, the people found little reason to quarrel with Bismarck or to question the wisdom of his political course. If Bismarck was guilty of nationalism, he shared this guilt with his age: nationalism was in its ascendancy everywhere, and in the struggle for political and economic power the universalistic tendencies of a more or less remote past were forgotten.

As an external symbol of its departure from the *grossdeutsch*-universalist and federalist ideology the new *Reich* adopted black, white, and red as its national colors, combining the Prussian black and white with the red of the Hansa city republics. The black, red, and gold of the Holy Roman Empire, of the followers of Jahn (cf. p. 442 sq.), of the Lützow Free Corps (cf. p. 448), of the revolution of 1848, and of the Austrian federalist movement was incompatible with the nationalistic aspirations of Bismarck's *Kleindeutschland.*

Bismarck's Foreign Policy (after 1871). William I, the new German emperor, and his trusted chancellor who had built the strongest nation on the European continent, found themselves immediately confronted with the task of allaying foreign apprehensions as to the future policies of Germany and therefore of convincing their neighbors that they had nothing to fear from a united and prosperous German nation. "We are satiated," declared Bismarck shortly after the Peace of Frankfurt. "It has always been my aim," he added, "to win the confidence of Europe and to convince it that German policy will be just and peaceful, now that it has repaired the *injuria temporum,* the disintegration of the nation." But aside from the widespread fear of further German expansionist aims, there were many dangerous tensions on the European continent which might precipitate an armed conflict at any time. It required the skill of a great statesman to neutralize these antagonistic forces and to steer the ship of State safely through many a threatening storm. Bismarck succeeded in this with the aid of a political pragmatism which never hesitated to shift friendships and alliances in accordance with the demands of changing political constellations and without much regard for abstract principles.

To isolate France and frustrate her desire for revenge, the German chancellor built a system of defensive alliances with Austria, Russia, and

Italy. In 1872 both Francis Joseph I of Austria and Alexander II of Russia visited Berlin, and Bismarck succeeded in engineering the *Dreikaiserbund* ('Three Emperors' League), a friendly accord among the three monarchs which, though it soon lapsed on account of the conflicting interests of Austria and Russia in the Balkans, was temporarily revived after the assassination of Alexander II in 1881. Friendship with the new Italian kingdom was fostered by the Berlin visit of Victor Emanuel II in 1873.

France, in the meantime, had rapidly recuperated from her defeat and had rebuilt her army, bringing it up to an effective strength of 471,000 men (as against Germany's 401,000), and adopting a new conscription law which provided for a five-year term of military service. Germany countered by adding to the fortifications of the frontier fortresses of Metz and Strasbourg. What Bismarck feared more than French rearmament, however, was a royalist restoration in France and a potential Franco-Austrian rapprochement. The Franco-German tension was eventually eased by the defeat of royalist and *revanche*-minded President MacMahon (1879) and the election of Gambetta, who was a Republican and in favor of a conciliatory policy toward Germany. The same end was ably pursued by Bismarck's ambassador to France, Prince Chlodwig zu Hohenlohe (1874–1885), the future German *Reichskanzler* (cf. p. 620). Hohenlohe was a scholar and statesman of international and liberal leanings, a south German federalist who was rooted in the universalist ideals of European culture and who for this reason had the reconciliation of Germany and France at heart.

German-Russian relations which had been friendly ever since the Wars of Liberation (cf. p. 446 sqq.) became strained after the Russian intervention in behalf of the oppressed Christian minorities under Turkish rule. Russia declared war on Turkey in 1877, and to discourage Russian ambitions aiming at Constantinople, England sent a fleet to the Black Sea, while Austria put an army into the field to check Russian moves in the Balkans. In 1878 Russia and Turkey signed the Treaty of San Stefano which guaranteed full independence to Serbia, Rumania, and Montenegro and recognized a "Greater Bulgaria," whose territory was to include the bulk of European Turkey and which was attached to the Russian sphere of influence. England and Austria, alarmed by this increase of Russian power, called for a revision of the Treaty of San Stefano and suggested to submit the issue to an international conference. It was a tribute to the newly won international prestige of the German empire and its chancellor that Berlin was chosen as the meeting place of the contending powers and that Bismarck was permitted to arbitrate the dispute, after he had declared that Germany was not interested in the Near-Eastern question and promised to act as an "honest broker."

The Congress of Berlin (1878) split Bulgaria into three parts, gave Bessarabia to Russia, and permitted Austria to administer the former Turkish provinces of Bosnia and Herzegovina. Although the achievements of the congress were hailed by Disraeli, the British prime minister and chief delegate, as "peace with honor," nothing was really settled, and the Balkans, whose representatives had not even been heard, were left seething with rivalries and unrest. The big powers were too much concerned with their own imperialist aims to judge objectively the issues at hand. While Lord Salisbury, the British foreign minister, shortly afterward regretted that England had "backed the wrong horse" at Berlin, encouraging Austrian expansion at the expense of Russia, Alexander II deeply resented the tripartition of his much coveted "Greater Bulgaria" into a northern independent region, a semiautonomous central section, and a southern Macedonian territory under Turkish control. The tsar blamed Bismarck for the Russian setback, and his veiled threats of war caused the German chancellor to look for a reliable ally to weather a possible Russian attack. Bismarck hurried to Vienna and concluded with the Austro-Hungarian Foreign Minister Andrassy the Austro-German Dual Alliance (1879), providing for mutual assistance in case of Russian aggression and for the benevolent neutrality of either party if one of the two nations should be attacked by France.

Meanwhile the French, in their attempt to extend their dominion in North Africa, occupied Tunis, a Turkish dependency, in 1881 and thereby thwarted the ambitions of Italy, which had hoped that this territory in the neighborhood of Sicily, located at the site of ancient Carthage, could be claimed as an Italian colonial possession on the "dark continent." Despite the fact that Bismarck, to keep France busy abroad and make her forget the loss of Alsace-Lorraine, had encouraged French expansion in Africa, he readily assured Italy of German support in case of a Franco-Italian clash in North Africa. Thus, in 1882, the *Dreibund* (Triple Alliance) of Germany, Austria-Hungary, and Italy was concluded, notwithstanding the Italian grievances against Austria on account of the "unredeemed" territories (*Italia irredenta*) of the southern Tyrol, Istria, and Trieste, whose Italian-speaking population was under Austrian rule. As in the case of the previous Austro-German *Zweibund,* it was agreed that the terms of the *Dreibund,* "in conformity with its peaceful intentions, and to avoid misinterpretation," were to be kept secret.

The second term of the Three Emperors' League expired in 1887, and as both Russia and Austria were adamant in their stand against a renewal, Bismarck, more than ever convinced that friendly relations with Russia were essential for the preservation of peace in Europe, concluded with Tsar Alexander III the secret *Rücksicherungsvertrag* (Reinsurance Treaty) of 1887. This treaty guaranteed mutual neutrality in case of a defensive war, but it was not renewed after its expiration in 1890.

Bismarck's system of alliances, although it had sporadically shown weaknesses and moved gradually toward disintegration, had succeeded in isolating France and in temporarily checking the French desire for *revanche*. This desire, however, was fanned to a new feverish heat by Boulanger, the French minister of war, who came into office after the fall of President Ferry in 1885. Ferry had cultivated the friendship of Germany and had thereby secured the undisturbed growth of the French colonial empire in Africa. In the face of a resurgence of French chauvinism and a threatening Franco-Russian rapprochement, Bismarck, in introducing the new Army Bill of 1887, reaffirmed in the *Reichstag* Germany's peaceful intentions: "We have no warlike needs," the chancellor said, "for we belong to what Metternich called satiated nations. We do not expect an attack from Russia. . . . The difficulty is not to keep Germany and Russia, but to keep Austria and Russia at peace. . . . We risk being called pro-Russian in Austria and pro-Austrian in Russia. That does not matter if we can maintain peace. Our relations with Austria rest on the consciousness of each that the existence of the other as a Great Power is a necessity in the interest of European equilibrium." Then speaking on the situation in the West, Bismarck declared: "We have no intention and no reason to attack France. . . . If the French will keep the peace till we attack, then peace is assured for ever. . . . But we have to fear an attack — whether in ten days or ten years I cannot say. War is certain if France thinks she is stronger and can win. This is my unalterable conviction. . . . If she won, she would not display our moderation of 1871. She would bleed us white, and, if we win, we would do the same to her. The war of 1870 would be child's play compared with a war of 1890 or whatever the date."

By 1887 Boulanger, who shortly afterward was tried *in absentia* for high treason and embezzlement and in 1889 committed suicide in Belgium, had been forced out of the French cabinet. However, in the same degree as Austro-Russian relations grew worse, the prospects for Franco-Russian friendship improved. Thus Bismarck found it necessary in the following year (1888) to review once more the European situation. It was his last major speech on foreign affairs in the *Reichstag*. "Like last year," he said, "I expect no attack. Yet the danger of coalition is permanent, and we must arrange once and for all to meet it. . . . We must make greater exertions than other nations on account of our position. Russia and France can only be attacked on one front; but God has placed us beside the most bellicose and restless of nations, the French, and He has allowed bellicose tendencies to grow up in Russia. We shall, however, wage no preventive war. Nevertheless, I advise other countries to discontinue their threats. We Germans fear God and nothing else in the world." This speech accompanied the introduction and passage of the last army bill endorsed by Bismarck. One month later Emperor William I died at the age of ninety-one, and after the short interval of the ninety-nine days' reign of his son, Frederick III (who succumbed to a cancerous throat ailment), William's twenty-nine-year-old grandson acceded to the throne as Emperor William II.

Bismarck's Domestic Policy (after 1871). The system of changing alliances and coalitions which served the German chancellor so well in conducting his foreign policy provided the pattern also for his dealing with domestic issues. As he could not rule against the will of a parliamentary majority, he sought alternating working agreements with the Progressives, the National Liberals, the Conservatives, and the Center party. Up to the time of William II's accession to the throne the domestic policies of Germany no less than her international policy bore the stamp of Bismarck's personality. In two specific instances, however, he failed to achieve his aims and instead strengthened the forces which he had intended to reduce to impotency. His fight against the "ultramontane" influence of the Catholic clergy resulted in a victory for the Church and a considerably strengthened Center party, and his antisocialist legislation had the effect of vastly increasing the socialist vote and of raising the factional representation of the Social Democrats in the Reichstag from nine seats in 1874 to thirty-five seats in 1890.

a) The "Kulturkampf."* Bismarck's attitude toward the Catholic Church was determined not by religious but by political considerations. The publication of the Syllabus of Pius IX** and even more the declaration of Papal Infallibility as promulgated by the Vatican Council had contributed to the creation of serious frictions between Church and State in Germany. The Center party in the Reichstag drew its strongest support from the Catholic population of the German South, among whom also the idea of Grossdeutschland (Greater Germany) had its deepest roots and where the critics of Bismarck's solution of the German Question had been most vociferous. In the state of Baden, which was ruled by the National Liberals, anticlerical legislation had been enacted as early as 1867.

Bismarck joined with the National Liberals in questioning the national loyalty and reliability of the Center party, the representative political organization of German Catholicism. Furthermore, he reproached the Center party for championing the cause of political and racial minorities, such as the Poles in Posnania and West Prussia, the Welfs in Hanover, and the French population of Lorraine, all equally opposed to the centralized administration in Prussia and in the Reich. Finally, ever apprehensive of potential hostile coalitions, Bismarck feared that in the eventuality of an international conflict involving Catholic powers, a politically organized Catholicism might sympathize with the enemy and thus hamper the German war effort.

German Liberalism, traditionally opposed to religious influences in politics and in education, welcomed the German chancellor's anticlerical campaign. Its hopes for a nationalized "romfreie Kirche" (a church free from Rome) received encouragement from the schismatic German Altkatholiken (Old Catholics) who had rejected the dogma of Papal Infallibility and had seceded from Rome in 1870. Their representatives were supported by Bismarck in

---

* The term, denoting a "struggle for civilization," was first used by Lassalle, later on by Rudolf Virchow, in an electoral manifesto of the Progressive party, and subsequently became the political slogan of anticlerical Liberalism.
** The Syllabus, published by the Papal State Chancery on December 8, 1864, contains a list of "the principal errors of our time." Specifically mentioned are among others, pantheism, naturalism, rationalism, indifferentism, socialism, communism, and liberalism.

their stand against the orthodox members of the German clergy and hierarchy.

The *Kulturkampf* began shortly after the foundation of the Second German Empire, reached its climax about 1875, and was gradually relaxed and finally called off between 1880 and 1887.

On July 8, 1871, the Catholic section of the Prussian ministry of culture and education was abolished, following the charge that its members had supported the Polish minority groups in Posnania and West Prussia. The *Jesuitengesetz* of 1872, which excluded all members of the Jesuit Order and affiliated congregations from the territory of the *Reich,* remained in force until 1917, although it was moderated in 1904. When the Vatican refused recognition to Cardinal Hohenlohe, the German envoy to the Holy See, Bismarck, referring to the historic contest between Henry IV and Gregory VII (cf. p. 71 sq.), declared defiantly: "Have no fear; to Canossa we will not go, neither in body nor in spirit."

In 1873 Adalbert Falk, the Prussian minister of culture and education, introduced the repressive *May Laws* which made all ecclesiastical education, discipline, and appointments subject to State approval and control. In the *Reich* civil marriage was made compulsory in 1875 (later on incorporated in the *Bürgerliches Gesetzbuch,* 1900). The Prussian *Brotkorbgesetz* (bread-basket law) of the same year canceled all State support for recalcitrant members of the clergy. Subsequently, all religious orders and congregations (with the exception of those in charge of the sick) were dissolved, the Catholics' right of organization and assembly curtailed, the Catholic press subjected to rigorous censorship, while many bishops and priests were fined, expelled, or imprisoned.

Bismarck tried to justify these repressive laws and measures in the Prussian *Herrenhaus* in 1873 by characterizing the struggle as "not a fight between faith and unbelievers, but rather the age-old contest between the kingship and the priesthood . . . ; the contest which filled the German Middle Ages down to the disintegration of the Empire; the contest which . . . found its medieval solution when the last heir of the illustrious house of Swabia died under the ax of the French conqueror, who was in league with the Pope."

The *Kulturkampf* was supported not only by Liberals, Protestant Conservatives, and "Old Catholics," but also by a group of Catholic nationalists (*Staatskatholiken*). On the other hand, it was opposed and condemned by many Protestant Conservatives (among them Crown Prince Frederick and his wife, and Empress Augusta), by the socialists, the French of Lorraine, the Poles of Posnania and West Prussia, and the Protestants of Hanover.

In 1878, confronted with the unexpected phenomenon of a greatly strengthened Center party and haunted by the specter of a parliamentary coalition of Centrists and Socialists, Bismarck began to retrace his steps and looked for an opportunity to start peace negotiations with Rome. His diplomatic retreat was made easier by Leo XIII, who succeeded Pius IX in 1879. The new pontiff, in his anxiety for the stabilization and pacification of social and international relations, was willing to meet the German chancellor halfway. Bismarck expressed his gratitude in a speech in the Prussian *Herrenhaus,* in which he paid tribute to Leo's love of peace and justice. "The Pope," he said, "is more pro-German than the Center party and . . . more interested in the consolidation of the *Reich* and the well-being of the Prussian state than the majority of the German *Reichstag* has been at times. . . . The Pope is not Welf or Polish, nor *deutsch-freisinnig* (German-liberal), and he has no leaning toward the Social Democrats. . . . He is simply Catholic. . . . He is free and represents the free Catholic Church. The Center party represents the Church in the service of parliamentarism and vote-getting intrigues. Hence I have chosen to address myself to the absolutely free Pope . . . because from the wisdom of Leo XIII and from his love of peace I expect more success for the internal peace of Germany than I did from the *Reichstag* and the Center party."

In enactments promulgated between 1881 and 1886 the previous legislative measures were so modified as to make them acceptable to the Vatican. The German Liberals who a little prematurely had hailed Bismarck as a second Luther had no further reason to applaud his dealings with Rome.

It was about this time that Bismarck started upon a new fiscal policy which called for protective tariff legislation and thus ran counter to the free-trade inclinations of the left-wing National Liberals. The payment of the French war indemnity had encouraged speculation on the stock market and resulted in overproduction in some industries, and the chancellor felt that the time had come to protect the German landowners, the producers of grain in eastern Germany, and the manufacturers, from the competition of foreign markets. To secure parliamentary approval of the new Tariff Bill he needed not only the votes of the Conservatives, on whom he could safely count in this matter of vital interest to them, but also those of the Center party. He therefore turned from the National Liberals, his onetime strongest supporters, and succeeded in gaining the backing of the Center party and its leader, Windthorst, for a program of moderate protectionism.

b) "Sozialistengesetz" and Social Legislation. For a second time Bismarck tried persecution as a weapon, in his fight against the rising tide of political socialism, and again he failed. But he had learned from past experience and therefore supplemented his antisocialist measures with a constructive program of social reform and social legislation.

The followers of the dialectic-materialist socialism of Marx and the romantic-idealist socialism of Lassalle (cf. p. 559) joined hands at the Convention of Gotha (1875) and together founded the Social Democratic party, whose tenets represented a compromise between the convictions of the two groups. The party adopted a program of progressive socialization, took a firm stand against the excessive increase of armaments, and opposed colonial imperialism. Since they ignored national boundaries and were eager to collaborate with their fellow socialists in foreign countries, they came to be regarded as *"vaterlandslose Gesellen"* (fellows without a country) and were believed by their political adversaries to constitute a threat to the healthy growth of the new Germany.

While Bismarck in an early meeting with Lassalle had shown an open mind for the just grievances of the working class, he denounced the demands of the Gotha program as "utopian nonsense." In 1878 two attempts were made on the life of William I, in the second of which the emperor was severely wounded. Although the perpetrators were radicals without socialist party affiliations, these incidents served Bismarck as an excuse to introduce his antisocialist bill, the *Sozialistengesetz*. The chancellor, confronted with a parliamentary majority unfavorable to the proposed harsh measures, had the *Reichstag* dissolved. When the newly elected representatives convened the bill was adopted with the votes of the Conservatives and National Liberals and renewed in 1880, 1884, and 1886, the last two times with the additional votes of the Centrists.

The Social Democrats, in the meantime, increased their vote from 500,000 in 1877 to 763,000 in 1887 and to 1,427,000 in Bismarck's last *Reichstag* of 1890. In the election of 1912 they obtained 110 seats (out of 397) and thus had become the strongest party in the *Reichstag*. This success was due not only to the antisocialist legislation (which was allowed to lapse long before 1912) but to the general social problems and conditions of the industrial age and to the able and high-minded leadership of August Bebel and Wilhelm Liebknecht. Bebel, for example, had enough sense of perspective to acknowledge ungrudgingly Leo XIII's efforts in behalf of social justice. "The Pope has stated," he said, "that the Church must work toward the goal of securing a just wage for the workingman. . . . And as the members of the Catholic clergy are in permanent touch with the working classes — far more so than the Protestants — Social Democracy has so far not succeeded in expanding as much among Catholics as among Protestants."

The *Sozialistengesetz* decreed the dissolution of all organizations which, by carrying on socialistic or communistic activities, were believed to constitute a danger to the public peace or aimed at the overthrow of the existing order. All meetings and demonstrations of such a nature were to be supervised and could be dissolved, and all subversive publications were prohibited. Entire districts could be placed under a state of limited emergency, and persons who were suspected of endangering public order could be denied domicile in these restricted areas. The law did not propose, however, to interfere with *Reichstag* debates, election speeches and campaigns, and the rights of suffrage. The *Sozialistengesetz*, like the anticlerical legislation, was gradually mitigated and finally discarded when, in 1890, a majority of Conservatives, Centrists, Progressive Liberals, and Social Democrats voted against its renewal.

Bismarck met the demands of the Social Democrats and the dissatisfaction of the proletarian masses positively by a comprehensive plan of *social legislation* which anticipated by several decades similar enactments in England

Otto von Bismarck, by Franz von Lenbach

Crown Prince Frederick William

and France, to say nothing of the much more laggard labor policy of the United States. The chancellor clarified his position in his *Reichstag* speech of April 2, 1881. "For fifty years," he declared, "we have been talking about the social question. . . . Free enterprise is no magic formula; the state can become responsible also for the things it fails to do. I am not of the opinion that the principles of *laissez-faire, laissez-aller,* pure *Manchestertum* in politics — 'let each man himself see to it that he gets along'; 'he who is not strong enough to stand will be run over and trodden down'; 'he that hath, to him shall be given, and he that hath not, from him shall be taken' — can be applied in the paternalistic monarchical state. On the contrary, I hold that those who oppose state intervention for the protection of the weak lay themselves open to the suspicion that they wish to use their strength . . . to gain support and to suppress others in order to establish a party rule. . . . Call this socialism, if you will, I do not care. . . . I desire to see our state, in which the vast majority are Christians, permeated with the doctrines of the religion we profess, especially with those regarding charity toward one's neighbor and compassion for the old and suffering."

The imperial message of November 17 of the same year announced the inauguration of comprehensive labor legislation. The Health Insurance Law, providing for half pay and medical attention for a period of six months in case of sickness, was introduced and adopted in 1883. The Accident Insurance Law, stipulating compensation for partially or totally disabled workers as well as a pension for the dependents of workers killed in the pursuit of their occupation, followed in 1884. The most far-reaching measure, the Old Age Pension Act, securing a retirement annuity for all workers over seventy and for those incapacitated at an earlier age, was passed in 1889. This vast program was supplemented in 1891 by the *Arbeiterschutzgesetz* (law for the protection of labor) which laid down rules for the enforcement of labor rest on Sundays and legal holidays, for State control of safety and health conditions in industry, for the protection of women in the labor market, and for the restriction and eventual abolition of child labor. The *Reichsversicherungsordnung* (federal insurance legislation) of 1911 unified and further implemented all the previous enactments.

Bismarck's Dismissal. Prince William of Prussia, the son of Frederick III and the favorite grandson of Queen Victoria of England, became German emperor and king of Prussia on June 15, 1888. Although before his accession to the throne he had shown great admiration for Bismarck's personality and work, frictions were soon to develop between the young, self-willed, and impetuous monarch and his chancellor. From his uncle, Frederick William IV, the new emperor had inherited the idea of the "divine right" and mission of kings and princes, but a lack of real self-assurance due to inexperience made him feel outweighed and overshadowed by Bismarck's genius. The desire for self-assertion and for popular acclaim caused him to bluster and blunder. Nevertheless, it seemed at first that William II was willing to fall in line with Bismarck's established policies. Heeding the advice of both his grandfather (William I) and his chancellor to cultivate friendship with Russia, he began his round of official state visits in St. Petersburg. As he was an ardent Anglophile, it needed no persuasion to convince him of the need for cordial relations with England. Early in 1889 Bismarck, with the emperor's approval, definitely suggested to Lord Salisbury, then British prime minister, a German-British alliance, arguing that "the peace of Europe can best be secured by a treaty between Germany and England, pledging them to mutual support against a French attack." Salisbury expressed hope for such an alliance in the future, but for the present he wanted "to leave the offer on the table, without saying yes or no." In the summer of the same year the German emperor paid his first visit to England, where he was received with cordiality and feted with great splendor. In 1890 Great Britain ceded to Germany the island of Heligoland, in exchange for the East African territories of Zanzibar, Wituland, and Uganda.

The occasion of the first open conflict between the emperor and his chancellor was a large-scale strike of miners in the Ruhr District (1889). William II, in the hope of increasing his popularity with the working class and their Social Democratic representation in the German *Reichstag* and Prussian *Landtag* by a policy of conciliation, invited a delegation of the miners to Berlin and in a blunt statement unequivocally affirmed the justice of their demands. Bismarck strongly disapproved and saw in the emperor's attitude a capitulation to the forces of radical socialism.

The open break between William and Bismarck occurred in 1890, consequent upon the frequent interferences of the emperor with the policies of Bismarck's cabinet and his direct dealings with individual cabinet ministers, over the head of the chancellor. Bismarck, determined to stop this dangerous procedure, appealed to a Prussian cabinet order of 1852 which stipulated that cabinet ministers could only report to the king after previous consultation with the prime minister. William's demand that this cabinet order be revoked was firmly rejected by Bismarck. The already tense situation was aggravated by a private visit which Windthorst, the Centrist leader, paid to Bismarck to discuss the political situation created by the recent *Reichstag* election, in which the Conservatives and National Liberals had suffered a severe setback, while the Social Democrats had emerged stronger than ever before. When the emperor reprimanded Bismarck for having received Windthorst without previous authorization by the sovereign, the chancellor blandly declared that he would receive any deputy of good manners any time, and that he would never submit to control over his own home. The conflict reached its climax when the emperor accidentally learned of the report of a subaltern consular official in Kiev concerning the movements of Russian troops. William angrily reproached Bismarck for having concealed from him this "terrible danger" and advised him to dispatch a strong warning to Austria. The sharp note containing this accusation was followed by a demand for immediate resignation. In a document which summarized the issues that had brought on the crisis and specified the reasons for submitting his resignation, Bismarck once more stressed the necessity of continued friendly relations with Russia, as any other course "would endanger all the important successes gained by the German Empire in the last decades under the rule of Your Majesty's two predecessors."

Bismarck retired to his estate of Friedrichsruh near Hamburg which during the remaining years of his life became the object of veritable pilgrimages of men and women from many regions and lands and from all walks of life. The first and greatest chancellor of the Second German Empire died on July 30, 1898.

The "New Course." The nominal successors of Bismarck in the Office of *Reichskanzler* during the next two decades were General von Caprivi (1890–1894), Prince Hohenlohe (1894–1900), and Prince Bülow (1900–1909). His actual successor, however, was the sinister Baron Fritz von Holstein who, even after his forced retirement as *Vortragender Rat* (assistant under-secretary) in the foreign office in 1906, retained his pernicious influence on German foreign policy to his death in 1909. The "gray eminence," as Holstein was nicknamed in court and diplomatic circles, was a shrewd and reckless politician, an expert in the manipulation of secret diplomacy, who despite his subaltern rank was the real power behind the throne of William II. Many of the erratic actions commonly attributed to the *Kaiser's* "personal regime" may be traced to the unseen direction of this master of political intrigue. To achieve his ends and impose his will on the emperor and the imperial cabinet, he exploited his knowledge of certain compromising private affairs of high-ranking personages, as well as the conflicting interests of such rival groups as the army, the navy, the heavy industries, the banking concerns, and the Pan-German nationalists. Together with Maximilian Harden (1861–1927), the highly talented but utterly cynical editor of the political journal *Die Zukunft* (the future), he employed his unquestionable skill to discredit the *Kaiser* and his regime at home and abroad.

The nonrenewal of the secret Reinsurance Treaty with Russia, on the ground that it was incompatible with the Austro-German alliance, was largely due to Holstein's hatred of Russia and his friendly feelings toward Austria. The immediate consequence was exactly what William I and Bismarck had dreaded, namely, a "cordial understanding" between Russia and France, leading eventually to the secret military alliance of 1894. Germany thus lost her pivotal position as mediator between the rival ambitions of Russia and Austria, and from a strategic point of view she suddenly found herself exposed on her eastern and western flanks.

As Holstein favored friendly relations with England, Caprivi was permitted to follow his own inclination in this regard and to continue the course charted out by Bismarck. However, for reasons of domestic policy the days of Caprivi's chancellorship were numbered. Yielding to liberal pressure, the German government had entered into trade agreements with a number of neighboring states (Austria-Hungary, Italy, Switzerland, Belgium, Russia, Serbia, Rumania) and subsequently lowered her protective tariffs. The resulting reduction of the prices for agricultural products made the agrarians feel themselves threatened in their vital interests, and in 1893 they formed the powerful *Bund der Landwirte* (Agrarian League) which was destined to play a role of increasing importance in the parliamentary life of Prussia and the *Reich*. The Liberals in turn joined the Social Democrats and Centrists in their opposition to a proposed increase of the armed forces. The new army bill was finally adopted by a newly elected *Reichstag,* but Caprivi resigned shortly afterward and was replaced in 1904 by the aged Prince Hohenlohe, the former German ambassador to France, who very reluctantly took over the burdens of his new office.

It seemed at first as if under Hohenlohe's chancellorship relations with England were to remain correct and even cordial, notwithstanding the fact that Germany's successful competition in the world markets and in the race for colonies (cf. p. 624 sq.) had begun to arouse anxiety and some misgivings in the British Isles. These feelings were intensified by imprudent and provocative utterances of the German emperor on several of his good-will visits to England. One year after Germany had celebrated the completion of the *Kaiser Wilhelm-Kanal* (1895) — linking the North Sea with the Baltic and thereby opening up a new, northern trade route — the first of several serious incidents occurred. William II dispatched the famous *Krüger Telegram* to Paul Krüger, president of the Boer Free State of Transvaal, in which he congratulated the Boer leader on having successfully repulsed the raid engineered by the English-born South African statesman Jameson. As the London Convention of 1884 had given Great Britain control over the foreign affairs of Transvaal, and as the action of the German emperor was coupled with the warning that Germany could not allow any attack on the independence of the Boer Free State, British reaction was naturally most unfavorable and hostile to Germany. Though the incident was soon smoothed over by diplomatic explanations and by an apologetic letter of Emperor William to Queen Victoria, it was never forgotten.

The "new course" in German foreign policy, which is usually dated from the time of Bismarck's dismissal, did not really become very conspicuous until 1897, the year in which Bülow became German minister of foreign affairs and Alfred von Tirpitz was appointed grand admiral of the German navy. Hohenlohe's moderating influence was nullified by the determination of the emperor and his chief advisers to embark on the ventures of a *Weltpolitik* which was to prepare the stage for World War I.

English sympathy was further alienated by William II's challenging declaration that Germany's future lay on the high seas, and that he would never rest until he had raised the German navy to the standard of the German army. When Bülow succeeded Hohenlohe as *Reichskanzler* in 1900, the challenge to British sea power became even more pronounced. The new naval building program of Tirpitz, which aimed at constructing a High Seas Fleet second to none, was met across the Channel with the announcement that England would launch two warships for each German one.

In France, meanwhile, the *revanche*-minded Théophile Delcassé had become minister of foreign affairs in 1898, while in England the Francophile prince of Wales had succeeded Queen Victoria in 1901 as King Edward VII. Although no formal treaty was as yet signed between the two powers, they were drawn together by the mutual sympathies of their political leaders as well as by their common opposition to Germany's "new course."

In 1902 Great Britain and Japan concluded a treaty of alliance which made it possible for England to withdraw part of her navy from the Pacific, while the Franco-British *Entente Cordiale* of 1904 released most of the units of the British Mediterranean fleet for duty in the North Sea. The Russian defeat in the Russo-Japanese War (1904–1905), revealing the weakness of tsarist Russia when forced to rely on her own resources, indirectly paved the way for the *Triple Entente* of Russia, France, and England, which was created in 1907 and officially announced by King Edward VII in 1908. Thus England had at long last been persuaded to relinquish her "splendid isolation," to join a powerful bloc of nations, designed to meet the combination of the *Dreibund*. This decisive step on the part of Great Britain was taken with much hesitation and only after the German emperor had consistently and obstinately refused to consider any limitation of the German fleet.

Europe was now divided into two hostile camps of almost equal numerical strength, but the power potential of the *Dreibund* was more apparent than real, as Italy's partnership in it had grown more and more halfhearted. Extremely vulnerable to an attack by sea, by virtue of her extended shore lines, she could ill afford to antagonize Great Britain. Therefore, while outwardly adhering to her commitments under the terms of the *Dreibund*, she was more than anxious to regain her freedom of action. At the same time the animosity against Austria was kept alive by the partisans of the *Irredenta* movement, who demanded that all Austrian territories inhabited by Italians or an Italian-speaking majority be returned to Italy.

Although the Triple Entente was conceived as a defensive alliance, to become practically effective only in case of overt military aggression, its creation was interpreted by Germany and Austria-Hungary as an actual "encirclement" which, while using intimidation as a temporary means, aimed ultimately at aggression. The growing mutual distrust between the two power blocs, fed by an increasing number of diplomatic incidents, added to the tension and spurred the nations on to redouble their efforts to outbid the armed strength of their opponents. The burden of armaments was reflected in the staggering increases of the national budgets and in the demand for higher taxes to meet the cost of the huge military appropriations.

The German people in their majority confidently followed the course traced out by their political and military leaders. While the Social Democrats and Progressives were often outspoken in their opposition to militarism and imperialism, they were, on the other hand, not insensitive to the danger of foreign aggression, and were determined to meet it at any time shoulder to shoulder with their compatriots. The parties of the Center and the Right (Centrists, National Liberals, and Conservatives) more or less openly supported a vigorous foreign policy. The only group which frankly clamored for national expansion by force of arms was that of the not too numerous but all the more noisy *Alldeutsche* (Pan-Germans). They even dreamed of incorporating into the German orbit the territories of politically separate but racially and linguistically related populations, such as those of Austria, Bohemia, Alsace, Switzerland, Holland, and Belgium. Their ambitions grew even bolder after Germany had taken the first steps toward the creation of a colonial empire (cf. p. 624 sq.). In 1891 they founded the *Alldeutscher Verband* (Pan-German League), an organization which publicly professed and propagated the Pan-German objectives.

The Pan-German call for a union with German Austria and the Sudeten Germans was bound to evoke memories of the *grossdeutsche* movement (cf. p. 530), but there was a vast difference between the advocates of *Grossdeutschland* and those of *Alldeutschland*. Whereas the former had in cosmopolitan spirit aspired to a federation of German states, whose Christian-universalist outlook and culture could bridge the antagonisms between eastern and western Europe and could thus become the nucleus of a world-wide federation, the latter strove for a nationalist Germanic empire of vast dimensions whose claims to power were to rest on the narrow concept of a supposed racial and cultural superiority. The Pan-German movement was thus at best a badly perverted application of the idea of *Grossdeutschland*.

In two instances at least the voices of the domestic critics of the German government's militaristic and imperialistic exploits were heard and sustained by large sections of the German population. In 1908 the indignation which was aroused by an unsigned interview with William II in the *London Daily Telegraph* — in which the emperor reaffirmed his pro-British sympathies, while at the same time accusing the German people of refusing to follow him on his conciliatory course — was so great that even Bülow was seriously perturbed and decided that the time had come to speak plainly to his sovereign. A government crisis, during which William II even mentioned the possibility of abdication, was resolved by the emperor's promise to observe more caution and tact in the future. However, in the following year Bülow, after being charged with having "betrayed" His Imperial Majesty during the critical *Reichstag* debates, was replaced by Theobald von Bethmann-Hollweg.

The second provocation of the home front occurred in the spring of 1914, when the imperial government decided to back an overbearing and misbehaving Prussian lieutenant of the garrison of the Alsatian town of Zabern by decreeing the sternest repressive measures against the aroused populace. This incident more than the many past political and psychological mistakes in the administration of the annexed province, made the *Reich* lose the sympathies of German Alsace. Public opinion was thoroughly shaken out of its habitual quiescence, and the abuses of militarism were severely indicted as never before.

Bethmann-Hollweg, the fifth *Reichskanzler* of the Second Empire, was a conservative with liberal leanings. He was a man of high ideals and a speculative bent of mind (the "chancellor-philosopher"), but was weak willed and therefore unable to hold his ground against the rising tide of militant German imperialism. The Prussian *Junkers* defeated his attempted reform of the Prussian *Dreiklassenwahlrecht* (cf. p. 529), and in the foreign field his efforts to reach a naval agreement with England were doomed to failure by the joint opposition of William II, Admiral Tirpitz, and the Navy League. Characteristically enough, when Lord Haldane, the British secretary of war, visited Berlin at Germany's request in 1912, the negotiations on the proposed naval truce were carried on by Tirpitz, not by Bethmann-Hollweg. It was Haldane's impression that "Tirpitz's school of thought will not be satisfied so long as it cannot dominate British sea-power."

The conversations dragged on and were further complicated by the simultaneous introduction of the new German Navy Bill. Germany's demand that England promise neutrality in a European war in exchange for a limitation of the German naval program was rejected by Great Britain on the ground that such a promise would be incompatible with her obligations to the other signatory powers of the Triple Entente. The drift toward an open break was only halted by the impact of the Balkan Wars of 1912–1913 (cf. p. 626 sq.), which made Germany and England join hands once more in a common attempt to prevent that conflict from developing into a general European war. Before the Balkan crisis Germany had flatly rejected the naval truce suggested by Lord Haldane, but now even Tirpitz hinted at the possibility of a ten to sixteen ratio of German and English capital ships.

However, this slight improvement in Anglo-German relations was more than outweighed by increasing tensions between Germany and France in the West, and between Austria and Russia in the East. Raymond Poincaré, like Delcassé an advocate of an anti-German policy of *revanche,* became prime minister of France in 1912 and succeeded to the presidency in 1913. France decided to raise the term of military service from two to three years, and almost simultaneously Germany adopted another army bill which set aside large appropriations for the further strengthening of the frontier fortresses, for the enlargement and improvement of the artillery, and for an increased gold reserve. The centenary celebration of the battle of Leipzig (cf. p. 451) in 1913 enabled the Pan-Germans to indulge in a frenzy of riotous nationalism, a demonstration which solidified the impression in the camp of the Triple Entente that a major conflict could not be held off much longer.

The Balkan Wars provided Germany with her last opportunity to act as mediator between Russia and Austria. However, the appointment of the Prussian General Liman von Sanders as reorganizer of the Turkish army was interpreted by Russia as a deliberate attempt on the part of

Germany to thwart any Russian advance in the direction of Constantinople and the Straits. The subsequent removal of Liman von Sanders from the command of the First Army Corps of the Turkish forces and his appointment as general inspector of the Turkish army was not enough of a concession to assuage Russian resentment.

Thus the seeds of war were sprouting in every part of Europe, and the international atmosphere was so heavily charged with inflammable matter that only a spark was needed to start off a general conflagration.

The Colonial Empire. As long as Bismarck remained at the helm of the second German empire he adhered to his policy of limited objectives. It was his intention to build Germany as a strong and unified continental power and he was averse to colonial ambitions and adventures. It was only reluctantly therefore that he finally yielded to the increasing demand for colonial markets, to relieve the economic pressure caused by the speedy industrialization of Germany after 1871. Owing to their belated achievement of political unity, the long prevalent agricultural bases of their economy, and their prolonged preoccupation with purely domestic problems, the Germans felt later than other nations the disturbing social and economic effects of the Industrial Revolution. When they finally appeared as industrial competitors and as claimants for overseas markets, the race for colonies was almost over, and the choicest territories had already been parceled out among the colonial empires of Spain, Portugal, Holland, England, and France.

From 1871 on, the dilemma experienced by other highly industrialized nations was brought home to Germany: the domestic food supply could no longer satisfy the needs of a growing population, and the urgency of increased imports of both food and raw materials produced the demand for colonial markets. As Germany, looking for open doors on other continents, became entangled in the intricate web of world economy, clashes with the colonial and imperialist interests of other powers were bound to occur.

In the eighties a merchant from Bremen had acquired control over some territories on the west coast of Africa and asked the German government for protection. Bismarck yielded to this request in 1884 and proclaimed a protectorate over what came to be known as German Southwest Africa. In the same year the West African regions of Togo and Kamerun were obtained by annexation. In 1885 East Africa, part of New Guinea, and some of the South Sea Islands (Marshall Islands) were added to the German colonial possessions. In 1899 the Caroline, Marian, and Palau Islands in the Pacific were purchased from Spain, and in 1900 a German protectorate was declared over the two largest Samoan Islands. The assassination of two missionaries in China had provided the German government with a welcome pretext to obtain from the Chinese government the port of Kiaochow and the coal fields of its rich hinterland on a ninety-nine year lease (1898). By the end of the century the German colonial empire comprised an aggregate area of over one million square miles and a native population numbering approximately twelve million.

German misrule in parts of the protectorate of Southwest Africa led to the violent uprisings of the Hereros and Hottentots in 1904. After their subjugation the economic exploitation of this colony proceeded apace. Immigration from the motherland, which in the beginning had to be stimulated artificially by the propaganda of the colonial office and of private *Kolonial-gesellschaften* (colonial associations, e.g., the German Africa Society, 1878), gradually began to flow more steadily, and in the end even the natives began to share to some extent in the higher cultural and economic standards of the colonizers. In 1912 the over-all trade returns from the German colonial empire amounted to about 240 million marks ($60,000,000), a sum total which is not too impressive considering the fact that both politically and economically the colonization had more often proved a liability rather than an asset to the motherland.

The Treaty of Versailles (cf. p. 651 sqq.) stripped Germany of all her colonies. They were nominally placed under the administration of the League of Nations, but actually were added as "mandates" to the colonial empires of the allied powers. The holders of such mandates were legally authorized to expropriate and expel all German nationals then living in these territories. With the exception of the South African Union they availed themselves of this privilege.

Colonial Frictions and International Crises. In the period from 1871 to 1895 the proportion of the rapidly growing German population to the available domestic resources was most unfavorable. Colonial expansion could thus be justified on economic grounds: partly from the need for new markets which were not closed by foreign protective tariffs, and partly from the desire to find outlets for the surplus population of the homeland. The stabilization of German economy during the final years of the nineteenth century, however, invalidated the force of these arguments. England in particular viewed with growing suspicion the renewed German demands for additional colonies. In her own case she regarded the possession of a colonial empire and the command of an adequate sea power for its protection as a matter of life or death, whereas in the case of Germany she recognized no such necessity and therefore interpreted the German demands as a deliberate challenge to the British empire. It is thus hardly surprising that international crises multiplied after 1895, many of them growing out of the rival colonial ambitions of Europe's great powers. And though many of these incidents were disposed of by arbitration or some compromise solution, each of them left a residue of bitterness and distrust which tended to heighten the tenseness of the international situation.

a) The Morocco Crises. The Congress of Berlin of 1884 tried to apportion spheres of influence and adjust rival colonial claims. Despite the fact that the British were considerably irritated by Germany's annexation of African territory bordering on some of their own colonial possessions, they finally agreed to recognize the German protectorates in 1890. Great Britain also acquiesced in France's penetration of Morocco (excepting the Spanish-owned strip of Mediterranean coast line, opposite Gibraltar), but this time Germany objected and thereby provoked three major diplomatic clashes which in each instance brought Europe to the very brink of war.

In 1903 an agreement was reached whereby Morocco was recognized as lying within the French, and Egypt as lying within the British sphere of influence. However, when France proceeded to the occupation of Morocco in 1905, Germany intervened, claiming that her interests had been completely ignored. William II, interrupting his sea voyage to Jerusalem, landed in Tangier on the Moroccan coast and categorically declared that he would be satisfied only with either the complete autonomy of Morocco or its administration under international control. As these demands met with the combined opposition of France and England, the German government proposed to submit the issue to an international conference.

The Algeciras Conference of 1906, while nominally recognizing the sovereignty of the Arab sultan of Morocco, granted France and Spain "police powers" to "maintain order" in the sultanate. At the same time the conference cemented further the Franco-British alliance.

The *second Morocco crisis* came in 1908, when French military police, in search of some deserters from the Foreign Legion, unlawfully entered the German consulate in Casablanca. Germany launched a vigorous protest, and the matter was finally referred for settlement to the Hague court of international arbitration (cf. p. 629 sq.). A compromise was reached by Germany's declaration that her interests in Morocco were exclusively economic, and by France's agreement to safeguard the economic interests of all powers in the Moroccan protectorate.

The *third crisis* occurred in 1911, after French forces had occupied the Moroccan capital city of Fez, following serious disturbances in the interior. Both Germany and Spain charged that this occupation violated the terms of the settlements of Algeciras of 1906 and of the Hague court of 1909. Germany underscored her diplomatic representations by dispatching the gunboat *Panther* to the south Moroccan port of Agadir (the *Panthersprung*). Again Great Britain placed herself firmly at the side of France, thus causing Germany to withdraw the *Panther* and making her agree to another compromise (1912) whereby she was assured freedom of trade in Morocco and was to receive a large slice of the French Congo (New Kamerun), in exchange for German recognition of the French Moroccan protectorate.

b) The Balkan Crises. Bismarck's successors did not share his conviction that the problems of the Balkans and the entire Near East "were not worth the bones of one Pomeranian grenadier." This policy of aloofness toward the Balkans had enabled him to mediate between the conflicting interests of Austria and Russia. The men, however, who were responsible for the "new course" of German foreign policy were soon attracted by the political and commercial possibilities of an extension of German influence into the Near East. This *Drang nach Osten* was bound to involve Germany sooner or later in the cross-purposes of Austrian and Russian imperialism.

In 1888, while Bismarck was still in office, German banking interests, capitalizing on the desire of influential political and military circles in Germany for a sphere of influence in Asiatic Turkey, obtained a Turkish concession to administer the railroad line running from Constantinople to Ismed, and to extend it to Ankara and Konya. This latter point was reached in 1896.

So far the German penetration of Turkey had been purely economic, but from then on the political interests began to predominate. William II, showing himself as indifferent as Bismarck to the complaints of the Eastern Christians against Turkish oppression, defied the concerted opinion of the great powers by making himself the champion of the sultan. In 1898 he journeyed to Constantinople, Syria, and Palestine, and at Damascus reassured the sultan and "the three hundred million Moslems scattered over the earth" that "the German Emperor will always be their friend."

In 1902 Germany was given permission by Turkey to extend the rail line to Bagdad, and from there to Basra and the Persian Gulf. The plans were thus laid for a new and much shortened trade route from central Europe to the Indian Ocean, and the Germans could proudly point to the "Berlin-Bagdad" scheme as being on a par with the much heralded British "Cape to Cairo" railway. Fear of Germany's preponderance in Turkey and her eventual control of the Bosphorus as well as of the route to India caused Great Britain and France to decline a German offer to have the Bagdad project financed and administered by an international consortium. Once more, on his visit to London in 1907, William II tried to ease British apprehensions by offering England control of the Persian section of the railway, but British insistence that the matter must be submitted to France and Russia for their approval nullified this conciliatory gesture. An agreement between Germany and England in this hotly disputed question was finally reached on June 15, 1914. The treaty was signed on July 27, only a few days before the outbreak of World War I. It provided for a German-British board of directors of the Bagdad company, and for cession to a British concern of a section extending from Basra to the Persian Gulf.

The fears of Great Britain and France of German domination in the Near East were not entirely justified, for the road from Berlin to Bagdad had to traverse the territories of the Balkans, the "powder magazine of Europe." It was a foregone conclusion that at least the Balkan Slavs would stubbornly oppose any Germanic penetration or domination. The waves of Slav nationalism were surging higher than usual, and the Serbs, encouraged by Russia, aimed at the creation of a Pan-Slav Balkan state. They strove to include the Slavic populations of Bosnia and Herzegovina, the provinces which, as stipulated by the Congress of Berlin (1878), were policed and partially administered by Austria, although constitutionally they were still under Turkish sovereignty. The Austrian government, alarmed by the Young Turkish revolution of 1908 and eager to forestall the rival claims of Serbs and Turks, annexed both provinces in the same year. Turkey, too weak to resist, was pacified by the payment of an indemnity. The infuriated Serbs, advised by Russia — still suffering from the aftereffects of her defeat in the Russo-Japanese War (1904–1905) — to avoid everything that might lead to an armed conflict, reluctantly abandoned their warlike preparations. Thus the first Balkan storm blew over.

New complications, however, arose in the Near East as an aftermath of the Turko-Italian War of 1911–1912 and led to the *First Balkan War* (1912). Encouraged by England to pursue her colonial exploits in Africa, Italy seized the Turkish possession of Tripoli and defeated Turkey in the ensuing conflict. The evident weakness of the Ottoman state tempted the Balkan states (Greece, Serbia, Montenegro, Bulgaria) to launch a combined attack on Turkey, which was despoiled of almost all its European possessions. But shortly afterward the victors fell out over the distribution of the spoils, and Bulgaria, turning on her erstwhile brothers-in-arms, was decisively beaten by them and forced to yield to Serbia and Greece most of her earlier gains, and part of her own territory besides.

At the Conference of London (1913), which terminated the *Second Balkan War,* Austria and Italy insisted on transforming the former Turkish province of Albania into an autonomous principality, thereby frustrating Serbia's desire for an outlet to the Adriatic.

Serbia and Greece emerged from the Balkan Wars with their territories almost doubled. Serbia received the larger part of Macedonia and some North Albanian regions, while Greece was given southern Macedonia, including Salonika, the western part of Thrace, Epirus, and most of the Aegean Isles. While Bulgaria linked her interests with those of Germany and Austria-Hungary, Serbia was fortified by her territorial gains in her Pan-Slav ideology and in her hostility toward Austria.

As the year 1913 drew to a close, conditions in the Near East were more fraught with dangers and explosive possibilities than before the outbreak of the Balkan conflict. The only ray of hope on the international horizon was the slight improvement in German-British relations which resulted from the mission of Lord Haldane and the progress in his negotiations on a naval truce and on the Bagdad railway.

Peace Movements. The final decades of the nineteenth century and the first decade of the twentieth witnessed not only an international armament race and a general intensification of aggressive nationalism, but also a certain crystallization of the sentiment in favor of a reduction of armaments, of international arbitration, and the creation of suitable instruments for the organization and maintenance of peace. Pacifists of various shades of political and religious conviction added their voices to those of the Vatican, the socialist labor movement, and left-wing liberalism to demand the substitution of international legal institutions for the latent anarchy of a precarious armed peace.

Religious pacifism has its home in England and the United States, and it was in the former country that the first peace societies were founded early in the nineteenth century. The London Peace Society was established in 1816, and the first peace society on the European continent was constituted at Geneva in 1830. The first international peace congress was held at Brussels in 1848, and on this occasion the demands for international arbitration and general disarmament were first advanced. After the Crimean War steps were taken to curb the abuses of unlimited national sovereignty and to humanize sea warfare. The fifteen nations attending the Geneva Convention of 1864 created the organization of the International Red Cross and adopted provisions for the humane treatment of wounded enemy soldiers and prisoners of war. These resolutions were later on incorporated in the codes of martial law of most civilized nations and were further implemented by the peace conferences of the Hague of 1899 and 1907. All these international gatherings were milestones on the way to the reconstruction and further elaboration of the principles of international law, which had never had much sway except in theory, but had completely fallen into abeyance in the age of princely absolutism and excessive nationalism.

Germany was the cradle of "classical pacifism," best documented in Immanuel Kant's tract *Zum ewigen Frieden* (*On Eternal Peace,* cf. p. 374) and conceived by him as "a scientific and practical conquest of the international system of power through the creation of an international system of law." The German *Friedensgesellschaft* (peace society) was founded at Berlin in 1892 by Alfred Fried, Helmut von Gerlach, and Ludwig Quidde. These individual and collective efforts in Germany and elsewhere were supplemented during and after World War I by the creation of several Catholic, Protestant, and interdenominational societies for the promotion of international peace.*

The hopes of the advocates of international peace through collaboration and arbitration were greatly strengthened by a manifesto of Tsar Nicholas II. In 1898 he invited the nations of the world to send representatives to an international conference at the Hague, to devise peaceful and legal ways and means to settle their differences. Although Germany did not refuse to participate in the conference, her attitude with regard to its proceedings and aims was as cool and even cynical as that of England had been on the occasion of a similar Russian initiative in the days of the Holy Alliance (cf. p. 459 sq.). William II was as outspoken as usual when he declared that he was willing to have Germany represented at the Hague in order not to be blamed in Russia and elsewhere for refusing, but that the best guarantee of peace was still the sharpened sword.

When the first Hague conference met in 1899, Prince Münster, the German

---

* The most important were the *Friedensbund deutscher Katholiken* (1917; parallel organizations in England, Holland, Switzerland, Poland, and the United States); Marc Sangnier's *Action internationale démocratique pour la paix* (Paris, 1921); the Protestant World League for friendship among the Churches (1914); the *Evangelischer Friedensbund* (1931); the League of Nations (1920-1946); and the United Nations (with UNESCO [United Nations Educational, Scientific and Cultural Organization], 1945-). German periodicals for the promotion of peace: *Die Friedenswarte* (organ *of the Friedensgesellschaft*); *Der Friedenskämpfer* (Cath.); *Die Zeit* (ed. by F. W. Foerster).

delegate, was specifically instructed by his government to vote against any measure proposing disarmament, and it needed the earnest persuasion of Henry White, the secretary of the United States embassy in London, to make Germany accept at least the Court of Arbitration. At the second Hague conference of 1907 England once more designated the question of disarmament as a matter of prime importance, and again the German government not only made its attendance conditional on the removal of this question from the agenda, but seriously jeopardized the success of the conference by her opposition to the principle of arbitration.

Reviewing the balance sheet of the Hague conferences in the *Reichstag* of the German republic in 1919, Count von Brockdorff-Rantzau, the German foreign minister, declared: "We admit that Germany's attitude at the Hague Conferences toward these two fundamental questions of disarmament and arbitration was an historic sin for which our entire nation must now do penance. It was due not merely to an exaggerated fear of the practical difficulties but to a false estimate of the respective values of might and right."

The Hague conferences owed their greatest and lasting achievement, the creation of the Permanent World Court of Arbitration, to the initiative and the political realism of George W. Holls, the secretary of the United States delegation. The weakness of the Hague Tribunal rested in the absence of any legal supranational power which could compel nations to submit their disagreements to arbitration as well as in the fact that the court itself was without any legal means to enforce its decisions. The chief gain, then, was almost entirely on the moral side: the creation of the Hague Tribunal aided in rallying large sections of world opinion in support of the idea of international justice, solidarity, and co-operation.

Germany As a World Power. Several motivating forces, some of them inherent in the national character, others attributable to historical and geographical circumstances, contributed to the phenomenal growth of the new German empire to a dominant position in Europe and in the world. The boom of 1871 and the crash of 1873 were followed by a speedy stabilization of German economy, a process in which the skillful exploitation of natural resources played a conspicuous part. But the construction of the imposing edifice of German agriculture, industry, and commerce required not only personal initiative and careful planning but even more a talent for large-scale organization and the will to unselfish and disciplined individual and collective action. A country with a soil of less than average fertility and an extremely narrow seaboard could overcome such handicaps only by superb teamwork and a rigid rationalization of its economic forces and resources. It proved a great boon that German private enterprise was traditionally accustomed to accept directives from above. And the fact that these directives were given by industrial and economic experts of more than average intelligence accounts in no small measure for the German success.

The industrial expansion of Germany after 1871 owed much to the willingness on the part of private and public financial agencies to take long-range views and not to shun major risks in providing the necessary credits. The German banking concerns, above all the *Deutsche Bank* (founded in 1870) and the federal *Reichsbank* (founded in 1875) played an important part in the industrial and economic progress of Germany. It was the *Deutsche Bank* which, for example, financed the Anatolian railway project of 1888 and thereby promoted the ambitious scheme of the Bagdad railway.

One of Germany's great early industrial *entrepreneurs,* the electrical engineer Werner von Siemens (1816–1892, cf. p. 553), creator of the German electrical industry, built between 1868 and 1870 the vast network of the Indo-European Telegraph System. In 1866 he invented the dynamo machine; in 1871 he exhibited in Berlin the first electric railway; and in 1881 he completed the first electric streetcar line in Berlin-Lichterfelde. Emil Rathenau (1838–1915), continuing the work of Siemens, acquired the Edison patents for electric bulbs in 1881 and, in 1883, founded the German Edison Company for Applied Electricity which later on developed into the world-renowned AEG (*Allgemeine Elektrizitätsgesellschaft:* General Electric Company).

Germany's vital coal and iron supply came from the mines of the Ruhr District, Upper Silesia, and the Saar region; that of iron ore from the rich deposits of Lorraine (annexed in 1871). The great Krupp works at Essen on the Ruhr, founded in 1811 by Friedrich Krupp (1787–1826), were developed by his son Alfred (1812–1887) into the world's mightiest armament factory (cf. p. 554). The latter's son, Friedrich Alfred (1854–1902), further expanded the vast undertaking, attaching to it the famous *Germania Werft* (shipbuilding yards) in Kiel on the Baltic Sea. In 1903 the huge concern was transformed into a joint-stock company with aggregate holdings of approximately $50,000,000, all the shares remaining in the possession of the Krupp family.

It was with the aid of such "coal and iron barons" as the Krupps and such competitive enterprises as those of Thyssen and Stinnes that Germany before the outbreak of World War I had managed to surpass England in the production of pig iron and to run a close second in the production of coal. In chemical research and applied chemistry she had achieved world supremacy. In several other branches of industry, such as the dye works of Ludwigshafen in Baden, the optical precision instruments of the Zeiss works in Jena, or the toy industries of Nuremberg, she set standards of ingenuity and high-class workmanship which were not matched anywhere in the world.

To utilize to better effect her internal waterways Germany built an ingenious system of canals, and to enlarge the volume of her overseas trade she embarked upon an extensive maritime building program, making the Hamburg harbor into the largest seaport, next to London. The main office of the Hamburg-America Line (founded in 1847; cf. p. 552) bore the symbolic inscription: *Mein Feld ist die Welt* ("My field is the world"). Its general director from 1899 to 1918 was Albert Ballin, who had worked his way up from very modest beginnings and whom William II came to honor with his friendship. Among the 439 ships with a total tonnage of 1,360,360 which the line owned on the eve of World War I was the mighty *Imperator* of 50,000 tons, launched in 1913. Bremen, Germany's second largest North Sea port, was the home of the North German Lloyd (founded in 1857; cf. p. 552) which in 1914 owned 494 seafaring vessels with a total tonnage of 983,000.

The closing decades of the nineteenth century showed an increasing tendency on the part of capitalistic enterprise to eliminate the shocks of unchecked competition by the concentration of capital in fewer hands. This tendency led in some countries to the creation of *trusts,* in others to the formation of *Kartells.* Germany preferred the *Kartell* to the *trust.**
The consequence of the *Kartell* system was the almost complete syndical-ization of the coal, iron, and steel industries by the end of the century. The advantages of the system were the prevention of waste and the co-ordination and unification of the industrial effort. The fact that Germany's manufacturing output more than trebled and her national income doubled during the reign of William II is in part at least attributable to this form of rationalized or "planned" capitalism.

World War I. The year 1914 found the great powers of Europe so en-meshed in a network of defensive alliances, and so inflexibly determined to maintain or extend their respective spheres of interest, that any serious international incident could be expected to touch off a major explosion. Such an incident occurred on June 28, when Archduke Francis Ferdinand, nephew of Francis Joseph I of Austria-Hungary, and heir apparent to the throne of the Dual Monarchy, was assassinated (together with his wife) while visiting the Bosnian town of Sarajevo. The assassin and his fellow conspirators were Bosnian nationals, but the crime had been inspired and planned by the chief of the publicity division of the Serbian general staff, who was also the presiding officer of the secret Serbian Organ-ization, *The Black Hand,* and closely linked with the Pan-Serbian society, *Narodna Obrana* (national defense). It is known from documentary evidence published by the Bolshevik regime of Russia that both the Serbian govern-ment and the Russian military attaché in Belgrade knew in advance of the preparations for the plot, and that the anti-Austrian movement among the Slavic subjects of the Austro-Hungarian monarchy had long been encouraged and materially supported by some of the highest Russian officials.

That the Pan-Slav movement, headed by Serbia, found such ready

---

* The ultimate objectives are identical in both forms of capitalistic concentration, but whereas in the *trust* the identity of the individual *entrepreneur* is lost, it is retained in the defensive *Kartell.* The result in either case is the accumulation of vast economic power in the hands of a small group of capitalists who are thereby enabled to lay down dictatorial rules concern-ing production, prices, credit, investments, interest rates, wage levels, etc.

response among the Slavs of the Austrian "succession states," and finally succeeded in creating a united front of anti-Austrian Slavs, was in part due to the failure of the Dual Monarchy to satisfy the justified civil and national aspirations of her Slavic subjects. Although about half of the population of Austria-Hungary were members of the Slavic race, the country was ruled by Germans and Hungarians (Magyars). Archduke Francis Ferdinand became the target of the Serbian nationalists precisely because he was known to favor concessions to the Austrian Slavs, and because the Serbian leaders were convinced that such a policy of conciliation would irreparably damage the Pan-Slav movement. It is the considered opinion of many of the critics of Austrian prewar policies that, if the dual system of the Austro-Hungarian monarchy had been transformed into a Danubian federation granting home rule to Czechs, Slovaks, Croats, and Slovenes, Pan-Slavism would have been deprived of one of its main arguments and incentives.

It was the pro-Austrian King Milan of Serbia who had written in the eighties of the nineteenth century: "If Austria could conciliate the Serbs within her territory by becoming a federal, instead of a dual monarchy, Serbia could join such a federation. In that case my kingdom would be content with the position occupied today by Bavaria, Saxony, and Wurtemberg in the German Empire. But in that case ten million Serbs would be united in one state, and our national unity would be effected. And since the other Balkan states would soon perceive the advantages gained from membership in this Austrian League of Nations, they might also join it."

The fact that none of the statesmen of modern Austria envisioned or attempted such a solution constitutes one of the tragic pages in the chapter of lost opportunities in the history of Austria and eastern Europe. Hence, the situation which prevailed in the summer of 1914, leading up to the climactic events of Sarajevo, presented a dangerous threat to the very existence of Austria-Hungary.

While Bismarck as late as 1887 had declared that "Germany recognizes Russian historic rights in the Balkans," the Germany of William II, as has been noted above (cf. p. 626 sq.), advanced its own ambitious schemes for the penetration of the Balkans, and thus it appeared that both Central Powers were ready to infringe upon the traditional Russian sphere of interest. This despite the fact that the German government had repeatedly tried to exert a restraining influence on the impetuous foreign policy of its Austrian ally. On the other hand, Germany obviously could not afford to hurt the sensibilities and alienate the sympathies of her only reliable partner in the *Dreibund*.

There is no doubt that the government of the Dual Monarchy acted in a very high-handed fashion in the course of events which followed the assassination of the archduke. The contents of the harsh ultimatum which Count Leopold von Berchtold, the Austrian foreign minister, dispatched to Belgrade on July 23 were made known to the German government only twenty-four hours prior to its transmission, and Serbia's conciliatory reply

— taking exception only to some minor points which the Serbian government wished to see submitted to the Hague Tribunal or an international
conference — was kept secret for three days. When William II finally was
informed of Serbia's submissive attitude he described the Austrian diplomatic
success as "a brilliant achievement, considering that only forty-eight hours
were allowed." And he continued his gratulatory remarks by saying: "It
is more than we could have expected. . . . It removes all reason for war."
In a letter addressed to Günther von Jagow, the German foreign secretary,
the emperor wrote in a similar vein: "After receiving the Serbian reply
which was handed to me this morning, I am convinced that the demands
of the Dual Monarchy have in substance been granted. The reservations
made on a few points of detail can in my view be cleared up by negotiation.
A most humiliating surrender has been effected before the eyes of the whole
world, and thus all ground for war has been removed." In a conversation
with Jagow in 1929 the British historian G. P. Gooch expressed the following judgment on the causes which led to the general European conflagration
of summer, 1914: "We think you could and should have pressed Austria
more strongly, just as you think we could and should have pressed Russia.
Each of us feared the loss of our friend and ally. The European system was
the main cause of the war. Germany was dragged in by Austria, England
and France by Russia." Jagow concurred in this view.

While the exchange of notes was taking place between Vienna and
Belgrade, the diplomatic and political mills were grinding in the other
European capitals. On July 20 Poincaré, the president of the French republic,
had paid a visit to St. Petersburg, and the military clauses of the Franco-
Russian alliance were then strongly reaffirmed. While telegrams were exchanged between Tsar Nicholas II and the German emperor, Russia had
begun preparations for a general mobilization, on July 25. William II
implored the tsar to halt the Russian troop movements in the direction
of the German and Austrian borders, and the tsar begged the kaiser to
help him "to avoid such a disaster as a general European war. In the name
of our old friendship, I implore you to do everything in your power to
prevent your ally from going too far." On July 25, Sir Edward Grey, the
British foreign secretary, proposed a conference of England, France, Germany, and Italy to work out a settlement by negotiation. But neither
Germany nor France showed any inclination to act upon this suggestion.

On July 28 the Austrian government, declaring itself unsatisfied by the
"evasive" Serbian reply, declared war on Serbia. Immediately the German
government urged Austria to disclaim any desire on her part to annex
Serbian territory. But the Dual Monarchy paid no heed to this request.
On July 29 the tsar ordered the general mobilization of the Russian army.
Following another fervent plea of the German emperor, this order was
temporarily rescinded, but reissued on July 30. Germany, while declaring
a "state of imminent danger of war," delayed mobilization, pending the
outcome of the emperor's personal appeal to the tsar. On July 31 a French

cabinet meeting affirmed the French government's readiness for war. On the same day William II demanded that Russia halt its mobilization within the next twelve hours. When twenty-four hours had passed without a Russian reply, the emperor announced in the evening of August 1 that a state of war existed between Germany and Russia. In the meantime, in the afternoon of that fateful day, the mobilization of the French and German armies had followed each other within a few hours. A German inquiry in Paris as to the intentions of the French government brought the response that France would be guided solely by her own interests. On August 3 Germany declared war on France. During the night from August 3 to August 4 German troops crossed the frontier of neutral Belgium. On August 4 England declared war on Germany, giving as the official reason for her action the German violation of Belgian neutrality of which both Germany and England were co-guarantors (cf. p. 525).

The German chancellor von Bethmann-Hollweg, who tried both to justify the invasion of Belgium as an act of self-defense (*"Not kennt kein Gebot"*: necessity knows no law) and to apologize for it by promising restitution after the war, did great and irreparable harm to the moral prestige of Germany when he referred to neutrality treaties as "scraps of paper." Actually Germany's invasion of Belgium was an essential and integral part of the strategy which had been devised by General Alfred von Schlieffen (1833–1913), who had intermittently been attached to the German general staff from 1866 on, and its chief from 1891 to 1906. Developing the military doctrines of Clausewitz and Moltke (cf. p. 534) on the tactics of a destructive *Blitzkrieg,* and adapting them to the requirements of the technical age, he had worked out a strategy (the *"Schlieffen Plan"*) which called for a lightning attack on France, enveloping Belgium and Holland in a vast flanking movement, while entrusting the defense of the eastern German frontiers to relatively small task forces. This plan was now put to the test by the order of Helmuth von Moltke (the nephew of the famous military strategist of the Bismarck era), the German chief of staff, without, however, including the Netherlands in the invasion thrust. As England, under the terms of a "gentlemen's agreement" between the French and British governments, had accepted, two days before Germany's invasion of Belgium, responsibility for the protection of the northern coasts of France, her entry into the war could hardly have been prompted solely by the German violation of Belgian neutrality.

To the very last moment Germany had clung to the hope of keeping England neutral, and as a consequence the British declaration of war came as a great shock, producing a violent emotional reaction, especially among the traditionally pro-English German liberals. The sentiments of the disappointed Anglophiles found an outlet in a somewhat artificial campaign of hate which manifested itself in the popular slogan *"Gott strafe England!"* ("May God punish England!") and in such documents as the famed German economist Werner Sombart's *Händler und Helden (Shopkeepers and*

Heroes) or the poet Ernst Lissauer's glowing *Hassgesang* (*Song of Hate*).

The second great disappointment for the German people, if not for their government, was Italy's declaration of neutrality on the ground that the terms of the *Dreibund* called for assistance in the case of a defensive war only, and that in any case Italian policy would be governed exclusively by her own *sacro egoismo*. Italy finally joined the Allies on May 23, 1915, by declaring war on Austria, after having been promised in the secret Treaty of London of April 26 much more than she could have hoped to obtain by bargaining with Austria.* She was promised the southern Tyrol to the Brenner Pass, the Austrian coastal regions, including Trieste, the Dalmatian Islands and the northern part of the Dalmatian coast, occupation rights in Valona, colonial possessions in Asia Minor, plus a guarantee that the papacy was to be excluded from participation in the future peace conference.

While the Central Powers were thus deserted by Italy right at the beginning of the war, their cause derived some additional strength in the first month of the conflict from Turkey's decision to fight on the side of Germany and Austria. The cause of the Allies, on the other hand, was aided by Japan's declaration of war against Germany on August 23, 1914.

The German people — not differing greatly in this respect from the populations in the enemy countries — were familiar only with the surface phenomena and not with the more obscure ultimate causes of the European conflict. They were therefore convinced that Germany had become the victim of a dastardly international plot and that the very existence of the "encircled" fatherland was at stake. Arrayed against the Central Powers was the world's greatest sea power and a potential man power almost three times superior to their own. The Central Powers were favored, on the other hand, by the tactical and strategic advantages of short communication lines and by the German superiority in military training, discipline, leadership, and striking power.

As the German people felt, or were made to feel, that war had been forced upon them, they arose as one man. Forgotten were all internal dissensions, and on August 1, 1914, the Social Democrats of the *Reichstag* faction joined the other parties in a unanimous approval of the war credits. Forgotten also (and not only in Germany) was the international solidarity and the pacifist creed of the proletarian masses. The international labor movement received perhaps its severest blow with the assassination of the great French socialist and pacifist Jean Jaurès, on the very eve of the war. As far as the German socialists were concerned, some of their leaders were among the first to enlist as volunteers. A wave of enthusiasm swept over the entire country, and the air was filled with patriotic slogans. The Kaiser's *"Ich kenne keine Parteien mehr: ich kenne nur noch Deutsche"* ("I no

---

* On May 10, 1915, the Dual Monarchy offered to Italy the cession of southern Tyrol, autonomy for Trieste, occupation rights in Valona, and *désinteressement* of Austria-Hungary in Albania.

longer know of political parties: I know only Germans") and Frederick the Great's *"Viel Feind', viel Ehr"* ("The more enemies, the greater the honor"), spoken in the tragic days of the Seven Years' War, were repeated by young and old, in homes, in workshops, in schools, and in churches.

By December, 1914, the mood of the people had undergone some changes. Spirits were still high, the war bulletins, given out in the characteristic lapidary style of Quartermaster General von Stein, were greatly encouraging, and victory celebrations were frequent. But, nevertheless, there was a general and as yet undefined feeling that something had gone wrong somewhere. It was known, for example, that French-British resistance before Paris and on the Marne river had upset the *Schlieffen-Plan*. It was not so generally known that the chief of staff, with victory almost within his grasp, had suddenly lost command of the situation, issued contradictory orders, and, by his hesitation and evident confusion, had made it possible for the enemy to convert the war of movement into a war of position. The opposing armies threw up entrenchments and formed a stationary double line which extended from the North Sea coast to the Swiss frontier.

In the December session of the German *Reichstag* Karl Liebknecht (the son of Wilhelm Liebknecht, the friend and associate of August Bebel; cf. p. 614) and seventeen fellow socialists voted against the new war credits. In March, 1915, the socialist opposition had increased to thirty-two, almost one third of the Social Democratic party. In the summer of the same year the dissenting party members seceded and formed the faction of Independent Socialists, the nucleus of the future Communist party (*K.P.D.: Kommunistische Partei Deutschlands*). The rifts in the political and social structure of Germany, which had been temporarily closed by the upsurge of patriotic feeling, began to reappear.

Meanwhile the war in the East had yielded important victories for the German armies. After initial successes of small Russian contingents in their advance upon East Prussia, the German forces under the command of Paul von Hindenburg (1847–1934), who had been called back from retirement, were victorious at Tannenberg (late August, 1914), annihilating the Russian Second Army trapped in the swamplands of the Masurian Lakes, and driving the Russian First Army back beyond the Russian frontier. In the summer and autumn of 1915 German troops under the command of General von Mackensen relieved the hard-pressed Austrian armies in Galicia and drove the Russians from Galicia and Poland with staggering losses for the enemy, taking over a million prisoners. The Central Powers were joined by Bulgaria in their drive on Serbia (October, 1915), and by the end of the year Balkan domination had been secured and land communication with Turkey established.

While the opposing armies were stalemated in the West and the Central Powers victorious in the East, the war on the sea, less spectacular and moving more slowly, proved in the end more effective in deciding the final outcome of the conflict. The major sea engagement took place on May 31,

1916, in the North Sea (Battle of Jutland), when the entire German High Seas Fleet under the command of Admiral Scheer managed to fight its way out of a trap laid by the British Admiral Jellicoe. Although victory was claimed by both sides, the British gave unsparing credit to the bravery and strategic ingenuity of the greatly inferior German forces in extricating themselves from an almost fatal predicament.

To meet the mortal danger of the British blockade, Germany early in 1915 declared the waters surrounding the British Isles as "zones of war," using the new weapon of the submarine boat to enforce a "counterblockade" by means of the destruction of increasing volumes of allied shipping space. German submarine attacks, initially confined to allied shipping, and temporarily relaxed after the strong protests of the United States which followed the sinking of the luxury liner *Lusitania* (May 7, 1915), were resumed in full force in January, 1917, when Germany embarked on a campaign of "unrestricted submarine warfare," threatening to destroy any and all belligerent and neutral vessels which entered specified danger zones in the proximity of the coastal waters of the allied powers. Although Germany came dangerously close to its goal — the destruction of a sufficient amount of allied shipping to hamstring the allied operations and force a conclusion of hostilities on German terms — the unrestricted submarine war was a desperate gamble, not only because it drew upon the *Reich* the odium of being insensitive to the injunctions of international law, but also and foremost because it alienated the remaining sympathies of the neutral powers and finally brought the most powerful of them, the United States, into the war on the side of the Allies.

The policy of unrestricted submarine warfare was itself an outgrowth of important changes in the German High Command, caused by the unexpected prolongation of the war and the gradually ebbing morale of the home front. General Erich von Falkenhayn, who had succeeded von Moltke as chief of staff, was dismissed in August, 1916, and replaced by Paul von Hindenburg. Erich Ludendorff, holding the position of quartermaster general, became second in command. Though nominally inferior in rank to von Hindenburg, Ludendorff was the superior strategist and, owing to his military prowess, came to wield a dictatorial power which was by no means confined to the military sphere, but made itself felt in the political sphere as well. A power politician by conviction, he was strongly influenced by the racial, anti-Semitic, and anti-Christian theories of Houston Stewart Chamberlain (1855–1927), Richard Wagner's son-in-law, a native of Great Britain, who had made Germany his adopted country. Ludendorff also maintained close ties with the Pan-Germans, supporting their annexationist war aims, and later on (1917) taking a hand in shaping the program and policies of the rightist and chauvinist *Vaterlandspartei*.

It was Ludendorff's conviction that the stalemate in the West could not be broken unless the morale of the enemy had first been weakened by the methods of ruthless and unrestricted submarine warfare. However, before this fateful course was definitively decided upon, the German government had extended some peace feelers, chiefly to induce the allied powers to make public their war aims. Yet these German overtures of December, 1916, were rejected by the Allies on the ground that they impressed them as "empty and insincere" and only intended to sow seeds of discord in their camp. The German peace initiative almost coincided with President Wilson's first note to the belligerents, in which he asked them to state the objectives they were fighting for. The demand of the American president caused some embarrassment among the allied powers, owing to the fact that (as was revealed in January, 1918, in the New York *Evening Post*) in autumn, 1916, they had concluded some secret treaties whose terms provided for considerable annexations in the East and West, proposed acquisitions of enemy territory which equaled if not exceeded in scope the Pan-German dreams of conquest. In their reply to the presidential note, however, the Allies mentioned as preconditions for peace negotiations only the restoration of the integrity of Belgium, Serbia, and Montenegro; the evacuation of the invaded regions of France, Russia, and Rumania; the liberation of the Italian and Slavic subjects of the Austro-Hungarian monarchy as well as of the non-Moslem populations "under the bloody tyranny of the Turks"; adequate compensation and indemnities, and definite guarantees for the future peace of Europe. These terms, formulated on the presupposition of the sole responsibility of the Central Powers for the war, and involving the dismemberment of Austria-Hungary, were unacceptable to an undefeated Germany and her partners.

The Russian February Revolution of 1917, staged by the socialist *Mensheviki,* and foreshadowing impending military collapse, seemed to work into Ludendorff's hands. To eliminate the eastern front by means of a series of steps which were aimed at effecting the rapid disintegration of Russia from within, the politico-military dictator of Germany decided to grant safe-conduct through the *Reich* to Lenin and other leaders of the radical *Bolsheviki,* who had been living in Swiss exile. The following November Revolution in Russia, plunging the country into utter chaos, had thus the full blessing of the German quartermaster general. In March, 1918, the Russians found themselves compelled to sign the humiliating Treaty of Brest-Litovsk, which ended the war in the East and deprived Russia of her Baltic provinces, Finland, Poland, the Ukraine, and some regions in the Caucasus.

The loss of Russia to the Allies was, however, far outweighed by the gain which was marked by the entry of the United States into the war on their side. Without the foolhardy continuation of unrestricted submarine warfare, in the face of mounting American resentment, United States participation in the struggle might never have gone beyond the financial engagements of private interests which had extended credits to the Allies in the amount of a billion and a half dollars. But the increasing losses of American life and property on the high seas, in addition to German diplomatic blunders and the obnoxious activities of German agents in the United States and in Mexico, finally turned the scales in favor of armed intervention. On April 6, 1917, the United States Congress declared war on the Central Powers.

Early in 1917 another unsuccessful peace offensive had been attempted by Emperor Charles I of Austria-Hungary, who had succeeded Francis Joseph I in 1916. The emperor had gained the conviction — and had so informed the German government — that Austria could not continue the fight beyond the autumn of 1917. He therefore had begun negotiations with the Allies, using as an intermediary his brother-in-law, Prince Sixte of Bourbon, who served as an officer in the Belgian army. But his peace efforts were frustrated by the adamant opposition of Germany on the one hand, and of Italy on the other.

In Germany, too, the sentiment in favor of a negotiated peace was steadily gaining ground and could no longer be stifled even by the most rigid censorship of the press and the attempted thorough regimentation of public opinion. On July 19, 1917, the German *Reichstag,* on the initiative of the Centrist deputy Matthias Erzberger, adopted with 212 votes of the Center party, the Socialists, and the Progressive Liberals against 126 votes of National Liberals and Conservatives the famous "peace resolution." This stated in part that "the Reichstag is striving for a peace of mutual understanding" and that "enforced cessions of territory as well as political, economic, and financial oppression are incompatible with a peace of this kind." It called for the creation of an international organization to guarantee the future peace of the world by means of political and economic collaboration. Erzberger's action had the strong moral support of the papal nuncio in Bavaria, Eugenio Pacelli, the future Pope Pius XII.

The reaction of the High Command was swift and decisive: the conciliatory Bethmann-Hollweg had to resign as chancellor to be replaced by Georg Michaelis, a docile and narrow-minded bureaucrat, who, during the brief period of his chancellorship, acted as Ludendorff's willing tool. Before the year 1917 ended he was forced out of office by an aroused *Reichstag.* But in the months that intervened between his assumption of office and his resignation he had managed to thwart another peace move which had been timed to coincide with and strengthen the peace resolution of the *Reichstag.*

This new peace offensive had issued from the Vatican. In August, Pope Benedict XV had addressed a note to the "Heads of the Belligerent Peoples," in which he had invited the governments at war to agree upon *seven points* from whose common acceptance a just and lasting peace might result. These points included drastic reduction of armaments, creation of an international institution for the arbitration of disputes among nations, provision of sanctions to be applied against any state which should refuse to submit to arbitration, guarantee of the freedom of the seas, complete and reciprocal condonation of all claims resulting from war damages and expenditures, restoration of all occupied territories to their legitimate owners, and co-ordination of all particular interests with the commonweal of human society, in a spirit of equity and justice. The chief negotiations on behalf of the papacy were carried on by Eugenio Pacelli.

The reaction of Chancellor Michaelis to these proposals was largely determined by his intense nationalism and his anti-Catholic bias. On July 24 the pope had dispatched a special preliminary note to the German government to find out in advance what its attitude would be with regard to the papal peace plan. On August 22 Michaelis wrote to Count Wedel, the German ambassador in Vienna: "In my opinion our endeavor must be to throw the odium of a possible failure of the Pope's mediation upon our enemies and show them to be in the wrong. . . . It is therefore my intention to proceed in this matter rather dilatorily."

In response to the papal note of August 1 the British government expressed its willingness to enter into peace negotiations, provided the German government were willing to offer specific guarantees for the restoration and future preservation of the independence and integrity of Belgium. The reaction in Germany to the papal initiative was unfavorable. Some influential newspapers spoke of "papal arrogance," and the Lutheran pastor Dr. Traub, as emissary of the Protestant "Evangelical League," stumped the country in an attempt to counteract the papal peace move, declaring that "as an Evangelical Protestant" he could not "see the end of the war in an untimely peace offered by the Pope in the very year of the jubilee of Luther's reformation" (1517). The German chancellor, making this view his own, subsequently resorted to procrastination, dissimulation, and even falsification to keep the contents of a special dispatch of the papal nuncio from the knowledge of the emperor and the imperial crown council. He furthermore explicitly refused to embody in his answer to the papal note any assurances regarding Belgian independence, assurances which, as he well knew, were an absolute prerequisite to any peace negotiations.

When Nuncio Pacelli received the preliminary draft of the German reply he realized at once that it foredoomed the papal peace move to failure. Reviewing the peace efforts of the Vatican of August, 1917, Archbishop Noerber of Freiburg wrote in 1919: "The war was definitely lost in the moment when the peace of reconciliation which Benedict XV tried to bring about was rejected for no other reason than that it had come from the Pope."

The last hope of the German *Wehrmacht* lay in forcing a decision in the West before the arrival of an expeditionary force from the United States. In October, 1917, while the Austrians routed the Italians at Caporetto, the Germans began preparations for a giant offensive to be launched in the spring of 1918. The privations of the fearful winter of 1917–1918 had brought the German home front near the breaking point. The limit of endurance was almost reached, and the general war weariness found expression in the oft-repeated phrase: *"Lieber ein Ende mit Schrecken als ein Schrecken ohne Ende"* ("Rather an end with terror than a terror without end"). But war weariness also spread among the front soldiers of the belligerents, and the French and Italian High Commands had to use ruthless force to crush several mutinies.

In January, 1918, Woodrow Wilson outlined in an address the "Fourteen Points" which he proposed as a basis for peace. Ludendorff, however, was determined to stake all on one last desperate gamble. In March, 1918, he led his armies in a gigantic assault against the French and British lines in the West, and at the cost of about half a million casualties the Germans reached the Marne river for a second time. But the exhaustion of the German armies provided the Allies with a sorely needed respite, and when Ludendorff, on July 15, launched his final offensive, designed to dislocate and definitively smash the enemy, the allied lines held. Regrouped and reorganized under the command of Marshal Foch, and reinforced by newly arrived powerful contingents from the United States, the Allies counterattacked and turned the second battle of the Marne (July 15 to August 2) into a decisive victory for their armies. On August 8 the British pierced the German lines east of Amiens, and during the following weeks the German forces were pressed back all along their extended front, losing another half million men in valiant rear-guard action.

On September 29, Ludendorff and Hindenburg informed the emperor that the war was lost and that a new German government, to be formed within the next twenty-four hours, must immediately ask for an armistice. During September and October Bulgaria and Turkey collapsed, and the Austrian empire was in a process of rapid disintegration. On November 4 the Dual Monarchy capitulated, Emperor Charles abdicated, and the Polish, Czech, Croat, and Slovene minorities rose in revolt and declared their autonomy.

Yielding to the demand of Ludendorff for an immediate armistice and the formation of a new government, the German emperor agreed to take the necessary steps to have the *Bundesrat* effect the transformation of the German *Reich* into a parliamentary and democratic monarchical State whose chancellor and cabinet were to be directly responsible to the *Reichstag*. On October 3 Prince Max von Baden, the nephew of the then ruling grand duke of Baden, known for his humanitarian work in behalf of the prisoners of war as well as for his democratic convictions, was asked to take over the office of chancellor. He replaced the aged Bavarian scholar and statesman, Count von Hertling, who had succeeded Michaelis.

Prince Max resolutely accepted the arduous task of forming a new government that had the backing of the *Reichstag,* and in his cabinet, in which he himself acted as foreign minister, he included for the first time two leading members of the Social Democrats (Philipp Scheidemann and Gustav Bauer). Pressed and practically coerced by Ludendorff, he finally abandoned his original plan of submitting a detailed blueprint for peace to Woodrow Wilson, and instead, contrary to his conviction, asked the American president for an immediate armistice, accepting as a basis for peace negotiations "the program laid down by the President of the United States in his message to Congress of January 8, 1918, and in his subsequent pronouncements."

Wilson's note of October 14 demanded as a prerequisite for peace "the destruction or reduction to virtual impotency of every arbitrary power anywhere that can . . . disturb the peace of the world." "The power," the note continued, "which has hitherto controlled the German nation is of the sort here described. It is within the choice of the German people to alter it." Wilson's note of October 23 spoke no longer of peace negotiations, but of the "surrender of the military masters and the monarchical autocrats of Germany."

Ludendorff, enraged by the tone and the demands of the American notes, abruptly reversed his decision and advocated continuation of the struggle. But on October 26 he had to yield to the demands for his resignation which were conveyed to him by the emperor. General Wilhelm Gröner, who took over the command of the German armies, was the first to mention to the emperor abdication as the only way to satisfy the stipulations contained in the American notes. The same course was suggested by Scheidemann in a letter addressed to Prince Max, who up to this moment had still clung to the hope of being able to save the monarchy.

In the meantime, dramatic moves were being enacted on the German home front. A revolutionary uprising had slowly but surely gained momentum, and on November 3 mutiny broke out among the naval squadrons stationed at Kiel. The rebellious sailors were soon joined by the workers, and quickly the revolt spread to the other German seaports. On November 7 several of the larger cities in northern and central Germany as well as Munich in the south joined the incipient revolution. In the latter city the establishment of a Bavarian republic was proclaimed by Kurt Eisner, one of the leaders of the radical wing of the Social Democrats. King Louis III of the ancient Wittelsbach dynasty was forced to renounce the throne. On November 9 the revolutionary wave was converging on Berlin. It was then that Prince Max, to avoid bloodshed and ensuing chaos, decided on his own responsibility to announce the abdication of the emperor. "The Chancellor," the proclamation read in part, "remains in office until the questions connected with the abdication of the emperor . . . and the setting up of a Regency have been settled. He intends to propose . . . the appointment of Herr Ebert to the chancellorship, and the framing of a bill to prepare elections for a German Constituent National Assembly."

Reluctantly, after much hesitation, and with grave misgivings William II, yielding to the advice of Generals Gröner and Hindenburg, decided to authorize the announcement of his abdication. On November 10 he crossed the border of Holland, to spend the remaining twenty-three years of his life in the Dutch health resort of Doorn. Thus, after a period of approximately five hundred years of uninterrupted rule, the Hohenzollern dynasty came to an end.

Declining for himself the office of *Reichsverweser,* which was offered him for the interim between the fall of the monarchy and the election of a National Assembly, Prince Max, before retiring from the political scene, persuaded the socialist leader Friedrich Ebert to accept the chancellorship of the German republic.

The Revolution. World War I had involved more than thirty nations, large and small, and approximately sixty-five million men had been under arms. Over eight million soldiers had lost their lives, and almost twenty-five million had been wounded or were among the missing. The total war expenditures have been variously estimated, but they must be figured in the proximity of one hundred and eighty billion dollars. German casualties amounted to one million six hundred thousand dead, over four million wounded, and over two hundred thousand missing. At the end of the war the German national debt stood at one hundred and seventy-six billion gold marks (forty-four billion dollars). The British blockade had caused increasing suffering among the civilian population of the Central Powers, and Germany alone counted about three quarters of a million deaths attributable to malnutrition. The privations of the last winter of the war had sapped the people's remaining strength and finally broken their will to resistance. Thus the defeat of the armies in the field coincided with the physical and moral breakdown of the home front. But the interrelation between the collapse of soldiers and civilians was only temporal, not causal, so that the *Dolchstosslegende* (the story of the home front "stabbing the army in the back," a malicious invention of the resurgent German militarists and rightists of later years) cannot be maintained in the light of historic facts.

The one consolation of the German people in their defeat and misfortune lay in their hope for a new era of political democracy and both social and international justice. Such a new era seemed to be reasonably assured by German acceptance of President Wilson's "Fourteen Points" and by the willingness of the German people to atone for the sins of their political and military leaders. It was this hope and this implicit trust in a saner and juster world order which acted as a moderating influence on the forces of revolution and eventually determined the triumph of constitutional government over leftist radicalism. Despite their many miseries and heartaches the Germans now breathed under a freer sky than they had for many decades, and they took a certain pride in putting their own house in order and in firmly resolving to gain back the confidence of the world.

The way, however, was difficult and dangerous. The first issue which the nascent Republic had to face was the internecine struggle between the Social Democrats (the majority group) and the Independent Socialists of the extreme Left. The workers and soldiers had made the revolution, and it was now a question whether the new Germany was to be ruled by a freely elected National Assembly or whether it was to follow the Russian model and be handed over to a proletarian class dictatorship. In the newly formed Workers' and Soldiers' Councils, meeting in Berlin on November 10, 1918, the Social Democrats received equal representation on a joint committee of the two socialist groups. It was due to the influence of the Social Democrats that the Proclamation of the Council of *Volksbeauftragte* (People's Commissars) of November 12 contained the provision that all future elections, including the one for a Constituent National Assembly, should be based on the universal suffrage of German men and women. Thus the democratic idea of equal popular representation had achieved its first and decisive triumph over those forces which advocated tyrannical class rule.

The twenty-two German monarchs, together with many of those political and military leaders who were linked with the monarchy by tradition and conviction, had disappeared almost overnight. Most of the kings and princes accepted their fate with good grace, and a few of them with a disarming sense of humor. But monarchical feeling had its firmest roots in the army and in the civil service, and it was in these quarters that the slowly growing resistance movement against the Republic found its strongest support. The traditional opposition to democratic ideas and institutions was of the most momentous import in the case of the judiciary, because many judges lacked the mental and psychological disposition to conduct political trials with impartiality. Thus, as a rule, the case of an accused democrat, liberal, or socialist was already prejudged when the hearing began. For the time being, however, these matters were of no immediate relevance. A small minority of the aristocrats and army officers openly sympathized with the revolution, while the majority withdrew for the moment from the scene of action, trying to avoid a premature showdown, and hoping for a comeback at some more opportune time. Ludendorff, for example, thought it the better part of wisdom to seek temporary refuge in Sweden.

The important thing, however, was that Generals Hindenburg and Gröner, who commanded the unreserved loyalty of the returning troops, placed themselves unequivocally at the disposal of the Republic, notwithstanding their sentimental attachment to the monarchical tradition of Germany. By putting the well-being of the nation above all personal considerations they set a noteworthy example and made possible a relative stabilization of the republican form of government.

The provisional government of the new German Republic was headed by the six socialists united in the *Rat der Volksbeauftragten,* with Friedrich Ebert acting as chancellor. The General Congress of Workers' and Soldiers' Councils, meeting in Berlin in mid-December, 1918, endorsed elections for a National Assembly by an overwhelming majority. Thus they delivered a strong rebuff to the dictatorial claims of the "Spartacus League," a group of left-wing extremists, who had been organized by Karl Liebknecht and Rosa Luxemburg in 1916 and had adopted the name of the leader of the rebellious slaves in ancient Rome (73–71 B.C.). A month earlier, a conference of the socialist-controlled State governments of Germany had likewise voted in favor of a National Assembly.

This consolidation of pro-democratic sentiment was materially aided by the united efforts of the Free (socialist) and Christian *Gewerkschaften* (Trade Unions, cf. p. 556) whose well-disciplined members were opposed to political and social radicalism. Their position had been strengthened by an agreement with the representatives of the German employers, negotiated on November 15, which, among other social gains, secured for the German workers the right of collective bargaining and the eight-hour day. It also provided for the establishment of committees of employees in all industrial plants, committees which were later to be centralized in a *Reichswirtschafts-rat* (Federal Economic Council; cf. p. 650 sq.). To facilitate the recovery of German economy the unions pledged themselves not to resort to arbitrary strikes. The Socialization Commission, appointed by the provisional government, met on December 5 and declared itself in favor of the maintenance of private property and opposed to expropriations and untimely experiments in socialization.

As was to be expected, this moderate and conciliatory policy of Majority Socialists and Trade Unions aroused the anger of the uncompromising radical minority. The Independent Socialists refused further co-operation, and before the elections for a National Assembly could be held the provisional government had to enlist the aid of General Gröner and the army to crush an uprising of the "Spartacus League" in Berlin (early January, 1919), in the course of which Karl Liebknecht and Rosa Luxemburg were brutally slain. In Bavaria, too, where the revolutionary movement from the outset had been headed by radical Independent Socialists under the leadership of Kurt Eisner, trouble was brewing. During the final year of the war, Eisner, a Berlin journalist who had moved to Munich in 1910, had organized a Bavarian underground movement and, in November, 1918, following the abdication of the king, had assumed the offices of prime minister and foreign minister of the Bavarian republic. In the hope of obtaining better peace terms from the enemy, Eisner advocated an abject and summary admission of German responsibility for the war and tried to force his opinion on the central provisional government in Berlin, threatening separate peace negotiations of Bavaria in case of refusal. This high-handed procedure as well as Eisner's ruthless suppression of the Bavarian opposition press aroused the indignation of Bavarian patriots and monarchist conservatives. In the elections for a provincial assembly of Bavaria (January 12, 1919) Eisner's Independent Socialists suffered a decisive defeat. The idealist doctrinaire had already resolved to hand in his resignation at the first meeting of the newly elected Diet, when on his way to the assembly he was assassinated by Count von Arco, a monarchist student of the University of Munich. The fact that Eisner was a Jew had contributed considerably to the violent opposition which was stirred up by his political actions.

Elections for the Constituent National Assembly were held on January 19, 1919. On February 6, the elected deputies met in the National Theatre of the city of Weimar, hallowed by the name of Goethe and the tradition of

German Humanism (cf. p. 403 sq.). The Germany which came into being at Weimar was henceforth known as the *Weimar Republic.*

The elections had given 163 seats to the Majority Socialists, 22 to the Independent Socialists, 91 to the Center party, 79 to the Progressives (renamed *Democrats*), 19 to the National Liberals (renamed *Deutsche Volkspartei:* German People's Party), 44 to the monarchist Conservatives (renamed *Deutschnationale Volkspartei:* German National People's Party), and 3 to minor political groups. Out of a total of 421 representatives, 333 supported the republican and democratic form of government (Majority Socialists, Centrists, Democrats), while 88 were either undecided (National Liberals) or outright antidemocratic and antirepublican (Conservatives). But it is interesting to note that even the monarchists of the extreme Right found it necessary to pay lip service to the democratic trend by adding the epithet *"Volk"* to their party label.

On February 11, 1919, Friedrich Ebert was elected *Reichspräsident,* an office which he held until his death in 1925. Gustav Scheidemann was appointed *Reichskanzler* of the Republic. A short-lived Bavarian Soviet dictatorship, proclaimed in April, 1919, which temporarily threatened to upset the fragile stability of the national government, was overthrown with the aid of Prussian and Swabian troops. On July 31 the Weimar Constitution — drafted by the provisional minister of the interior, Professor Hugo Preuss, formerly of the *Handelshochschule* (university for trade and commerce), Berlin — was adopted by a large majority of the National Assembly, against the opposition of the Independent Socialists, the German People's Party, and the German Nationals.

The Weimar Constitution. The committee to which Hugo Preuss's draft for the constitution of the German republic was referred for final action consisted of twenty-eight members representing proportionately the different political factions. It was headed by Konrad Haussmann, a distinguished member of the Democratic party. The compromise worked out by this committee struck a middle course between the tendency to centralize power in the federal government, and the particularist trend of the constituent states. The Constitution provided for a democratic republic of federated states. The individual states were henceforth known as *Länder* (lands). Article 13, which stated that federal law overrides state law, further reduced their still existing semiautonomy. Indicative of this limitation of state rights was the taking over of the German railway system by the *Reich* (a goal which Bismarck had failed to achieve), and Bavaria and Wurtemberg's surrender of their control of post and telegraph services.

The place of the former *Bundesrat* (cf. p. 547) was taken by the *Reichsrat,* in which the *Länder* were represented by members of their respective governments. And, to a larger extent than had been the case in the constitution of imperial Germany, a check was placed on the predominance of Prussia by the provision that no single *Land* was allowed more than two fifths of the total number of votes. Prussia held 26 out of a total of 66 seats, but only 13 of these 26 seats were filled by representatives of the Prussian government, while the remaining 13 were distributed among the administrations of the semiautonomous Prussian provinces.

The major change was not so much in the composition of the *Reichsrat* as in the title of its authority and power. While the old *Bundesrat* had derived its federal power from the Union of Princes, the *Reichsrat* derived its authority from the will of the people. In addition, its power as an administrative and legislative body was greatly restricted by the fact that both its enactments and its vetoes could be overruled by a two-thirds majority of the *Reichstag* or by popular referendum. With all its checks and balances to insure a division of power, the Weimar Constitution leaned toward a unicameral system, centered and anchored in the *Reichstag*.

Konrad Haussmann said of the Weimar Constitution that it was "born in suffering" and that it represented "the law of a people oppressed by the enemy." It reflected the mind of the German people in the hour of defeat, but also their hopes for a better future, and their determination to preserve both their unity and diversity within a legal framework that was to give reasonable assurance for the attainment of justice, progress, and peace. As stated in the Preamble, "this Constitution has been drafted and adopted by the German people, united in its *Stämme* (tribes), and animated by the desire to renew and strengthen its *Reich* on the bases of freedom and justice, to serve the cause of peace both within and without, and to promote the progress of human society."

In Article 1 emphasis is placed on the fact that "the supreme power of the *Reich* emanates from the people," while Article 4 declares that "the generally recognized rules of International Law are integral parts of German Law." Article 17 deals with Electoral Law, stating that "every *Land* is to adopt a Republican Constitution. The representatives of the people are to be elected by the universal, equal, direct, and secret suffrage of all German citizens, men and women (who have attained the age of twenty), in accordance with the principle of proportional representation." The adoption of the French system of proportional representation, while intended to make it possible even for smallest minorities to register their political and social convictions, actually tended to weaken rather than strengthen the parliamentary structure. It encouraged the formation of many small parties reflecting the particular interests of minority groups. Their votes were collected by districts, entered in a *Reichsliste,* and if they added up to the sixty thousand required for the election of a deputy, the minority obtained the status of a party and representation in the *Reichstag*.

Against the opposition of the monarchist-conservative deputies of the Right the Weimar Constitution adopted the colors black, red, and gold — the colors of the Holy Roman Empire and of the Revolution of 1848 — in place of the black, white, and red of the Empire of Bismarck and William II. The ancient black, red, and gold stood for the idea of *Grossdeutschland* (cf. p. 530), whereas the banner black, white, red symbolized the idea of

Bismarck's *Kleindeutschland*. The incorporation of German Austria in the federal organism of the *Reich* was envisaged by Article 2 of the Weimar Constitution, and Article 61 provided for Austrian representation in the *Reichsrat* in a consultative capacity. As early as November 12, 1918, the Austrian National Assembly had endorsed Article 1 of an Austrian Provisional Constitution, stating that "German Austria is a constituent part of the German Republic." Plebiscites held in several regions of German Austria gave evidence of overwhelming sentiment in favor of an *Anschluss*, but both at that time and in later years (cf. p. 669) the realization of this common aspiration of the advocates of *Grossdeutschland* was prevented by the uncompromising opposition of the Allies.

The *Reichspräsident* was to be elected for a period of seven years by the direct ballot of the people, and was re-eligible. His powers were in some respects greater than those wielded by the German emperor. Thus he could dissolve the *Reichstag,* even without the consent of the *Reichsrat,* a measure which in the Imperial Constitution had required the consent of the *Bundesrat.* He could invoke a popular referendum against decisions of the *Reichstag.* He was commander in chief of the armed forces, a power which the emperor had only exercised in time of war. Finally, he could be given extraordinary emergency powers under Article 48 of the Constitution. In case "public safety and order were seriously disturbed," the *Reichspräsident* could rule by decree laws, suspend certain *Grundrechte* (fundamental rights) — the right of *habeas corpus,* secrecy of the mails, freedom of expression, inviolability of the home and of private property, and the right of coalition — and could call on the *Reichswehr* to enforce his emergency decrees. While the exercise of such virtually dictatorial power was theoretically subject to endorsement by the *Reichstag,* this check was almost voided by the provision that the President could dissolve the *Reichstag* and, in the interim of the required sixty days between dissolution and re-election, could rule without a parliament. This article, obviously an offshoot of a period of insecurity and crisis, was later on to prove fatal to the very existence of the Weimar Republic (cf. p. 656 sqq.).

The second major section of the Constitution defined and circumscribed the *Grundrechte* or Bill of Rights and the correlative obligations of citizenship. In this part the spirit of the Weimar Constitution showed the closest kinship with the ideals of the Revolution of 1848 and the Frankfurt Parliament (cf. p. 530 sqq.). The *Grundrechte* were championed in particular by the Catholic Centrists, the Democrats, and the Majority Socialists. All *Grundrechte* were anchored in the dignity of the human person, their common denominator and *raison d'être*. Accordingly, the respective articles deal with those legal decrees and measures which were to safeguard social equality, personal freedom, and social justice. Class privileges were to be done away with. Titles of nobility were to become part of the family name, and no new ones could be conferred. Special guarantees were to protect the right of coalition, the rights of national minorities, the independence of the courts, democratic principles of education, freedom of the press, freedom of worship, and the rights of youth.

The Churches were designated as "corporations of public law," entitled to collect taxes from their members. In the case of the Protestant Churches this change of legal status meant liberation from subservience to the monarchist State whose head had in many instances held the power and exercised the functions of the episcopate. Although the Weimar Constitution tended toward the separation of State and Church, it provided for continued State support of the Churches, and several of the *Länder* subsequently entered into special "concordats" with the Holy See and the Protestant *Landeskirchen.**

The section dealing with education decreed the abolition of private preparatory schools and established a compulsory common *Grundschule* (basic school) of four grades for all children. Education in general was to aim at "moral training, public spirit, personal and vocational fitness, and, above all, the cultivation of German national character and of the spirit of international reconciliation."

The final and most comprehensive section of the Weimar Constitution was devoted to social and economic problems. Article 153 states that "property imposes obligations; it must be used in the service of the common good." This flexible concept of private property, striking a middle path between the capitalist-liberal idea of an absolute right of ownership and the socialist expropriation theory, harked back to the primitive Germanic and medieval Christian concept of a relative right to private ownership. It thus emphasized the communal component of private property and referred it to its ethical frame and term, the common good of all. The distribution of the soil, for example, was to be controlled by the *Reich,* and land that was needed for the social and economic good of the community might be expropriated or socialized. Entailed estates (*Fideikommisse*) were to be dissolved, and the unearned increment in the value of the soil was to be used for the benefit of the nation. Thus the *Reich* reserved for itself the right to socialize such private enterprises as it considered suitable and "ripe" for such conversion. In these instances the former owners were to be duly compensated.

The most important and socially most progressive innovation in the economic field was the creation of *Wirtschaftsräte* (Economic Councils), to culminate in a central *Reichswirtschaftsrat,* as outlined in Article 165. These economic bodies were to serve as instruments of social peace and social justice and were intended to supplement and complete the system of social legislation inaugurated by Bismarck (cf. p. 535 sqq.). The article stipulated

---

* Article 138 called for the commutation and eventual cessation of financial contributions of the State to the Churches, but State support was never discontinued, not even under National Socialism. Religious instruction in public schools was likewise continued, and the theological faculties at the universities were retained. A *Reich Concordat* with the Holy See was concluded in 1933.

that workers and employees were to "co-operate on an equal footing with employers in the regulation of wages and the conditions of labor, as well as in the general development of the productive forces." To achieve this end it was decreed that workers and employees were to receive "legal representation in the form of District Workers' Councils, Regional Workers' Councils, and a *Reich* Workers' Council." These chosen representatives of labor were then to "combine with the representatives of the employers . . . to form Regional Economic Councils and a *Reichswirtschaftsrat*. Bills dealing with basic social and economic questions shall be submitted to the *Reichswirtschaftsrat* before being presented to the *Reichstag.*" These legal directives were further implemented by the laws of February and May, 1920, the former providing for the election of a representative Workers' Council in all enterprises with more than twenty employees (*Betriebsräte*), the latter defining specifically the constitution and the functions of the *Reichswirtschaftsrat*. It was to consist of 326 members, proportionately representing agriculture, horticulture, forestry, fisheries, industry, trade, commerce, finance, communication and transportation, arts and crafts, and consumer interests. Twelve regional economic experts and twelve representatives of the *Reich* government completed the roster of this large and powerful organization.

With the creation of the *Reichswirtschaftsrat* the Weimar Constitution had, in theory at least, pointed a way to resolve the conflict between capital and labor, the two warring contenders in the "labor market," without resorting to the extremes of either excessive capitalist individualism or State socialism. The solution proposed, moreover, embodied much of the best social thinking of the Christian tradition of Europe and many of the suggestions contained in the social encyclicals of Popes Leo XIII and Pius XI.

The Treaty of Versailles. Prince Max von Baden's request for an armistice of October 5, 1918 (cf. p. 642) had been addressed to Woodrow Wilson and had expressed the desire on the part of Germany to accept the "Fourteen Points" as a basis of peace negotiations. The American president referred the German plea to the Allied Powers, and these in turn declared in a joint note to Washington "their willingness to make peace with the government of Germany on the terms of peace laid down in the President's address to Congress of January 8, 1918, and the principles of settlement enunciated in his subsequent addresses." The acceptance of the Allies was qualified, however, by two reservations, one relating to the freedom of the seas, the other to the problem of reparations. To those familiar with the spirit and the letter of the secret agreements and treaties (1915, 1916, 1917) concluded among the Allied Powers — regarding in particular the future disposal of the Rhineland, the German colonies, the Adriatic coast, Constantinople, and the Dardanelles — it must have been obvious even at that time that such far-reaching annexationist plans could hardly be reconciled with Wilson's "Fourteen Points." The French government, for example, had made it clear in September, 1916, that Germany should be deprived of the territory of the Saar and of the entire left bank of the Rhine. These regions were to be transformed into "autonomous republics" under French military supervision. Russia, in return for her approval of the French scheme, was to be given a free hand in the German East.

The note of the American State Department of November 5, 1918, conveyed to the German government the Allies' acceptance of the "Fourteen Points" in their qualified form. The German government in turn expressed its agreement, and a German Armistice Commission left for Paris. At the following "peace conference" the European Allies were represented by their Prime Ministers Lloyd George (England), Clemenceau (France), and Vittorio Orlando (Italy), while the chief spokesman for the United States was President Wilson, who had arrived in the French capital on December 13. Aside from these "Big Four," none of the thirty-odd "Allied and Associated Powers" played any conspicuous part in framing the peace treaties and in determining the future shape of the world's map.

The leader of the German delegation was Count von Brockdorff-Rantzau. He and his associates were excluded from participation in the negotiations, and the terms of the treaty they were asked to sign remained unknown to them up to the moment they were submitted for acceptance *in toto,* on May 7. The German delegates, held *incommunicado* behind barbed wire in a Paris hotel, were, however, permitted to hand in written remarks relating to questions of minor detail and to methods of the fulfillment of German obligations under the treaty.

On May 28, the Germans submitted a set of counterproposals and registered a vigorous protest against the violation of the Pre-Armistice Agreement as embodied in the "Fourteen Points." The answer of the Allies, termed their "last word," made some minor concessions and declared that in case the Germans refused to accept the peace terms as they then stood, the blockade would be continued and Allied troops would occupy the larger part of Germany. As the German High Command insisted that military resistance to invasion was out of the question, the German delegation finally yielded, and on June 22 the National Assembly, confronted with an Allied ultimatum with a time limit of twenty-four hours, accepted the Versailles Treaty against 138 opposing votes. The formal signing took place on June 28 in that same Hall of Mirrors of Versailles Castle where the German empire had been proclaimed on January 18, 1871.

The severest and most ignominious clause of the treaty, and the one to which the vote of the National Assembly had taken specific exception, was contained in Article 231, which stated that Germany acknowledged her and her allies' "responsibility for causing all the loss and damage to which the Allied and Associated governments and their citizens have been subjected as a consequence of the war imposed upon them" by the Central Powers. The German peace envoys had with a heavy heart accepted a dictated peace rather than lay their defenseless country open to invasion and the destruction of its national sovereignty. For thus having squarely shouldered their responsibility as the chosen representatives of the German people they were, before many years had passed, denounced as *November-verbrecher* (November criminals) by the domestic enemies of the Weimar republic.

Opposition to the treaty naturally was strong even among those who had voted for its acceptance. On June 20, Scheidemann resigned as chancellor. He was succeeded by his fellow socialist, Gustav Bauer. The Centrist Erzberger, the new minister of finance, had played an important part in the Armistice Commission and had recommended acceptance of the armistice terms, while to the socialist Hermann Müller, acting as the German pleni-potentiary in Versailles, had fallen the onerous and hateful task of putting his signature to the peace document.

According to the terms of the Armistice of November 11, 1918, Germany had to withdraw all her troops from the occupied territories in the West within a time limit of a few weeks. By the end of November this difficult military operation was completed. The withdrawal and the ensuing de-mobilization had proceeded in good order and without any breach of military discipline. During the same period 5000 locomotives, an equal number of motor trucks, 150,000 freight cars, and immense quantities not only of war material but of farm equipment, including horses (150,000), cattle (880,000), sows (15,000), sheep (897,000), and goats (25,000), had to be delivered to the Allies. These stipulations, too, were fulfilled.

To reimburse the victors for their shipping losses a large part of the German navy and merchant marine had to be handed over, and the German government had to pledge the construction within five years of approximately one million tons of new merchant ships, to be transferred to the Allies after completion (200,000 tons per annum). Added to this were large deliveries of coal, dyestuffs, and other chemical products; the German-owned ocean cables also passed into the hands of the victors. All German rivers were to be internationalized.

The food blockade was not terminated until July 12, 1919. On May 7 of that year Count von Brockdorff-Rantzau had indignantly referred to this fact in addressing the Versailles assembly. "The hundreds of thousands of non-combatants," the German chief delegate had stated, "who have perished since November 11, 1918, as a result of the blockade, were killed with cold deliberation, after our enemies had been assured of their complete victory."

The Treaty of Versailles deprived Germany of about one twelfth of her national territory and population. The German colonies were taken over by Great Britain, the British Dominions, France, Belgium, and Japan, to be administered as "mandates" under the League of Nations. Alsace and Lorraine were returned to France, while the former Prussian districts of Eupen and Malmédy were transferred to Belgium. The Saar region with its rich coal deposits was placed under the sovereignty of the League of Nations for a period of fifteen years, after which a plebiscite was to determine whether this territory should be united with France or with Germany.

■ Lost by Germany	German territory through plebiscite
▦ Saar District	▨ "Anschluss" prevented
▨ Occupied territory	▬▬▬ Demilitarized zone

From *Der Grosse Herder*, Herder, Freiburg i. Br.

The Treaty of Versailles.

In the East, Germany had to surrender those Polish regions which had been acquired by the partitions of Poland in the eighteenth century (cf. pp. 316, 322). To give Poland an outlet to the Baltic, the Allies created the "Polish Corridor" which separated East Prussia from the rest of Germany and thus became a cause of lasting resentment and multiplying frictions. The predominantly German city of Danzig in East Prussia was declared a "free city," but was incorporated in the Polish tariff system. Its economic life was gradually strangled by the development of the neighboring Polish sea and naval port of Gdynia which succeeded in monopolizing most of the overseas trade.

In October, 1921, the League of Nations divided German Upper Silesia, one of Germany's most important industrial centers, between Germany and Poland, notwithstanding the outcome of the plebiscite of March 20 which had indicated a clear majority in favor of Germany. The dividing line was drawn in accordance with the number of votes cast in the several disputed areas. Memel, the northernmost German city, was awarded to the republic of Lithuania, and Schleswig, in compliance with the expressed wishes of its population, was restored to Denmark.

The left bank of the Rhine was occupied by Allied troops, and Allied bridgeheads were established at Mainz, Coblenz, and Cologne, on the right bank of the river. The German army was to be reduced to a maximum strength of one hundred thousand men, including four thousand officers; the navy to six ships of the line of ten thousand tons each, six small cruisers, twelve destroyers, twelve torpedo boats, and fifteen thousand men, including fifteen hundred officers. The armed forces were to be welded into a strictly professional unit with specified time of service (twelve years for enlisted men, twenty-five years for the officers). The maintenance or construction of heavy guns, tanks, submarines, and military aircraft was prohibited, and all fortifications in the occupied zones of the Rhineland and up to thirty miles east of the Rhine had to be dismantled. The occupied territories were to be evacuated by the Allies in three successive stages within a period of fifteen years, subject to German fulfillment of her obligations under the Versailles Treaty. To "obtain the required guarantees," the Allies reserved for themselves the right to delay evacuation or to reoccupy already evacuated regions (Article 429).

In regard to the fallen imperial regime the German republic was required to hand over to Allied military courts the German "war criminals," including the *Kaiser* and some of the top generals of the army. However, this demand, which immediately aroused a storm of angry protest among Germans from the extreme Right to the moderate Left — a protest which was sustained by the papacy and several neutral countries — was never pressed and finally dropped altogether. Instead, trials of "war criminals" were to be conducted by the German Supreme Court in Leipzig. But by the time these proceedings were instituted, nationalist sentiment had been revived to such a degree that some of the "accused" (notably Hindenburg and Ludendorff) became the objects of popular ovations. More than one of these so-called "trials" was turned into a farce, and practically all of them ended in acquittals.

An Allied Reparations Commission was to assess the damages caused by Germany and to compute the sum total of indemnities and reparations which Germany was expected to pay. At a meeting of this commission in London, in April, 1921, this total was fixed at thirty-three billion dollars (one hundred and thirty-two billion gold marks). It took a decade to convince the political and economic leaders of the Allies of the necessity of scaling down this figure to an amount which could reasonably be exacted from Germany, without upsetting the precarious economic balance of victors and vanquished alike. When reason finally began to prevail, it was too late, because the Weimar Republic was already in its death throes.

It may be asked in conclusion: what actually had become of Woodrow Wilson's "Fourteen Points"? Six of them — relating to the evacuation and restoration of Belgium (VII); liberation of French territory and restoration of Alsace-Lorraine to France (VIII); autonomous development of the non-Germanic peoples of Austria-Hungary (X); self-determination of Rumania, Serbia, and Montenegro (XI); creation of an independent Poland with access to the sea (XIII); creation of a general association of nations, to afford "mutual guarantees of political independence and territorial integrity to great and small states alike" (XIV) — were either wholly or partially realized. The remaining eight points were either entirely discarded — (I) "open covenants, openly arrived at"; (II) freedom of the seas; (III) removal of economic barriers; (V) a "free, open-minded, and absolutely impartial adjustment of all colonial claims" — or so modified that little of the original substance was left.

This is what happened in regard to the guarantees that (IV) "national armaments be reduced to the lowest point consistent with domestic safety"; the demand for evacuation of Russian territory and an opportunity (VI) "for the independent development of the Russian people"; (IX) the promised "readjustment of the Italian frontier" in accordance with "clearly recognizable lines of nationality"; and the pledge of sovereignty for the Turkish portion of the Ottoman empire, plus a guarantee of autonomous development for the other nationalities under Turkish rule: Disarmament (IV) was carried out unilaterally by the vanquished under the terms of the peace treaties. In their attempts to overthrow the Soviets, the Allies repeatedly (1918–1920) interfered with the "independent political development of the Russian people" (VI). The Italian frontier readjustments (IX) placed over half a million Germans and Yugoslavs under Italian sovereignty. And the affairs of Turkey (XII) were finally settled not with the aid of the Allies but despite their adverse interference.

While in accordance with point X and the "principle of self-determination" the Austrian "succession states" were freed from Hapsburg rule and granted autonomy, the rump republics of German Austria and Hungary, under the terms of the treaties of Saint-Germain (September 10, 1919) and Trianon (June 4, 1920) were reduced to a small fraction of the former territories of the Austro-Hungarian monarchy. Both were economically and politically crippled and hedged in to such an extent that their "independent" survival was rendered difficult if not impossible.

The Fate of the Weimar Republic. Born under the most inauspicious circumstances, the German republic made a brave attempt to consolidate its as yet untested forces and to gain a firm footing at home and abroad. The choice of Friedrich Ebert as *Reichspräsident* had been a fortunate one.

The former harness maker was no imposing figure, but he embodied the very best character qualities of the German working and middle classes, and he even gained the respect of his enemies by the calm dignity, the good common sense, and the straightforward simplicity with which he discharged the duties and attended to the functions of his high office. The first *Reichspräsident* was typical in this regard of the officials of the Weimar Republic: while most of them lacked political genius and statesmanlike vision, they were clearheaded men of personal integrity and an abundance of good will, and they were animated by the strong desire to link the well-being of their own country with that of the community of nations and peoples. But being inexperienced in the art of political propaganda and the ritual of international diplomacy, they proved no match for the political demagogues at home and the political strategists abroad.

a) The Kapp Putsch. The young Republic was put to its first test in an uprising staged in March, 1920, by disgruntled monarchist and rightist reactionaries under the leadership of Wolfgang Kapp, an East Prussian landowner who, in 1917, had gained doubtful renown as founder of the annexationist *Vaterlandspartei.* Associated with Kapp were Captain Hermann Ehrhardt, commander of a marine brigade, and General Ludendorff, recently returned from his Swedish exile. Ehrhardt's marines had defied the order of the Inter-Allied Commission to disband; they had marched on Berlin and presented the government with an ultimatum, demanding new elections and active resistance to the dictate of Versailles.

The *Reich* government moved first to Dresden and then to Stuttgart, while the insurgents seized several ministries in Berlin and issued a proclamation abrogating the legality of the Weimar Republic and vesting all authority in Wolfgang Kapp. But this initial success was turned into dismal failure when General Hans von Seeckt, the *Reichswehr* commander, refused co-operation, and the government of the Republic called upon the German trade unions to organize a general strike. Some of the leaders of the *Putsch* were arrested, others went into hiding, and Kapp himself fled to Sweden.

The short-lived revolt had leaned on the armed strength of organized "Free Corps," semimilitary volunteer formations which had been recruited from returning soldiers and sailors and had been employed to aid in putting down communist uprisings in Germany and riots of Polish nationalists in the Silesian frontier districts. They now turned their fighting strength against the German republic, aiming to overthrow the Weimar regime and to free Germany from the shackles of Versailles. Gathering into their ranks large numbers of young men who had lived through the horrors of war and had in their disillusionment become disdainful of all civil law and order, they formed the nuclei of the future antirepublican "private armies" of the *Stahlhelm* (steel helmet), the SA (*Sturmabteilungen:* storm troops), and the SS (*Schutzstaffel:* protective guard; Hitler's bodyguard).

In the Ruhr District the partisans of Kapp ran into the armed resistance of communist labor battalions which quickly gained the upper hand and occupied several Rhenish cities. The *Reichswehr,* entering the Rhineland zone designated as "neutral" in the Versailles Treaty, put down the communist uprising after several bloody encounters. Although the *Reichswehr* had proceeded with the permission of the Allies, France used this incident as a pretext to occupy Frankfurt on the Main, "in the interest of the Allied occupation forces," an action which was strongly reproved by the United States, Great Britain, and Italy.

b) *Ruhr Invasion and Currency Inflation.* Elections for the first *Reichstag* of the Republic were held on June 6, 1920. The results broke up the parliamentary majority of the "Weimar coalition" of Social Democrats, Democrats, and Centrists, the parties which had voted for the acceptance of the Versailles Treaty and had dominated the National Assembly. The moderate parties, with the exception of the Centrists, were greatly weakened, while the Right and the extreme Left increased their representation, the German Nationals from 42 to 56, the German People's party from 22 to 62, and the Independent Socialists (Communists) from 22 to 81.

The cabinet headed by the Socialist Hermann Müller, which shortly after the *Kapp Putsch* had succeeded the Gustav Bauer cabinet, resigned after the *Reichstag* elections. A new government, representing more adequately the parliamentary situation, was formed under the chancellorship of the Centrist Konstantin Fehrenbach.

The major problem confronting the new chancellor and his cabinet ministers was that of reparations. In July, 1920, Fehrenbach went to Spa (Belgium) and three months later to Brussels to attend reparations conferences and obtain accurate information as to the payments, both in money and in kind, which Germany was expected to make. At both conferences Hugo Stinnes, a member of the German People's party and the leading German industrialist, protested sharply against the entire reparations policy of the Allies and even expressed himself to the effect that he would rather see Germany turn communist than submit to the demands of the Allies.

These demands were finally specified and handed to the German delegation at the London Conference of March 1, 1921. Germany was required to pay two hundred billion gold marks (c. fifty billion dollars) within a period of thirty years. The German refusal to accept these terms was followed by an Allied ultimatum and the occupation of some additional Rhenish cities. Fehrenbach resigned and was succeeded by Joseph Wirth, a member of the left wing of the Center party, who organized a new government on the basis of the Weimar coalition. Included in the Wirth cabinet was Walter Rathenau, the son of Emil Rathenau (cf. p. 631), the actual president of the AEG (*Allgemeine Elektrizitätsgesellschaft*), a prominent industrialist, an economic expert of more than average capacity, and a sincere believer in international understanding.

On May 11, 1921, the Wirth government accepted the London ultimatum, and Germany, aside from her continued deliveries in kind to France, paid a first reparations installment of one hundred and fifty million gold marks. Both Wirth and Rathenau were henceforth denounced by their domestic foes as the inaugurators of the German *Erfüllungspolitik* (fulfillment policy). Resentment against all those responsible for the signing of the Versailles Treaty reached a high pitch. On August 26, 1921, Matthias Erzberger was murdered in the Black Forest by members of the secret military *Organisation Konsul,* the first of many victims of the gradually emerging forces of counterrevolution and rightist reaction.

The devaluation of the German currency, which had begun during the war, was accelerated in the postwar years by the lowering of German productive capacity caused by territorial and property losses, the dwindling of foreign trade, the lack of international credits, and the payment of reparations. When the fall of the mark reached alarming proportions Germany demanded a moratorium on reparations (December, 1921), and in January, 1922, an international conference convened at Cannes on the French Riviera to straighten out the reparations tangle and stabilize the German financial situation. While the conference was in session, the moderate French cabinet of Aristide Briand was defeated, and the violently anti-German Raymond Poincaré became prime minister of France.

In April the Powers met again, this time at Genoa, and a Russian delegation was invited to take part in the negotiations. The Germans and Russians sprang a surprise on the world by signing the Treaty of Rapallo which waived all reparations and pledged friendship and economic cooperation between the two countries. The text of the treaty had been prepared by Maxim Litvinov, and the secret negotiations had been brought to a successful conclusion by Walter Rathenau, the German minister of reconstruction, and Chicherin, the Russian foreign commissar.

On June 24, Rathenau fell as the second victim of the *Organisation Konsul.* The assassins, when brought to trial, not only maintained that Rathenau had deserved death as a Jew and an *Erfüllungspolitiker,* but they cynically confessed that the execution of the "death sentence" had been necessitated by the very fact that a continuation of Rathenau's foreign policy would have proven advantageous to Germany and would thus have strengthened the prestige of the Weimar Republic.

Poincaré's appointment as French prime minister was followed by another German cabinet crisis. The Wirth government, finding itself compelled to inform the Allies of Germany's inability to meet the payments agreed upon after the London ultimatum of March, 1921, was sustained in its renewed plea for a moratorium on reparations and for an international loan by the British representative on the Reparations Commission. Wirth tendered his resignation on November 14, 1922, one day after he had dispatched his note to the Allies. Wilhelm Cuno, director of the Hamburg-America Line, was entrusted with the formation of a new coalition government which had the strong backing of German industry and consisted of members of the German People's party, the Centrists, the Bavarian People's party,* and the Democrats.

Poincaré viewed the Cuno government with even greater distrust than he had felt toward the Wirth cabinet. He declared himself opposed to any concessions in the question of reparations unless France were given tangible guarantee assets in the form of German State forests and mines in the Ruhr. He even raised again the question of the cession of the Rhineland to France and threatened occupation of the Ruhr in case Germany should fail to meet her reparations commitments.

When Germany, early in January, 1923, was declared in default on deliveries of timber and coal, French and Belgian divisions marched into the Ruhr and occupied the industrial key cities. The Ruhr occupation lasted from January, 1923, to July, 1925, and called forth strong British protests.

The attempt made by France to exploit the rich industrial assets of the Ruhr District was, however, hampered by a German policy of passive resistance and non-co-operation, as decreed by the German government on January 19. Germany's plight aroused increasing sympathy in the United States and Great Britain, and a *démarche* in Paris was undertaken by the Vatican. Thus France found herself not only in a partial economic stalemate but also in a diplomatic situation which became more and more untenable.

In the meantime, the disintegration of the German currency had become catastrophic. The German government had promised to reimburse German industrialists in the Ruhr for forced reparations deliveries and to compensate idle workers for their loss in wages. The printing presses worked overtime to turn out immense quantities of paper money without gold coverage, and soon Germany found herself engulfed in a mad whirlpool of uncontrolled inflation. Before long the equivalent of the dollar was quoted in millions and billions of paper marks. The speed with which the inflation proceeded was such that employees and wage earners had to be paid daily to allow them to catch up with the runaway prices. Even so, the fantastic amounts of paper earnings received became worthless within a few hours.

But what was a nightmare for the average German citizen turned out to be a field day for the holders of foreign currency. The country found itself overrun with foreigners who bought up commodities in such quantities and at such a rate that most stores were completely sold out in the early morning hours, and many were unable to replenish their stocks. The German and non-German holder of foreign currency could purchase industrial plants, ancient castles, land, and real estate for a mere trifle. Savings, insurance policies, and pensions were invalidated, and the entire German middle class was reduced to penury. Resentment against the *nouveaux riches* and

---

* The Bavarian People's party (*Bayerische Volkspartei*) had seceded from the Center party after the Revolution of 1918. This secession was caused by Bavarian opposition to the centralizing tendencies of the Center party as well as by the monarchist sentiment of Bavarian Catholics and their disapproval of the Weimar coalition of Centrists, Democrats, and Social Democrats.

ill feeling against foreigners were on the increase, and a wave of anti-Semitism swept over the country. The economic chaos proved a fertile breeding ground for cynicism, moral license, and political radicalism.

The Cuno cabinet did not survive the economic and financial crisis. It fell in August, 1923, and was replaced by another coalition government which once more included the Social Democrats and was headed by Gustav Stresemann of the German People's party.

c) The Stresemann Government and the Domestic Crisis. The new German chancellor stepped into a heritage that was anything but enviable: German economy and finance were in a state of confusion and exhaustion, and the country as a whole seemed to be on the brink of civil war. Gustav Stresemann (1878-1929), who had developed from an ardent nationalist into an equally determined advocate of international understanding, courageously faced the almost unsolvable problems with which his government was confronted and succeeded within a relatively short time in restoring order at home and securing a *modus vivendi* in the foreign field.

Convinced that the prolongation of the Ruhr struggle could only lead to national ruin, Stresemann called an end to passive resistance on September 26, 1923, and entered into negotiations with France. Thereupon voluntary German reparations deliveries were resumed, and conditions in the Ruhr District gradually returned to normality.

Stresemann's next immediate concern was the stabilization of the German currency. This difficult task was accomplished by the establishment of the *Rentenbank* which in turn issued a new *Rentenmark* (November, 1923), a currency which was not backed by gold but by a mortgage on the entire agricultural and industrial assets of Germany.

On November 23, the combined opposition of the Right and Left led to the fall of the Stresemann coalition government, but in the new cabinet headed by Wilhelm Marx of the Center party* Stresemann was given the post of foreign minister, an office to which he was returned again and again in the several coalition governments of the following years.

While holding the chancellorship of the *Reich,* Stresemann had also efficiently dealt with a triple threat of civil war. Both a monarchist-nationalist revolt of the *Fridericus Rex* movement in Pomerania and communist uprisings in Saxony, in the city of Hamburg, and in several other regions were crushed by the *Reichswehr.* The third threat, however, was the most formidable and the one which bore the earmarks of an organized counter-revolution. The abortive Munich "Beer Cellar *Putsch*" of November 9, 1923, staged jointly by Adolf Hitler and Erich Ludendorff, with the temporary connivance of the monarchistically inclined government of Bavaria, aimed at the abolishment of parliamentary institutions, the suppression of civil liberties, the expropriation of the Jews, and the summary liquidation of political opponents.

---

* This cabinet as well as the following three (1923-1926) renewed the Cuno coalition of German People's party, Centrists, Bavarian People's party, and Democrats.

Adolf Hitler (1889-1945), a native of the Austrian town of Braunau, after having failed in his early attempts as an art student and painter in Vienna, had moved to Munich in 1912. In 1914, he enlisted as a volunteer in a Bavarian infantry regiment. A rabid Pan-German, anti-Semite, and anti-communist, he blamed the Weimar Republic and an international Jewish conspiracy for the lost war, the Treaty of Versailles, and all the subsequent evils which had befallen Germany. In 1919, he and a small band of sympathizers created the NSDAP (*Nationalsozialistische Deutsche Arbeiter-partei:* National Socialist German Workers' party) which gathered a steadily mounting number of recruits from the ranks of uprooted and disillusioned intellectuals, members of the impoverished middle classes, soldiers, and workers. Combining the self-righteousness of the monomaniac fanatic with the persuasive oratory of the revivalist and the cunning of the mass psychologist and political spellbinder, Hitler succeeded in welding his following into a disciplined militia which was bound to the *Führer* by unconditional fealty. Capitalizing on both the nationalist and socialist trends fostered by the political and economic pressures of the postwar years, he held out to the masses the seductive bait of "National Socialism."

The Munich *Putsch* was preceded by the *Führer's* solemn vow that within twenty-four hours he would be master of Germany or dead. However, twenty-four hours later he was neither master of Germany nor dead, but lying flat on the ground in Munich's Odeon Square, trying to dodge the bullets of the Bavarian police. In falling to the ground he had wrenched his shoulder and was carried off by a party physician. Two days later he was taken into custody. The Hitler *Putsch* failed because both the Bavarian government and the *Reichswehr* had refused at the last moment to endorse the extremist program of the *Führer* and his associates.

On April 1, 1924, Hitler was sentenced to serve five years in the fortress of Landsberg in Bavaria, but he was pardoned and released before the year had ended. He had used the months of confinement to write *Mein Kampf,* the future "Bible" of National Socialism, and he emerged from Landsberg with the halo of the political martyr.

Although the Stresemann government had weathered the economic and political crises, it was reproached by the Right for having liquidated passive resistance in the Ruhr, and by the Social Democrats for having been too lenient with the enemies of the Republic. The result of these accusations was the withdrawal of the Social Democrats from the coalition and the above-mentioned emergence of the first Marx cabinet.

d) The Dawes Plan, the Treaty of Locarno, and the Young Plan. Notwithstanding the fact that rightist and leftist radicalism in Germany made some headway during the years following the Ruhr invasion, the period during which Stresemann directed Germany's foreign policy was generally characterized by increasing international co-operation and by a growing willingness on the part of the Allies to aid in Germany's recovery and to restore her to full equality in the family of nations. The spirit of Versailles gradually gave way to what was hopefully called the "spirit of Locarno."

Upon the request of the German government the Reparations Commission appointed two committees of financial and economic experts to deal with the problems of currency stabilization and economic rehabilitation. Charles Gates Dawes, who later became the United States vice-president in the administration of Calvin Coolidge (1925–1929) and was awarded the Nobel Peace Prize in 1925, was the chairman of the first committee. He was a coauthor of the "Dawes Plan" which represented the first attempt to settle the problem of reparations on a purely economic basis, divorced from political considerations. The plan, as adopted on August 16, 1924, by the Conference of London, stipulated that Germany was to pay two and a half billion marks (c. six hundred million dollars) per annum over an as yet unspecified number of years, but provisions were made for reduced payments during the first few years. The sums required for these annual payments were to be raised by mortgages on German railroads and industries, by contributions out of the budget of the German government, and by foreign credits and loans. After a period of five years the annual payments were to be readjusted on the basis of a prosperity index, that is, on the basis of a re-examination of the German capacity to pay. The total German transfer of reparations payments during the five years the Dawes Plan remained in operation amounted to approximately eight billion marks (c. two billion dollars).

The Dawes Plan furthermore called for a reorganization of the German *Reichsbank,* making this institution independent of the State, establishing its control over the circulation of currency and, for a period of fifty years, giving it a monopoly for the issuance of bank notes. The *Direktorium* of the *Reichsbank* was to be composed of fourteen members, seven of them Germans, and the remaining seven representing the United States, Great Britain, France, Italy, Belgium, Holland, and Switzerland.

A second Marx cabinet was formed after the *Reichstag* elections of March 9, 1924. The moderate parties returned weakened, while the extremists of the Right and Left had increased their strength. Nevertheless, the *Reichstag* adopted the Dawes Plan on August 29. Shortly afterward the hope of obtaining a stronger backing for the government's policy of international understanding prompted the *Reichspräsident* to decree the dissolution of parliament and order a new election. The *Reichstag* which convened in December actually indicated in its composition the more conciliatory spirit of the Conference of London and the Dawes Plan: the extremists of the Right and Left lost heavily, while the government parties gained a comfortable majority. The election had also without doubt been influenced by the change of government in England and France. In the former country the labor cabinet headed by Ramsay MacDonald had come into office, while in France the Socialist Edouard Herriot had become president of the Republic.

Nevertheless, political and parliamentary stability in Germany was anything but assured. Progress in the "restoration of Germany to equality among the nations" was much too slow to suit the impatient agitators and politicians of the German Right. To many supporters of the moderate parties it seemed fair and reasonable enough to accede to the Nationalists' bid for representation in the government, thus giving them a chance to make good their claims. It was hoped that the responsibility of office might put an end to their destructive and demagogic criticism and engage them constructively in the rebuilding of Germany and the cementing of international relations.

It was such considerations that led to the resignation of the second Marx cabinet and the formation of a new government, in which the German Nationals obtained representation. Hans Luther, who leaned toward the moderate Right and had held posts as food minister and finance minister in previous cabinets, assumed the office of *Reichskanzler* (January, 1925).

On February 28, 1925, *Reichspräsident* Ebert died. In the following election (April 26) by popular ballot the aged General Field Marshal von Hindenburg, the candidate of the Right, obtained the majority of votes over Wilhelm Marx, the candidate of the parties of the Weimar coalition, and Ernst Thälmann, the candidate of the Communist party. The Centrist Marx was beaten by the decisive vote of the Catholic Bavarian People's party.

Though a conservative Prussian army officer, who had been trained and made his military career under the Hohenzollerns, Hindenburg disappointed all those who had voted for him in the hope of an early swing to the Right and an eventual restoration of the monarchy. He kept his oath of office loyally and gave strong moral support to the policies inaugurated by Gustav Stresemann. It was only after Stresemann's premature death in 1929 that the soldier-president gradually succumbed to the influence of rightist and reactionary politicians.

The crowning achievement of Stresemann's tireless efforts in behalf of the pacification of Europe and international co-operation was the negotiation of the *Locarno Pact.* In this treaty, which was signed by Germany and the Western Allies on October 16, 1925, Great Britain, France, Italy, Belgium, and Germany jointly guaranteed the inviolability of the Franco-German borders as established by the Treaty of Versailles. The only flaw in this international agreement — and, as history was to demonstrate, a major one — was that it left the question of Germany's eastern frontier unsettled. The reason for this omission was Germany's unwillingness to recognize as final the situation created by the "Polish Corridor" and the separation of Danzig from the body of the *Reich* (cf. p. 654). German refusal to follow up French suggestions for the signing of an "eastern Locarno" caused the French government to enter into new military alliances with Poland and Czechoslovakia.*

* After World War I the Allies created Czechoslovakia to satisfy the national aspirations of the Czechs and Slovaks. The new nation consisted of parts of the former Dual Monarchy of Austria-Hungary (Bohemia, Moravia, Austrian Silesia, North Hungary, and Lower Austria) and some districts of the former Prussian province of Silesia. The population of Czechoslovakia included approximately 44 per cent Czechs, 16 per cent Slovaks, almost 25 per cent Germans, and several ethnic and linguistic islands of Magyars, Ruthenians, and Poles.

The very substantial positive achievements of the Locarno Pact are to be credited to the close collaboration and combined good will of Gustav Stresemann, Aristide Briand, and Sir Austen Chamberlain: the foreign minister of Germany, and the prime ministers of France and England. In recognition of this fact they were awarded the Nobel Peace Prize for the year 1926. The initiative, however, had come from Stresemann, who had first discussed the possibilities of the plan with Lord d'Abernon, British ambassador in Berlin, who in turn had finally succeeded in convincing the British prime minister of the epochmaking significance of Stresemann's offer.

On November 27, 1925, the Locarno Pact was endorsed by the *Reichstag,* against the votes of the German Nationals, the National Socialists, and the Communists. Even before the signing of the pact the "spirit of Locarno" had borne fruit in the withdrawal of the last Franco-Belgian occupation troops from the Ruhr (1925). The first (Cologne) Allied occupation zone in the Rhineland was evacuated in January, 1926. This was followed by the withdrawal of the Inter-Allied Military Control Commission and the extension of an invitation to Germany to join the Council of the League of Nations.

As far as the German Right was concerned, the Pact of Locarno was, however, nothing to be proud of or grateful for. As Germany at Locarno had voluntarily renounced all claims to Alsace-Lorraine, the signing of the treaty was termed a betrayal of national interests, and the ratification had been preceded by a campaign of personal vilification against Stresemann. The brown-shirted legions of Adolf Hitler, brandishing the *Hakenkreuz* (swastika) banner, and the monarchist-chauvinist *Stahlhelm,* an organization of German war veterans, loyal to the black-white-red of the imperial standard, registered their protests in noisy demonstrations. The supporters of the Weimar Republic countered with mass meetings and parades of the semimilitary contingents of the *Reichsbanner* (founded in 1924), chiefly recruited from liberal and socialist groups and carrying the black, red, and gold banners of the Republic. The Communists on their part were parading their own private army, the *Rotfront,* taking their cues from Moscow and waving the red flag with the hammer and sickle emblem of the Third International.

Obviously, there was small evidence of the "spirit of Locarno" in the violent quest for power of these rival groups. Germany by this time was not only on the way to regaining her former stature as a world power but was also economically on the road to recovery. Therefore, the growth of political dissension and radicalism on the domestic scene must be attributed to the tardiness of the Allies in restoring the occupied zones to German sovereignty, their unwillingness to effect an early relaxation of the burdens of reparations, their refusal to live up to their promise of international disarmament, and their reluctance to remove from the German people the stain of the unfortunate war guilt clause of the Versailles Treaty. The work of peace-loving statesmen, such as Stresemann and Briand, was rendered increasingly difficult by the phalanx of ill will to which the chauvinists of all European nations, including Germany, contributed their weighty share. Thus Stresemann's fervent plea for solidarity in international affairs as well as Briand's call for the creation of a United States of Europe evoked even less response among their own countrymen than across the national boundaries.

On December 10, 1926, the day on which Germany was welcomed as a member of the League of Nations, Stresemann addressed the Geneva Assembly, declaring that "it cannot be the purpose of the Divine world order that men should direct their supreme national energies against one another. . . . He will serve humanity best who, firmly rooted in the traditions of his own people, develops his moral and intellectual gifts to the best of his ability, thus reaching out beyond his own national boundaries, and serving the whole world." These were lofty words, and they were uttered by a man who was anything but a starry-eyed idealist. Stresemann was a man of practical affairs who had learned in the hard school of political experience that even in politics crime does not pay, and that any sound nationalism and true political realism must take account of universal moral principles and incentives if the national State itself is not to fall victim to an international anarchy engendered and sustained by the unchecked will to power.

The acceptance of the Dawes Plan had been followed by a remarkable recovery of German economy, aided by large scale investment (*c.* sixteen billion dollars) of foreign capital in German industry, public utilities, housing enterprises, and public works. By 1929 both the German national income and industrial production were nearly twice what they had been before the period of inflation. New industrial concerns (*Kartelle*) came into being, savings accounts increased, and in 1927 employment figures were the highest attained since the end of the war. The government could even lower the income-tax rates and raise the salary scale of the civil service.

The bright colors of this picture of Germany's economic and financial status are, however, somewhat delusive. What looked like genuine prosperity was largely an artificially stimulated economic overexpansion, and this artifact rested on unsound foundations. It could only be maintained as long as the flow of foreign credit continued unabated, but was bound to collapse as soon as world prices declined and the international financial situation forced the withdrawal of foreign capital. In 1929, Germany's total indebtedness to foreign creditors amounted to twenty-nine billion marks (*c.* seven billion dollars).

The new crisis set in with the crash of the stock market in the United States in October, 1929, and the ensuing upheaval in world economy. Even before this critical climax was reached it had become evident that German commitments under the Dawes Plan exceeded the financial and productive capacity of the country and that a readjustment of reparations payments had once more become necessary. Preliminary negotiations in 1927 and

1928 led to the appointment of a special committee in January, 1929, to study the possibilities of a definitive settlement of the problem of reparations. In May, 1929, the *Young Plan,* so named after Owen D. Young, the United States representative and chairman of the Reparations Committee of experts, was completed and presented to an International Conference, meeting at the Hague in August of the same year.

The Young Plan fixed the total of German reparations at 34,9 billion gold marks (*c.* 8,5 billion dollars) and provided for (1) payment of definite annuities covering the period from 1929 to 1988, following a gradually rising scale which was to reach its peak with an annuity payment of approximately two and a half billion marks in 1966; (2) creation of the Bank for International Settlements in Basel (Switzerland), to execute the transfer of payments and to act as a clearinghouse for international war debts; (3) reduction and eventual cancellation (after ten years) of reparations in kind; (4) termination of foreign control over German finances; (5) abolishment of the office of the General Agent of Reparations; (6) complete evacuation of the occupied territories in the Rhineland not later than June 30, 1930.

Meanwhile the German political situation had again undergone some important changes. The success of Stresemann's foreign policy was reflected in the *Reichstag* elections of May, 1928, in which the Social Democrats gained over two million votes and the German Right was considerably weakened. The new party constellation permitted the formation of a coalition government which included the Social Democrats and was headed by the Socialist Hermann Müller. Arrayed against it were the German Nationals, the National Socialists, and the Communists.

On August 27, 1928, Stresemann scored another triumph of his policy of international reconciliation: most of the larger nations of the world, including Germany, put their signatures to the Briand-Kellogg Pact of Paris, outlawing aggressive war and pledging the solution of all international conflicts by peaceful means. The chief shortcomings of the pact were its failure to define aggressive war and to provide for adequate sanctions against aggressors.

In view of the continued successes of the much maligned *Erfüllungspolitik* the German parties of the Right felt that one by one their arguments against the Weimar Republic were losing ground. Already the very structure of the Versailles Treaty, the mainstay of their relentless fight against successive German governments, was crumbling, and soon their opposition would be deprived of its object. These circumstances worked for an ever closer collaboration between the parties of the Right, especially after, late in 1929, the German Nationals had made Alfred Hugenberg — the main shareholder of the powerful *Hugenberg Konzern* which through its ownership of a large chain of newspapers, magazines, news agencies, telegraph companies, and motion-picture enterprises (UFA) controlled a large section of German public opinion — their party chairman.

Gustav Stresemann died on October 3, 1929, without having been able to witness the final adoption of the Young Plan by the *Reichstag* (March 12, 1930). Even before his death the joint forces of Hugenberg's German Nationals and Hitler's National Socialists had initiated a popular referendum "against the War Guilt Lie and the Young Plan," asking punishment for the "traitors" who had participated in framing this latest scheme for a reparations settlement. The referendum was held on December 22, 1929, and the initiative was defeated by a large majority of the voters. From then on large amounts donated by Hugenberg and his fellow industrialists, many of whom had made huge fortunes during the period of inflation, went into the coffers of the National Socialist party. These sums were largely used to recruit new storm-troop members from the ranks of the destitute and unemployed, and to defray the expenses of organization and propaganda.

e) The Brüning Government and the End of the Weimar Republic. The economic world crisis which came in the wake of the financial crash in the United States made itself felt in Germany by the flight of capital, the withdrawal of foreign credits, and the rising unemployment figures (almost seven million in 1930). Growing unemployment was in part caused by the far-reaching "rationalization" processes in which German industry had been engaged in the preceding years, and in part also by the abrupt discontinuation of reparations deliveries in kind. The cabinet headed by Hermann Müller, bent upon carrying out certain budgetary reform measures designed to make Germany less dependent on foreign capital, failed to gain the necessary parliamentary backing. As President Hindenburg refused to decree the dissolution of the *Reichstag,* the cabinet resigned, and the task of forming a new coalition government devolved upon Heinrich Brüning who, in 1929, had become the parliamentary leader of the Center party. The new chancellor, though anxious to obtain a broad parliamentary backing, was himself one of the spokesmen of the right wing of his party and came more and more under the influence of those rightist and ultraconservative groups whose spokesmen held key positions in the cabinet.

The Brüning government, which had assumed office on March 30, 1930, obtained a vote of confidence with the aid of the German Nationals, against the opposition of the Social Democrats, the extreme Left, and the extreme Right. The German Nationals felt indebted to Brüning for his extension of a large-scale farm relief program which had been initiated by the preceding cabinet and which benefited the agrarian interests of various agricultural sections of Germany. The temporary rift which the affirmative vote of Hugenberg's party caused in the *bloc* of German Nationals and National Socialists — a *bloc* which dated back to the common opposition to the Young Plan — seemed to justify Brüning's hope of isolating the National Socialists. When, however, during June and early July, the cabinet introduced legislation designed to balance the budget, the German Nationals swung back into opposition, and the government failed by eight votes to obtain a majority. On July 18, the *Reichstag* was dissolved.

In the elections held on September 14, 1930, the National Socialists cashed in on the economic crisis, raising their party's representation to 107 seats, as against 95 in the preceding *Reichstag,* and 12 in 1928. From a small and noisy group of demagogues the followers of Adolf Hitler had grown into the most powerful party with a popular backing of 30 per cent of the electorate. The Communists likewise scored heavily, and from then on the extreme Right and Left were closely, albeit negatively, united in their will to destroy German democracy and the Weimar Republic. In most other respects National Socialists and Communists were mortal enemies and fought each other with ever increasing violence. The "party line" for the German Communists was decreed by Moscow in 1931: they were told to co-operate with all the enemies of the Weimar Republic.

In the same year (1931) German Nationals, National Socialists, and *Stahlhelm* joined forces at a meeting in Braunschweig to form under Hugenberg's leadership the rightist "Harzburg Front" against the Brüning government. However, it became increasingly evident that the political struggle in Germany was turning into a contest between Brüning and Hitler. The *Führer* had been successful in enlisting the support of many conservative Christians by stressing the pledge of the original party platform of 1921, to uphold and defend "positive Christianity." These converts apparently failed to see that many of the other specifically listed aims of the party program flagrantly contradicted such an assertion.

Chancellor Brüning could hold himself in office only with the support of the Social Democrats who, realizing that the choice for Germany was from now on between a moderate authoritarian conservatism and a radical rightist dictatorship, reluctantly gave their backing to a series of *Notverordnungen* (emergency decrees). These decree laws, issued by a *Präsidialkabinett* (presidential cabinet) under Article 48 of the Constitution (cf. p. 649), were to cope with the grave financial and economic situation, on the one hand, and were to curb political radicalism and save what was left of the Weimar Republic, on the other.

The prestige both of the Weimar Republic and the Brüning cabinet was further undermined by determined Allied opposition to an Austro-German customs union negotiated by Ernst Curtius, the German foreign minister, and Johann Schober, the Austrian vice-chancellor, and announced on March 25, 1931. The initiative had come from Austria, but it was generally understood that the governments of both Germanic nations envisaged a future complete economic union and an eventual political *Anschluss,* to redeem Austria from the fatal predicament into which she had been driven by the Treaty of Saint-Germain (cf. p. 656). After England, France, and Italy had registered their protest, the matter was referred to the Hague Tribunal which by an eight-to-seven vote decided against the Austro-German plan.

In the course of the year 1931 the German economic situation also showed further signs of deterioration. The flight of capital, the export of gold, and the withdrawal of foreign credit continued apace, and on July 1 President

Hoover, responding to a personal appeal of *Reichspräsident* Hindenburg, announced a one year's moratorium on all intergovernmental war debts. During the month of July the huge *Nordwolle Konzern* (North German Wool Company) failed, involving in its collapse some of the leading German banks. The German government temporarily closed all banks and immediately issued drastic decrees for the control of foreign exchange, cash payments, and check clearings, with the result that in August the crisis had been mastered and normal banking operations could be resumed. The revolutionizing effect, however, of the government decrees was an almost total nationalization of German finance.

Shortly after the announcement of the Hoover moratorium the Young Plan Advisory Committee and a group of economic experts, working in conjunction with the Bank of International Settlements, arrived at the conclusion that Germany could not be expected to resume reparation payments. They decided that the German economic crisis had to be viewed as an integral part of the world crisis and could therefore be solved only by concerted international action. Finally, the Conference of Lausanne (convened in June, 1932, shortly after the fall of the Brüning government) decided that after a final payment of three billion marks, to be transmitted at the end of three years, all future German reparations should be canceled.

The Brüning government and with it the Weimar Republic could point to some significant achievements both in the domestic and foreign fields. The second major financial and economic crisis of the Republic had been beaten by means of stringent deflationary measures, albeit at the heavy cost of government-decreed reductions of salaries, wages and rates of interest, and the imposition of higher taxes. The government had assumed control over the banks, and all foreign currency in excess of two hundred marks had to be surrendered to the *Reichsbank*. Protective laws prohibited the import of many agricultural products, including butter. Prices for food-stuffs were high, while the general standard of living had been lowered. On the other hand, the overhauling of the entire economic and financial structure of the *Reich* and the radical curtailment of government and private spending had lent additional weight to the government's plea of January, 1932, for the complete cessation of reparations payments and for the cancellation of a large proportion of private indebtedness as well.

It had been demonstrated, furthermore, that the economic problems were directly linked with the political problems and that a stabilization of world economy could only be hoped for if the spirit of Versailles were liquidated at long last. If, then, the enemies of the Weimar Republic did not want to lose out completely they had to make haste, especially in view of the fact that the Genoa Disarmament Conference of February, 1932, gave evidence that there were good prospects of a favorable decision in regard to this last one of Germany's major grievances.

The last chance for the obstructionists of the German Right and extreme Left came with the expiration of President Hindenburg's term of office on May 5, 1932. In view of the tense political situation in Germany an attempt was made to have a two-thirds majority of the *Reichstag* amend the Constitution so as to permit Hindenburg to continue in office for another year, without calling a special election. However, the refusal of Hitler and Hugenberg to concur in such a move made a presidential election mandatory.

In 1928, Hindenburg had been elected to the presidency by the parties of the Right with the aid of the Bavarian People's party. In 1932, the Prussian soldier and monarchist, who had become almost a symbol of the Weimar Republic, campaigned against the enemies of this same republic: against Hitler, the candidate of the National Socialists; Colonel Düsterberg, the candidate of the German Nationals and the *Stahlhelm;* and Thälmann, the candidate of the Communists. Hitler at the time was a man without a country, having lost his Austrian citizenship as a former member of the Bavarian army. He was naturalized, however, by the National Socialist government of Braunschweig.

The first ballot was indecisive. In the second balloting (April 10) Hindenburg obtained nineteen million votes, the absolute majority. Hitler received thirteen million, and Thälmann three million. The candidate of the German Nationals and the *Stahlhelm* had withdrawn in the second race in favor of the National Socialist *Führer.*

Four days after the presidential election General Gröner, minister of the interior and of defense in the Brüning cabinet, decreed the suppression of the private armies of the National Socialists. The result was that in the subsequent elections for the Diets of Prussia and several other German "lands" the National Socialists emerged as the strongest party. General Gröner was forced to resign as *Reichswehrminister,* retaining however the portfolio of minister of the interior.

On May 30, 1932, Chancellor Brüning was dismissed by Hindenburg. In the morning hours of that day he had presented for the President's signature a decree calling for the breaking up of bankrupt *Junker* estates in East Prussia, to provide settlements for German farmers. The *Reichspräsident* had gradually been maneuvered into a position where he had to choose between his bourgeois chancellor and the members of his own caste.

On his eightieth birthday Hindenburg had been presented by rightist German industrialists with the huge ancestral family estate of the Hindenburgs in East Prussia (Neudeck), and the aged President enjoyed spending his days of rest in the circle of his *Junker* friends and neighbors, the owners of the surrounding estates and farm lands. They had finally convinced him that what Germany needed was a strong and ruthless regime. Not only was Chancellor Brüning not the man of the hour, but he was even advocating a policy of "agrarian bolshevism"! Thus, when Brüning submitted his scheme for the parceling of *Junker* estates, the president believed he held the evidence that his friends were right. Brüning had to go.

On May 28, 1932, Franz von Papen, the wily diplomat and rightist politician, the leader of the right wing of the Center party and co-owner of the influential Berlin Centrist newspaper *Germania,* had met with Adolf Hitler to discuss the political situation and the possibilities of joint rightist action. The aristocratic von Papen had little liking for the self-made *Führer* and former lance corporal, but, like Hugenberg and many of the industrialists and *Junkers,* he intended to use Hitler's oratorical and organizational talents to further his own political schemes. Hitler made his "toleration" of a Papen cabinet and any future co-operation contingent on two conditions: the *Reichstag* must be dissolved, and the order suppressing the SA and SS formations must be rescinded.

On June 1, Franz von Papen was appointed chancellor, on the special recommendation of General Kurt von Schleicher, who had long held important posts in the *Reichswehr* ministry and who, as a friend of Hindenburg's son Oskar, had had a hand in the making and unmaking of Brüning. He now was given the portfolio of *Reichswehrminister* (minister of defense) in the Papen cabinet.

On June 4, three days after von Papen's appointment as chancellor, Hitler's first condition for "toleration" and collaboration was fulfilled: the *Reichstag* was dissolved. The second condition was met on June 16: the SA and SS formations were legalized. The decree which outlawed them had really never been enforced.

On July 20, von Papen deposed by an unconstitutional presidential decree the democratic government of Prussia, filling all posts in the administration of the State and the municipalities, including the police force, with rightist officials. The Prussian delegates to the *Reichsrat* were likewise replaced by antirepublicans. Von Papen himself assumed the office of *Reichskommissar* for Prussia.

In the *Reichstag* elections of July 31 the National Socialists received 230 seats, thus more than doubling their strength, and the Communists 89, while the parties of the middle lost correspondingly. The Papen cabinet was largely composed of civilian and military aristocrats and therefore nicknamed "the barons' cabinet." It represented a party coalition of the moderate Right which, without the support of the National Socialists, could rally behind it only 42 of the *Reichstag* deputies. The combined National Socialist and Communist vote, on the other hand, commanded an absolute majority which could obstruct any positive action of the legislative branch of the government. Under these circumstances, and as Hitler had already withdrawn his pledge of "toleration," the cabinet could only rule by decrees countersigned by a docile *Reichspräsident,* and by further bending and twisting the ominous Article 48 of the Constitution.

In September, 1932, the *Stahlhelm,* with von Papen's approval, staged a mammoth parade in Berlin, in which 150,000 war veterans marched, pledging unswerving allegiance to the black-white-red standard of the Hohenzollern monarchy.

The untenable parliamentary situation caused the president to decree the dissolution of the *Reichstag* and to call for new elections. The cancellation of German reparations and the progress in the disarmament talks (cf. p. 670) — to be credited to the foreign policy of Stresemann and Brüning, but taking effect during the early days of von Papen's chancellorship — swung about a million National Socialist votes to the support of the Papen cabinet and another million to the parties not represented in the government. Thus in the elections of November 6, 1932, the National Socialists lost altogether two million three hundred thousand votes and thirty-five *Reichstag* seats.

It was at this juncture that General Kurt von Schleicher reappeared on the scene. He had convinced himself that the reactionary von Papen could not be expected to endorse any extensive program of social reform and public works such as in his opinion could alone save Germany from political and social chaos. On November 17, von Papen resigned, and von Schleicher was appointed chancellor, minister of defense, and *Reichskommissar* for Prussia.

The Schleicher cabinet honestly tried to create a broad front for the tasks of reconstruction. The chancellor called for the transformation of the *Reichswehr* into a democratic people's army and tried to enlist the support of the trade unions and of all other groups which had the true interests of Germany at heart. But both the Social Democrats and the Center party, albeit for different reasons, refused to co-operate. The Social Democrats saw in the new chancellor merely the representative of the hated military caste, and the Centrists had not forgiven Schleicher his share in the overthrow of the Brüning government.

In the meantime, an important meeting between Hitler and von Papen had taken place in Cologne, in the residence of Baron von Schröder, one of the leading German bankers. Papen and some of his political friends and associates had long toyed with the idea of establishing a "corporate state," a type of functional or vocational social order, in which the interests of all social groups were to be welded into an organic and "solidaric" structure. They were even naïve enough to believe that the corporative order as outlined in Pius XI's encyclical *Quadragesimo Anno* (1931) could be harmonized with the "corporatism" of Mussolini's Italy and with the demands of the National Socialist program. They failed to see that the "solidarism" envisaged by the papal encyclical had its frame and term in the free development and perfection of human personality, that it rested on the premise of free service and voluntary association and acknowledged the sanctions of divine, natural, and moral law. Fascist and National Socialist "corporatism," on the other hand, was centered in the absolute power of the State or the Race and proposed the *Gleichschaltung* (co-ordination) of individuals and groups by means of physical and spiritual coercion and regimentation. Hitler, however, was too shrewd to disappoint prematurely this wishful thinking of the Papen group and of those Roman Catholics who had only recently constituted themselves as a subdivision of the National Socialist party.

Acting upon such rather fantastic premises, von Papen used his influence with Hindenburg to persuade the president that the National Socialists should be given a share in a government of a sufficiently conservative stamp to enable it to exert a controlling influence on the National Socialist hotspurs.

The *Reichstag* adjourned on December 9, 1932. Between January 17 and January 28, negotiations between von Papen, Hugenberg, and Seldte (the *Stahlhelm* leader) had brought agreement as to the composition of the new government. On January 28, von Schleicher was dismissed and von Papen commissioned by the president to work out a compromise with Hitler. On January 30, Hitler was appointed chancellor, taking the oath of office to support the Weimar Constitution. The event was celebrated in the evening with a torchlight parade of SA troops marching through the Brandenburg Gate and the Wilhelmstrasse, with Hindenburg and Hitler in the reviewing stand.

The Hitler cabinet included, aside from the *Führer* himself, only two National Socialists. Joseph Göbbels was appointed minister of propaganda and public enlightenment, and Hermann Göring became a minister without portfolio (*ohne Geschäftsbereich*). Von Papen was made vice-chancellor and *Reichskommissar* for Prussia; Hugenberg, minister of agriculture; Seldte, minister of labor; General von Blomberg, minister of defense. Baron von Neurath was retained as foreign minister, and Count Schwerin von Krosigk as minister of finance.

As the government commanded no parliamentary majority, the president decreed the dissolution of the *Reichstag* and set March 5 as the date for new elections. On February 27 a fire of mysterious origin destroyed the *Reichstag* building in Berlin. A feeble-minded Dutch communist, named van der Lubbe, was found on the premises in a dazed condition. He was arrested, "confessed" having set fire to the building, and was later executed.

On February 28, President Hindenburg, again invoking Article 48 of the Constitution, signed a decree "for the Protection of the People and the State," which served as a cover to justify the arrest of thousands of communists, the suppression of the communist press, and the eventual proscription of the Communist party. A supplementary decree established the SA and SS formations as organs of the military police.

The following election campaign turned into a field day for the parties of the Right: communist and socialist meetings were dissolved, their newspapers confiscated; gatherings and publications of Centrists and Liberals were under close surveillance; and all radio stations were operated and controlled by National Socialist functionaries.

The elections were preceded, accompanied, and followed by rioting and bloody excesses. The National Socialists won 288 seats (43 per cent), as against 196 in the previous *Reichstag*. The German Nationals, the Center party, and the Social Democrats suffered only minor losses, while the Communists lost one fifth of their deputies. National Socialists and German Nationals combined polled 51 per cent of the total vote, thus holding a slim majority.

The immediate sequel of the election was a mass persecution unequaled in German history: large numbers of communists, socialists, liberals, Catholics, and Pacifists were arrested, beaten, tortured, and either murdered or sent to concentration camps. State and municipal governments were ousted and replaced by National Socialist administrations. However, the final act of the drama needed for its consummation a screen of legality: The government could obtain dictatorial powers only by a change of the Constitution, for which a two-thirds majority of the *Reichstag* was required. This requirement was fulfilled by outlawing the Communist party, thus preventing the elected Communist deputies from taking their seats in the *Reichstag*.

On March 23 this "rump parliament" convened in the Kroll Opera House in Berlin and passed with the votes of the Right and the Centrists the *Ermächtigungsgesetz* (Enabling Act) which conferred dictatorial powers on Hitler's cabinet for a period of four years. On July 14 all political parties with the exception of the NSDAP were either dissolved or they disbanded "voluntarily."

On August 2, 1934, President Hindenburg died. Shortly afterward Hitler abolished the title of *Reichspräsident* and assumed personally the title and office of *Führer und Reichskanzler*. This step, too, had to be "legalized" by a "plebiscite": the *Führer und Reichskanzler* received a "popular endorsement" of almost 90 per cent. The Weimar Republic had come to an inglorious end.

Here the account of Germany's political destinies must break off, for the time being. What followed—the "revolution of nihilism" (Rauschnig), the captivity, first of Germany, and later on of Europe, under the Nazi yoke, World War II, the defeat and prostration of Germany — is of too recent date to be seen and evaluated in its true proportions and to permit the detached objectivity required for a historical analysis.

It may suffice therefore to state that from 1933 on the iron rule of the National Socialist *Totalstaat* extended to all departments of public life, culture, and education, and to the most intimate concerns and relations of private and family life. While all civil and human rights were totally abrogated, all duties and responsibilities converged in the *Führer,* the embodiment of *Volk* and *Reich*. Citizenship was limited to "Aryans," and the *Nürnberg Laws* eliminated all Jews from the political, economic, and cultural life of the German *Volksgemeinschaft* (folk community). As has been stated, "positive Christianity" was given a boost in the party program, and freedom was promised to all religious creeds "as far as they do not endanger or are in conflict with the moral ideas of the Germanic race," while at the same time a subtle, insidious, and relentless war of extermination was waged against Christian citizens, churches, and groups of all denominations; while party officials declared Germanism and Christianity as mutually exclusive, and thousands upon thousands of innocent victims lingered and died in concentration camps. The innocent and the guilty: they all became victims of a gospel of hate and the "will to power," embodied in a regime which glorified war and conquest as necessary and normal outlets for a nation's vigor and as "legitimate" means to national glory.

Chapter 17

CULTURAL TRENDS

The Age of Crisis. Baron Karl vom Stein, the leader of the social and political reform of Prussia (cf. p. 432 sqq.), had written in the early twenties of the nineteenth century: "We are overpopulated; we have overreached ourselves in production and manufacture, and we are overfed; our administration has become more and more materialistic, and we have reduced everything to a lifeless mechanism." At about the same time the usually optimistic Goethe had visualized a mankind which would become "more shrewd and more intelligent, but hardly better or happier." He believed he saw "a time approaching when God will no longer be pleased with man, when once again He will have to smash His creation to pieces in order to rejuvenate it."

As the nineteenth century ran its course and turned into the twentieth, such isolated voices of gloom were echoed by many of the prominent thinkers of the West, and the word "crisis" appeared more frequently in learned publications and disputations. In Germany, Paul Lagarde (1827–1891), Friedrich Nietzsche (1844–1900, cf. p. 695 sq.), and Julius Langbehn (1851–1907) were among the first to indict the moral and spiritual bankruptcy of the modern age, and to unmask what Robert M. Hutchins has called the "twin myths of progress and utility." Lagarde, professor of Oriental languages at the University of Göttingen, called for the creation of a new German *Volksgemeinschaft* (people's community) on a religious and moral basis, and was bitterly opposed to political and economic liberalism, moral relativism, and philosophic materialism. Deploring the encroachments of the *Naturwissenschaften* (natural sciences) and of the "scientific method" upon the *Geisteswissenschaften* (human studies; humanities), he wrote in 1881: "The predominance of natural science is partly due to the fact that *Geisteswissenschaft* has little to show for itself but the dressed-up subjectivity of individuals and groups, so that honest thinkers develop a loathing for it. . . . The nullity of human kind is at present so pronounced that even the religious urge has taken refuge in the natural sciences. But though the prevalent scientific hypotheses are noisily proclaimed as exact science, they are nothing but scientific dogmas. What do we nonscientists learn in our universities but theories, high-sounding phrases, and empty words? . . . Our judgments on literature, music, and philosophy are such as we find in compendia and review factories; our judgments on political matters are nothing but the spawn of those reptiles who pollute our cities. We have so much education that we no longer have access to ideas."

And Julius Langbehn, in his provocative book *Rembrandt als Erzieher (Rembrandt, the Educator,* 1890), joined Lagarde in his fight against the materialism of the age. He praised religious faith, *Volkstum* ("folkishness," national culture), and great art as supreme character builders and asserted in the opening lines that "the spiritual life of the German people finds itself at present in a slow process of decline. Science and knowledge succumb to ever increasing specialization. In thought and literature epoch-making personalities are lacking. The Fine Arts, though distinguished by significant individual accomplishments, have lost the character of monu-mentality and with it their most compelling force. We have plenty of musicians, but composers and performers of talent are rare. Architecture is the axis of art, as philosophy is the axis of all scientific thought, but at the moment we have neither a German architecture nor a German philoso-phy. The great masters are dying out; *les rois s'ent vont* (the kings dis-appear). . . . There is no question but that in all this the democratizing, levelling, and atomizing spirit of this century expresses itself. The entire culture and education of the present age is historical, 'Alexandrian,' retrospec-tive; we are less concerned with the creation of new values than with the registration of old ones. And the greatest weakness of our modern culture is truly this: it is scientific and wants to be scientific, but the more scientific it becomes the less creative it will be."

More radical and more penetrating in his criticism than either Lagarde or Langbehn was Friedrich Nietzsche. In the midst of the delusive prosper-ity, the joyful exuberance, and the noisy nationalism of the *Gründerzeit* (foundation period) which followed the victorious war against France and the proclamation of the German empire (cf. p. 546), he raised his voice in solemn warning: "Of all the evil consequences," Nietzsche wrote in 1873, "which have come in the wake of the latest war with France, the worst is perhaps a widespread, yea even universal mistake: the mistake, namely, of public opinion that German civilization too was victorious in that conflict." Such a delusion, he feared, would eventually "turn the German victory into defeat, yea into the very extirpation of the German spirit in favor of the 'German Empire.' "* He lamented the "unspeakable impoverishment and exhaustion of our existence," and he believed he recognized undercurrents of destructive forces which were prone to endanger the proud edifice of the new Germany: "We are living in an atomic age, an atomistic chaos. Today everything is determined by the coarsest and most evil forces, by the egotism of an acquisitive society and by military potentates. . . . A revolu-tion is unavoidable, and it will be an atomistic revolution." And the preface

---

* Cf. *Unzeitgemässe Betrachtungen* (I).

of *Der Wille zur Macht* (*The Will to Power*) contained the following prophetic passage: "My work," Nietzsche stated programmatically, "shall contain a summary judgment on our century, on the entire modern age, on the kind of civilization which we have attained. . . . What I am going to narrate is the history of the next two centuries. I shall describe what will of necessity come about: the advent of nihilism. . . . Our entire European civilization has long been moving with a tortuous tension, a tension which has been growing from decade to decade, toward the final catastrophe."

About a generation later, Nietzsche's attempt to diagnose the crisis of the modern age and to "narrate the history of the next two centuries" was repeated by Oswald Spengler (1880–1936) in his *Der Untergang des Abendlandes* (*The End of the West,* I and II; 1917 and 1922), a work which sings the swan song of Western civilization and preaches a funeral oration over its allegedly decomposing corpse. For Spengler the modern crisis is a phenomenon inherent in every culture organism: *"Zivilisation"* as such is the end phase of *"Kultur,"* signifying the exhaustion of the culturally creative energies and their replacement by the rationalizing and mechanizing tendencies of science and technology. For him cultural organisms are plantlike growths following in their evolution universal biological laws; they thus pass necessarily through the successive stages or "seasons" of spring, summer, autumn, and winter, and their end or death is both predictable and **inevitable.**

No attempt is made by Spengler to mitigate or overcome the crisis of the age: he merely describes its symptoms. But this description and the philosophy of history on which it rests are themselves symptoms of the crisis and of that spirit of the age which had been penetratingly analyzed by Spengler's precursors, especially by Nietzsche. Spengler's "scientism" and biologism fail to recognize the essential distinction between human nature and physico-mechanical nature, between that which is materially and biologically pre-determined and that which owes its growth to the self-determination of free human agents, between the causality which rules in the natural sciences and the personal and moral imperatives which determine the course of history and the related *Geisteswissenschaften.* Thus Spengler is simply a consistent positivist and materialist when, in his book *Der Mensch und die Technik* (*Man and Technology,* 1931), he arrives at the conclusion that man is a *Raubtier* (beast of prey), that ideals are indicative of cowardice, that man, the "knowing priest of the machine age," is creative not by virtue of his mind, but by virtue of his hand, and that therefore he is not a rational animal but at best a rationalizing brute.

Cultural "crisis" is in the last analysis the manifestation of a lack of confidence in established cultural values and standards. In this respect the crisis of modern Germany is identical with the crisis of modern Europe and America. It is a crisis which, having its roots in significant shifts in the system of values, involves civilization in all its branches: the State, society, economics, education, art, literature, philosophy, and religion. No doubt, both Nietzsche and Spengler had sensed this all-embracing nature of the crisis of their age. But whereas for Nietzsche's basic cultural optimism the mind of Western man could advance to new shores by means of the vitalization of its unused recuperative resources, by means of an *"Umwertung aller Werte"* (transvaluation of all values), for Spengler's cultural pessimism the crisis was indicative not of a transition but of the impending *finale* of Western civilization. To both authors, however, it appeared as the tragedy of modern civilization that the scientific age, which had promised peace, security, and liberation from all illusions and superstitions, was producing on all sides a growing instability and was multiplying revolutionary upheavals; that modern civilization was creating a universe which, to use Aristotle's words, could be inhabited only by beasts or by gods, a universe from which man therefore was excluded. When Nietzsche felt it his "terrible duty" to announce to the world "the death of God," when the romantic longing of his heart projected itself into the chimera of the *"Übermensch,"* the *"blonde Bestie,"* and when he proclaimed the insatiable "will to power" as the new ethical code of the "superman" of the future," he provided the precise pattern for Spengler's historic naturalism and biologism.

It was his intense romantic idealism that made Nietzsche say that "the best in us is derived from the sentiments of the past. The sun of our life has set, but the sky still glows with its light, although we no longer see it." His classical-humanist education had taught him to acknowledge and revere the continuity of the Graeco-Roman-Christian heritage of European thought and culture. He recognized in the Western tradition a common stock of ideas by means of which even minds of vastly differing convictions had been able to communicate with each other. And he was all the more disturbed by the revolutionary impact of the age of positivistic science and philosophy which had "atomized" modern mankind by depriving it of those normative and axiological criteria without which a rational system of thought and moral action was impossible.

Nietzsche's description of the predicament of modern civilization became in Spengler's pessimistic view the fatal predicament of modern man: he who had been the master of nature had been reduced to serfdom and slavery by the machine age. The means were revolting against the ends: in a universe constituted exclusively by mechanical and physical laws everything was materially predetermined, and there was no room left for the self-determination of a human person. If both human life and subhuman nature were immersed in such a universe of brutal and morally indifferent facts, the "why?" of the metaphysician and the "ought" of the moralist, the questions as to the nature of being and the ends of doing, became equally meaningless. "The saying 'this ought to be,'" wrote Spengler, "must be replaced by the inexorable 'this *is* so.' . . . A proud skepticism discards the sentimentalities of the nineteenth century. . . . Skepticism is the only philosophical attitude still possible for this age and worthy of it."

According to Spengler, what we are witnessing today is the spectacle of a machine age defeating its own ends. The tired mind of the West seeks escape and refuge either in sports or in exotic religious cults which were scorned and disdained in the age of Darwin. While some of the intellectual leaders are beginning to rebel against their destiny, against the mechanization of life, the masses, having completely succumbed to the spirit of the age, are irretrievably lost. This civilization of "Faustian man" will soon be destroyed and forgotten, as dead and forgotten as are the highways of the Romans, the Chinese Wall, and the palaces of Memphis and Babylon. Spengler therefore admonishes his contemporaries to heed the example of Achilles: let us rather have a short life, full of action and fame, than a long life void of meaning and content. Our fate is inevitable; a return is impossible; optimism is sheer cowardice. Let us then stand firmly at the posts where destiny has placed us, knowing that we. are lost, without hope and without redemption. To be able to do this is the mark of our greatness.

The merit of Spengler's diagnosis of the age of crisis and of his counsels of despair lies in his merciless analysis of the "spirit of the age" and in the consistency with which he proceeds from certain given premises to seemingly inescapable conclusions. That his cultural pessimism itself is one of the symptoms of the crisis which he describes is further evidenced by the fact that he fails to see the flaws in the premises. If the premises of materialism and naturalism are correct, then Spengler's conclusions are logical and legitimate. If man's distinguishing mark is his hand, then he achieves his greatest triumph in the creation of "millions and billions of horse-power." But if man's distinguishing marks are his intellect and free will, then the entire picture changes, and the essentially different premises call for essentially different conclusions. If the crisis of the age issues from man's confused mind, from his sick heart, and from his perverted volitional and emotional life, then he and his civilization are not irretrievably lost, because human nature at any historical juncture will be able to rouse itself, to challenge the "spirit of the age" and to recover the wholeness and balance of a truly human life and civilization.

Economic Forces. Viewing with deep concern the turning away of the new German empire from the ideals of the past, the Prussian historian Heinrich von Treitschke (1834–1896, cf. p. 592) said in the German *Reichstag* in November, 1871: "You may believe a teacher of youth who has had an opportunity to watch the younger generation: it must shake the soul of even the most optimistic of us when we see on all sides increasing self-indulgence, materialism, and the abandonment of the ideal values of life." And the realistic novelist Wilhelm Raabe (cf. p. 590 sq.) wrote in one of his books: "Thus the money bag had burst open in the German lands, the thalers were rolling in the streets, and too many hands were eager to grab them. It almost seemed as if this were the greatest gain which the united fatherland had derived from its great world-historic success."

a) Industry. The symptoms of crude materialism to which the above-mentioned complaints allude were most conspicuous during the final decades of the nineteenth and the first decade of the twentieth century. They reflected the transformation of Germany from an agrarian to an industrialized country. This social and economic development was in part determined by the rapid increase of the population, which rose from forty-one million in 1871 to almost sixty-eight million in 1914.* During the same period the city population was growing steadily at the expense of the countryside: while in 1871 two thirds of the German people had lived on the land, in 1914 two thirds lived in big or medium-sized cities.** Industrial mass production gradually penetrated into the rural districts, often superseding the home industries and peasant crafts.

Both Bismarck's policy of protective tariffs (1879) and Caprivi's commercial treaties with neighboring countries (1891) aimed at aiding the development of German industry and effectively served their purpose. The gradual integration of Germany's national economy in the complex structure of world economy likewise stimulated industrial enterprise and strengthened German capitalism.

The industrial expansion of Germany, however, proceeded by no means in a straight upward movement: it was repeatedly retarded by economic slumps and depressions. Thus, the boom of the *Gründerzeit* (1871–1872) was followed by *"der grosse Krach"* (big crash) of 1873. It took Germany some time to recover from this economic disaster, a recovery which was hampered by the competition of other highly industrialized European nations. Between 1873 and 1879 it was generally believed that a policy of free trade would benefit German economic interests, but this view was gradually reversed, and the steady and almost uninterrupted advance of German industry began with the adoption of protective tariffs (1879) and was accelerated by the conclusion of international trade agreements (1891). Prince Bülow, Caprivi's successor in the office of *Reichskanzler* (cf. p. 620 sq.), merely stated the facts when he wrote shortly before the outbreak of World War I: "The industrialization of Germany . . . proceeded from the end of the eighties on with a vehemence which was equalled only by the industrial development of the United States."

The rise of Germany as a leading industrial power was prepared for and aided by an astounding increase in the production of pig iron, the adoption of new mechanical inventions and machines, such as the steam turbine and the Diesel motor, and by pioneering work in the electrical and chemical industries. During the first decade of the twentieth century Germany took the lead in the manufacture of artificial dyes made from coal tar, such as

---

* The territorial losses of World War I reduced the population figures to approximately sixty-three million (1925).
** In 1871, 36.1 per cent of the German population lived in places with 2000 or more inhabitants; in 1880, 41.4 per cent; in 1890, 47 per cent; in 1900, 54.4 per cent; in 1910, 60 per cent; in 1925, 64.4 per cent. In 1871, 4.8 per cent lived in "big cities" (of 100,000 or more inhabitants); in 1890, 12.9 per cent; in 1900, 16.2 per cent; in 1910, 21.3 per cent; in 1919, 24.9 per cent; in 1925, 26.2 per cent; in 1928, 27.9 per cent. Thus, in 1928, almost one third of the population lived in big cities. While in 1871 Germany had 8 big cities, in 1910 it had 44, and 48 in 1928.

alizarin and indigo. During the war years (1914–1918), when the Central Powers were cut off from the outside world, German chemists learned how to gain nitrogen from the air and thus developed a high production volume of artificial fertilizers and explosives. While in 1913 Germany had imported 971,000 tons of saltpeter from Chile and Peru, the new method of nitrogen fixation made her not only capable of satisfying all the demands of the domestic market, but made possible in the postwar years the export of large surplus quantities of nitrogen. The manufacture of artificial silks and dyes opened up new fields in the textile industries, although German textile production never matched that of England and the United States.

Germany's industrial advance was accompanied and followed by a corresponding expansion of domestic and foreign trade and the development of an extended and highly efficient transportation system. The German railroad lines, for example, measured 62,500 kilometers in 1917, as compared with 19,600 kilometers in 1870. Motor transportation on land and in the air made similar strides and, owing to Count Ferdinand Zeppelin's invention of the rigid dirigible airship (1900), Germany for several decades held the lead in this type of air transportation.

b) *Agriculture.* German agriculture was in a favorable position during the period immediately following the Franco-Prussian War. The productivity of the soil had been heightened by the use of artificial fertilizers and the application of phosphoric acid and potash. The management of farm lands was improved and simplified by the introduction of farm machinery. In 1874, the first *landwirtschaftliche Hochschule* (agricultural university) was opened in Berlin. The German Agricultural Society, founded in 1884, promoted and spread the knowledge of technical agricultural methods and devices, especially by means of publications and periodic exhibitions. Agricultural co-operatives facilitated the purchase of seed grains and fertilizers, the acquisition of machines, the sale of farm produce, and the procurement of money at a low rate of interest.

While these developments greatly benefited German agriculture, the German farmer of the late seventies began to feel more and more the effects of foreign, especially Russian and American, competition. Simultaneously he suffered from the increasing pressure of the industrial age which tended to sacrifice agricultural to industrial interests. Caprivi's commercial treaties favored German industry but resulted in hardships for German agriculture. Prince Bülow's new protective tariffs of 1902, on the other hand, largely repaired the damage, and during the decade preceding World War I German agriculture enjoyed a reasonable amount of prosperity. The war naturally caused a temporary agricultural crisis, but the postwar inflation proved a boon to many German farmers: they were able to liquidate their indebtedness, while at the same time their lands and homesteads retained their value as stable assets.

c) *"Handwerk und Gewerbe"* (*Handicrafts and Trades*). The industrial methods of manufacture worked to the disadvantage of the established handicrafts and trades and destroyed many of the home industries and independent *Handwerker*. This process was speeded up by the trade regulations of 1869 and 1871 which abolished the still prevalent trade restrictions of the *Zünfte* (guilds) and decreed complete *Gewerbefreiheit* (freedom of trade). The opposition of the *Handwerker* led to a series of legal enactments (between 1878 and 1897) which partially incorporated certain features of the guild system, reintroduced the *Meisterprüfung* (master's certificate), and made obligatory the procurement of a *Befähigungsnachweis* (aptitude credential, 1908).* These measures actually saved the independent crafts and trades from extinction and guaranteed a high quality of individual performance, especially in the industrial arts and crafts.**

d) *The "Spirit" of Capitalism.* The adverse effects of capitalism and industrialism were analyzed and severely criticized by leading German economists and sociologists. Max Weber (1864–1920) believed he had discovered the ideological roots of capitalism in the *Berufsethos* (vocational ethics) of Calvinism and Puritanism, which placed an ethico-religious premium on "success" in business and on the accumulation of a maximum of economic goods, not to provide leisure and comfort but as an external sign and guarantee of divine favor. Thus, according to Weber, economic activity as such, which had been viewed with suspicion by the theologians and moralists of the precapitalistic era, was endowed with an ethico-religious accent, and immoderate acquisitiveness, formerly condemned as a social vice, came eventually to be regarded as a manifestation of Christian virtue. Weber thus attributed to the capitalistic *Ethos* the creation of the *Homo Oeconomicus* (economic man) whose economic activities were "autonomous" in the sense that they were completely divorced from the exactions of the natural and moral law. Subsequently, in the period of economic liberalism (cf. p. 549 sq.), the capitalist *entrepreneur* looked to the liberal-capitalist State for the protection of the claimed "absolute" right of ownership.

The anticapitalist critique of Werner Sombart (1863–1941) followed a similar line of reasoning. He accused capitalism of having caused the disintegration of family life and of having destroyed the ethical foundations of business life. As negative factors he mentioned in particular the mechanization of labor, the widening cleavage between employers and employees,

---

* The *Gewerbeordnung* (trade regulation) had its legal basis in the enactments of 1869, 1900, and 1929. A qualified *Gewerbefreiheit* was guaranteed in Article 151 of the Weimar Constitution.

** The following are the German technical terms (some of them untranslatable) commonly used to designate the different phases and aspects of *Gewerbe*: (1) *Hauswerk*: the transformation of raw materials in an independent *Hauswirtschaft* (home economy); (2) *Lohnwerk*: paid work, performed with individually owned tools, either in the house of the client (*Stör*) or in the worker's own home; (3) *Verlag*: a group of independent *Handwerker*, working for the same employer; (4) *Manufaktur*: work performed by *unselbständige Arbeiter* (dependent workers) in a manufacturing enterprise; (5) *Fabrik* (factory): work performed by *unselbständige Arbeiter* in an industrial plant, especially machine production in light and heavy industries. These different phases do not necessarily follow each other in a historical sequence, but often co-exist side by side.

the intensification of the class struggle, and the general dehumanization of social relations.

These and similar indictments make capitalism appear as a kind of inverted Marxism because, like Marxism, it adheres to a purely utilitarian and materialistic system of values. It enthrones economics as a supreme ruling power and subordinates to this economic absolutism all cultural, moral, and spiritual activities and interests.

The accuracy of this interpretation seems to be borne out by the fact that in the capitalistic era, culminating in the years preceding World War I, increasing numbers of the younger generation turned from scientific and intellectual vocations and professions to economic and financial pursuits. Science no less than art and literature became largely subservient to capitalistic interests. Those, on the other hand, who refused to follow the general trend condemned themselves to tragic isolation or expended their vitality in fruitless spiritual rebellion. Literature and the arts came more and more to be regarded as luxuries which could be enjoyed only by economically satiated gourmets. While the servile writer and artist might prosper as a hack, responsible and truly creative minds were frequently forced into an eccentric and Bohemian existence, their works reflecting the lack of a popular response.

Technology. Capitalism and industrialism are inseparably linked with the technological development of the modern age. Technology, too, is characterized by its utilitarian and exclusively this-worldly interests. It is free from ethical preoccupations and determined by purely practical and rational-scientific calculations. It excels in the invention of labor-displacing machinery and has thereby contributed to the aggravation and complication of the social problem. On the other hand, it has been praised by such an astute observer as the German physicist Friedrich Dessauer (1881–) as "the greatest earthly power, the root and communal foundation of cultural progress, the liberator of man from the threatening forces of nature . . . unlocking the doors of the universe. . . . It has vastly enlarged the individual sphere of influence and activity and has transformed the ego-centered thinking and doing of man so as to make him a servant of society and humanity. . . . By reducing progressively the immense distances between man and man it has been able to raise the masses to a higher level of spiritual existence."

In Dessauer's optimistic view technology thus appears as a potent factor in the process of human liberation, democratization, and unification. In this positive evaluation of technology Dessauer, the Roman Catholic, is in agreement with most of the leaders of socialism, but in striking disagreement with Spengler. It is interesting to note that the papal social encyclicals no less than Marx and Bebel blame the economic egotism of the ruling classes rather than technological advance for the degradation of the workingman. Bebel in particular saw in the victory of technics over nature a powerful stimulus for the social and cultural advancement of the proletariat. He

expected from the steadily rising volume of production numerous benefits
for the working class, such as shorter hours of work and more time for
recreation and education.

There is no doubt that most of the critics of technology and the machine
age were not blind to the many material advantages and the great poten-
tialities of the new methods of production and distribution. Their attacks
were usually aimed not at technology as such, but rather at that confusion
of means and ends which turned man from a master into a servant of the
machine. It was generally recognized that technology had opened up new
vistas for creative human endeavor, but deeper minds insisted that technology by itself could not provide the incentives or point the way to higher
cultural standards. This important reservation was made by Heinrich von
Treitschke, who wrote in his *German History of the Nineteenth Century:*
"One has spoken of technology and the facilitation of transportation and
communication as if they by themselves constituted civilization, while actually they only offer the *means* for cultural progress. Future generations will
not ask to what extent we were able to speed up the transmission of letters
but rather whether we had any great human ideas to communicate."* In
other words, while technology places new means at the disposal of man, it is
indifferent with regard to cultural and moral ends.

Materialism and "Idealism." Although the *neudeutsche Kultur* of the
decades between the foundation of the Second Empire and World War I
(1871–1914) owed its physiognomy largely to material forces and accomplishments, there was no lack of idealistic and even romantic interests and yearn-
ings. But it appears that the ideal aims and ends themselves were derived
from material presuppositions and from the one-sided materialistic preoccupations of the age. Idealism was extolled privately and publicly, in State
and Church, in schools and universities. It was a household word in the
circles of nationalists and Pan-Germans and among all those historians,
educators, preachers, politicians, and military men who wrote and spoke
high-soundingly of the eternal mission of *Deutsche Kultur* when what they
really meant was *Machtpolitik* and *Realpolitik*. And this materialistically
colored "idealism" was especially rampant among the upper classes, the
new aristocracy of money and property. "The same generation," wrote Alfred
Lichtwark, the Director of the Hamburg Art Gallery, in 1905, "which has
acquired the new goods, was only in exceptional instances capable of also
attaining to the new culture for whose service these goods were destined.
Wealth, too, needs tradition, and there was no tradition of wealth in
Germany. . . . In our country one can be very rich, very uneducated, and
unwilling to make any sacrifice for cultural ends, without becoming an
object of contempt. . . . There has perhaps never been an upper stratum
of society with as little cultural significance as in present-day Germany. In

---

* *Deutsche Geschichte des 19. Jahrhunderts,* Vol. V, p. 426.

spiritual and intellectual vitality and interest it lags behind the middle and lower classes."*

Lichtwark himself, of course, and others of a similar mind prove that it would be unjust to indulge in any sweeping generalizations. There have always been many scholars, teachers, preachers, writers, and artists of rank in the new German empire who vigorously opposed both the crude materialism and superficial idealism of their age. But their warnings went largely unheeded as long as the nation as such remained in the grip of a materialistic, utilitarian, and one-sidedly practico-political philosophy of life. On the whole, the contemplative *"Volk der Dichter und Denker"* (people of poets and thinkers) had become a people of political, social, and economic action and was very proud of having accomplished this transformation.

Wissenschaft (Science and Knowledge). As has been previously stated, the new Germany which came into being in 1871 retained and even amplified its leadership in the natural sciences (cf. p. 559 sqq.). Science not only supplied agriculture, industry, and technics with new methods and tools, but entered into a close alliance with nonscientific branches of knowledge, such as philosophy, psychology, historiography, and literary criticism, disciplines which for better or worse availed themselves of the "scientific method."

a) "Naturwissenschaften" (Natural Sciences). Theoretical and physical *chemistry* were given a more solid foundation by the research of Walter Nernst (1864–1941), Albert Einstein (1879–1955), Arnold Sommerfeld (1868–1951), and Fritz Haber (1868–1934). In the latter's opinion, "the accomplishments of the past fifty years have raised German organic chemistry to such heights that the world has almost come to regard chemistry as a German science."

In *physics,* Heinrich Hertz (1859–1894), a pupil of Helmholtz (cf. p. 562) and one of the last great representatives of the "classical physics" of the nineteenth century, perfected theoretically and experimentally the science of electrodynamics and made important contributions to Maxwell's theory of electricity. He discovered the electromagnetic waves *("Hertzsche Wellen")* and thereby laid the foundation for the epoch-making development of wireless telegraphy and radio communication. The revolutionary effects of Albert Einstein's Theory of Relativity and Max Planck's (1858–1947) Quantum Theory transcend in their significance the limited sphere of physical science and are beginning to exert a profound influence on epistemology and even on metaphysics. According to Planck, "the transformation of the physical world picture which has taken place during the past two decades is one of the most thoroughgoing changes that have ever occurred in the evolution of a science. . . . The Quantum Theory has

---

* *Der Deutsche der Zukunft,* p. 8.

finally shattered the much too narrow frame of our former world view."*

Hardly less revolutionary are the recent changes in the fields of biology, anthropology, and psychology. The neovitalism of Hans Driesch (1867–1941), harking back to the Aristotelian "entelechy," has resurrected the idea of plan, design, or "final cause" as prime factors in the evolution of organic life.** Max Scheler's (cf. p. 593 sq.) "metaphysical" anthropology aims at a new understanding of the human person as a *"Leib–Seele–Einheit"* (body-soul unity). The *Ganzheitspsychologie* (Gestalt psychology, structural psychology) of the Berlin and Würzburg schools as well as Sigmund Freud's (1856–1939) psychoanalysis, Alfred Adler's (1870–1937) individual psychology, Carl G. Jung's (1875–) analytic psychology, and Igor A. Caruso's (1914–) and Wilfried Daim's (1923–) different brands of psychotherapy have revolutionized psychological research and contributed to a deeper understanding of the central core of human personality and human behavior.

Whatever will be the ultimate impact of these new scientific theories on modern civilization, this much is certain: they have seriously disturbed and upset the naïve self-assurance of the complacent scientism and agnosticism of the age of Dubois Reymond and Ernst Haeckel (cf. p. 565).

b) Geisteswissenschaften.† In some of the above-named scientific theories, such as Scheler's "metaphysical anthropology," Alfred Adler's "individual psychology," Jung's "analytic psychology," or Caruso's and Daim's "existential psychotherapy," *Naturwissenschaft* has almost become an aspect of *Geisteswissenschaft.* In other words, the former relationship between these two groups of disciplines has practically been reversed: whereas by the latter part of the nineteenth century natural science in its rapid expansion had absorbed into itself every activity and manifestation of the human self, the opening decades of the twentieth century have begun to accentuate once more the basic values and creative impulses of human individuality and personality. This shift of emphasis had its ultimate sources in a changing outlook upon life and a subsequent re-examination of the nature of human knowledge. Such a radical reorientation of thought led of necessity to spirited controversies between the representatives of *Naturwissenschaft* and those of *Geisteswissenschaft,* resulting in a clarification of the mutual relationship of these disciplines and in a redefinition of their respective terms and methods.

1. *Krise der Wissenschaft.* The critical examination of the relative rank and value of the different branches of science and knowledge started from the contention of some German thinkers that different epistemological approaches were required for adequate interpretations in the spheres of science and culture. In view of the exaggerated claims of the natural sciences

---

* *Das Weltbild der neueren Physik* (1929), p. 16.
** Cf. *Die Philosophie des Organischen* (Engl. trans., *The Science and Philosophy of the Organism* (London: A. and C. Black, 1929).
† The term came into general use after the publication of Wilhelm Dilthey's *Einleitung in die Geisteswissenschaften* (1883).

and the encroachments of the "scientific method" on nonscientific modes of human knowledge, the neo-Kantian philosopher Heinrich Rickert (1863–1936) tried at the turn of the century to demarcate the boundary line between *Naturwissenschaft* and *Kulturwissenschaft,* with special reference to the historical disciplines.* A different subject matter, he asserted, requires a different method of approach. The generalizing natural sciences progressively eliminate the distinctive marks of individuality. But it is precisely the individuality and uniqueness of historical and cultural events which characterize the subject matter of the historical and cultural disciplines. The historian is intensely interested in the objects of his research precisely because of their unique and individual nature, and this interest must be satisfied by a method of research which recognizes and responds to the need for a discipline of equal rank with natural science. This discipline, according to Rickert, is *Geschichtswissenschaft* (the "science" of history).

Rickert's argument, however, was not merely aimed at the claimed infallibility and omnipotence of natural science, but equally at those historians who, appropriating the "scientific method," had tried to develop a *Historismus* ("historicism") free of all presuppositions, value judgments, and philosophic interpretations (*voraussetzungslose Wissenschaft*). This attitude had gradually led to a leveling relativism which eventually invaded all the provinces of human life and action, denying the possibility of abiding values and normative judgments in State and society, law and customs, literature and art, philosophy and religion. It was in opposition to this relativization of history and human life that Nietzsche's friend, the classical philologist Erwin Rohde (1845–1898), praised the rugged one-sidedness of men like Nietzsche. "We need such men," he argued, "if we are not to be driven into insanity by the diabolic doctrine that all things have their two sides. In this doctrine lies the whole curse of our 'historicism,' our faithlessness, our faint-heartedness." And Nietzsche himself asserted in his essay *On the Advantages and Disadvantages of History in regard to Life*** that "the oversaturation of an epoch with History makes it hostile and dangerous to life." In his opinion, this kind of "historicism" paralyzed the culturally creative energies and begot first irony and in the end an even more dangerous cynicism.

As, paradoxically enough, the maligned "historicism" itself was born of a desire for "objective" historical truth and could point to great accomplishments in matters of factual research, the dispute obviously was not so much concerned with the ultimate goal as with the problem of the most suitable and promising means and methods to be adopted in the pursuit of that ultimate end.

The real issue of the debate and the cause of the "crisis" was the

---

* Cf. especially *Die Grenzen der naturwissenschaftlichen Begriffsbildung* (1896) and *Kulturwissenschaft und Naturwissenschaft* (1899).
** Cf. *Unzeitgemässe Betrachtungen,* II.

irreconcilable conflict in the scientific and the philosophico-metaphysical concepts and interpretations of "truth." Was truth identical with the phenomenal world of scientific facts, as the scientists claimed, or did it, as the nonpositivist thinkers asserted, transcend these phenomenal data of sense perception? The representatives of the new *Geisteswissenschaft* rejected both scientific phenomenalism and philosophic positivism (cf. p. 594 sq.) and, partly under the influence of German idealistic philosophy (cf. p. 499 sqq.), partly inspired by Bergson's (1849–1941) intuitionism and Bolzano's and Brentano's neo-Aristotelianism (cf. p. 692 sq.), called for a "resurrection of metaphysics." The liberal Protestant theologian and *Kulturphilosoph* Ernst Troeltsch (1865–1923), after having carried in his writings the premises of historicism and relativism to their extreme and ultimately self-contradictory conclusions, found toward the end of his life a metaphysical reorientation of his thinking and a way out of the blind alley of historicism in the religious and philosophical views of his friend Friedrich von Hügel (1852–1925), a British Catholic thinker of German ancestry. He became convinced that "skepticism only *seems* to be a necessary consequence of the modern intellectual situation and of modern historicism" and that "it can be overcome by those ethical and ideal forces which emerge from history itself and are mirrored and concentrated in ethical norms.* Others, like Wilhelm Dilthey (cf. p. 691) and, later on, Max Scheler (cf. p. 593 sq.) and Martin Heidegger (cf. p. 694), following the lead of Herder, Goethe, the romantic philosophers (cf. p. 499 sqq.), and Nietzsche, advocated a *Lebensphilosophie* which was to reunite *Wissenschaft* and *Leben* and create a new cultural synthesis by means of an all-embracing and metaphysically anchored philosophy of life and civilization.

2. *"Literaturwissenschaft"* (*Literary Criticism*).   The *"Krise der Wissenschaft"* produced some interesting developments in the field of literary criticism, running largely parallel with the general trend of thought from scientific positivism to a resurgence of metaphysical speculation.

From the eighteenth century on, German literary criticism passed through three principal stages. The first phase was marked by an idealistic awakening under the influence of Platonic and neo-Platonic thought, as mediated in part by Lord Shaftesbury (1671–1713), and embodied in a profoundly personalized manner in the works of Leibniz, Herder, Schiller, Goethe, and the romantic writers and thinkers. The second phase may be described as strictly positivistic or antimetaphysical. It revealed the influence of the doctrines of Auguste Comte (cf. p. 566 sq.) and Karl Marx (cf. p. 556 sqq.) and of the methods of both natural science and dialectic materialism. Comte's principles of the *philosophie positive* were applied to literary and art criticism by Hippolyte Taine,** whose approach to works of literature and art intended to be purely scientific and positivistic. Literature and art, like science, "neither condemn nor pardon; they merely state and explain

* Cf. *Die Überwindung des Historismus* (1924), p. 44.
** Cf. *Histoire de la littérature anglaise* (1864) and *Philosophie de l'art* (1865).

facts." The *"milieu"* or *"température morale"* of a literary work or a work of art is constituted by the general state of manners and customs, and the *milieu* produces literary and art forms by way of a Darwinian evolution, eliminating the unfit elements and adopting those which conform to the environmental atmosphere or climate.

Taine's principle of "natural selection" in literature and art was introduced into the methodology of German literary history and criticism by Wilhelm Scherer (1841–1886).* He and his influential school of literary historians abandoned all idealistic and metaphysical criteria of interpretation and thus established the predominance of the positivistic method in German literary research.

The third phase of German literary criticism, dating from the beginning of the twentieth century, reflects the gradual turning away from positivism and the return to some of the principles and methods of the classical and romantic eras, but within a set of intellectual and cultural circumstances which had been rendered much more complex by the problems posed by modern science and by the resultant critical situation of the *Geisteswissenschaften.*

Wilhelm Dilthey (1883–1911),** though still under the spell of positivism, developed on the bases of Hegel's and Rickert's philosophy of history a new method of literary interpretation which emphasized *Verstehen* (understanding) rather than *Beschreibung* (description). His acute insight into the process of literary creation led him to a deeper penetration of the personalities of such German authors as Lessing, Goethe, Hölderlin, and Novalis, and to a novel exegesis of their works. Although in perpetual search of spiritual realities, Dilthey lacked some of the philosophical and methodical tools to comprehend fully the spiritual forces of cultural history. It is fortunate, therefore, that his artistic vision frequently carried him farther than his "scientific" conscience would have given him permission to go.

In the element of artistic vision, superadded to ratiocination and descriptive analysis, contemporary German literary criticism occasionally rejoins and even metaphysically transcends the great tradition of the classical and romantic age. In the work of Joseph Nadler (1884–),† for example, the virtues of the metaphysician, the artist, and the scientist are found in happy union. It is historians and critics of Nadler's type that point the way to an end of sterile specialization, to a future synthesis of the still separated branches of knowledge, and to their hierarchical integration in a harmonious structure of science, knowledge, and wisdom.

3. *Philosophy.* The epistemological problem concerning the possibility and validity of knowledge, its types and degrees, as corresponding to different

---

* Cf. *Geschichte der deutschen Literatur* (1883).

** Cf. especially *Das Erlebnis und die Dichtung* (1906) and *Einleitung in die Geisteswissenschaften* (1883).

† Cf. especially Nadler's monumental *Literaturgeschichte der deutschen Stämme und Landschaften* (4 vols., 1912–1928).

disciplines, received particular attention within the sphere of strictly philosophic speculation. Hermann Cohen (1842–1918) and Paul Natorp (1854–1924), the founders of the neo-Kantian Marburg School, inquired into the principles and premises of scientific knowledge and clearly delimited and circumscribed in their critical analysis the specific tasks of philosophic research. Both scholars devoted great effort to the elucidation of Kant's (cf. p. 371 sqq.) profound but much disputed concept of the "noumenon" or thing-in-itself, and they like every other neo-Kantian claimed to offer the one and only authentic interpretation of the master's ideas.

Nicolai Hartmann (1882–1950), too, started from Kant's idealistic theory of knowledge but, turning against philosophic idealism, he arrived in the end at epistemological realism and laid the foundations for a new realistic metaphysics and ontology.* Hartmann's philosophy thus marks an important turning point in German speculative thought. He consciously reverts to the pre-Kantian and pre-Cartesian tradition of Aristotelian and Thomistic realism. His epistemology like that of Thomas Aquinas starts from the immediate givenness of the object of knowledge. For him as for the medieval philosopher "the relation between subject and object is an ontological one, and it is in the fact that this relation inheres in 'being as such' that the solution of the problem must be sought."

Nicolai Hartmann's return to philosophic realism was in part caused by his temporary association with a group of German thinkers who followed the intellectual leadership of Edmund Husserl (1859–1938), the founder of the school of Phenomenology,** who was himself indebted to the Aristotelianism of Franz Brentano (1838–1917). A priest and at one time a distinguished member of the theological faculty of the University of Würzburg, Brentano had come into conflict with the ecclesiastical authorities and had finally been suspended from his priestly office and relieved of his academic duties. From 1874 to 1895 he was a lecturer at the University of Vienna, and after that lived in retirement in Florence and Zurich.

Brentano's commentaries on the psychology of Aristotle, his theory of value, and in particular his investigations on the nature of justice represent important and lasting contributions to contemporary thought. Among the thinkers whom he attracted to his lectures was Edmund Husserl, a native of Moravia, who, originally a mathematician, had been converted to philosophy by the brilliant oratory and personal persuasive power of Friedrich Paulsen (1846–1908).

Husserl's Phenomenology† is indebted, next to Brentano, to the keen speculation of the Bohemian Catholic theologian, philosopher, and mathe-

---

* Cf. especially *Grundzüge einer Metaphysik der Erkenntnis* (1925).

** Many of the members of this school reside at present in the United States, where they edit *Philosophy and Phenomenological Research* (New York, 1940 sqq.), the successor to the *Jahrbuch für Philosophie und phänomenologische Forschung*.

† Cf. especially *Ideen zu einer reinen Phänomenologie und phänomenologischen Philosophie* (1913); English trans., *Ideas: General Introduction to Pure Phenomenology* (London: Allen and Unwin, 1931).

maticïan, Bernhard Bolzano (1781–1848). Because of the universality of his preoccupations and interests, Bolzano was known as the "Bohemian Leibniz."* Bolzano's *Wissenschaftslehre* and Brentano's "descriptive psychology" were systematized by Husserl and further elaborated by Max Scheler, Nicolai Hartmann, and Martin Heidegger. All the members of the phenomenological school found in the writings of the two older philosophers (Bolzano and Brentano) welcome support for their attack on the prevalent "psychologism" of Christoph Sigwart (1830–1904) and Benno Erdmann (1851–1909), both followers of Herbert Spencer, and on the exaggerated idealism of the neo-Kantian schools of Heidelberg, Freiburg, and Marburg (Windelband, Rickert, Cohen, Natorp).

Phenomenology soon became the most conspicuous philosophic trend in such prominent centers of German thought as Munich, Berlin, Freiburg, and Marburg, and helped to strengthen the antipositivist movements in France, England, and the Americas.

Phenomenological research stressed the primary importance of "essences" and concentrated its efforts on the analysis of the data of "pure consciousness" as objects of a *Wesensschau* (intuition of essences) which tries to penetrate to the "pure" phenomena underlying the empirical surface phenomena of sense perception. Although Husserl himself never overcame entirely the position of Kantian idealism, he furnished his pupils the methodological tools for a constructive criticism of both epistemological idealism and psychological positivism. It is the conviction of most contemporary philosophers who have adopted the phenomenological method that "it has no necessary connection with philosophic idealism and seems even incompatible with it."**

Among Husserl's disciples, Max Scheler (1875–1928)† and Martin Heidegger (1889–)‡ present the most interesting development. The influence of these thinkers extends far beyond Germany and is especially noticeable in France, Spain, Mexico, and South America. In his *Lebensphilosophie,* his anthropological views, and his concept of human personality Scheler was influenced by Nietzsche (cf. p. 695 sq.), while he owed the basic tenets of his moral philosophy to the teachings of St. Augustine, and those of his metaphysical speculation to Bergson and Husserl. If Husserl's phenomenology had been chiefly concerned with the analysis of "pure consciousness," Scheler's main interest centers in the phenomenological description of the emotions. He claims for man an "axiological sense" or an organ of emotive intuition and evaluation which carries him into the realm of essential and objective values and ultimately determines his position in the

* Cf. especially Bolzano's *Wissenschaftslehre* (1837; new ed., 1929).
** Cf. the author's translation of Oswaldo Robles, *Propedéutica Filosófica* (*The Main Problems of Philosophy*) (Milwaukee: The Bruce Publishing Company, 1946), p. 34.
† Cf. *Vom Ewigen im Menschen* (1921) and *Die Stellung des Menschen im Kosmos* (1930).
‡ Cf. especially *Sein und Zeit* (1927); *Vom Wesen des Grundes* (1929); *Was ist Metaphysik?* (1929); *Brief über den Humanismus* (1947); and *Holzwege* (1950).

universe. Values are thus cognized by the spontaneous activity of "emotional consciousness" rather than by the acts of "intellectual consciousness." All values are "intentional objects of pure sentiment," and those values which embody objectively the aims of the pure sentiments of personality rank highest in the hierarchical scale. At one time a convert to Catholicism, Scheler construed later in life under the influence of Schelling (cf. p. 501 sq.) a pantheistic and radically dualistic metaphysics, in which God was conceived as emerging out of the self-redeeming urges of human life and culture.

Martin Heidegger, whose philosophy, like that of Hartmann, aims at a new "fundamental ontology" *(Seinslehre),* and whose "existentialism" in its more negative aspects was appropriated by the French philosopher, Jean-Paul Sartre, shows in the several phases of his intellectual formation the influence of such widely diverging thinkers as Aristotle, St. Augustine, Duns Scotus, Pascal, Kant, Hegel, Rickert, Dilthey, and Kierkegaard. His thought is thus one of the most striking and startling expressions of an age of speculative uncertainty and intellectual crisis.

Heidegger is primarily concerned with the phenomenological analysis and the metaphysical exploration of *human existence.* In the concept of *"Angst"* (anguish), which he adopts from Kierkegaard's writings, he claims he has discovered a new transcendental medium of metaphysical knowledge. In his "existence," which is chained to *Zeitlichkeit* (temporality) and *Geschichtlichkeit* (historicity), man is caught between the two abysses of temporal transitoriness and nothingness. The being of man is thus *Sein zum Tode* (a "being unto death," a "being unto nothingness"). Human *"Angst"* denotes the experience and expresses the tragic situation of man. It aims at an objective world of essences, but it never reaches beyond the limited and fragmentary nature of human existence. In *"Angst"* and *"Sorge"* (care) man attends to things temporal and becomes hopelessly involved in them, although out of the depth of his being he cries out for a world of abiding values. But in this very experience of his forlornness, of a constantly menaced existence, in the very proximity of not-being and death, Heidegger's human being acquires or discovers the deepest significance of his selfhood.

As Heidegger, in the works published up to this date, has confined himself to a phenomenological inquiry into the *being of man,* without having yet attained to his original objective, the phenomenology of *being as such,* it would be presumptuous and premature to pass a final judgment on his philosophy. It would certainly be unjust to judge him by the misinterpretations and the mental and moral aberrations of some of his self-styled disciples.

A neo-positivist reaction against the "resurrection" of metaphysical speculation in Germany is represented by the "School of Vienna," some of whose members are, at present, residents of the United States and occupy leading positions in American universities. Catering to the empirical and pragmatic bent of the Anglo-Saxon mind, they have managed to command a respect and a following which they at no time enjoyed either in Austria or in

Germany. The "logical empiricism" of this group (Schlick, Carnap, Neurath, Wittgenstein, Reichenbach) claims to be a "scientific philosophy," restricting the field of philosophically "meaningful" questions to experimentally verifiable data, subject to semantic analysis and expressed in logico-mathematical symbols. Whatever cannot be so verified and demonstrated (ideas, moral concepts and judgments, rational inductions and deductions, etc.) is said to be void of meaning and is shoved aside as superstition and tautological trickery. This extreme form of neo-positivism can only be understood when seen as a justifiable corrective of some of the abuses of Hegelian and post-Hegelian idealism (cf. p. 502 sqq.). "Logical empiricism" is justified in recalling philosophy from vague abstractions and generalizations to concrete data, but it succumbs to the fallacies of an opposite extreme when it tries to make of philosophy a purely compilatory discipline and a mere adjunct of science.

The antimetaphysical and in fact antiphilosophical radicalism of the "logical empiricists" illustrates in a very practical manner those dangers of an uninhibited "scientism" which had been first recognized by Friedrich Nietzsche (1844–1900). "What I got hold of at that time," Nietzsche had written in the preface to the second edition of *The Birth of Tragedy,** "was something terrible and dangerous, a problem with horns, not necessarily a bull, but certainly a new problem: the problem of science itself, science comprehended for the first time as something problematical and highly questionable." Thus it appears that Nietzsche, though never a systematic philosopher himself, had first discerned the essential difference between the scientist and the philosopher and had categorically emphasized the basic distinction between scientific and philosophic aims and methods.

For Heinrich Rickert (cf. p. 689), who was guided by Nietzsche's poetic and philosophic intuitions in his systematic differentiation between *Naturwissenschaft* and *Kulturwissenschaft,* the preacher of the "Superman" and the "Will to Power" was above all a *Lebensphilosoph,* that is, a philosopher who castigated the separation of both science and philosophy from *life* and advocated a revitalized and personalized *Wissenschaft.* Such a demand, however, was highly unpopular.in an epoch of scientific specialization, on the one hand, and an abstract, devitalized metaphysics, on the other. It is hardly surprising, therefore, that Nietzsche during his lifetime was not taken very seriously by either scientists or philosophers.

And yet there is no doubt that Friedrich Nietzsche, though often self-contradictory and harshly dissonant in his views, was a thinker in whose sensitive mind and passionate heart all the intellectual vibrations and radiations of the age were gathered and reflected as in a focus. None of the professional philosophers of the Second Empire has, positively and negatively, exerted a comparable influence on all the branches of German

---

* *Die Geburt der Tragödie aus dem Geiste der Musik* (1886; the first edition had been published in 1871).

thought and culture. His heroic fight against the tremendous odds of an "atomized" society and a disintegrating civilization, his tragic isolation, and his final descent into the listless night of insanity, make him both a witness and a victim of the crisis of the age.

Philosophy was for Nietzsche "love of wisdom" in the Socratic sense, and the philosopher, if he was deserving of his title, was the friend and lover of wisdom. Possessed of the distinctive philosophic character marks of *Redlichkeit, Heiterkeit,* and *Beständigkeit* (integrity, serenity, and consistency), he was first of all called to realize in his own life the virtues of a philosophic existence, and then to shape all human conduct in the image of the true philosopher. This was to be the way of life of *Zarathustra,** the hero of his philosophico-poetic masterpiece, the symbol of Nietzsche's new man and teacher, who first withdraws into solitude to ripen to maturity in communion with nature, and to acquire moral fortitude in his intercourse with the eagle and the serpent, and then returns eventually into the world to spread the glad tidings of the new ethics of the *Übermensch.* This new "Superman," wholehearted in his will and unbroken in his spirit, is now prepared to set about the gigantic task of bringing about the *"Umwertung aller Werte"* (transvaluation of all values). He has banished mercy and compassion from his "heroic" soul, and his ethical code is the *"Wille zur Macht"* (will to power). With Nietzsche, Zarathustra fights against the *décadence* of the bourgeois society of the *fin de siècle,* against a corruption of human values which both the author and his hero blame on the emasculation wrought by the "slave morality" of Christianity, a morality which, according to Nietzsche, is born of the *ressentiment* which the weakling feels in the presence of the lordly power of the master.

To see Nietzsche's anti-Christian polemics in its true perspective it is necessary to point out that the inventor of the *Übermensch* and the advocate of the *Herrenmoral* was the son of a Lutheran pastor and a disciple of Schopenhauer. His idea of Christianity bore the impress of Luther's pessimistic view of human. nature (cf. p. 219), on the one hand, and of Schopenhauer's (cf. p. 505 sq.) Buddhistically tainted Christianity, on the other. The Christianity which Nietzsche reproaches for its pure otherworldliness and its lack of moral stamina is certainly not the religion lived, preached, and instituted by Christ.

The unstinted praise which Nietzsche lavished on the "subterranean" instincts of life, and his consecration of all sorrow and suffering in the embrace of a this-worldly eternity, a cyclical perpetual recurrence of all things (*"Wiederkehr des Gleichen"*) — ideas with which the poet-philosopher crowns his *Weltanschauung* — represent a desperate attempt to attain to an integrated world view on the basis of atheistic naturalism. To bring about such a future integration of life and civilization he regarded as the supreme task and duty of the philosopher, the "physician of culture."

---

* Cf. *Also sprach Zarathustra* (4 parts, 1883–1891).

It was Nietzsche's conviction that humanistic culture had utterly failed to live up to its promises and that the originally Christian impulses of Humanism not only shared in this failure but were ultimately responsible for it. To escape, however, the snares of skepticism, cynicism, and nihilism, Western man must let the dead bury their dead and look toward a future in which new values will have to be wrested from the vital forces of the earth, values which will once more determine "the measure, currency, and weight of all things."

The final phase of Nietzsche's controversy with the "spirit of the age" and with the menacing forces of darkness in his own mind was marked by an outcry for a synthesis of "Dionysos and Christ," the personification of the splendor of this life and of the glory of the life beyond, and the profoundest longing of his soul was perhaps revealed in his call for "a Caesar with the soul of Christ."

Nietzsche's message to the age of crisis was above all a great challenge: his deification of telluric forces and his simultaneous merciless dissection of the actually existing culture were signalizing the crossroads to which modern mankind had advanced. The alternative was either a wholehearted new paganism or an integral Christianity.

In 1920, the German Catholic philosopher Peter Wust (1884–1948) published a book entitled *Die Auferstehung der Metaphysik* (*The Resurrection of Metaphysics*), in which manifestly the positive and constructive elements of German idealism and of the speculative thought of Nietzsche and Scheler fused with the ancient tradition of the *Philosophia Perennis*. Wust's attempt at such a synthesis was one of several symptoms of a *rapprochement* between modern secular philosophy and that Graeco-Christian heritage of ideas which had on the whole remained unaffected by the teachings of extreme rationalism, idealism, positivism, and materialism. It seemed to Peter Wust that modern man had "cheated himself out of the ultimate reason for his existence"; that he resembled a lonely wild animal, "roving restlessly hither and thither in the desert which is Western Civilization, hideously crying out his hunger and thirst for eternity."

The neo-scholastic or neo-Thomistic revival, which found an eloquent spokesman in Wust,* claimed that the critical realism of the time-tested scholastic philosophy (cf. p. 141 sq.) was fully able to cope with the complexities of modern thought, and to attain to that philosophic synthesis which so far had escaped modern thinkers and modern systems. Theodor Haecker (1879–1945), a disciple and inspired translator of Søren Kierkegaard, had been led to the scholastic tradition by his study of the personality and the works of Cardinal Newman. He went so far as to state that "the highest type of the European and American intelligentsia is on its way home to the natural and supernatural truths of the *Philosophia Perennis."* And, in 1924, the German neo-Kantian philosopher Arthur Liebert, then

---

* Other leading German and Swiss Neo-Thomists are Denifle, J. M. Scheeben, Ehrle, Hertling, Baeumker, M. Grabmann, Pesch, Mausbach, Geyser, J. Gredt, Jansen, E. Przywara, Hans Urs von Balthasar, O. Karrer, etc.

president of the *Kantgesellschaft,* asserted in an address, delivered at the International Philosophical Congress in Naples, that the neo-scholastic program did not call for the imitation and repetition of outworn doctrines, but was a vital philosophy, capable of facing and solving many of the problems of modern thought and modern science. He further objected to the fashionable designation of Kant and Thomas Aquinas as representatives of criticism and dogmatism, respectively, and called Thomism an indispensable complement of modern critical philosophy.

According to Martin Grabmann (1875–1948), the most prominent Thomistic theologian and philosopher of the University of Munich, scholastic and neo-scholastic philosophy "stress and make secure the natural powers of human thought; they guard the independence of philosophy in its own domain and draw a clear line of demarcation between faith and knowledge." And Grabmann is in essential agreement with all the neo-scholastics in asserting that respect for the fundamental doctrines of tradition does not preclude far-reaching adaptations to modern intellectual and scientific needs and conditions; that neo-scholasticism rejects both absolute traditionalism and absolute relativism; that exclusive traditionalism means petrifaction and death, while exclusive relativism means indifference to values and ultimately the dissolution of the very concept of being. For Erich Przywara, S.J., therefore, the essential requisite of scholastic philosophy is "to go through the world, seeking what was lost rather than hurling condemnations and execrations. The only determining factor in its attitude toward all individual philosophies must be the untiring quest for the kernel of truth they contain. . . . Its anathemas are never directed against *contents* of truth, but against the idolization of particles of truth. Accordingly, its method consists not in drawing the greatest possible number of boundary lines or in digging the deepest possible trenches, but in looking everywhere for the sheen of the all-pervading *Logos*."

This admonition of the German Jesuit philosopher reflects the spirit of Leo XIII's encyclical *Aeterni Patris* (1879). This encyclical, signalizing an authoritative endorsement of and providing a powerful incentive for the neo-scholastic movement, bore fruit in the foundation of the *Institut Supérieur de Philosophie* of Louvain (Belgium) and similar centers of scholastic studies in various European and American countries, and found an institutional representation in Germany in the Albertus Magnus Academy of Cologne (1922).

Religious Forces and Movements. The surface phenomena of the intellectual, moral, social, and cultural unrest of the modern age had as their deepest source and cause a religious crisis which manifested itself in many and often contradictory movements, all pointing to the undeniable fact that most of the traditional spiritual and moral values of the Western World had become problematical.

In Germany, the period after 1871 witnessed both the radical affirmation of the tenets of antireligious materialism and the re-examination and eventual unconditional reassertion of religious faith and dogma. In between these mutually exclusive positions there was a broad sphere of religious liberalism, ranging from halfhearted lip service to the ideologies of the past to a feverish search for new religious dispensations and cults.

When, in 1872, David Friedrich Strauss had challenged many of his contemporaries with the categorical assertion, "We are no longer Christians,"* Alfred Dove, one of the younger historians of the Second Empire, replied with equal emphasis: "No, we are still Christians, and now more than ever we want to be Christians." It was nevertheless an incontrovertible fact that the secularization of society and culture was proceeding at a rapid pace, especially among the working classes, where the impact of industrialism had been strongest and the inroads of materialism largest.

a) German Protestantism. To halt the progress of secularization proved particularly difficult for the Protestant denominations, because they were doctrinally divided between the orthodox and liberal factions. During the early years of the regime of William II the Lutheran orthodox church, which had commanded great influence by virtue of its association with the highest Berlin court circles, was gradually forced to yield to the advancing forces of theological liberalism. This trend was signally strengthened by the appointment of the liberal Adolf von Harnack (1851–1930), a close friend of William II, to the foremost chair of Lutheran theology at the University of Berlin.

In 1892, the German Lutheran church was severely shaken by the so-called *Apostolikumstreit* (dispute concerning the Apostles' Creed), growing out of the refusal of Pastor Christoph Schrempf of Wurtemberg to use the Apostles' Creed in the administration of the sacrament of baptism. A group of students of theology of the University of Berlin drew up a petition to the *Oberkirchenrat* (supreme church council) to ask for the permanent elimination of the Apostles' Creed from the Lutheran liturgy, but they were advised by Harnack to postpone their action.

The *freireligiöse* (free religious) movement in German Protestantism gained additional strength early in the twentieth century. It was chiefly represented by Karl Jatho and Gottfried Traub, two liberal Lutheran pastors, who commanded a large following but, after severe clashes with the *Oberkirchenrat,* were suspended from office. Jatho and Traub were joined in their fight against Lutheran orthodoxy by the philosopher Arthur Drews who, in his book *Die Christusmythe* (1909), denied the historical existence of Christ, and by the brothers Ernst and August Horneffer, who were disciples of Nietzsche. In the years preceding World War I the attacks of independent Protestant groups upon institutional or "confessional" Protestantism gained such momentum that the orthodoxy seemed to be fighting a hopeless and losing battle. While in the first decade after the Franco-Prussian War the Protestant theological faculties of some of the leading

---

* Cf. *Der alte und der neue Glaube* (1872).

German universities were still dominated by orthodox theologians, the liberal theological "Left" gradually acquired more and more chairs toward the close of the century. Under the leadership of Albrecht Ritschl (1822–1889) of the University of Göttingen, Protestant dogmatic theologians devoted themselves in increasing numbers to *Religionswissenschaft* and *vergleichende Religionsgeschichte* (comparative history of religion), thus introducing the virtues and vices of "historicism" and the "scientific method" into the field of theology.

World War I and its aftermaths produced a strong reaction against theological liberalism and "historicism." While, on the one hand, German Protestantism began to take an active part in the "ecumenical movement" — working for a world-wide reunion of the separated Christian churches, and demonstrating this desire impressively at the international Church conferences of Stockholm (1925) and Lausanne (1927) — it was, on the other hand, called back to the fundamentals of Christian faith by the *Theologie der Krise* (Crisis Theology) or "dialectical theology" of a group of Swiss and German theologians, who followed the leadership of Karl Barth (1886–).*

The "dialectical theology" of Karl Barth and his associates was equally opposed to the secularizing tendencies of theological liberalism and to the sterile dogmatism of Lutheran and Calvinist orthodoxy. The new movement, Calvinistic in origin, wanted to endow the Christian message with the fervor and rigor of that unconditional supernaturalism which Barth claimed for the original creeds of Calvin and Luther. The Barthian theology is "Crisis Theology" because it makes man aware of the precariousness of his existence, and it is "dialectical" because it asserts to have its sole ground and *raison d'être* in that Divine Revelation which forces a human response in the form of an all-decisive "yes" or "no." While the Word of God is said to be an eternal affirmation, the word of sinful man is perpetual negation; while God is Eternal Life, man's existence is a "being unto death"; while God is all Holiness, man is all sinfulness.

Being antihumanistic and anti-idealistic, "Crisis Theology" takes issue with the representatives of German humanism and idealism, especially with Schleiermacher's (cf. p. 507 sq.) doctrine of a divine immanence in nature, and with Hegel's (cf. p. 502 sqq.) pantheism. This uncompromising attitude had been anticipated by Søren Kierkegaard (1813–1855), Barth's theological ancestor, and in that Danish thinker's lifelong two-front battle against Hegelianism, on the one hand, and against the liberal secularism of the Danish-Lutheran State Church, on the other (cf. p. 595 sq.).

From his opposition to theological liberalism and Hegelian pantheism, Kierkegaard developed a neo-Lutheran theology which declared war on all philosophy. In particular he rejected the idea of making Christianity a historically conditioned phase in the dialectical self-realization of the

---

* Cf. especially *Der Römerbrief* (1918) and *Christliche Dogmatik* (12 vols., 1927 sqq.). Other theologians either temporarily or permanently associated with Barth are Emil Brunner, W. Thurneysen, Friedrich Gogarten, and Erik Peterson (who became a Roman Catholic in 1930).

Weltgeist. To him the appearance of Christ and of Christianity signified a unique event of absolute and incomparable value and validity, an event which imposed upon a disciple the fearful responsibility of "becoming a Christian," that is, a follower of Christ. In denouncing "historicism," he was denouncing the finite as against the infinite, the service of time as against the service of eternity.

What then, in Kierkegaard's view, was the position of Christianity in the world and in his own age? "Christianity," he insisted, "is a reality, but Christendom is nothing but an optical illusion." And to his *Journals* he entrusted this reflection: "There must be another reformation, and this time it will be a horrible reformation. Compared with this coming reformation that of Luther will appear as a mere jest. Its battle-cry will clamor for the remnants of faith on earth. And we shall witness millions becoming apostates: truly a fearful reformation. We shall recognize that Christianity is practically non-existent, and it will be a horrible sight to behold this generation, pampered and lulled to sleep by a childishly deformed Christianity — to see this generation wounded once again by the thought of what it means to become a Christian, to be a Christian."

Kierkegaard thus had become the prototype of an "existential" thinker, that is, one who attains to absolute clarity as to where in human life he as an individual experiences the fullest depth of reality, and who expresses this experience in his life and in his work. And it is this same "existential" consistency which is harshly reaffirmed in Karl Barth's "Crisis Theology," which wants to be strictly a *Theologia Crucis,* upholding both Luther's metaphysical dualism between the finite and the infinite and Calvin's Divine Absolutism, which condemns and elects by eternal decree, regardless of human effort or merit. Here, too, is found the radical break with the humanist-idealist doctrine of a divine immanence in the world and in man, on the one hand, and with the Thomistic doctrine of an *analogia entis* and God's ontological indwelling in His creation *"per essentiam,"* on the other.

Karl Barth — before he was deprived by the National Socialist regime of his chair at the University of Bonn, and expelled from Germany in 1934 — had had a large following among German youth. After resuming the teaching of theology at the University of Basel, he continued to watch with deep concern from the vantage point of his native Switzerland the life-and-death struggle of Christian Germany against its "ungodly rulers," trying at the same time to arouse the consciences of Christian men and women in Europe and the Americas to a realization of the acute crisis of contemporary Christendom.

For a long time Barth's doctrines and efforts had not been taken very seriously by both the leading orthodox and liberal German church groups: the Lutheran orthodoxy in the North and Northeast; the "United Church," consisting of the joint Lutheran and Calvinist denominations in central and southern Germany; and the liberal theologians, who had their chief spokesmen in the theological faculty of the University of Marburg. All these theological camps were under attack by the Barthians, because in none of them was theology any longer a living spiritual force molding the thoughts and lives of the people.

It is, however, the never explained paradox of Barthian theology that it advocates a moral and cultural reformation, although its premises of an absolute divine transcendence and a metaphysically evil world, seen exclusively *sub ratione peccati* (under the aspect of sinful corruption) seem to leave no room for cultural activities of moral or spiritual value. From the outset, therefore, it had been clear to Barth's Protestant and Catholic critics that his *Credo* had so overstated the "negative theology" of certain neo-Platonically inclined Christian mystics that the divine First Cause necessarily crushed completely the culturally and morally significant activities of all secondary causes and agents. The order of grace effaced the order of nature, precluding the possibility of a "natural theology" or theodicy, and thus destroying the contiguous relationship of nature and supernature as seen by Catholic theology and Thomistic philosophy. According to the latter, "grace does not efface nature, but rather supports it and leads it to perfection" (*gratia supponit et perficit naturam*). If Barth's theological and metaphysical premises were accepted *in toto,* Christian dogmatics would be turned into a doctrinal body of incomprehensible paradoxes, and Christian faith could save itself only by a *Sprung* (leap) into a *"credo quia absurdum."*

Yet even though the "Theology of Crisis" became involved in some insoluble contradictions (as illustrated, for example, by the controversy between Karl Barth and Emil Brunner, the latter pleading for the elaboration of a "natural theology"), it had without any doubt served to rarefy and clarify the religious atmosphere in German Protestantism. The integral supranaturalism of Barth was soon to collide head on with the equally uncompromising religious naturalism of the *Deutsche Glaubensbewegung* (German Faith Movement) and the Germanized Christianity of the *Deutsche Christen.* While the neo-paganism of the former asserted that Germanism and Christianity were mutually exclusive and went so far as to call Christianity "the religious Versailles of the Germans," the latter, less consistent, wanted to retain a racially "purified" Christianity and eventually proclaimed the identity of the "Third Reich" with the kingdom of God on earth ("one People, one State, one Church, one *Führer*"). In 1934, the Protestant literary critic Karl Kindt, writing in the periodical *Die neue Literatur,* ventured the opinion that God had created Karl Barth and the *Deutsche Christen* to demonstrate "that the one and indivisible truth cannot be taken apart without the most disastrous effects."

It was realistically acknowledged in the opposing camps that an unbridgeable abyss separated the Kierkegaard-Barth position from that of the "German Christians" and the "German Faith Movement." The leaders admitted that it was useless to call for peace where there is no peace and where there cannot be peace. They thus subscribed to Kierkegaard's "either — or." However, in between these extreme positions, the "United Lutherans," including several Calvinistic groups, closed their ranks and re-examined their basic beliefs. In the midst of the religious turmoil that followed the National Socialist revolution they looked for a theological *via media:* on the one hand, they declared their willingness to co-operate, to an extent delimited by the exactions of their Christian conscience, with the totalitarian State and, on the other, they opposed vigorously any *Gleichschaltung* of State and Church. Under the leadership of such men as Martin Niemöller they founded the *Pfarrernotbund* (pastors' emergency league) and organized the *Bekenntniskirche* (Professing Church), and were prepared to suffer persecution, torture, and death for their religious convictions. "The assertion," they declared defiantly, "that the voice of the nation is the Word of God is blasphemy. . . . It is the mission of the Church to educate men for the Kingdom of Christ, not for the German *Reich.* A Church which serves two masters is untrustworthy in every word it preaches. . . . Earthly, material values must not be placed above eternal values. The true meaning of the Gospel must not be interpreted in such a way as to make it pleasing and acceptable to the desires of men. We call heresy the assertion that Christ is the prototype of Nordic Man. We call heresy the Germanization of Christianity. The Christian Church does not and cannot distinguish between baptized Jews and baptized Gentiles. . . . We solemnly deny the State the right to govern the Church, to appoint or depose ministers or to meddle with questions of Church doctrine. Today, the very foundations of Christianity are shaken by error and confusion. This is the time of the great temptation."

Such quotations, to which many more of a similar tenor might be added, illustrate the type of crisis through which German Protestantism is passing, a crisis whose outcome will perhaps decide the future of Protestantism the world over. It is Karl Barth's conviction that the Christian Church must once again cast its lot with the Christian martyrs of the catacombs. He believes that not since medieval times have Christians in every part of the globe faced a situation of more monumental simplicity: a situation which poses questions of such unequivocal clarity that the answers should be easy and self-evident.

b) German Catholicism. In a compendium entitled *Deutschland unter Wilhelm II,* which appeared shortly before the outbreak of World War I and surveyed the several aspects of German civilization under the Second Empire, it was stated by a Roman Catholic contributor: "If anyone has good reason to be grateful to His Majesty, it is the Catholic Church, which has abundantly enjoyed the good graces of the Imperial Sovereign and has been permitted to co-operate in the accomplishment of great national tasks." Notwithstanding the essential correctness of this optimistic estimate, the Catholic Church in Germany underwent several minor crises, some of which. e.g., the *Kulturkampf* (cf. p. 611 sq.), affected German Catholics directly and exclusively, while others reflected more universal religious problems and situations.

Out of the opposition of some groups of German Catholics to the Vatican Council's (1869–1870) definition of Papal Infallibility grew the schismatic movement of *Altkatholizismus* (Old Catholicism) which, though it looked at first rather menacing, remained without serious consequences.

The "Old Catholics" claimed to stand firmly on the principles of the undivided universal Church of the first Christian millennium; they re-affirmed the dogmas of the Trinity, the divinity of Christ, and the absolute authenticity of scriptural Revelation, but rejected the authoritative nature of ecclesiastic "tradition," the dogma of the Immaculate Conception, the primacy of the Roman pontiff, and the infallibility of the pope in *ex cathedra* pronouncements on matters of faith and morals. In addition, they leaned toward the Lutheran interpretation of Mass and Eucharist and demanded the use of the vernacular in the liturgical services. Finally, they denied the obligatory character of priestly celibacy and of the reception of the sacraments; permitted cremation; and refused to accept the Roman Catholic teachings on indulgences, the veneration of saints and images, processions, pilgrimages, sacramentals. The "Old Catholic" constitution provided for independent national churches headed by an episcopate which shared its administrative powers with a synodal council composed of clergy and laity. The movement spread from Germany to some other countries, especially to Austria, Switzerland, Poland, and North America. In 1877, the *Altkatholiken* were represented in Germany by 120 parishes with a membership of 53,640. Old Catholicism was officially recognized and financially supported by the states of Prussia, Baden, and Hessen and was favored by special legislation during the years of the *Kulturkampf*.

About the turn of the century a philosophico-theological movement known as "modernism," which had its origins in France, Italy, and England, began to exert a profound influence on a number of leading German Catholic theologians and laymen. Partly for apologetic reasons the "modernists" tried to adapt religious doctrine and practice to modern scientific theories and to the social and cultural conditions of the age. In its German form *Modernismus* combined the *Gefühlstheologie* (the subjective-emotional theology) of Schleiermacher (cf. p. 507 sq.) with biblical criticism and a Darwinian interpretation of the history of dogma and religion. The leaders of the movement (Döllinger, Merkle, Loisy, Tyrrell, etc.) defined religious dogma as a purely symbolic expression of religious truths, to be constantly readjusted to the changing aspects of cultural evolution. Sacraments were explained as fixations of the natural urges of man for a sensuous representation and practice of religious doctrine, and the Church was said to owe its origin to the natural urge of human beings for spiritual intercourse and religious communion. Faith and knowledge were declared as not only completely autonomous in themselves, but as intrinsically contradicting each other.

Pope Pius X, in his encyclical *Pascendi* (1907), designated Modernism as "the sum total of all heresies." The condemnation of the modernist teachings and the censuring and indexing of the writings of several modernist theologians and philosophers was followed by a special papal decree (*Motuproprio Sacrorum antistitum*) of 1910, which demanded of all clerical teachers in Catholic seminaries, schools, and universities, as well as of all pastors and other church officials, the solemn renunciation of all those views that had been singled out as heretical in the encyclical of 1907 (*Antimodernisteneid*). This rigorous measure definitively sealed the fate of the modernist movement.

As a result of the modernist controversy there prevailed for some time an unfortunate tendency among the most conservative groups of German Catholics to denounce as *modernistisch* authors and books which were merely unconventional or marked by originality of thought. This tendency is well illustrated by the so-called *Literaturstreit* (dispute on literature) which followed the publication of Carl Muth's (1867–1944) critical appraisal of Catholic *belles lettres* at the turn of the century.* The future editor of *Hochland,* which was to become one of the leading periodicals of the German Catholic intelligentsia, had asked whether Catholic literature was on a par with the literary production of non-Catholic authors, and had answered in the negative. He had criticized the largely apologetic or purely didactic and moralizing nature of Catholic *belles lettres* and had exhorted Catholic writers to "come out of the ghetto" and face courageously and positively the complex intellectual, moral, and social problems of the modern age.

The attitude of defensive apologetics, which had to a greater or lesser extent prevailed from the time of the Reformation on, had led to a literary isolationism and provincialism which were unwilling and unable to enter into competition and a fruitful exchange of ideas with non-Catholic literary groups and movements. Catholic literature and literary criticism thus were often lacking in vitality and seriousness of effort, and the tendency prevailed to judge literary works by their good intentions and sincere religious devotion rather than by standards of artistic excellence. Many of the works of Catholic authors were "Catholic" only in a narrow and feeble sense and without that breadth and depth which derive from a truly universal view of reality and which are forever exemplified in Dante's immortal poem.

In the face of violent attacks and cries of *"Modernismus,"* Carl Muth carried on the good fight and finally won out. It is in a considerable degree due to this lonely and undaunted *Kulturkämpfer* that Germany possesses today a Catholic literature of high rank, and that German Catholicism, stepping forth from its "ghetto," has become one of the most positive and creative forces in contemporary civilization.

Favored by the political and social constellations of the period following World War I — especially by the increasing influence of the Center party in national and international affairs and by the high quality and exemplary organization of the Catholic daily press — German Catholicism greatly

---

* Cf. Carl Muth, *Steht die katholische Belletristik auf der Höhe der Zeit?* (1898).

increased its material and spiritual assets. Its leading part in the *Catholic Action* movement and in the realization of the tasks of the "lay apostolate," as outlined in several papal encyclicals, was specially commended by Pope Pius XI.*

The freedom of action which the Catholic Church enjoyed under the Weimar Republic made possible the creation of new archbishoprics, bishoprics, and abbeys, and the foundation or reclamation of monastic settlements, many of which had been expropriated and secularized early in the nineteenth century (cf. p. 325).** All of these gains, however, were wiped out by the persecution of the Church which followed the revolution of 1933.

One of the fruits of the "monastic spring" of the early years of the Weimar Republic was the growth of the Catholic *liturgical movement*. Though international in character, it assumed in Germany the dimensions of a popular religious revival under the leadership of the Benedictine abbeys of Maria Laach in the Rhineland and Beuron in the valley of the upper Danube. Without ever leaning on any formal organization, the liturgical movement gradually penetrated into ever widening circles of clergy and laity, gaining a particularly strong foothold among the various Catholic youth groups. Officially sanctioned and encouraged by Pius XI's Constitution *Divini cultus sanctitatem* of 1928, it aimed at a deeper understanding of the liturgy of the Church as the center and cultic expression of Christian faith and life. Translations of liturgical texts and explanations of the liturgical rites, the study of the history of the liturgy, and the fostering of liturgical architecture and the allied arts of painting and music were to instill the liturgical spirit (the *"sentire cum Ecclesia"*) in individual devotion and community service and thus to make the liturgy a living reality in the daily lives of the people.

c) Religious Fermentation. Aside from those religious forces which carried some of the spiritual unrest of the age of crisis into the established churches, there were others, either opposed to institutional religion altogether or attempting to clothe religious ideas in new cults and rituals. While the members of these movements were united in their protest against the "soulless" materialism of modern civilization, they disagreed as to the means to be adopted to combat and overcome the materialistic trend.

The longing for new "absolutes" and for a faith which could unify the *Weltanschauung* of modern man was as articulate in the antirational creeds of religious cranks and enthusiasts as in the circles of serious, God-seeking intellectuals. According to the neo-Kantian philosopher Arthur Liebert, "all our being and all our possessions must of necessity be shattered, unless we have some norms and standards with which to reorient our existence toward a supratemporal and supernatural value." The turning away from

---

* Cf. Leo XIII, *Sancta Dei Civitas* (1880) and *Sapientia Christianae* (1890); Pius X, *Acerbo nimis* (1905); Benedict XV, *Maximum illud* (1919); and Pius XI, *Ubi arcano* (1922).

** Between 1918 and 1933, 1337 new religious settlements (orders and congregations) were established in Germany.

positivism becomes therefore "a moral commandment." Religion alone "can resolve the tensions and antinomies of human life. The problem of religion, therefore, has become the *Schicksalsfrage* (all-decisive question) of our time." This view was shared by all those educators, artists, and writers who called for a moral regeneration on the basis of a religious renascence.

A religious renovation was also advocated by several groups of religious socialists and pacifists, pleading for a human society united by the bond of an "undogmatic" faith. While the sincerity of religious socialism cannot be doubted, its program was too vague and its reasoning too loose to be persuasive beyond the numerically small circles of its immediate adherents.

Similar limitations of an intellectual and moral nature attached to the proselytizing efforts of those who sought the solution of the riddles of life in the revised and revamped teachings of occultism and spiritism. Nevertheless, the feeling of religious homelessness and insecurity, intensified by the experiences of war and revolution, made such doctrines and cults attractive to many who were looking for a religious haven, but were unwilling to accept any of the traditional creeds.

In the seventies and eighties of the nineteenth-century serious-minded scholars, such as Gustav Fechner (cf. p. 566), Friedrich Zöllner, and Baron Karl Du Prel, strongly defended the authenticity of spiritistic and mediumistic phenomena. In the nineties the occultistic movement derived encouragement from the publication of Karl Kiesewetter's *History of Modern Occultism*. After the turn of the century the Munich physician, Baron von Schrenck-Notzing, and the philosopher Konstantin Österreich aroused new scientific interest in the problems of "mediumism," spiritistic "materializations," and the general phenomena of "parapsychology" by their critical-experimental investigations.

The preoccupation of German nineteenth-century scholars with the literature, philosophy, and religion of India brought in its wake a popularization of Buddhistic and theosophical doctrines and practices. A derivative of East Indian and American theosophy was Rudolf Steiner's (1861–1925) "anthroposophy," a mystico-theosophical system, which in the years following World War I attracted tens of thousands of enthusiastic adepts in Germany and Switzerland and which to this day commands the unfaltering allegiance of groups of disciples in Europe and North America.

Rudolf Steiner, a native of Croatia, of Catholic parentage, had become known as an interpreter of the philosophic ideas of Goethe and Nietzsche when, in his endeavor to trace the evolution of the human spirit, he availed himself of the principles elaborated in Goethe's *Metamorphosis of Plants* and established on this basis a gnostico-theosophical anthropology. In 1902, he was appointed general secretary of the German section of the Theosophical Society at Adyar (India) but, after some doctrinal quarrels with Annie Besant, he seceded from that organization and made himself the independent leader of the German Anthroposophical Society (1913). An artist by avocation, Steiner drew the blueprints for the weird structure of the *Goetheanum,* the Anthroposophic Temple at Dornach near the Swiss city of Basel, a work in whose completion anthroposophic architects, sculptors, and painters co-operated. The *Goetheanum,* dedicated to the memory of Goethe, was to be a *freie Hochschule für Geisteswissenschaft,* a "free university" serving the cultivation of "art, letters, medicine, and the natural sciences."

Steiner's "anthroposophy" (the perfect knowledge concerning man) is a synchretistic system of thought, borrowing ideas from Buddhistic, Christian, gnostic, Manichaean, and theosophical sources. Its *"Geisteswissenschaft"* requires a methodical esoteric training which proceeds by way of the successive stages of "preparation, illumination, and initiation," from "imagination to inspiration and intuition," to culminate in the perfectly adequate understanding of human and cosmic nature. In the "temple" of this highest knowledge man is said to learn the truth about the eternal laws of life and about the divine essence of his own being. The evolutionary phases of the human "microcosm" run parallel with the evolution of the "macrocosm" (the world cosmos). This dual evolution is pushed forward periodically by inspired religious leaders, the greatest of whom is the *"Sonnenwesen Christus"* (Christ, the "sun principle"). The individual human being advances through a series of purgative incarnations which in turn are determined by the law of *Karma* (the accumulative sum total of man's moral acts). The entire system is anchored in a blind faith in the spiritual authority of the inspired "leader" and thus tends to withdraw its basic tenets from the scrutiny of critical examination on the part of the disciple.

The amazing temporary success of Steiner's anthroposophy, constituting one of the startling paradoxes of the age of science and technology, justifies an attention which is hardly warranted by its intellectual and religious content. During the hectic years of the postwar period the followers of Rudolf Steiner filled the largest lecture halls in such cities as Munich, Stuttgart, and Basel. Protestant theologians, philosophers, men of letters, artists, scientists, representatives of industry and commerce were gathering in large numbers around this strange and impressive figure, all eager to be handed some infallible recipes for the ardently desired regeneration of modern society. Those who were privileged to witness the manifestations of the anthroposophic movement as critical observers could discover a psychological pattern which was duplicated several years later when another "leader," whose birthplace was located in close proximity to that of Steiner, appeared on the German scene, to turn the aspirations of the masses from the "astral spheres" to the more tangible realities of "blood and soil."

d) "Jugendbewegung" (Youth Movement). Also of a vaguely religious nature was that spontaneous revolutionary movement about the turn of the century with which part of the younger generation in Germany registered their protest against an industrialized and mechanized civilization centered in big cities, and against "conventional lies" of modern bourgeois society.

The German *Jugendbewegung* grew out of a Rousseauan "back to nature" longing, a call for simplicity, truthfulness, consistency in thought and deed, and genuine *Gemeinschaft* (social and communal spirit), as against the sophistication, artificiality, halfheartedness, and selfishness of the liberal-capitalist era. A romantic yearning of youth for a natural and even primitive life in forest and field led at the beginning of the twentieth century to the formation of the first *Wandervogel* (birds of passage) groups. The members pledged abstinence from alcohol and tobacco and dedicated themselves to a self-imposed discipline and to the cultivation of the values of German *Volkstum* ("folkish" values and habits). In the revival of folk songs, folk dances, and folk music, in the nomadic roaming across the country-side, and in the devotion to the ideals of true *Kameradschaft* German youth expressed its desire for a thorough emancipation from the conventions and the external discipline of home and school.

In 1913, the *Freideutsche Jugend* (Free German Youth), composed of thirteen of the youth groups, met on the *Hohe Meissner* in the Hessian mountains to celebrate the centenary of the Wars of Liberation (cf. p. 446 sqq.) and to proclaim the "autonomy" of German youth. Emphasizing the nonpolitical nature of their movement, the famous *Meissner Resolution* formulated the ideals of the groups represented, stating that the *Freideutsche Jugend* proposed to shape the lives of its members in accordance with the demands of "self-determination, personal responsibility, and inner truth-fulness." The values of human personality were thus strongly endorsed and the subjection of man to the dehumanizing influence of a materialistic society severely condemned. All forms and rules of life were acknowledged as binding only if they grew out of the real substance of human nature and expressed man's deepest individual and social aspirations.

World War I not only disrupted the normal evolution of the German Youth Movement, but thoroughly changed it in many of its aspects. While, on the one hand, the movement gained in passionate self-assertion and con-crete elaboration of some of its aims — with the establishment of "free" schools, *Jugendburgen* (youth castles), *Jugendherbergen* (youth hostels), *Volksbildungsheime* (educational centers), *Werkwochen* (weeks devoted to work, intellectual intercourse, and recreation), *Bücherstuben* (reading centers), — it fell a prey, on the other hand, to multiplying factional divisions of a political and sectarian nature, and was finally absorbed by the ideologies of warring political parties. The Catholic youth movement, whose spiritual growth had proceeded in intimate contact with the liturgical movement (cf. p. 706), was unified in 1915 in the *Grossdeutsche Jugend* and a few affiliated groups, composed largely of students of secondary schools and universities. After the National Socialist revolution the entire youth movement was *"gleichgeschaltet"* in the Hitler Youth, and its ideal impulses were shrewdly harnessed to the pseudo religion of the totalitarian State.

The balance sheet of the German Youth Movement shows on the positive side the wholesome effects of a return to simpler tastes and more natural modes of life as well as many of the benefits derived from a keen sense for the many weaknesses and inconsistencies of contemporary civilization. On the negative side it shows the unhealthy consequences of an exaggerated and uncritical esteem for the limited values of adolescence, of an unjustifiable conceit, and of a tendency toward libertinism and extreme subjectivism.

Art, Literature, and Music. The pictorial, plastic, literary, and musical arts of the late nineteenth and early twentieth century mirror the intellectual, moral, social, and religious forces which animate and agitate the age of crisis. Germany shows herself quite as capable as in the past of adding her own creative impulses to those foreign elements which she transforms and nationalizes in the process of adaptation. And, as so often in the past, she occasionally assumes a position of cultural leadership, providing inspiration for the artists, writers, and composers of other lands.

a) Architecture. As Gottfried Semper (cf. p. 573) had predicted in 1854, the principles of a new architectural style were derived from the applied arts and crafts. The eclecticism which prevailed in the seventies of the nineteenth century, and which was marked by the unimaginative repetition of historically dated styles (neo-gothic, neo-renaissance, neo-baroque), gradually gave way to a desire for new and original architectural forms which were to embody the spirit of the modern age. The fulfillment of this desire was first realized in the decorative arts, where an antihistorical and "purist" movement arose in opposition to the borrowed pomp and colossal sham of the buildings and monuments of the *Gründerzeit* and the early decades of the "Wilhelminian" era. This blustering architecture had completely obscured the inner relationship between form and function, and its stucco façades with their extravagant ornamental trimmings had paid no heed to organic structure and artistic decorum.

The new movement in German architecture was indebted to the art theories of the romantic British reform-socialists John Ruskin (1819–1900) and William Morris (1834–1896). Both strove to save the integrity of the artisan and the craftsman from the disastrous effects of the mass-production methods of the machine age. While in their nostalgic "pre-Raphaelite" attachment to medieval art forms they were still history-minded, they conceived of the artistic process not so much in terms of imitation as of original re-creation. And their efforts found an enthusiastic response among German artists and art theorists. At the turn of the century, some of their ideas took shape in the German *Jugendstil,** a decorative style which espoused simplicity of artistic design, but soon violated its own principles by a languid and overly ornate lineament.

While the eccentricities of the *Jugendstil* were soon forgotten, its insistence on simplicity, modernity, and *Materialgerechtheit* (purity and right use of building materials) were to become important ingredients of contemporary German "functional" architecture. The German architects, aware of the tectonic and aesthetic possibilities of the new building materials: iron, steel,

---

* The *Jugendstil* owes its name to the linear technique which was the most characteristic element in Otto Eckmann's (1865–1902) contributions to the German art magazine, *Jugend.*

reinforced concrete, and glass, succeeded in creating an artistic idiom for the revolutionary changes in science, industry, and economy, and at the same time provided an adequate answer to the social needs of the industrial age. The style of the *Neue Sachlichkeit* (new objectivity), reflecting the growing depersonalization and collectivization of modern life, utilized to great advantage the new devices of engineering and the mechanical sciences to achieve a new monumentality in architectural design, while simultaneously contributing to the improvement of living and housing conditions in the crowded areas of the big cities.

The development of the functional style in German architecture proceeded in several phases, each of them associated with the names of some of the leading architects. One of its earliest and most impressive examples was Alfred Messel's (1853–1909) Wertheim department store in Berlin, completed in 1904. It was modern in its huge steel frame of blocklike appearance, but traditional in the neo-gothic design of the surface ornament. Regional elements and the interrelation of architecture and landscape received strong emphasis in the buildings of Hermann Muthesius (1861–1927) and Ludwig Hoffmann (1852–1931). Meanwhile H. Tessenow (1876–1950) and especially Peter Behrens (1868–1940) achieved an impressive simplicity by means of a strictly abstract-geometrical design, devoid of any kind of ornamentation. Behrens' building for the *AEG* (General Electric Company) in Berlin offered a striking example of a purely rational and functional architectonic structure of cubes and planes. It thus became a kind of paradigm of that international style which owes its characteristic features to the genius of the engineer and in which the form of the building depends entirely on the intrinsic dynamics of the materials of construction: steel, glass, and concrete. The chief German representative of this style came to be Walter Gropius (1883–), whose *Bauhaus* at Dessau was completed in 1926, to serve as an experimental workshop for the development of architecture and interior decoration. The replacement of the massive walls by huge sheets of glass permits illumination of the interior from all sides and thereby gives expression to a new concept of "publicity" which, as it progressively invades even the privacy of the home, symbolically illustrates the dwindling importance of private and personal life.

The development of German secular architecture was paralleled in its main aspects by ecclesiastic buildings. The church architects of the early twentieth century tried to replace the retrospective and imitative historical architectural experiments of the nineteenth century by new modes of construction, taking advantage of the new building methods and materials. They were anxious to embody the timeless Christian content in new forms. Thus the many recent *Catholic* church buildings in Germany are indicative of the attempt to adapt ground plan and interior to the spiritual incentives of the liturgical and Catholic Action movements (cf. p. 706): the place of the liturgical sacrifice is conceived as a broad unit centered in the high altar, and integrated by a greatly enlarged choir space. As was the case in the early Christian basilica (cf. p. 54), the hall-like character of the interior emphasizes the communal unity of the congregation. Decorative adornments are reduced to a minimum and always subordinated to the simple and massive proportions of the total spatial order. The trend toward simplicity and spatial unity is usually even more pronounced in the new *Protestant* church buildings, where it found strong support in ecclesiastical tradition.*

b) *Painting and Sculpture.* In architecture both the collective tendencies and the technical genius of the industrial age could express themselves most convincingly. Whenever the other arts tried to become in a similar manner carriers of the scientific-technical spirit, they fell short of their goal because of the inadequacy of their means and methods. In painting and sculpture no less than in the literary arts the late nineteenth and early twentieth century was a period of "movements" and abstract theories rather than of creative ingenuity and great individual artists and writers. And these movements, following each other more and more rapidly, were in them-selves symptoms of the intellectual, moral, and emotional instability of their protagonists, of their frantic search for new methods, new techniques, new sensations. Their craving for originality at any price and their endless theorizing often made them oblivious to any rule and norm aside from those imposed by the fixed ideas of their own inflated ego. As a result, the movements which they sponsored remained mostly unintelligible to the majority of their contemporaries, and their sponsors were thus hampered in the communication of an intended message or a professed creed.

There were, however, notable exceptions, especially in the earlier and less radical phase of the development toward modernism. Wherever the *Gehirnkunst* (brain art) engendered by the *Zeitgeist* had not led to the atrophy of heart and soul, romanticism still proved a potent force. Hans Thoma (1839–1924), for example, a son of the Black Forest and its healthy peasant culture, remained in his poetic and romantic realism always close to the thinking and feeling of the common people. His south German and Italian landscapes, his genre paintings and his still lifes continued the romantic tradition of Schwind, Richter, and Böcklin (cf. p. 578 sq.), but were modern in their freedom from any academic canon, in their vivacity and realistic observation. As director of the art gallery of Karlsruhe (Baden) Thoma encouraged the development of a genuine *Heimatkunst* (regional art), while keeping an open mind with regard to modern trends.

Another heir of German romanticism was Max Klinger (1857–1920), who at one time was widely acclaimed as the most popular master of the *fin de siècle,* but whose limitations as a painter and sculptor are today generally

---

* Outstanding contemporary *Catholic* German church architects: Hans Herkomer, Dominikus Böhm, Gottfried Böhm, Ludwig Ruff, C. Holzmeister, T. Burlage. *Protestant* architects: G. Bestelmeyer, F. Höger, Otto Bartning, O. Dörzbach. The Catholic painter Willy Oeser, in his monumental religious wall paintings, mosaics, and altarpieces, has succeeded in creating an artistic style which eminently fits the austerity of this architecture.

Church in Bischofsheim Near Mainz. Dominikus Böhm, Architect

The Shell House in Berlin

admitted. His works, burdened with too many literary allusions, are peculiarly German in their mixture of romantic-symbolist and naturalistic-descriptive elements. With Richard Wagner he shared the desire to transcend the boundaries of any particular art form and to make all the arts fuse in a *Gesamtkunstwerk* (cf. p. 495). As most of Klinger's works lack that formal perfection to which he obviously aspired, it is hardly surprising that he made his most valuable contributions to modern German art in his brilliant graphic sketches, where he could give free reign to his often riotous imagination and to his predilection for fantastic and symbolic-mystical themes. It is in these sketches that he developed a chiaroscuro technique and a nervously dynamic lineament which pointed forward to the pictorial styles of impressionism and expressionism. This new technique appears at its best in Klinger's dramatic graphic narratives and in his *Brahms Phantasies*.

The antihistorical and antimetaphysical trends of the late nineteenth century found their artistic expression in *naturalism* and *impressionism*. Under the dominant influence of the natural sciences the German artists, following the French example, turned against the traditional academic rules and against the romantic-idealistic thought content of the art of the earlier nineteenth century. Their "back to nature" movement was no longer concerned with ideas, but with "facts" and "things." While for the naturalists these "things" themselves were still of primary importance, the impressionists stripped even the "thing" of its substantiality, retaining only the optical surface appearance, the sensed values of light, shade, and color, their composition and ever 'changing variations and combinations.

Reviving the eighteenth-century "sensism" of David Hume, the German physicist and philosopher Ernst Mach (1838–1916) provided the speculative basis for an impressionistic epistemology by reducing all reality to a "bundle" of sense perceptions. The world of objects thus became an aggregate of the restless flux and flow of sensations and "impressions," and art became the ability to reproduce these sensed data. Impressionism thus applied to art the principle of positivist philosophy (cf. p. 594 sq.).

Both naturalism and impressionism were antihistorical, antimetaphysical, and antiacademic; both were opposed to any allegorical or symbolic or even philosophical interpretation of reality, simply because both regarded ideas as fictions and phantasms and therefore as meaningless. But whereas naturalism was animated by a revolutionary social fervor — an attitude which accounts for its sympathy with the poor, its criticism of social conditions and institutions, and its characteristic *Armeleutemalerei* (the portrayal of social misery) — impressionism, aside from its vehemently defended aesthetic creed, had no thesis to advance, no cause to sponsor, no ideas to represent. Thus it was as much beyond love, hatred, and passion as "beyond good and evil." Its interest in life was purely *sachlich* (objective), and its art accordingly was "art for art's sake" in the narrowest sense. But it was precisely this exclusive preoccupation with strictly technical-artistic problems that enabled the impressionist to make important discoveries in the limited sphere of sense perception and to depict in his "plain air paintings" of light and color those finest and most delicate nuances which had been beyond the reach of the traditional studio painters.

Naturalistic subject matter and impressionistic technique often fuse in the paintings of Max Liebermann (1847-1935) and Fritz von Uhde (1848-1911). Liebermann, a native of Berlin, shows in the realistic technique and subject matter of his earlier works close kinship with French and Dutch naturalism and realism. Starting out with the portrayal of groups in a setting of semidark interiors, he gradually develops a distinctly personal style of impressionistic landscape painting. The human and social elements in his early canvasses disappear more and more in his cool and factual pictorial renditions of figural and scenic observations, representing chance perceptions without any prearranged structural design. The human person is dissolved in the functional objective relations of luminous planes and in the vibrations of a fluid atmosphere.

While Liebermann was determined in the choice and treatment of his subject matter by the moral indifferentism of a Jewish-liberal *milieu,* Fritz von Uhde, an army officer and the son of a high Protestant church official, made his impressionistic style subservient to a religious and social thesis. His portrayal of Christ as the friend and companion of the socially disinherited scandalized the Protestant orthodoxy, but was acclaimed by socialists and freethinkers. His attempted "socialization" of Christianity was at the same time a rejection of the hieratic idealism of ecclesiastical art. His paintings introduced the Gospel message in a missionary spirit into the simple social relationships of everyday life.

The humanitarian and social thesis was even stronger, although dissociated from the religious component, in the graphic works of Käthe Kollwitz (1867-1946). A member of the socialist party and animated by a deep sympathy with proletarian misery, this woman dedicated her great artistic talent to the single task of a passionate indictment of social injustice. In some of her etchings, as for example in the dramatic scenes depicting the uprising of the Silesian weavers (a theme suggested by Gerhart Hauptmann's drama, cf. p. 732), Käthe Kollwitz rose above any partisan creed to a timeless symbolization of human suffering.

Impressionism in the strict sense, which had celebrated its greatest triumphs in France, the land of its origin, was represented in Germany, aside from Liebermann, by Lovis Corinth (1858-1925) and Max Slevogt (1868-1931). Corinth followed the French impressionists in the dissolution of the tectonic pictorial form and in the depersonalization of the human model. Like Peter Paul Rubens he showed himself enamored of lustrous human flesh, depicting the human nude in endless variations of pose and posture. But while he shared with Rubens the virility of the brush stroke and the ability to vivify his canvasses with the sensuous splendors and the brutal vitality of nature, he lacked the Flemish master's artistic culture and aristocratic restraint. Thus Corinth's religious paintings, unlike those of Rubens, were religious only in name: his interest remained centered in problems of technical dexterity and unrelated to the spiritual significance of his subject matter.

The talent of the Bavarian-born Max Slevogt asserted itself most vigorously in the impromptu creation of brilliant and refreshing coloristic compositions and in the art of book illustration. A master of chiaroscuro, he succeeded in achieving a maximum of expressiveness with a minimum of characteristic line drawing, thus confirming Liebermann's saying that *"zeichnen ist die Kunst, wegzulassen"* (drawing is the art of omission), that is, skill in selecting the essential and omitting the accidental. In 1902, the second year of his stay in Berlin, Slevogt created one of the great masterpieces of German impressionism, the dazzling painting entitled *The White Andrade,* in which he portrayed the famous Portuguese singer in the title role of Mozart's *Don Giovanni.* In its graceful elegance, in the sparkle of golden and silken hues, and in its flashy stage setting, the dramatic-musical quality of Slevogt's art appears at its very best.

The end phase of both French and German impressionism was characterized by an attempt to restore to painting a solid structural form and composition. It was the genius of the great French "post-impressionists" Cézanne and Gauguin and of the Dutch painter van Gogh that finally led the way in the abandonment of the flat impressionistic surface patterns and in the reconquest of a well-defined three-dimensional space. But this newly conquered space no longer obeyed the optical requirements of linear perspective: it was an impressionistically conceived space, constructed by means of functionally interrelated and receding color planes. However, it was the ecstatic-visionary, thoroughly individualistic, and essentially Germanic art of van Gogh rather than the constructivist formalism of Cézanne and Gauguin that was destined to become the greatest inspiration of German *expressionism.*

In its loud and vehement self-assertion, its emphasis on inner experience, and its abstract form-language, the expressionistic movement was typically German or, more precisely, North German. With few exceptions its chief representatives were *Obersachsen.** Although German expressionism claimed to be, and in many respects actually was, the antithesis of impressionism, it remained indebted to the technical innovations of the impressionists. But whereas both naturalists and impressionists had extolled external nature at the expense of mind and ideas, the expressionists idolized mind and contemned nature. To manifest his intellectual sovereignty over the objective external world, the expressionist not only distorted the natural object and arbitrarily destroyed its formal beauty, but he arrived finally at purely abstract patterns. He composed "symphonic" arrangements of lines and kaleidoscopic color schemes and thus approached a style of purely

---

* North Germans, among others: Emil Nolde, Kirchner, Schmidt-Rottluff, Erich Heckel, and Max Pechstein. South Germans: Oskar Kokoschka, Paul Klee, Franz Marc, and Willy Oeser.

ornamental and decorative character. His crude stylizations were not primitive or naïve in the true sense but rather symptoms of nervous fatigue, and his proclaimed kinship with the artistic language of peasants, children, and savages was a manifestation of that same sentimental urge which had started Gauguin on his flight to the South Sea Islands in search for an escape from his own sophistication.

This intellectual sophistication finally prevailed over the creative impulses of the earlier German expressionists. In the end the movement parodied and satirized itself in the aesthetic monstrosities of the German cubists, futurists, constructivists, and dadaists. The latter derided abstract expressionism by reducing their own "compositions" to a jumble of absurd and meaningless associations of line scrawls and color patches. All these extremist movements, originating in the years following World War I and during the inflation period, reflected in their nihilistic and cynical aspects the crisis through which the nations of Europe were passing.

The gradual social and economic reconstruction of Germany under the Weimar Republic produced as its parallel phenomenon in art a healthy reaction against the *Gehirnkunst* of the expressionists in the form of a new realism which took its cue from the *Neue Sachlichkeit* in architecture. This meant a return to nature and matter-of-fact objectivity, on the one hand, and an accentuation of searching and often cruel social criticism, on the other. Thus, the graphic art of George Grosz (1893–1959) mercilessly dissected the militarist and capitalist pseudo culture of bourgeois society, while in Max Beckmann's (1884–1950) paintings the human soul appeared dissolved psychoanalytically into bundles of complexes and reflexes, so that the human physiognomy is turned into a grotesquely formless grimace. Or the human being is depicted as a robot in whose head and heart a clockwork performs its automatic functions.

The development of German *sculpture* parallels in the main that of architecture and painting. The partly classical, partly realistic spirit of Hans von Marées (cf. p. 578) was alive in the statues of Adolf von Hildebrand (1847–1921), whose friendship with Marées was to prove of great significance for contemporary German sculpture. He was born in Marburg, educated in Switzerland, and artistically matured in Italy. Hildebrand worked conscientiously in the tradition of the great Renaissance master Donatello and remained forever enamored of classical formal beauty, without relinquishing nature as his most trustworthy guide. His art theory was as much the fruit of many studio talks with friends and fellow artists as of his own creative efforts. Its ingenious application may best be appreciated in such masterpieces as the Wittelsbach Fountain in Munich or the equestrian statue of Bismarck in Bremen.*

The sculptures of August Gaul (1869–1921) and Georg Kolbe (1877–1947) adopted and continued Hildebrand's naturalism, but not his classical ideal-

---

* Cf. Adolf von Hildebrand, *Das Problem der Form* (1893; *The Problem of Form in Painting and Sculpture*, Engl. trans., New York: Stechert, 1907).

ism. Kolbe advanced from naturalist-impressionist beginnings to a sensitive and rhythmically balanced expressionism. The influence of medieval Gothic statuary formed one of the constituent elements in the works of Bernhard Hoetger (1874–) and Wilhelm Lehmbruck (1881–1919). The former added heavy Germanic accents to the loose impressionistic style of his French teacher, Auguste Rodin, while the latter developed a spiritually refined sculptural expressionism on the basis of the firm tectonic pattern of Aristide Maillol's French post-impressionistic sculptures. The kinship with the spiritual content, albeit not with the external form, of medieval Romanesque and Gothic was even stronger in the works of Ernst Barlach (1870–1938), whose cubic wood sculptures defied any of the accepted stylistic categories of modern art. On a journey to Russia, undertaken in 1906, Barlach discovered the metaphysical substance of his artistic creed in the extended horizons of the Russian plains and in the simplicity and unbroken vitality of Russian peasant life. Henceforth Barlach's plastic and graphic as well as his considerable literary production became multiform variations of this experience. The simple creatures whom he modeled with tender love are implanted in the motherly earth, the timeless children of God and nature.

c) *Literature.* In the seventies of the nineteenth century the poetic realism of the generation of Hebbel and Ludwig (cf. p. 585 sqq.) had outlived itself. Some of its representatives were still alive and productive, but they had lost their audience. Literary tastes were at a very low ebb in the complacent *Gründerzeit,* and the reading public was satisfied with the sugary and sentimental rehash of hackneyed forms and contents of classical and romantic ancestry. A flood of *Unterhaltungsromane* and labored *Professorenromane* testified to the exhaustion of the novel, while the stage cultivated an anemic neo-classicism and moralizing French thesis plays in the manner of Scribe and Sardou; and lyric poetry relished the pseudo simplicity and forced gaiety of mass-produced drinking, soldier, and student songs.

In the meantime, however, the physiognomy and rhythm of German life had begun to change: in the years following the Franco-Prussian War the material wealth of the new German empire had poured largely into the big cities and was contributing to the increase of the social cleavage between capitalists and proletarians. Marxian socialism became a strong force in German life and soon also in German literature.

Among those who heralded the rise of a new literature of social significance was Theodor Fontane (1818–1898). A native of the Mark Brandenburg, he had spent the greater part of his life as a journalist when, at the age of sixty, he published his first novel. As a keen and rather detached observer he described the social transformations which were taking shape in his Prussian homeland. With a mild and melancholy skepticism he viewed the "transvaluation of all values," questioning as much the validity of tradition as the legitimacy of progress. From Darwin he had learned the "law" of the survival of the fittest by means of "natural selection," and from Taine the rules imposed upon human life by the forces of the *milieu*. Man accordingly could not be a free agent, and the moral law, far from being absolute, had to be adapted to the changing situations determined by heredity and environment. Thus Fontane came to regard all values as man-made and subject to the varying requirements of human needs and wants. As everything had two sides, nothing and no one could be said to be absolutely right or absolutely wrong. The world which unfolds itself in Fontane's novels, therefore, and the human beings who populate this world are never determined in their actions by enduring natural or supernatural norms but invariably by chance and circumstance, which add their prodigious weight to the inherent weakness of human nature. There is no longer any room for either heroic action or tragic guilt. The attitude of *tout comprendre c'est tout pardonner* (to understand all is to pardon all) became the source of Fontane's irony and of his soft-spoken bourgeois humanism.*

Two other precursors of the coming literary revolution were the Austrians Ludwig Anzengruber (1839–1889), the playwright, and Marie von Ebner-Eschenbach (1830–1916), the novelist. Anzengruber, a masterly dramatic technician, had inherited Hebbel's realism (cf. p. 586 sq.), and continued and perfected the traditional Viennese *Volksstück* (folk drama). His peasant tragedies and comedies, occasionally pointedly anticlerical and bordering on the melodramatic, excelled in the art of individual characterization and were revolutionary in their trenchant social criticism.**

In her measured and cultivated prose Marie von Ebner-Eschenbach portrayed with warm and rich feeling the aristocratic and popular traditions of the society of the Hapsburg empire.†

The credit for having introduced realism on the German stage and for having thereby prepared it to play its significant part in the literary revolution of the eighties, belongs to Duke George II of Meiningen and his troupe of actors and stage designers. Under the duke's personal direction the *Meininger* made the most painstaking efforts to impart to the dramatic setting a realistic accuracy which resulted from minute historical research. The troupe's Berlin performance of Shakespeare's *Julius Caesar* (1874) was an epoch-making event in the history of the German stage, and the decisive reform of the theaters of the *Reich* capital dates from that year.

The *Deutsches Theater* in Berlin, under the directorate of Adolf L'Arronge (1838–1908), was opened in 1883, marking another important step toward the victory of dramatic realism. To the realistic settings of the *Meininger*

---

* Cf. the social novels *Effi Briest* (1895; Engl. trans. in *German Classics of the 19th and 20th Centuries,* New York: 1913–1915, Vol. 12) and *Der Stechlin* (1898). Of great charm are his *Wanderungen durch die Mark Brandenburg* (1862–1882), a travelogue in four volumes. His ballads show Scotch influence.

** Cf. the dramas *Der Pfarrer von Kirchfeld* (1871, with *Kulturkampf* thesis); *Das Vierte Gebot* (1878; *The Fourth Commandment,* Engl. trans., Pittsburgh: 1912); and *Die Kreuzelschreiber* (1872, comedy). The novel *Der Schandfleck* (1877) tells the moving story of a village King Lear.

† Cf. *Dorf- und Schlossgeschichten* (1883); *Das Gemeindekind* (1887; *The Child of the Parish;* Engl. trans., New York: Bonner [1893]); *Parabeln, Märchen und Gedichte* (1892).

was now added the cultivation of correct enunciation and polished declamation. In the staging of plays requiring elaborate and spectacular sets and the handling of huge masses of actors (*Volksszenen*), the *Meininger* and, to a lesser extent, L'Arronge anticipated some of the devices which later on established the fame of Max Reinhardt (1873–1943), the "magician of the stage," whose overemphasis on the sensuous and optical elements of the scene, however, often tended to distort or obscure the literary values of the drama.

The actual conquest of the German stage by the new realistic or naturalistic movement in German literature was signalized by the foundation of the Berlin *Freie Bühne* in 1889. Both in its name and in its artistic creed and repertory it followed the model of André Antoine's Paris *Théâtre Libre* (1887–1895). Among the first plays offered to a selected audience of literary connoisseurs were Ibsen's *Ghosts* and Gerhart Hauptmann's *Vor Sonnenaufgang* (*Before Sunrise*). In the theater riots which followed both performances two worlds clashed in irreconcilable antagonism. The naturalistic revolutionaries had challenged the conservatives and traditionalists and, for the time being, *naturalism* had become the passionately defended creed of the younger generation of writers.

German naturalism, in its dramatic creations as well as in its novels and lyrics, had received inspiration from several foreign authors but, above all, from Emile Zola (1840–1902). In his literary theory the French naturalist had followed in the footsteps of his predecessors Balzac, Flaubert, and the brothers Goncourt. Their program called for the application of positivistic and "scientific" principles to literary creations. "Truthful" literature must be scientifically composed literature, that is, a literature in which man appeared as the end product of the forces of heredity and environment. On the speculative bases of materialistic philosophy and scientific theory Zola and his German disciples arrived at a redefinition of art which, in the formulation of Zola, was *"un coin de la nature, vu à travers un tempérament"* (a corner of nature, seen through the medium of a temperament). But in proportion as the individual "temperament" was dissolved or reduced to a bundle of sensory reflexes, the "corner of nature" became all important. In the end the accurate photographic description of the natural object remained as the sole preoccupation of the naturalistic writer.

However, to this purely factual-scientific interest in reality, as suggested by Zola, the German naturalists added an ethico-social component for which the Scandinavians (Ibsen, Björnson, Jacobsen) and the Russians (Turgenev, Tolstoi, Dostoevski) provided the themes. As a consequence, the "corner of nature" was no longer any chance aspect of reality, but one which represented in a condensed form the darkest and most sordid features of life, preferably the *milieu* of a proletarian existence.

This selective method was even retained in the "consistent" naturalism of Arno Holz (1863–1929) and Johannes Schlaf (1862–1941). In the early nineties, at a time when the Austrian poet and critic Hermann Bahr

(1863-1934) was predicting "the end of naturalism," Arno Holz was still busy trying to outline the proper requisites of a consistently naturalistic style. In his opinion, "art has the tendency to be nature." Consequently, naturalistic art, that is, "true" art must strive to be *sachlich* (objective) and close to science. The task of the epic and dramatic writer exacts the most stringent observation of objects, without any attempt at metaphysical interpretation, and without giving any room to the free play of imagination. Nature itself must speak, and the writer's only concern must consist in registering its voice. As to lyric poetry, it must dispense with rhyme, meter, and verse; it must be freed even from those free rhythms which express the emotions and passions of the individual poet, so that it may completely obey the dictation of the external object.

Holz's naturalistic theory of art and literature was thus surely "consistent" enough. But its convincing force was limited to those who accepted with Holz the positivistic concepts of "truth" and of "nature." To those who refused to affirm the "scientific" premises and bases of art and literature the naturalistic theory proved much too narrow.

With one-sided rigor naturalism had presented a picture of man, society, and nature which differed essentially from the view taken by the humanistic idealism of the classical and romantic periods. There human culture had been envisaged as proceeding from a harmonious interplay of human and natural forces. The disenchanted world of the naturalistic writers, on the other hand, had handed man and society over to a telluric determinism. Groping in vain for an axiological center which might impart meaning to a spiritless and depersonalized life, the succeeding generation of writers sought and eventually found escape in a more or less unreal world of shadows and surface appearances. Thus literary *impressionism* came into being as an outgrowth of the desire to transcend the crude domination of matter and as an attempt to sublimate the bitterness of the struggle for existence in detached and unreflecting moods and in exciting sensory and emotive experiences. While *pictorial* impressionism (both in art and literature) enjoyed the thrills provided by colorful series of optical apperceptions, *psychological* impressionism (*symbolism*) indulged in the dissection of inner experiences, and *musical* impressionism (both in literature and music) clung to the tonal-acoustic values of rhythmical sound.

Although these several types of impressionistic literature are rarely found in their purity, but usually mix and overlap, the works of some authors fall readily into one of the three categories. The technique of pictorial impressionism, for example, is easily recognized in the colorful prose sketches of the Viennese Peter Altenberg (1859-1919), whose moody subjectivism (*Wie ich es sehe,* 1896) sounded a keynote of the impressionistic view of life. Psychological and symbolical impressionism is represented in a characteristic variation of personal temper and regional *milieu* in the novels and dramas of Arthur Schnitzler (1862-1931), the Viennese writer and physician.

Schnitzler's works typify in their psychoanalytical technique the *fin de siècle décadence* of cosmopolitan Vienna. His principal characters are frivolous melancholics who play with life and love, which for them are at best mildly exciting pastimes offering ever new opportunities for nervous stimulations and erotic adventures. Schnitzler himself shared to a large extent the subjectivism and relativism of his characters, and he frankly confessed that he too found himself unable to accept any obligatory ethical norms or standards. "I have neither the courage nor the temperament nor the simplicity to adhere to any faith or party," he wrote. And his friend Hugo von Hofmannsthal, in a prologue written for Schnitzler's playlet *Anatol*, expressed in sad though beautiful verse the make-believe texture of psychological impressionism:

> Also spielen wir Theater,
> Spielen unsre eignen Stücke,
> Früh gereift und zart und traurig,
> Die Komödie unsrer Seele,
> Unsres Fühlens heut und gestern,
> Böser Dinge hübsche Formel,
> Glatte Worte, bunte Bilder. . . .*

Musical impressionism is also ably represented in Hugo von Hofmannsthal's (1874-1929) poems and lyrical dramas. But the melodious rhythmicality of his verse is even surpassed in the early lyrics of Stefan George and in the consummate melodious beauty of the poetry of Rainer Maria Rilke. The latter's art rises above all stylistic categories by virtue of its accomplished union of rich content and immaculate form.

The musical impressionists, sometimes referred to as neo-romanticists, owed a great deal to the symbolism of French and Belgian authors, such as Verlaine, Baudelaire, Huysmans, Maeterlinck, and Verhaeren. Among their German models Friedrich Nietzsche (cf. p. 695 sq.) ranks foremost, and it is from him that they learned once more about the creative possibilities of language and about the rhythmical dynamism of words and verbal patterns.

Even where he chose the dramatic form Hugo von Hofmannsthal was essentially a lyricist who expressed his profound experience of the transitory and enigmatic character of life in a symbolic verse language of great beauty and formal perfection. The moods of melancholy resignation and the twilight hues of the sensed evening glow of Western culture prevail. "We desire not,"

---

* Thus we enact our own plays:
Prematurely ripened, tender and sad,
We enact the comedy of our souls,
The todays and yesterdays of our feelings.
In smooth words and multi-colored images
We compose a pretty formula for evil things. . . .

Schnitzler's best known works include the plays *Anatol* (1893; Engl. trans., New York: 1911); *Liebelei* (1896; *The Reckoning*, Engl. trans., New York: 1907); *Der grüne Kakadu* (1899; *The Green Cockatoo*, Engl. trans., London: 1913); the novel *Der Weg ins Freie* (1908; *The Road to the Open*, Engl. trans., New York: 1923), and several volumes of novelettes.

he wrote, "the invention of stories but rather the rendition of moods; not contemplation, but representation; not entertainment, but impression."

Hofmannsthal's modern versions of some of the great dramas of Greek antiquity (Sophocles' *Oedipus* and *Electra*) and of Austrian, Italian, and Spanish medieval and baroque plays (*Jedermann; Das Kleine Welttheater; Das Salzburger Grosse Welttheater*) offered Max Reinhardt unique opportunities for the display of a veritable phantasmagoria of brilliant stage effects, often achieved within the natural setting of a public square or against the background of monumental cathedral architecture. Notwithstanding some distressing neurotic distortions which the Viennese author occasionally allows himself in the portrayal of leading characters, these grand spectacles show Hofmannsthal as one of the legitimate heirs of the medieval and baroque morality play and as a late German representative of a genuine world literature and world culture. With his *libretti* for Richard Strauss's impressionistic operas (*Rosenkavalier; Ariadne; Josephslegende*) he made an important contribution to the development of the post-Wagnerian *Musikdrama*.*

Hofmannsthal had originally been loosely associated with a group of poets and writers (the *Kreis der Blätter für die Kunst*) who followed the leadership of the Rhenish author Stefan George (1868–1934). The ways in which George conceived of the poet and of the verbal media of literary expression were new and unheard of only for a generation which had forgotten the accomplishments of German classicism and romanticism. The naturalistic profanity and vulgarity of form and content had left its unmistakable traces on German language and literature. In opposition to the "socialization" of literary values, George and many other symbolist-impressionist writers joined in Horace's dictum *"Odi profanum vulgus et arceo"* (I hate the profane crowd and keep away from it). For George and his school the poet, endowed with the high-priestly qualities of aristocratic leadership, had to stand as a lonely prophet against his time and against the spirit of the age.

In the historic soil of George's native Rhineland the heritage of Roman and Christian antiquity had fused with the introspectiveness of northern spirituality in the form of a broad and highly cultured Catholicism. These historical forces in unison were originally alive in Stefan George. Thus, in a period which lacked spiritual direction and discipline, this Rhenish poet, with his insistence on *Gestalt*, presented a rare phenomenon. In proportion as the romantic moods and remotely Christian reminiscences of his early poetry subsided, there arose in their place an eroticism which pretended to emulate the Greek glorification of divine beauty incarnate in the human form and which finally received its fixation in the *"Maximin-Erlebnis."* The

---

* The *Kleine Dramen* (*Der Tod des Tizian; Der Tor und der Tod*, etc.), though products of his early youth, are among Hofmannsthal's most accomplished works (*Death and the Fool;* Engl. trans. in "Poet Lore" 24 [1913]; *The Death of Titian;* Engl. trans. in *German Classics*, Vol. 17).

physical beauty of a friend who died in the flower of youth thus became the symbol of an idolatrous aesthetic cult. This Maximin cult in turn set the pattern for the oblations offered by George and his *Kreis* at the altars of great historical *Gestalten,* in whom "the divine" appeared *verleibt* (embodied) and the bodily *vergottet* (divinized). As literary manifestations of their cult the disciples of George wrote the biographies of Plato, Caesar, Dante, Shakespeare, Goethe, and Nietzsche.

The members of the *Kreis* set themselves apart from other literary movements, and to accentuate their being different as well as to emphasize the importance of form, rhythm, and sound they created their own typography and orthography, omitting punctuation and abandoning the capitalization of nouns. The hieratic structure and the messianic ambitions of the George school were truncated by the only too obvious intellectual and moral limitations of its individual representatives. "George lacks," wrote the contemporary literary historian, Fritz Strich, "some of the most essential and enduring human qualities. He had to conjure up the past because he and his age had lost the creative power to form timeless symbols of human existence out of their own substance. No truly creative literary accomplishments have emerged from George's *Kreis.*"

Those works which were inspired by George's *Führertum* and which can claim more than passing attention were either translations or of a scholarly rather than poetic nature. Thus both George and his disciple Rudolf Borchardt translated Dante. George translated Baudelaire's *Fleurs du Mal* and Shakespeare's *Sonnets.* Friedrich Gundolf (1880–1931), the author of standard biographies of Caesar, Goethe, and George, presented a new translation of Shakespeare's dramas. Ernst Bertram wrote a highly original biography of Nietzsche, Kurt Hildebrandt one of Plato, and Ernst Kantorowicz that of the Hohenstaufen emperor, Frederick II. All these authors made important contributions to the interpretation of historic personalities and, by virtue of their synthetic understanding of historical events, enriched the methodology of historical and literary criticism. Moreover, both the expressionist and neo-realist movements in German literature were decisively influenced by the vitality of George's verse and by his exaltation of the poet's calling. The shortcomings in George's work and in his *Führertum,* however, may well be summed up in the prophetic words of Friedrich Hebbel (cf. p. 586 sq.), who wrote in his *Diaries:* "It becomes ever more clear to me that only what proceeds from God can be made the subject matter of the highest art. . . . Even in Goethe's *Faust* that which is built on magic is transitory; for a time will come when even the memory of magic and sorcery will be forgotten."*

The poetry and prose of Rainer Maria Rilke (1875–1926) marked both the fulfillment of and the victory over impressionism. Rilke, the descendant of Carinthian Catholic noblemen, was born in Prague, and the picturesque

* The best of George's poetry is contained in the volumes *Das Jahr der Seele* (1897), *Der Siebente Ring* (1907), *Der Stern des Bundes* (1907), and *Das Neue Reich* (1929).

romantic charm of that ancient Bohemian city permeates his early impressionistic and folk-song-like lyrics. Like the sculptor Barlach (cf. p. 719) he experienced the spell of the boundless horizons of the Russian and North German plains, and he matured as a literary disciple of Russian and Scandinavian writers and under the steadying personal influence of the French sculptor, Rodin.

In the *Stundenbuch* (*Book of Hours*, 1905) Rilke professes in sublimely beautiful verse a cosmic-pantheistic religion, in which all individual things and beings appear as temporal fixations of eternal cosmic waves and rhythms. While the three major parts of this work (*Vom mönchischen Leben; Das Buch von der Pilgerschaft; Das Buch von der Armut und vom Tode*) are clothed in the symbolism of monastic life, the contents suggest not the mystical surrender of the self-centered ego to the Deity but rather a cosmic expansion of the *ego* and its final dissolution in the divine *All*. Similarly, the *Marienleben* (*Life of Mary*, 1913) celebrates the mother of Christ as a symbol of the spiritual *ego* giving birth and form to the divine.

All the works which Rilke wrote before World War I reflect both his search for and his flight from God. "But the road that leads to Thee," the poet confessed, "is fearfully long, and the track is laid waste because no one has travelled it for so long."*

After ten years of silence Rilke, in 1923, published the *Sonette an Orpheus* and the *Duineser Elegien*,** songs which in their melancholy beauty reflect the experiences of war and revolution and are filled with a heroic despair and the presentiment of death. The mythical singer Orpheus becomes the symbol of a superhuman existence embracing and harboring the antithesis of life and death: "Only in that dual realm sings a gentle voice the songs of eternity." The *Elegies* delve once more into the mystery of life. What is man? He is past and future, life and death; the eternal quest of the "I" for the "Thou," the unstilled longing for God surging against the inexorable actualities of time, world, and death. Human existence is *"Sein zum Tode"* (being unto death) in Rilke's poetry as much as in Heidegger's philosophy (cf. p. 693 sq.).

Rilke's linguistic and metrical form was the medium of his metaphysical urge for the infinite. It expresses an endless movement toward an infinitely distant goal and in its restless rhythmical flux presses on beyond time, space, and *Gestalt*. In form and content this poet appears as the late-born heir of the great culture of Europe who on the highest artistic level and in precious language sang the swan song of German romantic idealism and man-centered humanism.

German literary *expressionism* came into being about the end of the first decade of the twentieth century. Like naturalism, it was endowed with the impetuosity and aggressive radicalism of a literary revolt. It was intimately

---

* *Aber der Weg zu Dir ist furchtbar weit*
  Und, weil ihn lange keiner ging, verweht. — (*Stundenbuch*).
** *Duinese Elegies* (in the original with Engl. trans., London: Hogarth, 1930).

linked with parallel movements in the other arts and had its roots in a changing philosophy of life which left its impress on German civilization in its entirety.

But the expressionistic movement in German literature was even more short lived than either naturalism or impressionism. Flourishing and spending its energies during and following World War I, it came to a surprisingly premature end in the middle twenties of this century. The literary harvest was relatively small, and only a very few works reached the stage of literary perfection. Some critics even assert that the entire movement exhausted itself in pretentious poses, inarticulate outcries, neurotic gestures, and helpless stammerings. An unbiased appraisal, however, will arrive at more positive conclusions.

German literary expressionism voiced the indignation and passionate protest of a generation of writers who felt they had been born into social conditions and were condemned to live in cultural surroundings which they experienced as disgraceful and utterly inhuman. They therefore were united in the idealistic resolve to use their literary talents to change these conditions and surroundings. Furthermore, what was later on termed *Neue Sachlichkeit* (cf. p. 711), the new realistic simplicity in art and literature, the monumental form in functional architecture, the religious fermentation, and the dynamic wave of the Youth Movement (cf. p. 708 sq.) — all this was nourished and fanned by the spirit of expressionistic thinking and writing.

It was an axiomatic assertion of the expressionistic visionaries that their own world was to be in every respect the exact antithesis of the actually existing world of their fathers. Thus the fanatical will to "transvaluate all values" (Nietzsche) captured their hearts and poured from their lips, making them oblivious to the limitations of time and space, tradition and history, logic and grammar, and to any and all of the petty realities of the external world. Instead, the inner world of the soul, the mind, and the spirit was to rule supreme. In short, the expressionistic writers were profoundly convinced that they were burdened with the task or entrusted with the mission of renewing the face of the earth, of reshaping the history of the world.

The expressionistic movement had reached its peak when a defeated Germany seemed politically and socially nothing but a heap of ruins. But far from being dismayed or even surprised by such a spectacle, the expressionist intelligentsia took pride in having actively contributed to the downfall of imperial Germany and in having had its share in the subsequent political and social revolution.

The pronounced *pacifism* espoused by the several expressionistic groups amply justified such claims. Handicapped in their activities and utterances by a rigid censorship, many of the expressionists had taken up residence in Switzerland, and many others had their radical propaganda printed and published abroad and then secretly distributed in Germany.

The literary revolution in *Berlin* used the pages of the two periodicals,

Aktion and *Sturm,* for their manifestoes against power politics and their defense of humanitarianism and cosmopolitanism. In Berlin, too, were gathered the "activists," led by Kurt Hiller and Heinrich Mann (1871–1950), the elder and less famous (though hardly less talented) brother of Thomas Mann. The philosophy of activism, written by Leonhard Nelson revealed its close kinship with the democratic constitutionalism of the French and American Revolutions. The professed radicalism of many activist leaders remained, however, largely confined to the printed page. Assailing the *art for art's sake* slogan of the impressionists, they proposed to make art and literature servile tools of political and social ideas. Unlike Zola, they carefully refrained from mingling with the poor and miserable whose lot they bewailed in impassioned pleas. Thus their voices, coming from the safe and icy distance of aristocratic seclusion, had a feeble and shallow sound, giving the lie to the talkative protestations of their "love for mankind."

The intellectual cleavage and (temporary) personal antagonism between the two Mann brothers illustrated almost dramatically the clash between German literary conservatism and revolutionary radicalism. While Thomas Mann (cf. p. 734 sq.) was esteemed by some of the younger writers as the distinguished heir of Germany's classical and romantic tradition, as the disciple of Goethe, Wagner, Schopenhauer, Nietzsche, and the great Russian novelists, Heinrich Mann was the idol of a rebellious and irreverent literary clique whose members were inspired by the ideology of Western democratic liberalism. And at the very moment when the events on the battlefields of Europe seemed to turn the scales completely in favor of the latter group, Thomas Mann, in his *Betrachtungen eines Unpolitischen* (1918), made a final and almost desperate attempt to exonerate the Prussian conservative world of his Hanseatic forebears, a world in which he still wished to believe and which he therefore defended against the ruthless attacks of the Western *"Zivilisationsliteraten."*

In the German South the *Münchener Kammerspiele* (Munich Little Theater) achieved fame for its sponsorship of the expressionistic *drama*. Homage was paid there to August Strindberg (1849–1912), the great Swedish playwright, who more than any other writer fathered German dramatic expressionism. His influence was strongly felt in the eccentric plays of Frank Wedekind (cf. p. 734), in Karl Sternheim's satirical and cynical comedies; and in the spectacular, technically brilliant *Denkspiele* of Georg Kaiser. The performance of Reinhard Goering's pacifistic drama *Seeschlacht* (*Sea Battle,* 1917) was followed by the first of a series of theater riots, in which pacifist and nationalist sentiments clashed.

The most promising of the pacifist-expressionist playwrights was Fritz von Unruh (1885–). Coming from an ancient family of the Prussian nobility and counting among his ancestors many distinguished Prussian generals, he had attended the Imperial Military Academy in close companionship with the Prussian princes. He served as an officer in the war, and had both lost and found himself and his life aim in the horror and anguish of the trenches before Verdun. While his early dramatic production, especially the colorful *Louis Ferdinand* (1913) was in temper and atmosphere (though not in its thesis) akin to some of the plays of Heinrich von Kleist (cf. p. 483 sq.), his postwar dramas gave voice to tortured and defiled humanity. His passionate longing envisaged a new daybreak when the idols of militarism and nationalism would be unmasked and the idea of a mankind united in brotherly love would be universally accepted.*

The stirring socialist dramas of Ernst Toller (1893–1939) were written in a similar vein. His *Masse Mensch* (1920), presenting a poignant indictment of both militarist and communist dictatorship, continued a dramatic pattern in which the collective dynamism of the masses replaces the individual hero, a substitution for which Gerhart Hauptmann's *Die Weber* had provided the paradigm. During the "white" counterrevolution which overthrew the short-lived Soviet dictatorship of Bavaria (1919), Toller was apprehended and sentenced to five years' imprisonment in a Bavarian fortress for his share in Kurt Eisner's (cf. p. 646) socialistic experiment. A political exile after 1933, he took his own life in 1939, in a New York hotel.**

The expressionistic *Weltanschauung* clearly reflected some of the political and social changes as well as the intellectual crisis through which the German nation was passing. The stress which the expressionists placed on human and spiritual-personal values made them disdainful of materialism and positivism. But their spiritualistic subjectivism was as one-sided and unrealistic as had been the materialistic "objectivity" of their naturalist and impressionist antagonists. The inflated *ego* of the expressionist soon became forgetful of *la terre sacrée,* of the reality of matter and nature, and thus his deep longing for an objective realm of values beyond the sphere of a self-centered idealized individualism remained in the main unfulfilled.

Franz Werfel (1890–1945), a native of Prague and a citizen of Vienna prior to Hitler's annexation of Austria, was one of the few initial members of the expressionistic movement who outgrew the metaphysical narrowness of the school and attained to that integrated view of reality which had been anticipated by the French philosopher Bergson and which finally became the common property of the German phenomenological, neo-realist, and neo-Thomist thinkers (cf. p. 697 sq.). In literature as in the arts this neo-realism appeared in the form of the *Neue Sachlichkeit* (cf. p. 711) and in its attempted synthesis of the antithetical positions of naturalism and impressionism, on the one hand, and expressionism, on the other. In a programmatic speech delivered in 1931 and entitled *Realismus und Innerlichkeit* Franz Werfel called for the restoration of a hierarchic order of values in which

---

* Cf. *Opfergang,* a prose epic (1916; Engl. trans., *The Way of Sacrifice,* New York: A. Knopf, 1928), and the dramas *Ein Geschlecht* (1916), *Platz* (1920), *Heinrich aus Andernach* (1925), and this writer's school edition of *Prinz Louis Ferdinand* (New York: Oxford University Press, 1933).

** Cf. *Seven Plays* (New York: Liveright Publishing Corp.); *No More Peace* (New York: Farrar & Rinehart, 1937); *Pastor Hall* (New York: Random House, 1939); and the autobiography *I Was a German* (New York: W. Morrow & Co., 1934).

matter and spirit, nature and supernature were to receive due consideration. His own later works, especially the drama, *Paulus unter den Juden (Paul among the Jews,* 1926; Engl. trans., Mowbray, 1928), and his novels *Barbara oder die Frömmigkeit; (The Pure in Heart,* Engl. trans., New York, 1931), *Der veruntreute Himmel (Embezzled Heaven,* Engl. trans., New York: Viking Press, 1940), and *Das Lied von Bernadette (The Song of Bernadette,* Engl. trans., New York: Sun Dial Press., 1942) were milestones on the road to such an integral literary realism.*

The neo-realist synthesis demanded and partially realized by Werfel naturally found its strongest support among German *Catholic writers* whose works are grounded in the experienced polarity of subject and object, nature and supernature, reason and faith.

In 1912, the convert Reinhard Johannes Sorge (1892–1916), who died in the battle of the Somme, had written the drama *Der Bettler (The Beggar),* the first of many ecstatic dramatic confessions of the expressionist movement. In his short life Sorge traveled the long road from the creed of Nietzsche's Zarathustra to a view of life which permitted him to pronounce "Judgment on Zarathustra" *(Gericht über Zarathustra,* 1921). In between he had written several dramatic works in the vein of the medieval morality play. In this revival of the strictly religious play Sorge was followed by the Austrian Max Mell (1882–1958),** the South German Leo Weismantel (1888–), and others.

Ruth Schaumann (1899–) and Gertrud von Le Fort (1876–), both outstanding as lyricists and novelists, and both converts, represent contemporary German Catholic literature at its highest level. Ruth Schaumann, in her work as a sculptor and graphic artist as much as in her writings, reveals a prodigious poetic imagination and a tenderness of feeling which are nourished by her personal experience of the sacred realities of love, motherhood, the human soul, and God. Gertrud von Le Fort's literary style, on the other hand, is more objective and her view of the world more retrospective, enabling her to form timeless culture symbols of Christian truths. In the majestic psalmody of her *Hymnen an die Kirche* individualism and universalism fuse, and the human soul, immersed in the rhythmical sequence of the ecclesiastical year, experiences its own existence as organically linked with the *Corpus Christi Mysticum.* In the novel *Der Papst aus dem Ghetto* (1930; *The Pope from the Ghetto,* Engl. trans., New York: Sheed and Ward, 1934) she tells in the unemotional style of the old chronicles the moving story of Cardinal Petrus of the Jewish family of Pier Leone who, as Anacletus II, the antipope, plunged the Church into the schism of 1130. This narrative views the problem

---

* Other prominent representatives of the *Neue Sachlichkeit* are the lyricists Gerrit Engelke, Jakob Kneip, Adolf von Hatzfeld, and Richard Billinger; and the novelists Joseph Roth, Oscar Maria Graf, Alfred Döblin, Emil Strauss, Hermann Hesse, Erwin Guido Kolbenheyer, Joseph Magnus Wehner, Paul Alverdes, Ernst Wiechert, Franz Kafka, Hans Carossa, Hermann Stehr.

** Cf. *Das Apostelspiel* (1923; Engl. trans., Methuen, 1934); *Das Schutzengelspiel* (1923); *Das Nachfolge-Christi-Spiel* (1927).

of Judaism and of the Jewish people in its profound religious significance and sees its solution in Israel's free acceptance of God's providential design. The novelette *Die Letzte am Schafott* (1931; *The Song at the Scaffold,* Engl. trans., New York, 1933) relates the martyrdom of 17 Carmelite nuns at the time of the French Revolution, painting against the dark background of a general breakdown of human hopes and values the overpowering reality of divine grace. In *Das Schweisstuch der Veronika* (*The Veil of Veronica,* 1928) and its sequel, *Der Kranz der Engel* (*The Angels' Wreath,* 1948) the action takes place in present-day Rome, the main theme being the meeting of paganism and Christianity in the Eternal City: Rome, the great pagan mother of nations, the city of sublime and enduring beauty, bearing in her womb the secrets of the glories of nature and mind; and that other Rome, the radiant monstrance of the world, the mother of all spiritual blessings, in whose presence the splendors of the pagan city pale, because in the heartbeat of the true *Roma Aeterna* abides the secret of the living God.

After having thus roughly sketched the most important literary movements flourishing in the years which intervened between the foundation of the Second Empire and the end of the Weimar Republic, there remains the task of giving an appraisal of the literary work of some individual authors who resolutely cut across the boundary lines of schools and cliques. While in their philosophy of life and in their artistic-technical means they are no less representatives of the spirit of the age than the members of literary groups, they often succeeded in expressing a common set of social and cultural experiences in a vigorous and distinctly personal style.

Gerhart Hauptmann (1862–1946),* whose beginnings were more or less loosely associated with the naturalistic movement, manifested even in his earliest dramatic production an understanding of human nature and social situations which transcends the narrow doctrinairism of a photographically correct naturalism. His drama *Vor Sonnenaufgang* (1889; *Before Dawn,* Vol. 1), though naturalistic in the accurate description of the sordid *milieu* of a corrupt Silesian family of peasant *parvenus,* derives its moving force from the author's compassion with the fate of his characters. Helen, who in the midst of the debasing influences of her environment has preserved her moral integrity and believes she has found a way of escape in her love for a social-democratic apostle of temperance, takes her own life when her lover, an all-too-faithful adept of the theories of heredity and environment, refuses to marry into a family of drunkards. The main characters of this and the two following plays, *Das Friedensfest,* 1890; *Einsame Menschen* (1891; *The Reconciliation; Lonely Lives,* Vol. 3), are products and victims of external circumstances, unfree in their

---

* Cf. *The Dramatic Works,* New York: Viking Press, 1912–1917; 1924; 1929; 9 vols.

actions, and driven on to their doom by the pitiless forces of heredity and *milieu*. Their actions are no more and no less than *Schmerzreaktionen* (pain reactions). They are weak but not guilty, and therefore not tragic in the accepted sense of the term. However, Hauptmann's *milieu* and character analysis implies not only compassion with these victims of a capitalist-materialist *Weltanschauung*, but at the same time a social criticism and a moral indignation deriving from the religious-pietistic idealism indelibly implanted in the author by the atmosphere and the family traditions of his Silesian homeland.

Gerhart Hauptmann's international fame was firmly established with his drama *Die Weber* (1892; *The Weavers*, Vol. I), in which the historical uprising of the Silesian weavers of 1844 offered the playwright a unique opportunity to depict with great dramatic skill the cumulative dynamism and destructive power of the impoverished proletarian masses. The fact that Hauptmann, himself the grandson of a Silesian weaver, could draw on personal recollections gave the drama an added and convincing force and made it the most authentic social play of contemporary German literature.

"Straight at the heart of German discord" aimed Hauptmann's *Florian Geyer* (1896; Vol. 9), his second drama of social revolution. As the Silesian weavers had risen against their capitalist exploiters, so the hapless peasant masses of the early sixteenth century, under the leadership of the imperial knight Florian Geyer, revolt in the Great Peasants' War (cf. p. 240 sq.) against the German knights and princes. Defying the naturalistic dogma, which had banished history from the stage, Hauptmann wrote a historical drama, but one which carried a stirring message for his German contemporaries. The peasant revolt is crushed and drowned in blood because of the disunity of the several groups and their unwillingness to subordinate themselves to the better judgment of their chosen leader.

In the plays *Fuhrmann Henschel* (1898; *Drayman Henschel*, Vol. 2) and *Rose Bernd* (1903; Vol. 2) the fate of the main characters is no longer determined by heredity and environment but by the unrestrained inner forces of will and instinct. The former drama develops August Strindberg's and Frank Wedekind's favorite theme, the victory of female brutality over masculine weakness and inertia. *Rose Bernd*, on the other hand, seizes upon a popular *Sturm und Drang* (cf. p. 394 sq.) motif, the self-destruction of a woman who has murdered her newborn baby. The symbolistic and romantic elements which enter into the naturalistic setting of the verse drama *Hanneles Himmelfahrt* (1894; *The Assumption of Hannele*, Vol. 4) become dominant in the theme and style of *Die versunkene Glocke* (1896; *The Sunken Bell*, Vol. 4). This is Hauptmann's poetically most accomplished play, in which the fate of Heinrich, the bell founder, becomes a symbol of the destiny of the great artist who, in Hauptmann's opinion, must find in closest communion with nature a compensation for his human and social loneliness.

Hauptmann's succeeding plays deal partly with legendary, partly with historical subjects. *Der arme Heinrich* (1902; *Poor Henry,* Vol. 4) introduces modern psychological motivations into Hartmann von Aue's (cf. p. 152 sq.) medieval tale of the leprous knight who has been promised health by the voluntary sacrifice of a pure maiden, but is finally cured by divine grace. *Der weisse Heiland* (1920; *The White Savior,* Vol. 8) pictures with gross historical bias Montezuma as the "savior" who is put to death by fanatical and gold-hungry Spaniards.

Among Hauptmann's prose works the novels *Der Narr in Christo, Emanuel Quint* (1910)* and *Der Ketzer von Soana* (1918)** stand out; the former for its warmth of human feeling and its original treatment of a religious theme, the latter for its qualities of style. Emanuel Quint is a Moravian God-seeker who attempts to relive the life of Christ in the Silesian mountains, but who, in his pietistic subjectivism and in the growing confusion of his mind, ends by identifying himself with the Saviour, and dies as an outcast in utter loneliness. The story of the *Heretic of Soana* is a panegyric of pagan naturalism, in which the anarchical force of instinct is polemically opposed to the intellectual and moral exactions of Christianity. A young Italian priest forsakes his religious calling to spend the rest of his life as a shepherd in the unbridled freedom of nature. The repulsiveness of the theme is not sufficiently mitigated by the artistic proficiency with which it is developed. Hauptmann's conception of paganism is as distorted and unreal as his idea of Christianity. In none of his many works has he ever succeeded in overcoming the vacillating and vague pantheism and sentimental humanitarianism which from the outset characterized his somewhat ill-balanced philosophy of life.

It was the protest against the relativistic softening of metaphysical and moral values and norms that made Paul Ernst (1866–1933), the one-time socialist, a most determined opponent of naturalism and impressionism and an impassioned advocate of a literary conservatism resting on "the unity of vital experience, social action, faith, and a common ethnic and national destiny." In the treatise *Der Weg zur Form* (1906) Ernst offered a theoretical exposition of his dramatic principles, demanding a return to the spirit and form of Greek and German classical drama which both, in his opinion, had been characterized by a vital union of aesthetic, metaphysical, and moral values. Moral relativism, he asserted, had destroyed the very foundations of the genuine drama by its denial of the absolute nature of good and evil, a negation which had made a tragic conflict impossible. Greek tragedy had succumbed to the moral relativism of Euripides, "the destroyer of the myths" (Nietzsche). Similarly, the classical German drama had been destroyed by the immoralism or amoralism of the naturalists and impressionists: "The sophists ruined the drama of antiquity by their doctrine of the relativity of moral concepts. And the naturalistic drama of

---

* *The Fool in Christ, Emanuel Quint* (Engl. trans., New York, 1911).
** *The Heretic of Soana* (Engl. trans., New York, 1923).

our time is no longer a drama in the true sense because, characteristically enough, it is closely linked with sociological positivism. . . . The essence of being human consists not in our faculty of understanding, but in our capability of discerning ultimate values. . . . Only man can be moral, and therefore all human greatness rests on morality."

Ernst's exclusive interest in the aesthetic and moral components of art and literature set him apart from the expressionists, on the one hand, and from the contemporary religious writers, on the other. While the former placed subjective-spiritual experience above moral content, the latter attempted to ground moral goodness in the superior values of meta-physical and religious truth.*

The antinaturalism of Frank Wedekind (1864–1916) sprang from entirely different roots. With the vehemence of a temperament unchecked by any traditional standards of morality he advocated in his partly serious, partly grotesque dramas the free reign of sexual instincts, convinced "that natural processes are never indecent, but either useful or harmful, reasonable or unreasonable." An inverted bourgeois, Wedekind declared a war to the finish on all "bourgeois morality," borrowing from Nietzsche his call for a new *Herrenmoral* "beyond good and evil," and his plea for the breeding of a new race of "noble human animals." Lacking a moral standard of measurement, Wedekind's social criticism remained purely negative and destructive, unable to create true dramatic symbols of a new order and meaning of reality. The freedom of the individual which he preached had no counterpart in objective moral values and was corroded by the author's cynicism and Bohemian snobbery.**

The contrast between art and life, between the existence and *milieu* of the artist and the bourgeois, became the central problem of the novels of the brothers Heinrich and Thomas Mann. The theme was suggested by the blood heritage of the two authors, the sons of a patrician Hanseatic father and a Creolean mother. While Heinrich Mann[†] attempted to resolve the art-life antinomy by a twofold escape, first into Bohemianism, and afterward into activist-social expressionism (cf. p. 727 sq.), Thomas Mann (1875–1955) sought the solution of the problem in a humanistically ennobled *Bürgertum*. Thus Heinrich's way led from a cult of sensuous beauty to social satire, and Thomas proceeded from the experience of the lonely and life-hungry artist (*Tonio Kröger*, 1903; Engl. trans. in *German Classics of the 19th and 20th Centuries*, Vol. 19) to an artistic culture which was sustained by social responsibility (*Königliche Hoheit*, 1909; *Royal Highness*, Engl. trans., New

---

* Cf. Ernst's drama *Brunhild* (1909) and the novel *Saat auf Hoffnung* (1915), both contained in *Gesammelte Schriften* (19 vols., Munich, 1928 sq.).

** Cf. the dramas *Frühlings Erwachen* (*The Awakening of Spring*, 1891; Engl. trans., Brown, 1919); *Erdgeist* (*Earth Spirit*, 1895; Engl. trans., New York, 1914); *Der Marquis von Keith* (1901); in *Gesammelte Werke* (9 vols., Munich, 1912 sqq.).

† Cf. the novel, *Die kleine Stadt* (1909; *The Little Town*, Engl. trans., New York: Houghton, 1931), the best among Heinrich Mann's earlier works; and the socio-political satire, *Der Untertan* (1918; *The Patrioteer*, Engl. trans., New York, 1921).

York, 1926) and a belief in a conservative political democracy. Although both authors surpassed the naturalistic novel by virtue of their deeper and broader understanding of the conflicts inherent in human life and civilization, they tended to satirize or neutralize these conflicts without ever attaining to a metaphysical or cultural synthesis.

Out of the dual endeavor of conscientious factual analysis and sympathetic human understanding was born the melancholic-skeptical irony with which Thomas Mann views the actions of his major characters. Autobiographical features are no less conspicuous in his stories than in his four long novels and his historical play *Fiorenza* (1905). In *Buddenbrooks* (1901; Engl. trans., New York, 1924) Mann, at the age of twenty-five, traced the decay of a patrician family of the Hansa city of Lübeck (the author's birthplace), driving home his thesis that biological and physical health are threatened and eventually doomed by the virus of art and culture. Young Hanno Buddenbrook, biologically unable to carry on the solid patriarchal traditions of his ancestors, is "infected" with music. *Der Zauberberg* (1924; *The Magic Mountain*, Engl. trans., New York, 1927), picturing life in a Swiss Alpine sanatorium for consumptives as a symbolic cross section of decadent European society, almost morbidly underscores Mann's often professed neo-romantic "sympathy with death," introducing psychoanalysis as a technical means of characterization. Hans Castorp, the scion of a patrician family of the city of Hamburg, who succumbs to the spell of the "magic mountain," and whose intended brief visit to the mountain resort extends to a period of seven years, is saved from a life of make-believe and utter unreality when he follows the call to arms, meeting death on the battlefields of World War I. The epic tetralogy *Joseph und seine Brüder* (1933 sqq.; *Joseph and His Brothers*, Engl. trans., New York, 1934 sq., 4 vols.) uses a biblical theme for a sophisticated exposition of typically modern psychological and sociological problems and offends by its flippant rationalizations of scriptural texts and personages. *Dr. Faustus* (the "Life of the German Composer Adrian Leverkühn," Engl. trans., New York: A. Knopf, 1949), finally, attempts a psychological and metaphysical interpretation of the ultimate meaning of German history, the German people, and the German mind.

The novelette *Mario und der Zauberer* (*Mario and the Sorcerer*, 1930) more than any of Mann's major works gives evidence of the fact that the author was well aware of the dark and dangerous irrational forces which were closing in on Germany on the eve of the National Socialist revolution. But it appears extremely doubtful whether the revolver shot which in the end kills the sorcerer provides an adequate answer or a really "satisfactory solution." It is quite certain, on the other hand, that Mann's thin-blooded humanism was incapable of offering a more positive answer or a more substantially human solution.

d) *Music.* The spirit of German classicism and romanticism exerted a more enduring influence on contemporary German music than on the plastic, pictorial, and literary arts. Not only was the classico-romantic musical tradition kept alive, but its continuity was enriched by the creative genius of some great masters who proved fully equal to the task of entering into the great heritage bequeathed to them.

The neo-romanticism of Richard Wagner's music dramas (cf. p. 493 sqq.) had conquered the Western World, so that its influences prevailed not only in the post-Wagnerian opera but also in symphony, chamber music, choral music, and *Lied*. Still, the classical tradition of German music experienced a vigorous revival in *Johannes Brahms* (1833–1897), a native of Hamburg who, after romantic beginnings, developed a distinctly North German classicism of striking originality.

The heavy and severe style of many of Brahms's compositions reveals a typically low-German inclination toward the balladesque and the tragic, elements which prevent his works from being easily accessible to non-Germanic audiences. The richness of his harmonic technique derives from his familiarity with the ancient church modes, while he owes his mastery of vocal polyphony to the influence of Johann Sebastian Bach and the early Dutch masters. From both Palestrina and Bach he drew inspiration for his choral and hymnic music and for his madrigals and concertos, while from Beethoven he learned the logical-synthetic interlinking of themes and motifs. Thus the classical elements prevail, but the romantic components are not lacking. They are manifest in the poetic inspiration of many of his works, in the temperamental rhythm and emotional vivacity of his Hungarian dances and gypsy songs, and in his admiration for medieval and Catholic forms of art and cultic worship. Romantic also is his longing. for southern climes and cultures and the mood of a melancholy, unstilled yearning which permeates especially the works of the Viennese period.

In an age which in art and culture paid homage either to listless traditionalism or restless progressivism, Brahms enlivened the sense for lasting forms and values, setting in his own life and work the example of a healthy balance and artistic discipline.*

In his independence of Richard Wagner's style and *Weltanschauung* Johannes Brahms stands almost alone. He had few disciples and founded no school. The heirs, successors, and imitators of Wagner, on the other hand, were numerous. Among them Hans Pfitzner (1869–1949) stands out as the only one who combined in his operas the three major elements of the Wagnerian music drama: the romantic mysticism of *Lohengrin,* the erotic mysticism of *Tristan,* and the *Parsifal* theme of religious asceticism and salvation by redeeming love (*Erlösungsdrama*).

Pfitzner is Richard Wagner's most legitimate heir, and the purely ideal romantic dreamworld of his operas appears almost as an anachronism in the midst of the materialism of a technical-utilitarian age. In his music-dramatic version of Hartmann von Aue's medieval epic *Der arme Heinrich* (1895) he shows himself as the modern master of the Christian *Erlösungs-*

---

* The works of Brahms include 17 pieces for chamber music, 4 symphonies, 4 concertos, 10 sonatas, and many choral compositions (among them *Deutsches Requiem*).

drama. As a genuine neo-romanticist he combines the charm of the medieval legend with the refinement of modern psychological penetration. His instrumentation broadens and deepens the polyphonic individualism of the post-Wagnerian orchestra by the objective patterns of the medieval *discantus* and the church modes.

The opera *Palestrina* (1916), the musical dramatization of the genesis of the Renaissance master's famous *Missa Papae Marcelli,* contains Pfitzner's artistic *credo:* it is a Faustian drama of the lonely creative artist in the midst of an unfeeling and unresponsive world. In this work as well as in his mature chamber music the composer revives the musical Gothic of Josquin des Près, fusing it with the intricate counterpointal technique of eighteenth-century classicism and with the spiritual animation of German romanticism. The passionate sensualism of Wagner gives way in Pfitzner's music to restrained emotions and occasionally to an ascetic austerity.*

Musical naturalism and impressionism in Germany is most skillfully and colorfully represented by *Richard Strauss* (1864-1949). He achieved world fame with his opera *Der Rosenkavalier* (1911), a work which in its lyrical gaiety leans strongly toward the Viennese operetta, for which *Johann Strauss* (1804-1849),** *Franz von Suppé* (1820-1895), and *Karl Millöcker* (1842-1899) had created the indigenous and lasting pattern.

With *Salome* (1905; text by Oscar Wilde) and *Elektra* (1909; text, as in most of the following Strauss operas, by Hugo von Hofmannsthal, cf. p. 723 sq.) the composer made his most important contributions to the naturalistic operatic style. Both works are actually musical caricatures of the main characters they portray. The clever and exciting tonal effects serve to underscore the psychopathological elements, and the carefully calculated nuances of a lavish orchestration are designed to register and illustrate the most minute nervous reflexes. Wagner's great art of musical characterization is replaced by an episodic and mosaiclike picturesqueness which no longer pays attention to dramatic development and thus dilutes and dissolves the structural form.

The blurring of form and contour and the prevalence of color and *Stimmung* (mood) are most conspicuous in Strauss's impressionistic program music, especially in his tone poems,† which are hardly more than aggregates of brilliant and startling musical *aperçus* or sketchy aphorisms without any tectonic unity. In the *Alpensymphonie* the musical "program" faithfully renders the tonal effects suggested by an alpine scene, including not only the phenomena of nature but even the sound of cowbells. But Strauss's perfect command of all the technical registers of orchestration and

---

* Pfitzner's compositions include, aside from his operas and chamber music, numerous orchestral and choral works, cantatas (*Von deutscher Seele,* 1921), and *Lieder.* He wrote several books in violent protest against modernistic music (*Gesammelte Schriften,* 1926–1929).

** Cf. *Die Fledermaus, Der Zigeunerbaron, Eine Nacht in Venedig,* etc.

† Cf. *Also sprach Zarathustra, Don Juan, Ein Heldenleben, Tod und Verklärung, Alpensymphonie.*

composition can hardly atone for the lack of that profound and comprehensive view of reality which is the indispensable requisite of great art
and which Richard Wagner had in mind when he said: *"Ich kann den
Geist der Musik nicht anders als in der Liebe fassen"* (In Love alone can
I comprehend the true spirit of music).

This deepest love of reality in its plenitude, seen as the handiwork of its
divine Maker, was the prime motivating force in the works of *Anton
Bruckner* (1824–1896), Austria's greatest musical genius since Schubert's
time, and the most accomplished modern master of that monumental
symphonic form which Beethoven had created. Bruckner's music is the
naïve, unreflected language of the human heart, and both his sacred and
secular compositions are permeated by his childlike Catholic faith, by the
sturdiness of his ancestral peasant *milieu,* and by the idyllic beauty of his
homeland, the landscape of Upper Austria. In the mystic-ecstatic transport
of his music Bruckner reveals his kinship with Franz Liszt (cf. p. 493 sq.),
although his religious experience has deeper roots and expresses itself in
simpler and purer forms. All of Bruckner's works are an affirmation of
life: jubilant "feasts of sound" which find the answer to all the dark and
perplexing problems of human existence in the supreme clarity of that "dear
Lord," to whom the composer dedicated his last (ninth) symphony (*"an
den lieben Gott"*).*

The serene religious harmony which in Bruckner's music triumphs over
all tragic discord remains a never satisfied longing in the compositions of
Gustav Mahler (1860–1911), a native of Bohemia, whose international
reputation as conductor (Budapest, Hamburg, Vienna, United States)
equaled his fame as a composer. Mahler surpasses Bruckner in the firm
and often grandiose tectonic structure of his works and in his melodious,
though eclectic, versatility. Having received his initial inspiration from
Beethoven, he completed the form of the choral symphony which Beethoven
had inaugurated with his Ninth Symphony, and he pointed the way to
a powerful musical expressionism in his own Ninth Symphony and in the
Lied von der Erde (*Song of the Earth*).

Mahler's music is perhaps the purest musical documentation of the
cultural crisis of the turn of the century and of the ever repeated attempts to
resolve the conflict between *Ich* and *Welt,* between individualism and social
collectivism. Filled with a missionary passion for the socialization of the
metaphysical and ethical values of music, Mahler wanted to carry his
message to the masses by creating the *"Sinfonie des kleinen Mannes"* (the
symphony for the little people), by lifting the events of everyday life into
the sphere of the sublime, and by striving for the simple grandeur of the
folk song.

Mahler's symphonies express and reflect in successive phases his desperate

---

* Bruckner's compositions include nine symphonies (the ninth unfinished), three Masses, one
Requiem, one *Te Deum,* one quintet for strings, and several choral and liturgical works.

struggle to free himself from the discords which threatened his own life. A God-seeker in an irreligious age and environment, he invokes the healing and redeeming powers of Faith in the Second Symphony, of Love in the Third Symphony; he flees into the world of dreams in the Fourth; turns his energies to the social tasks of an active life in the Fifth; and, finally, resigns himself to the seemingly inescapable tragedy of life in the Sixth Symphony. This resignation and the romantic "sympathy with death" resound once more with strongest emotional accents in the *Kindertoten-lieder* and in his swan song, the *Lied von der Erde*.

The breadth and depth of both Bruckner's and Mahler's human and artistic penetration of reality was not reached by *Max Reger* (1873–1916), the Bavarian composer, whose exuberant vitality lacked the intellectual acumen which could have acted as a steadying and balancing influence on his unruly talent. Reger's compositions are both conservative and "modernistic," and his historical significance lies in the fact that he combined the classical forms of absolute music with revolutionary innovations in producing chromatic and enharmonic effects. He is undoubtedly the greatest contemporary master of the art of linear counterpoint, and in his magnificent organ music, especially in his fugues and double fugues, he proves himself a loyal and convincing disciple of Johann Sebastian Bach. Yet all too often Reger's scintillating and impetuous temperament arbitrarily disrupts the rigid firmness of this classical frame and expresses itself in the erratic forms of a bulging baroque expressionism.*

Musical *expressionism* as a distinct style growing out of a new and revolutionary theory was introduced into German music by *Arnold Schön-berg* (1874–1951), a native of Vienna, who succeeded the Italian "futurist" Busoni as director of the Berlin *Hochschule für Musik* and took up residence in the United States in 1933.

Two major phases may be distinguished in Schönberg's development as a composer. In the first he shows himself as a neo-romanticist and enthusiastic follower of Richard Wagner (cf. the choral work *Gurrelieder,* the string sextet *Verklärte Nacht,* and the *Chamber Symphony*). The works of this period, though rich in melodic invention and bold in their polyphonic structure, are lacking in logical coherence and give vent to an unrestrained emotionalism. The second phase is characterized by a fully developed expressionistic style which, indulging in daring cacophonic experiments and disregarding most of the traditional laws of harmony and melody, tends to make Schönberg's compositions purely abstract and therefore unintelligible to the uninitiated (the choral work *Friede auf Erden, Stefan George Lieder, Pierrot Lunaire Lieder, Serenade,* etc.). This type of

---

* Reger's compositions include orchestral works (*Hiller Variations, Mozart Variations,* Romantic Suite, four tone poems, two concerti, choral-orchestral pieces), chamber music (eleven sonatas, seventeen preludes and fugues, five string quartets, etc.), works for piano and organ, about 200 *Lieder,* and *a capella* choruses.

musical expressionism obviously parallels the development toward pure abstraction in literature, painting, and sculpture.

The latest works of Arnold Schönberg thus illustrate on the highest level the fact that contemporary German music, too, was eventually forced to yield to the tendencies inherent in the age of crisis and to mirror even in its most earnest and sincere representatives the progressive disintegration of those values which had constituted the spiritual and moral substance of the German and European past. The artist who is compelled to move as it were in an empty space, unaided by the vital and concrete forces of a *Volkskultur,* which alone could provide the proper frame for his creative work and the proper response to his artistic genius, finds himself isolated in an anonymous no man's land. The historian, on the other hand, who refuses to pose as a major or minor prophet of gloom or cheer, will voice the conviction expressed in Fritz von Unruh's latest novel, namely, that "The End is Not Yet," basing his optimism on that perpetual recuperative power of the human spirit which he finds amply documented in the pages of German history.

BIBLIOGRAPHY

Alexander, Edgar, *Adenauer and the New Germany* (New York: Farrar, Strauss & Cudahy, 1957).

Alker, Ernst, *Geschichte der deutschen Literatur von Goethes Tod bis zur Gegenwart* (Stuttgart: Cotta 1949-50), 2 vols.

Allers, Rudolf, *The New Psychologies* (New York: Sheed & Ward, 1933).

Allgemeine deutsche Biographie, ed. Freiherr Rochus von Liliencron, and others; Bayerische Akademie der Wissenschaften (Leipzig: Duncker und Humblot, 1875–1912), 56 vols.

Ancelet-Hustache, Jeanne, *Master Eckhart and the Rhineland Mystics*. Trans. by Hilda Graef (New York: Harper Torchbooks, 1957).

Andreas, W., *Deutschland vor der Reformation* (Stuttgart: Deutsche Verlagsanstalt, 5th ed. 1948).

Angelloz, J. F., *Rainer Maria Rilke: Leben und Werk*. Trans. by Alfred Kuoni (München: Nymphenburger Verlagshandlung, 1955).

Artz, Frederick B., *The Mind of the Middle Ages. An Historical Survey: AD 200-1500,* 3rd ed. (New York: Knopf, 1958).

Bab, Julius, *Das Theater der Gegenwart* (Leipzig: J. J. Weber, 1928).

Bahr, Hermann, *Expressionism,* trans. R. T. Gribble (London: Henderson, 1925).

Balthasar, Hans Urs von, *Karl Barth. Darstellung und Deutung seiner Theologie* (Köln: Jakob Hegner, 1951).

Barraclough, Geoffrey, *The Origins of Modern Germany* (Oxford: B. Blackwell, 1946).

―――― *Die kirchliche Dogmatik* (Zollikon-Zürich, Evangelischer Verlag, 1945-59), 4 double vols.

Barth, Karl, *Epistle to the Romans,* trans. Edwyn C. Hoskins (New York: Oxford University Press, 1933).

Bauhaus, 1919–1928, ed. Herbert Bayer, Walter Gropius, and Ise Gropius (New York: The Museum of Modern Art, 1938).

Bebel, F. August, *My Life,* trans. anon. (London: Allen & Unwin, 1912).

Becker, Otto, *Bismarcks Ringen um Deutschlands Gestaltung*. Herausgegeben und ergänzt von A. Scharff (Heidelberg: Quelle & Meyer, 1958).

Bekker, Paul, *Beethoven*. Trans. from the German by M. M. Bozman (New York: Dutton, 1932).

―――― Richard Wagner: *His Life in His Work*. Trans. by M. M. Bozman (New York: Norton, 1931).

Bethmann-Hollweg, Theobald von, *Reflections on the World War,* trans. G. Young (New York: Harper, 1920).

Bieber, H., *Der Kampf um die Tradition: Die deutsche Dichtung von 1830-1880*. (Stuttgart: J. B. Metzler, 1928).

Bielschowsky, Albert, *Life of Goethe,* trans. W. A. Cooper (New York: L. Putnam, 1905–1908), 4 vols.

Bismarck, Otto von, *Bismarck, the Man and the Statesman:* being the *Reflections and Reminiscences* written and dictated by himself, trans. A. J. Butler, Smith (London: Elder, 1889), 2 vols.

────── *The Kaiser vs. Bismarck,* suppressed letters by the Kaiser and new chapters from the autobiography of the Iron Chancellor (New York: Harper, 1921).

Bocheński, I. M., *Contemporary European Philosophy.* Trans. from the German by D. Nicholl and Karl Aschenbrenner (Berkeley and Los Angeles: University of California Press, 1956).

Boehme, Jakob, *Aurora,* trans. J. Barker and D. S. Hehner, Watkins (London, 1914).

Braig, Friedrich, *Heinrich von Kleist* (München: Beck, 1925).

Brandenburg, Erich, *From Bismarck to the World War: A History of German Foreign Policy, 1870-1914,* Trans. by A. E. Adams (London: Oxford University Press, 1933).

Braun, Otto, *Von Weimar zu Hitler* (Zürich and New York: Europa-Verlag, 1940).

Brecht, Arnold, *Prelude to Silence. The End of the German Republic* (New York: Oxford University Press, 1944).

Brock, Werner, *An Introduction to Contemporary German Philosophy* (Cambridge: University Press, 1935).

Brentano, Franz, *The Origin of the Knowledge of Right and Wrong,* trans. C. Hague (Westminster: Constable & Co., 1902).

Bruce, Maurice, *The Shaping of the Modern World.* Vol. I: *Ends and Beginnings; The World to 1914* (London: Hutchinson, 1958).

Bülow, Bernhard von, *Imperial Germany,* trans. Marie A. Lewenz (New York: Dodd, Mead, 1917).

────── *Memoirs,* trans. F. A. Voigt (New York: G. P. Putnam's Sons, 1935), 4 vols.

Burckhardt, Jacob, *The Civilization of the Period of the Renaissance in Italy,* trans. S. G. C. Middlemore (New York: Charles Scribner's Sons, 1878).

Butler, Dom Cuthbert, O.S.B., *Western Mysticism* (London: Constable & Co., 1927).

Cambridge Medieval History (New York: Macmillan, 1926–1936), 8 vols.

Cambridge Modern History. Planned by Lord Acton; edited by Sir A. W. Ward, Sir G. W. Prothero, and Sir Stanley Leathes (New York: Macmillan, 1911-34), 14 vols.

Cambridge Modern History, The New, (I): *The Renaissance.* Edited by G. R. Potter (New York: Cambridge University Press, 1957); (II): *The Reformation.* Edited by G. R Elton (New York: Cambridge University Press, 1958). (VII): *The Old Regime* (1713-63). Edited by J. O. Lindsay (New York: Cambridge University Press, 1959).

Carlyle, R. W., and A. J., *History of Mediaeval Political Theory in the West* (New York: G. P. Putnam's Sons, 1916), 6 vols.

Carsten, F. L., *Princes and Parliaments in Germany from the Fifteenth to the Eighteenth Century* (New York: Oxford University Press, 1959).

Chamberlain, Houston Stewart, *The Foundations of the Nineteenth Century,* trans. J. Lees (New York: Lane, 1912).

Clark, James M., *The Great German Mystics, Eckhart, Tauler and Suso* (Oxford: 1949).

Clark, R. T., *The Fall of the German Republic* (London: Allen & Unwin, 1935).

Clausewitz, Karl von, *On War,* trans. O. J. Matthijs Jolles (New York: Random House, 1943).

Collins, James, *History of Modern European Philosophy* (Milwaukee: Bruce, 1954).

Comte, Auguste, *Cours de philosophie positive* (Paris, 1830–1842), 6 vols.

Conant, James B., *Germany and Freedom: A Personal Appraisal* (Cambridge, Mass.: Harvard University Press, 1958).

Coudenhove-Calergi, R., *Pan-Europe,* Introd. by N. M. Butler (New York: Alfred A. Knopf, 1926).

Craig, Gordon A., *From Bismarck to Adenauer: Aspects of German Statecraft* (Baltimore, Md.: Johns Hopkins Press, 1958).

Creizenach, W., *Geschichte des neueren Dramas* (Halle A. S.: M. Niemeyer, 1918-23, 2nd ed.), 3 vols.

Czernin, Graf von, *In the World War,* trans. anon. (New York: Harper, 1920).

Daniels, Dom Augustinus, *Eine lateinische Rechtfertigungsschrift des Meister Eckhart* (Münster: Aschendorff, 1923).

Dante, Alighieri, *The Latin Works of Dante,* trans. A. G. Ferrers Howell and Philip H. Wicksteed (London: J. M. Dent, 1904).

Dawson, Christopher, *The Age of the Gods* (London and New York: Sheed & Ward, 1933).

——— *The Judgment of the Nations* (New York: Sheed & Ward, 1942).

——— *The Making of Europe* (New York: Sheed & Ward, 1934).

Dawson, William H., *The Evolution of Modern Germany* (New York: Scribner's Sons, 1908).

——— *The German Empire, 1867-1914, and the Unity Movement* (New York: Macmillan, 1919).

——— *Germany under the Treaty* (London: Allen & Unwin, 1933).

——— *A History of Germany* (London: E. Benn, 1928).

Dehio, Georg, *Geschichte der deutschen Kunst* (Berlin: W. de Gruyter, 1930-32), 8 vols.

——— *Handbuch der deutschen Kunstdenkmäler.* New edition by Ernst Gall (Berlin: Deutscher Kunstverlag, 1935 sqq.),

Dehio, Ludwig, *Germany and World Politics in the Twentieth Century* (New York: Knopf, 1959).

Delatte, Dom Paul, O.S.B., *The Rule of St. Benedict,* trans. Dom Justin McCann, O.S.B. (London: Burns, Oates & Washbourne, 1921).

De Maistre, Joseph, *Essai sur le principe générateur des constitutions politiques* (Paris, 1810), Vol. I, Oeuvres complètes.

——— *Les Soirées de St. Petersburg, ou Entretiens sur le gouvernement temporal de la Providence* (Paris, 1821), Vols. IV and V, Oeuvres complètes.

Denifle, H., O.P., *Luther and Lutherdom,* trans. R. Volz (New York: Holy Name Society, 1917).

Denzinger, Heinrich, and Bannwart, Clemens, S.J., *Enchiridion symbolorum, definitionum et declarationum de rebus fidei et morum* (Freiburg: Herder, 1922).

Diebold, Bernhard, *Anarchie im Drama* (Frankfurt a.M.: Frankfurter Verlagsanstalt, 3rd ed., 1925).

Diesel, Eugen, *Germany and the Germans,* trans. W. D. Robson-Scott (New York: Macmillan, 1931).

Dilthey, Wilhelm, *Das Erlebnis und die Dichtung* (Berlin and Leipzig: Teubner, 10th ed., 1929).

—— *The Essence of Philosophy.* Trans. from the German by S. A. Emery and Wm. T. Emery (Chapel Hill: University of North Carolina Press, 1954).

—— *Gesammelte Schriften* (Leipzig: Teubner, 1914-1958), 12 vols.

Dobert, Eitel Wolf, *Deutsche Demokraten in Amerika. Die Achtundvierziger und ihre Schriften* (Göttingen: Vandenhoeck·& Ruprecht, 1958).

Driesch, Hans, *Man and the Universe,* trans. W. H. Johnston (London: R. R. Smith, 1930).

—— *The Science and Philosophy of the Organism* (London: A. & C. Black, 1929).

Droz, Jacques, *Les Révolutions allemandes de 1848* (Paris: Presses Universitaires de France, 1957).

Dürer, Albrecht, *Records of Journeys to Venice and the Low Countries,* trans. R. Tumbo, Jr. (Boston: Merrymount, 1913).

Ehrenberg, R., *Capital and Finance in the Age of the Renaissance:* a Study of the Fuggers and Their Connections, trans. H. M. Lucas (New York: Harcourt, Brace, 1928).

Ehrismann, Gustav, *Geschichte der deutschen Literatur bis zum Ausgang des Mittelalters* (München: Beck, 1918, 1922, 1935), 3 vols.

Einhard (Eginhardus, Abbot of Seligenstadt), *Life of Charlemagne,* in *Early Lives of Charlemagne,* trans. A. J. Grant (New York: Oxford University Press, 1922).

Eloesser, Arthur, *Modern German Literature,* trans. C. A. Phillips (New York: Alfred A. Knopf, 1933).

Engel, Gabriel, *Gustav Mahler* (New York: The Bruckner Society of America, 1932).

Engels, Friedrich, *Ludwig Feuerbach and the Roots of the Socialist Philosophy,* trans. Austin Lewis (Chicago: Kerr, 1903).

—— *The Peasant War in Germany,* trans. M. J. Olgin (New York: International Publishers, 1935).

—— *Principles of Communism,* original draft of the Communist Manifesto, trans. Max Bedacht (New York: Daily Worker, 1925).

Epstein, Klaus, *Matthias Erzberger and the Dilemma of German Democracy* (Princeton, N. J.: Princeton University Press, 1959).

Erzberger, Matthias, *The League of Nations: The Way to the World's Peace,* trans. B. Miall (New York: Hodder, 1919).

Euler, Heinrich, *Die Aussenpolitik der Weimarer Republik* (Aschaffenburg: P. Pattloch, 1957).

Eyck, Erich, *Bismarck and the German Empire* (London: Allen & Unwin, 1950).

—— *Geschichte der Weimarer Republik* (Erlenbach-Zürich, 1954-56), 2 vols.

Fabre-Luce, A., *Locarno: The Reality,* trans. Constance Vesey (New York: Alfred A. Knopf, 1928).

Falk, Minna R., *History of Germany from the Reformation to the Present Day* (New York: Philosophical Library, 1957).

Feuerbach, Ludwig, *The Essence of Christianity,* trans. Marian Evans (London: Chapman, 1854).

Fichte, Johann Gottlieb, *The Way Towards the Blessed Life,* trans. W. Smith (London: Chapman, 1844).

—— *Addresses to the German Nation,* trans. R. F. Jones and G. H. Turnbull (Chicago: Open Court, 1922).

—— *The Science of Knowledge,* trans. A. E. Kröger (Philadelphia: Lippincott, 1868).

—— *The Vocation of Man,* trans. W. Smith (Chicago: Open Court, 1931).

Fife, Robert H., *The Revolt of Martin Luther* (New York: Columbia University Press, 1957).

Fischer-Galati, Stepgen A., *Ottoman Imperialism and German Protestantism,* 1521-1555 (Cambridge, Mass.: Harvard University Press, 1959).

Flenley, Ralph, *Modern German History.* With 2 additional chapters on the War of 1939-45 and the Post-War Years (London: Dent, 1959).

Foerster, Friedrich Wilhelm, *Europe and the German Question* (New York: Sheed & Ward, 1940).

Foerster-Nietzsche, Elisabeth, *The Life of Nietzsche,* trans. A. M. Ludovici (New York: Sturgis, 1912–1915).

—— *The Lonely Nietzsche,* trans. P. V. Cohn (London: Heinemann, 1915).

—— *The Young Nietzsche,* trans. A. M. Ludovici (London: Heinemann, 1912).

Franz, G., *Der deutsche Bauernkrieg* (München & Berlin: R. Oldenbourg, 4th ed., 1956), 2 vols.

Freud, Sigmund, *The Ego and the Id,* trans. Joan Riviere (London: Woolf, 1927).

—— *General Introduction to Psychoanalysis,* trans. anon. (New York: Boni & Liveright, 1920).

Freytag, Gustav, *Pictures of German Life,* trans. Mrs. Malcolm (London: Chapman, 1862, 1863), 4 vols.

Friedensburg, F., *Die Weimarer Republik* (Hannover: Norddeutsche Verlagsanstalt O. Goedel, 1957 [new edition]).

Froebel, F. W. A., *Chief Writings on Education,* trans. S. S. F. Fletcher and J. Welton (New York: Longmans, Green, 1932).

Fülöp-Miller, René, *Power and Secret of the Jesuits,* trans. F. S. Flint and D. F. Tait (New York: G. P. Putnam's Sons, 1930).

Gasquet, F. A., Cardinal, *The Rule of St. Benedict* (London: Chatto & Windus, 1925).

—— *Monastic Life in the Middle Ages* (London: G. Bell & Sons, 1922).

Gebhardt, B., *Handbuch der deutschen Geschichte.* 8th edition by H. Grundmann (Stuttgart: Union Verlag, 1958-59), vols. 1, 2, 4.

Germany. A Companion to German Studies. Edited by Jethro Bithell (London: Methuen, 5th revised ed., 1955).

German White Book Concerning the Responsibilities of the Authors of the War, trans. Carnegie Endowment (New York: Oxford University Press, 1924).

Germany, the Federal Constitution of, April 16, trans. Edmund J. James (Philadelphia: University of Pennsylvania, Series in Economy and Public Law, No. VII, 1899).

——— *Preliminary History of the Armistice,* official documents published by the German National Chancellery, trans. Carnegie Endowment (New York: Oxford University Press, 1924).

Giedion, S., *Walter Gropius* (New York: Reinhold Publishing Corporation, 1954).

Gierke, Otto von, *Natural Law and the Theory of Society,* trans. Ernest Barker (New York: Macmillan, 1934).

Gilson, Etienne, *Reason and Revelation in the Middle Ages* (New York: Charles Scribner's Sons, 1938).

——— *The Spirit of Mediaeval Philosophy,* trans. A. H. C. Downes (New York: Sheed & Ward, 1936).

——— *The Unity of Philosophical Experience* (New York: Charles Scribner's Sons, 1937).

Gilson, Etienne, *Christian Philosophy in the Middle Ages* (New York: Random House, 1955).

Goethe, Johann Wolfgang von, *Works,* Weimar ed., ed. N. H. Dole (Boston: Nicolls, 1915), 14 vols.

——— *Conversations of J. P. Eckermann With Goethe,* trans. S. M. Fuller (Boston: Hilliard, Gray, 1852).

Goetz, W., *Translatio Imperii: Ein Beitrag zur Geschichte des Geschichtsdenkens und der politischen Theorien im Mittelalter* (Tübingen: J. C. B. Mohr, 1958).

Göhring, Martin, *Bismarcks Erben 1890-1945. Deutschlands Weg von Wilhelm II. bis Adolf Hitler* (Wiebaden: Franz Steiner, 1958), 2nd ed. 1959.

Golay, John Ford, *The Founding of the Federal Republic of Germany* (Chicago: University of Chicago Press, 1958).

Gooch, George P., *Studies in Modern History* (New York: Longmans, Green, 1931).

——— *Germany* (New York: Charles Scribner's Sons, 1925).

Gordon, Harold J., *The Reichswehr and the German Republic, 1914-26* (Princeton, N. J.: Princeton University Press, 1957).

Grabmann, Martin, *Introduction to the Theological Summa of St. Thomas Aquinas,* trans. J. S. Zybura (St. Louis: Herder, 1930).

———*Die Kulturwerte der deutschen Mystik des Mittelalters* (Augsburg: Benno Filser, 1923).

——— *Thomas Aquinas, His Personality and Thought,* trans. Virgil Michel (New York: Longmans, Green, 1928).

Gregorovius, F., *History of the City of Rome in the Middle Ages,* trans. Annie Hamilton (London: G. Bell & Sons, 1894–1902).

Gregory of Tours, *History of the Franks,* trans. O. Dalton (London: Clarendon Press); selections, trans. Ernest Brehaut (New York: Columbia University Press, 1916).

Grimmelshausen, H. J. C., *The Adventurous Simplicissimus,* trans. A. T. S. Goodrick (New York: Dutton, 1924).

Grisar, Hartmann, S.J., *Luther,* trans. E. M. Lamond (St. Louis: Herder, 1913–1917).

——— *Martin Luther, His Life and Work,* ed. Arthur Preuss (St. Louis: Herder, 1935).

Gropius, Walter, *The New Architecture and the Bauhaus,* trans. P. M. Shand (New York: Museum of Modern Art, 1937).

Haeckel, Ernst, *The Riddle of the Universe,* summarized by Vance Randolph (New York: Vanguard Press, 1926).

Haecker, Theodor, *Virgil, Father of the West,* trans. A. W. Wheen (New York: Sheed & Ward, 1934).

Haller, Johannes, *Epochs of German History,* trans. E. W. Dickes (New York: Harcourt, Brace, 1930).

—— *France and Germany, the History of 1000 Years,* trans. Dora von Beseler (London: Constable & Co., 1932).

Hamann, Richard, *Die deutsche Malerei im 19. Jahrhundert* (Leipzig and Berlin: B. G. Teubner, 1914).

—— *Geschichte der Kunst von der altchristlichen Zeit bis zur Gegenwart* (Berlin: T. Knaur, 1933).

—— *Der Impressionismus in Leben und Kunst* (Marburg: Verlag des Kunstwissenschaftlichen Seminars, 1923).

—— *Kunst und Kultur der Gegenwart* (Giessen: Münchowsche Verlagsbuchhandlung, 1922).

Hamerow, Theodore J., *Restoration, Revolution, Reaction: Economics and Politics in Germany, 1815-1871* (Princeton, N. J.: Princeton University Press, 1958).

Hartmann, Eduard von, *The Philosophy of the Unconscious,* trans. C. Coupland (London: Trübner, 1893).

Hartmann, Nicolai, *Ethics,* trans. Stanton Coit (New York: Macmillan, 1932), 3 vols.

Hartung, F., *Deutsche Geschichte im Zeitalter der Reformation, der Gegenreformation und des dreissigjährigen Krieges* (Berlin: W. de Gruyter, 1951).

Hauptmann, Gerhart, *The Dramatic Works,* ed. Ludwig Lewisohn (New York: Viking Press, 1912–1929), 9 vols.

Hauser, Oswald, *Deutschland und der Englisch-Russische Gegensatz,* (1900-1914). (Göttingen: Musterschmidt Verlag, 1958).

Hayes, Carlton J. H., *A Political and Cultural History of Modern Europe* (New York: Macmillan, 1932–1938).

Haym, Rudolf, *Die romantische Schule* (Berlin: Weidmannsche Buchhandlung, 5th ed., 1928).

Hegel, G. W. F., *Early Theological Writings.* Trans. by T. M. Knox (Chicago: University of Chicago Press, (1948).

—— *Encyclopedia of Philosophy.* Trans. and annotated by Gustav E. Mueller (New York: Philosophical Library, 1959).

—— *Phenomenology of Mind,* trans. J. B. Baillie (New York: Macmillan, 1931).

—— *The Philosophy of History.* Trans. by J. Sibree; Introduction by C. J. Friedrich (New York: Dover Publications, 1956).

Hegemann, Werner, *Frederick the Great,* trans. Winifred Ray (New York: Alfred A. Knopf, 1929).

Heidegger, Martin, *Holzwege* (Frankfurt a.M.: V. Klostermann, 1952).

—— *An Introduction to Metaphysics.* Trans. by Ralph Manheim (New Haven: Yale University Press, 1959).

—— *Sein und Zeit* (Tübingen: M. Niemeyer, 8th ed., 1957).

Heiden, Konrad, *A History of National Socialism* (New York: Knopf, 1935).

Heine, Heinrich, *Works,* trans. G. Leland (London: Heinemann, 1891–1905), 12 vols.

Henderson, W. O., *The State and the Industrial Revolution in Prussia, 1740-1870* (Liverpool: University Press, 1958).
—— *The Zollverein* (London: F. Cass & Co., 1939), 2nd ed., 1959.
Hettner, Hermann, *Geschichte der deutschen Literatur im 18. Jahrhundert.* Edited by G. Witkowski (Leipzig: P. List, 1929).
Hildebrand, Adolf von, *The Problem of Form in Painting and Sculpture,* trans. Max F. Meyer, and R. M. Ogden (New York: Stechert, 1932).
Hindenburg, Gert von, *Hindenburg, 1847-1934; Soldier and Statesman,* trans. Gerald Griffin (London: Hutchinson, 1933).
Hindenburg, Paul von, *Out of My Life,* trans. A. Holt (New York: Cassell, 1933).
Hodges, Herbert A., *The Philosophy of Wilhelm Dilthey* (London: Routledge & K. Paul, 1952).
Hofer, Walter, *Geschichte zwischen Philosophie und Politik* (Basel: Verlag für Recht und Gesellschaft, 1956).
Hohenlohe-Schillingsfürst, Fürst zu, *Memoirs,* ed. F. Curtius (New York: Macmillan, 1906), 2 vols.
Holborn, Hajo, *A History of Modern Germany: The Reformation* (New York: Alfred A. Knopf, 1959), vol. I.
Holthusen, H. E., *Rainer Maria Rilke.* Trans. by J. P. Stern (New Haven: Yale University Press, 1952).
Holtzmann, Walther, *Beiträge zur Reichs- und Papstgeschichte des Hohen Mittelalters: Ausgewählte Aufsätze* (Bonn: Röhrscheid Verlag, 1957).
Hrotsvitha of Gandersheim, *The Plays of Roswitha,* trans. Cyph. St. John, i.e., Christabel Marshall; with introd. by Cardinal Gasquet (London: Chatto and Windus, 1923).
Huch, Ricarda, *Der dreissigjährige Krieg* (Wiesbaden: Insel Verlag, new ed., 1957), 3 vols.
Huizinga, J., *The Waning of the Middle Ages* (London: E. Arnold & Co., 1924).
—— *Erasmus* (New York: Charles Scribner's Sons, 1924).
Humboldt, Alexander von, *Works* (New York: Appleton, n.d.), 9 vols.
Humboldt, Wilhelm von, *The Sphere and Duties of Government,* trans. J. Coulthard, Jr. (London: Chapman, 1844).
Jacobsen, Hans-Adolf, *1939-1945, Der zweite Weltkrieg in Chronik und Dokumenten* (Darmstadt: Wehr und Wissen Verlagsgesellschaft, 1960).
Janssen, Johannes, *History of the German People at the Close of the Middle Ages,* trans. M. A. Mitchell and A. M. Christie (St. Louis: Herder, 1925), 17 vols.
Jarrett, Bede, O.S.B., . *Social Theories of the Middle Ages* (London: E. Benn, 1926).
Jaspers, Karl, *The Idea of the University.* Edited by K. W. Deutsch. Trans. by H. A. T. Reiche & H. F. Vanderschmidt (Boston: Beacon Press, 1959).
—— *Man in the Modern Age,* trans. Eden and Cedar Paul (New York: Holt, 1933).
—— *Nietzsche: Einführung in das Verständnis seiner Philosophie* (Berlin & Leipzig: W. de Gruyter, 1936).
—— *The Question of German Guilt.* Trans. by E. B. Ashton (New York: Dial Press, 1947).

Jones, W. Tudor, *Contemporary Thought of Germany* (London: William Norgate, 1930, 1931), 2 vols.

Kahn, Robert A., *The Habsburg Empire:* A Study in Integration and Disintegration (New York: Frederick A. Praeger, 1957).

Kant, Immanuel, *Critique of Aesthetic Judgment,* trans. J. H. Bernard (New York: Macmillan, 1914).

—— *Critique of Practical Reason.* Trans. by Lewis White Beck (New York: The Liberal Arts Press, 1959).

—— *The Critique of Pure Reason,* trans. Max Müller (New York: Macmillan, 1907).

—— *The King's Two Bodies: A Study in Mediaeval Political Theology* (Princeton, N. J.: Princeton University Press, 1957).

—— *Perpetual Peace,* trans. Helen O'Brien (London: Sweet & Maxwell, 1927).

Kantorowicz, Ernst, *Frederick II, 1194-1250,* trans. E. O. Lorimer (London: Constable & Co., 1931).

Karrer, Otto, *Meister Eckehart. Das System seiner religiösen Lehre und Lebensweisheit.* Textbuch aus den gedruckten und ungedruckten Quellen (München: Verlag Josef Müller, 1926).

Kessler, Harry Graf von, *Walter Rathenau, His Life and Work,* trans. W. D. Robson-Scott and Lawrence Hyde (New York: Harcourt, Brace, 1930).

Ketteler, Wilhelm Emmanuel, Freiherr von, Bischof, *Schriften,* ed. Johannes Mumbauer (München: J. Kösel and F. Pustet, 1924), 3 vols.

Kierkegaard, Sören, *Christian Discourses,* trans. Walter Lowrie (New York: Oxford University Press, 1939).

—— *The Concept of Dread.* Trans. by Walter Lowrie (Princeton: Princeton University Press, 1944).

—— *Either/Or: A Fragment of Life.* Trans. by David F. Swenson. Lillian M. Swenson, and Walter Lowrie (Princeton: Princeton University Press, 1944).

—— *Fear and Trembling,* trans. Robert Payne (New York: Oxford University Press, 1939).

—— *The Journals,* trans. Alexander Dru (New York: Oxford University Press, 1938).

—— *Papirer* (Copenhagen: Nordiskforlag, 1909-34), 18 vols.

—— *The Present Age,* trans. Alexander Dru and Walter Lowrie (New York: Oxford University Press, 1940).

—— *The Journals of S. K.* (New York: Oxford University Press, 1938).

—— *Samlede Vaerker* (Copenhagen: F. Hegel & Son, 1901-06), 14 vols.

—— *Stages on Life's Way,* trans. Walter Lowrie (Princeton: Princeton University Press, 1940).

—— *Training in Christianity.* Trans. by Walter Lowrie (Princeton University Press, 1944).

Klemperer, Klemens von, *Germany's New Conservatism: Its History and Dilemma in the Twentieth Century* (Princeton, N. J.: Princeton University Press, 1957).

Kogon, E., *Der S. S. Staat* (München: Karl Alber, 1946).

Kohn, Hans, *The Mind of Germany* (New York: Charles Scribner's Sons, 1960).

Körner, Joseph, *Bibliographisches Handbuch des deutschen Schrifttums* (Bern: A. Francke, 3rd ed., 1949).

Kosch, Wilhelm, *Deutsches Literaturlexikon* (Bern: A. Francke, 2nd ed., 1947-58), 3 vols.

Lamprecht, Karl, *Deutsche Geschichte* (Berlin R. Gaertner, 1902-09), 12 vols.

Lange, Victor, *Modern German Literature, 1870-1940* (New York: Ithaca, N. Y.: Cornell University Press, 1945).

Leibniz, G. W., *Monadology and Other Philosophical Writings,* trans. R. Latta (Oxford: Clarendon, 1898).

———— *Philosophic Writings,* sel. and trans. M. Morris (New York: Dutton, 1934).

Leo XIII, Great Encyclical Letters of (New York: Benziger Bros., 1903).

Lessing, Gotthold Ephraim, *Laocoön,* trans. Sir Robert J. Phillimore (New York: Dutton, 1905).

Loewenstein, Prince Hubertus zu, *The Germans in History* (New York: Columbia University Press, 1945).

———— *The Tragedy of a Nation: Germany 1918–1934* (New York: Macmillan, 1934).

Lortz, Joseph, *Die Reformation in Deutschland* (Freiburg i.B., Herder, 1949), 2 vols.

Lowrie, Walter, *A Short Life of Kierkegaard* (Princeton: Princeton University Press, 1942).

Luther, Martin, *Works,* ed. Eyster Jacobs (Philadelphia: United Lutheran Publishers, 1915–1932), 6 vols.

———— *Werke; kritische Gesamtausgabe,* ed. J. K. F. Knaake, G. Kawerau, E. Thiele, and others (Weimar: Hermann Böhlau, 1883 sqq.).

Lutz, Ralph H., *The German Revolution of 1918–1919* (Stanford University, Calif.: Stanford University Press, 1922).

———— *The Fall of the German Empire, 1914–1918* (Stanford University, Calif.: Stanford University Press, 1932).

Malleus maleficarum, ed. Jacob Sprenger, trans. Rev. Montague Summers (London: John Rodker, 1928).

Mann, Golo, *Deutsche Geschichte des 19. und 20. Jahrhunderts* (Frankfurt: S. Fischer, 1958).

Manschreck, Clyde L., *Melanchthon: The Quiet Reformer* (Nashville, Tenn.: Alingdon Press, 1858).

Marx, Karl, *Capital, the Communist Manifesto, and Other Writings,* ed. Max Eastman (Modern Library, 1932).

Mau, H. and Krausnick, H., *German History, 1933-1945: An Assessment by German Historians.* Trans. from the German by A. and E. Wilson (London: O. Wolff, 1959).

Max, Prince of Baden, *Memoirs,* trans. W. M. Calder and C. W. H. Sutton (London: Scribner; Constable, 1928).

Meinecke, Friedrich, *Die Entstehung des Historismus.* Edited by Carl Hinrichs (München: R. Oldenbourg, 1959).

———— *The German Catastrophe: Reflections and Recollections* (Cambridge: Harvard University Press, 1950).

Meissner, Hans Otto, and Wilde, Harry, *Die Machtergreifung. Ein Bericht über die Technik des nationalsozialistischen Staatsstreichs* (Stuttgart: Cotta, 1958).

Meister Eckhart, *Die deutschen und lateinischen Werke* (Stuttgart: Deutsche Forschungsgemeinschaft, 1936 sqq.).

———— *Selected Treatises and Sermons*. Trans. from Latin and German by James M. Clark and John V. Skinner (London: Faber & Faber, 1958).

Merker, Paul and Stammler, Wolfgang, *Reallexikon der deutschen Literaturge-schichte* (Berlin: W. de Gruyter, 1925-31), 4 vols.

Metternich, Fürst von, *Memoirs*, trans. Gerard W. Smith (New York: Harper, 1881), 5 vols.

Migne, Jacques-Paul, *Patrologiae cursus completus*, a chronological collection of the works of all fathers, doctors, and authors of the Church (Paris, 1844–1880), 382 vols.

Mirbt, Carl, *Quellen zur Geschichte des Papsttums und des römischen Katho-lizismus* (Tübingen: J. C. B. Mohr, 1924).

Moltke, Helmuth von, *Essays, Speeches, and Memoirs* (New York: Harper, 1893), 2 vols.

Moltmann, Günter, *Amerikas Deutschlandpolitik im zweiten Weltkrieg. Kriegs-und Friedensziele 1941-1945* (Heidelberg: Carl Winter, 1958).

Mommsen, W., *Geschichte des Abendlandes von der französischen Revolution bis zur Gegenwart* (München: F. Bruckmann, 1951).

Montalembert, Comte de, *The Monks of the West* (London: John C. Nimmo, 1896), 6 vols.

Monumenta Germaniae Historica, founded by Reichsfreiherr Karl vom Stein, ed. Georg Heinrich Pertz and others; *Scriptores* (SS) *rerum Germanicarum in usum scholarum* (German translation, sel., *Geschichtsschreiber der deuts-chen Vorzeit,* 1884–1928, 96 vols.).

Mosse, L. E., *The European Powers and the German Question* (1848-71), *with Special Reference to England and Russia* (New York: Cambridge University Press, 1958).

Muschg, Walter, *Die Zerstörung der deutschen Literatur* (Bern: A. Francke, 3rd ed., 1956).

Nadler, Josef, *Literaturgeschichte der deutschen Stämme und Landschaften* (Regensburg: J. Habbel, 4th ed., 1938-41).

Nadler, Joseph, *Literaturgeschichte Österreichs* (Salzburg: O. Müller,. 2nd ed., 1951).

Newlin, Dika, *Bruckner, Mahler, Schönberg* (New York: King's Crown Press, 1947).

Nichols, Alden J., *Germany after Bismarck: The Caprivi Era, 1890-1894* (Cam-bridge, Mass.: Harvard University Press, 1958).

Nicholas of Cusa, *Opera omnia,* ed. Ernsa Hoffmann and others (Leipzig: Felix Meiner, 1932 sqq.).

Nietzsche, Friedrich Wilhelm, *Complete Works,* ed. O. Levy (New York: Macmillan, 1925), 18 vols.

Olden, Rudolf, *Stresemann,* trans. R. T. Clark (New York: Dutton, 1930).

Olivero, F., *Rainer Maria Rilke. A Study in Poetry and Mysticism* (Cambridge, Eng.: W. Heffer & Sons, 1931).

Otto, Bishop of Freising, *The Two Cities: a Chronicle of Universal History to the Year 1146 A.D.,* trans. C. C. Mierow (New York: Oxford University Press, 1928).

Pastor, L. F. August, Freiherr von, *The History of the Popes From the Close of the Middle Ages,* trans. F. I. Antrobus, R. F. Kerr, and Dom Ernest Graf (London: K. Paul, Trench and Trübner, 1906–1941), 24 vols.

Paulsen, Friedrich, *The German Universities and University Study,* trans. F. Thilly and W. Elwang (New York: Charles Scribner's Sons, 1906).

Pinder, Wilhelm, *Vom Wesen und Werden deutscher Formen.* Vol. I: *Holbein d.J. und das Ende der altdeutschen Kunst.* Vol. II: *Die deutsche Kunst der Dürerzeit* (Text). Vol. III: *Die deutsche Kunst der Dürerzeit (Bildband).* (Frankfurt: H. F. Menck, 1951-57).

Pinson, K. S., *Modern Germany, Its History and Civilization* (New York: Macmillan, 1955).

Pius XI, Sixteen Encyclicals of His Holiness, 1926–1937 (Washington: National Catholic Welfare Conference, 1937).

Planck, Max, *The Universe in the Light of Modern Physics,* trans. W. H. Johnston (London: Allen & Unwin, 1931).

Ploetz, Karl, *Epitome of Ancient, Mediaeval, and Modern History,* trans. H. Tillinghast (New York: Houghton Mifflin Co., 1925).

Pollock, James Kerr, *Germany in Power and Eclipse: The Background of German Development* (New York: Van Nostrand, 1952).

Propyläen-Kunstgeschichte (Berlin: Propyläen-Verlag, 1925-39), 10 vols.

Propyläen-Weltgeschichte. Edited by W. Goetz (Berlin: Propyläen-Verlag, 1930-33), 10 vols.

Propyläen-Weltgeschichte, Neue. Edited by Golo Mann (Berlin: Propyläen-Verlag, 1960-   ), planned in 10 vols.

Przywara, Erich, S.J., *An Augustine Synthesis* (London: Sheed & Ward, 1936).

Pufendorf, Samuel Freiherr von, *De jure naturae et gentium,* trans. C. H. and W. A. Oldfather (New York: Oxford University Press, 1934).

—— *De officio hominis et civis juxta legem naturalem,* trans. F. G. Moore (New York: Oxford University Press, 1927).

Quint, Josef, *Meister Eckehart: Deutsche Predigten und Traktate* (München: Carl Hanser, 1955).

Ranke, Leopold von, *History of the Reformation in Germany,* ed. R. A. Johnson (New York: Dutton, 1905).

—— *History of the Popes,* trans. E. Fowler (New York: Colonial Press, 1901), 3 vols.

Rassow, Peter (Ed.), *Deutsche Geschichte im Überblick* (Stuttgart: J. B. Metzler, 1953).

Ritter, Gerhard, *Stein: Eine politische Biographie* (Stuttgart: Deutsche Verlagsanstalt, 3rd ed., 1958).

—— *Friedrich der Grosse* (Heidelberg: Quelle & Meyer, 3rd ed., 1954).

—— *The German Resistance: Carl Goerdeler's Struggle Against Tyranny.* Trans. by R. T. Clark (New York: Praeger, 1959).

—— *Die Neugestaltung Europas im 16. Jahrhundert* (Berlin: Verlag des Druckhauses Tempelhof, new ed., 1950).

Robertson, John G., *A History of German Literature* (Edinburgh: W. Blackwood, 3rd ed., 1959).

—— *Life and Work of Goethe* (London: G. Routledge & Sons, 1932).

Rosenberg, Arthur, *A History of the German Republic.* Trans. by I. F. D. Morrow & Marie Sieveking (London: Methuen, 1936).

Sauvigny, Bertier de, *Metternich et son temps* (Paris: Hachette, 1959).

Schacht, Hjalmar, *The Stabilization of the Mark,* trans. Ralph Butler (London: Allen & Unwin, 1927).

——— *The End of Reparations: The Economic Consequences of the World War,* ed. G. Glasgow (London: Cape, 1931).

Scheidemann, Philipp, *The Making of the New Germany: Memoirs,* trans. J. E. Michell (New York: Appleton, 1929).

Schiller, Friedrich von, *Works,* ed. N. H. Dole (Boston: Niccolls, 1915), 10 vols.

Schnabel, Franz, *Deutsche Geschichte im neunzehnten Jahrhundert* (Freiburg im Br.: Herder, 1929 sqq.), 4 vols.

Schnürer, Gustav, *Kirche und Kultur im Mittelalter* (Paderborn: Ferdinand Schöningh, n.d.).

——— *Katholische Kirche und Kultur in der Barockzeit* (Paderborn: Ferdinand Schöningh, 1937).

——— *Die Anfänge der abendländischen Völkergemeinschaft* (Freiburg: Herder, 1932).

Schopenhauer, Arthur, *The World as Will and Idea,* trans. R. B. Haldane and J. Kemp (London: Trübner, 1896), 3 vols.

Schweitzer, Albert, *Johann Sebastian Bach,* trans. E. Newman (New York: Breitkopf & Haertel, 1911), 2 vols.

Soergel, Albert, *Dichtung und Dichter der Zeit* (Leipzig: R. Voightländer, 6th ed., 1922).—Neue Folge: *Im Banne des Expressionismus* (Leipzig: R. Voightländer, 1925).

Spengler, Oswald, *The Decline of the West,* trans. F. Atkinson (New York: Alfred A. Knopf, 1934).

——— *The Hour of Decision,* trans. F. Atkinson (New York: Alfred A. Knopf, 1934).

——— *Man and Technics,* trans. F. Atkinson (New York: Alfred A. Knopf, 1932).

Spitta, Julius, *Johann Sebastian Bach,* trans. C. Bell and J. A. F. Maitland (New York: Novello, 1899), 3 vols.

Srbik, Heinrich von, *Aus Österreichs Vergangenheit, von Prinz Eugen zu Franz Joseph* (Salzburg: O. Müller, 1949).

——— *Geist und Geschichte vom deutschen Humanismus bis zur Gegenwart* (München: F. Bruckmann, 1950-51).

——— *Metternich, der Staatsmann und der Mensch* (München: F. Bruckmann, 1954), 3 vols.

Stahl, Ernst Ludwig, *Heinrich von Kleist's Dramas* (Oxford: B. Blackwell, 1948).

Stammler, Wolfgang, *Deutsche Literatur vom Naturalismus bis zur Gegenwart* (Breslau: F. Hirt, 2nd ed., 1927).

——— *Von der Mystik zum Barock* (Stuttgart: J. B. Metzler, 2nd ed., 1950).

Stegemann, Hermann, *The Mirage of Versailles,* trans. R. T. Clark (New York: Alfred A. Knopf, 1928).

——— *The Struggle for the Rhine,* trans. G. Chatterton-Hill (London: Allen, 1928).

Steiner, Rudolf, *The Philosophy of Freedom,* trans. A. Hoernlé (New York: G. P. Putnam's Sons, 1916).

——— *An Outline of Occult Science,* trans. Max Gysi (New York: Rand, McNally, 1914).

Steinhausen, Georg, *Deutsche Geistes-und Kulturgeschichte von 1870 bis zur Gegenwart* (Halle: Max Niemeyer, 1931).

——— *Geschichte der deutschen Kultur.* Neu bearbeitet und erweitert von Dr. Eugen Diesel (Bibliographisches Institut: Leipzig, 1936), 2 vols.

Stresemann, Gustav, *Essays and Speeches,* Pref. Sir Austen Chamberlain; trans. Chr. R. Turner (London: Butterworth, 1930).

——— *Diaries, Letters, and Papers,* trans. Eric Sutton (New York: Macmillan, 1935).

Strich, Fritz, *Goethe and World Literature* (New York: Hafner, 1949).

Stutz, Ernst, *Oswald Spengler als politischer Denker* (Bern: Francke Verlag, 1958).

Suso, Henry, *Little Book of Eternal Wisdom* and *Little Book of Truth.* Trans. with Introduction and Notes by James M. Clark (London: Faber & Faber, 1953).

Sybel, Heinrich von, *The Foundation of the German Empire by William I,* trans. Marshall Livingston Perrin and others (New York: T. Y. Crowell, 1890–1898), 7 vols.

Tacitus, *The Germania,* trans. Arthur Murphy (New York, 1909, in *The Classics,* pp. 354–424).

Taut, Bruno, *Modern Architecture* (London: The Studio, 1929).

Tawney, R. H., *Religion and the Rise of Capitalism* (New York: Harcourt, Brace, 1926).

Taylor, H. O., *The Classical Heritage of the Middle Ages* (New York: Macmillan, 1935).

Theologia Germanica. Introduction and Notes by Joseph Bernhart. Trans. from the German by Susanna Winkworth, revised by Willard R. Trask (London: Victor Gollancz, 1951).

Thimme, Anneliese, *Gustav Stresemann. Eine politische Biographie zur Geschichte der Weimarer Republik* (Hannover: Norddeutsche Verlagsanstalt O. Goedel, 1957).

Thomas Aquinas, St., *Opera omnia,* ed. Cardinal Thomaso Maria Zigliara and others (Rome: Typographia Polyglotta, 1882–1930), 15 vols.

——— *Basic Writings,* ed. Anton C. Pegis (New York: Random House, 1944), 2 vols.

——— *On the Governance of Rulers,* trans. Gerald B. Phelan (New York: Sheed & Ward, 1938).

Treitschke, Heinrich von, *History of Germany in the Nineteenth Century,* trans. Eden and Cedar Paul (New York: McBride, 1915–1919), 7 vols.

Treue, Wilhelm, *Deutsche Geschichte von den Anfängen bis zum Ende des zweiten Weltkrieges* (Stuttgart: Alfred Kröner, 1958).

Troeltsch, Ernst, *Christian Thought, Its History and Application,* ed. Baron F. von Hügel (New York: Doran, 1923).

——— *Protestantism and Progress,* trans. W. Montgomery (New York: G. P. Putnam's Sons, 1912).

——— *Social Teaching of the Christian Churches,* trans. Olive Wyon (London; New York: Macmillan, 1931), 2 vols.

Tymms, Ralph, *German Romantic Literature* (London: Methuen, 1955).

Valentin, Veit, *1848: Chapters of German History,* trans. E. T. Scheffauer (London: Allen & Unwin, 1940).

——— *The German People* (New York: Alfred A. Knopf, 1946).

Wagner, Richard, *Prose Works,* trans. W. A. Ellis (London, 1892–1899), 8 vols.
───── *My Life,* trans. anon. (New York: Dodd, Mead, 1924).
Waidson, H. M., *Jeremias Gotthelf: An Introduction to the Swiss Novelist* (Oxford: B. Blackwell, 1953).
Walter, Bruno, *Gustav Mahler* (New York: Knopf, 1958).
Walzel, Oskar, *German Romanticism,* trans. A. E. Lussky (New York: G. P. Putnam's Sons, 1932).
Wandruszka, Adam, *Das Haus Habsburg: Die Geschichte einer europäischen Dynastie* (Stuttgart: F. Vorwerk Verlag, 1956).
Watkin, E. T., *Catholic Art and Culture* (New York: Sheed & Ward, 1944).
Wattenbach, W., *Deutschlands Geschichtsquellen im Mittelalter* (Weimar: H. Böhlaus Nachfolger, 1952-53), 2 vols.
Weber, Max, *Gesammelte politische Schriften.* Zweite erweiterte Auflage mit Geleitwort von Theodor Heuss, Ed. by J. Winkelmann (Tübingen: J. C. Mohr, 1958).
───── *The Protestant Ethic and the Spirit of Capitalism,* trans. Talcott Parsons (New York: Charles Scribner's Sons. 1930).
───── *The Nemesis of Power: The German Army in Politics* (New York: Macmillan, 1953).
Wheeler-Bennett, John W., *Wooden Titan; Hindenburg in Twenty Years of German History* (New York: William Morrow, 1935).
Wiese, Benno von, *Friedrich Schiller* (Stuttgart: J. B. Metzler, 1959).
Wilhelm II, *The Kaiser's Memoirs,* trans. R. Ybarra (New York: Harper, 1922).
Wilms, Hieronymus, *Albert the Great,* trans. Adrian English and Ph. Hereford (London: Burns, 1933).
Woelfflin, Heinrich, *Principles of Art History,* trans. M. D. Hottinger (New York: Holt, 1932).
Worringer, Wilhelm, *Form in Gothic,* trans. H. Read (New York: G. P. Putnam's Sons, 1927).
Wust, Peter, *The Crisis in the West,* trans. E. I. Watkin (London: Sheed & Ward, 1931).
Zentner, Wilhelm, *Anton Bruckner: Leben und Werk* (München: Schnell & Steiner, 1946).
Zimmern, H., *The Hansa Towns* (New York: G. P. Putnam's Sons, 1891).
Zoepfl, Friedrich, *Deutsche Kulturgeschichte* (Freiburg im Br.: Herder, 1929, 1930), 2 vols.

INDEX

Aachen, Treaty of (1748), 314
Absolutism, economic, *see* Mercantilism; political theory of, 304–306, 327 sq; princely, 303–306
Adrianople, battle of, 23
Agriculture, German, modern, 683
Albert the Great, O.P., St., xvi, 143–145
Albigenses, 135
Albrecht II, 166
Albrecht the Bear, 111
Alexander I, Tsar of Russia, 446 sqq, 455, 536
Algeciras Conference, 626
Allied Powers, secret agreements and treaties of, 651 sq
Alsace, Germany's loss of, 453
Alsace-Lorraine, German annexation of, 545
Altenberg, Peter, 722
Altkatholiken, see Old Catholics, German
Anabaptists, 227, 230; "kingdom" of, 242; teachings of, 241
Anacreontics, 349, 408
Angles, 21, 27
Anglo-Saxons, 27, 28; conversion of, 37
Antiquity, Science of, 402 sq
Anton Ulrich of Brunswick, Duke, 348
Anzengruber, Ludwig, 720
Apostolikumstreit, 699
Architecture, Carolingian, 53; contemporary German, ecclesiastic, 711 sq; "functional," 573 sq, 711 sq; Gothic, xv, 148–150; "Gothic revival" in, 570–573; late Gothic, 193; modern German, 570–573; Romanesque, 81–82, 149
Arianism, 22
Ariovistus, 20
Aristotle, 143 sq; *Poetics* of, 381 sq; on social theory, 376
Armeleutemalerei, 715
Arminius (Hermann), 20
Armistice, terms of, 653
Arndt, Ernst Moritz, 339, 447, 470, 479 sq
Arnim, Achim von, 470, 477 sq
Arnold, Gottfried, 366 sq
Art, Baroque, 341; medieval theory of, 156 sq; religious, decline of, 278; Romantic, 487–491; secular (sixteenth century), 278 sq; and technology, 573 sq
Aryan race, theory of, 564
Attila, 25
Augsburg, "Confession of," 210, 232; Diet of (1518), 209; Diet of (1530), 210;

Diet of (1548), 211 sq; Diet of (1555), 212; "Interim" of, 211 sq; League of (1686), 308; Religious Peace of, 213
Augustine, St., xi, 24, 36, 44, 53
Ausonius, 7
Austerlitz, battle of, 325
Austria, military reforms in, 443 sq; rebellions in, 526 sq; rise of, 168 sq; war aims of (1813), 449 sq
Austria-Bavaria, origins of, 114
Austrian War of Succession, 314
Austro-Hungarian monarchy, creation of, 308
Austro-Sardinian War, Prussia's attitude in, 536

Baader, Franz von, 390, 600
"Babylonian Captivity" of Papacy, 164, 171, 172; end of, 173
Bach, Johann Sebastian, 350 sq, 493; and Brahms, 736; and Reger, 739
"Balance of power," restoration of (Congress of Vienna), 455
Balkan Crises and Balkan Wars, 626–628
Banking, beginnings of, 131; late Middle Ages, 188; modern, 554–556
Barbarossa, Frederick, *see* Frederick I
Barlach, Ernst, 719
Baroque, arts and crafts, 337–345; church architecture of, 341 sq; early, high, and late, 342; fusion of arts in, 341; literature, 346–349; music and opera, 350–354; painting, 345; religious art of, 341; stagecraft, 347
Baroque culture, 330–354; origins of, 330; and Papacy, 330; political aspects of, 330 sq; religious aspects of, 336 sq; social significance of, 331 sq
Barth, Karl, dialectical theology of, 700–703
Basedow, Johann, 377 sq
Basilica, early Christian, 54, 82
Bastarnians, 4; migrations of, 19
Bauer, Gustav, 642, 653
Baur, F. Chr., 596 sq
Bavarian People's Party (*Bayerische Volkspartei*), 660 n
Beaumarchais, Pierre de, 368
Bebel, August, 614
Beckmann, Max, 718
Beethoven, Ludwig van, life and works of, 426–428
Beguinage, 125

Henry V, 73–74, 89
Henry VI, 92 sqq
Henry VII, 163
Henry the Lion, 90, 111
Henry the Proud, 89
Herbert of Cherbury, Lord, on Natural Religion, 357
Herder, Johann Gottfried, xvi, 200, 385 sq, 392, 488; life and works of, 396–398
Heredity, theory of, 563–565
Heresy, extermination of, 136
Herschel, Friedrich Wilhelm, 388
Hertling, Georg von, Count, 642
Hertz, Heinrich, 687
Heyne, Christian Gottlob, 403
Heyse, Paul, 583
High German, and Low German, 33
Hildebrand, Lay of, 57
Hiller, Kurt, 728
Hindenburg, Oskar von, 672
Hindenburg, Paul von, 637, 638, 642, 643, 645, 672, 674; re-election of, 671; Reichspräsident (1925), 664
Historicism, 689 sq; theological, 700
Historiography, modern German, 591 sq; sixteenth century, 275 sq
Hitler, Adolf, 661 sq, 665, 668, 669, 672; appointed Chancellor, 674; imprisonment and release of, 662; naturalization of, 671; and von Papen, 673
Hobbes, Thomas, 304
Hofer, Andreas, 444
Hoffmann, E. Th. A., 470, 478
Hoffmann, Ludwig, 711
Hoffmann von Fallersleben (A. H. Hoffmann), 528
Hofmannsthal, Hugo von, 723 sq
Hohenlinden, battle of, 325
Hohenlohe, Chlodwig zu, Prince, 608, 619 sq
Hohenzollerns, branches of, 310; end of dynasty of, 643
Holbein, Hans, the Younger, xv, 194–198, 391
Hölderlin, Friedrich, 474 sq
Holstein, Fritz von, Baron, 619
Holy Alliance, 459 sq, 511
Holy Office, founding of, 136
Holy Roman Empire, xiv; dismemberment of, 290; of the German Nation, 62, 63
Holz, Arno, "consistent" naturalism of, 721 sq
Hoover moratorium, 670
Hrotsvitha of Gandersheim, 85
Hubertusburg, Peace of, 314 sq
Hugenberg, Alfred, 667 sq, 671, 672, 674
Humanism, Christian, 26, 62; German, 248–253; centers of, 248 sq; the New, 398, 403 sq, 440
Humanity, Comte's "religion" of, 567
Humboldt, Alexander von, 559 sq
Humboldt, Wilhelm von, 403, 456, 591; educational reform of, 339–442
Hume, David, 371 sq, 385
Hungarian Magyars, conversion of, 110

Hungarians, 65, 67
Hungary, partition of (1541), 208; rebellion of, 526 sq
Huns, 19, 22, 23, 25
Huss, John, 176 sq; excommunication and burning of, 177
Husserl, Edmund, phenomenology of, 692 sq
Hussite Wars, 176–178
Hutten, Ulrich von, 251 sq; and Erasmus, 252

Iconoclast Controversy, 47
Idealism, German, xiv–xv; German, *Classical*, 391–428; and materialism, modern German, 686 sq; philosophic, 499 *n;* philosophic systems of, 499–507
Ignatius of Loyola, St., 254–257
Illuminati, Order of, 371
Immermann, Karl, 581
Imperial Deputation, Principal Decree of (1803), 325
Impressionism, German, painters of, 716 sq
Indo-European nations, 3
Industrial Revolution, 548–551; impact on religion of, 598; and literature, 583
Industry, German, 553 sq; expansion of, 681–683
Inflation, German, 659–661
Innocent III, Pope, 93, 94, 107; on serfdom, 118
Inquisition, founding of, 136; procedure of, 136
Interest, prohibition of, 129 sq
"International," 559
Interregnum, 92, 96; end of, 162

Jahn, Ludwig, 464; "Turnvater," 442 sq
Jansenism, 336
Jaurès, Jean, assassination of, 636
Jerome, St., 23
Jesuit Order, 213, 463; and education, 257; founding of, 257 sq; *ratio studiorum* of, 259
Jesuitengesetz (1872), 612
Jews, persecutions of, 130, 176; persecution of (1933), 675
John of Austria, Archduke, *Reichsverweser,* 531
John of the Cross, St., monastic reform of, 336
John of Saxony, Elector, 210
Jordanus of Saxony, O.P., 144
Joseph II of Hapsburg, Emperor, 320, 389; anti-ecclesiastical policies of, 375
Jugendbewegung, see Youth Movement, German
Jugendstil, German, 710
Jung-Stilling, Johann, 390
Junkers, Prussian, 513, 514; and Brüning, 671
Jutes, 21, 27

Kaiser, Georg, 728
Kalmar, Union of, 120